WAUGH ON WOMEN

WAUGH ON WOMEN

Jacqueline McDonnell

Duckworth

First published in 1985 by
Gerald Duckworth & Co. Ltd.
The Old Piano Factory
43 Gloucester Crescent, London NW1

ISBN 0 7156 2006 1

British Library Cataloguing in Publication Data

McDonnell, Jacqueline
    Waugh on women.
    1. Waugh, Evelyn—Criticism and interpretation
    I. Title
    823'.912   PR6045.A97Z/

    ISBN 0-7156-2006-1

Photoset in North Wales by
Derek Doyle & Associates, Mold, Clwyd
Printed and bound in Great Britain by
Ebenezer Baylis & Son Ltd, Worcester

Contents

For Dennis
with love

Preface

This is the first study to give a comprehensive view of the women in Evelyn Waugh's novels. I use the word 'study' because although it points critical conclusions it also uses a great deal of biographical material. This material has been necessary to the understanding of the women characters, and also to show that Waugh was not, as has been contended, a pure fantasist.

The world that Waugh's women occupied was very much a real one – the only one he felt able to write about: 'The sad thing is that "Metroland" is my world that I have grown up in and I don't have any other except at second hand or at a great distance' (*Letters* p. 206). It was a world that Waugh admired at the beginning of his writing career, one that emancipated society women were determined to treat on their own terms. Waugh did not entirely agree with this attitude, but he marvelled at it, and his first heroine, Margot Beste-Chetwynde, has a freshness and a wickedness about her which are entirely believable and devastatingly charming. So successful is she as a character that one is prepared to forgive her her sins.

Over the years Waugh's women characters (apart from Julia Stitch, who was the real and very extraordinary figure of Lady Diana Cooper) changed. Their 'sins' could not so easily be forgiven, and Waugh's hostility to womankind comes to the surface: he often denigrates his heroines' looks, their intelligence and their outlook on life.

His opinions were deeply influenced by his disastrous first marriage, and the unhappy relationships before his successful marriage to Laura Herbert. His bitterness prevails in such characters as Brenda Last and Celia Ryder.

The human frailty of his female characters was not to be tolerated; adulteresses in particular had to be punished. And many of Waugh's women are exterminated, or lose the partner they desire, or – like Julia Flyte – have to choose between man and God.

In the early books Waugh succeeds entirely; a line of dialogue, a line of description, evoke a world. But when he tries to picture love – that 'hooded stranger' in *Work Suspended*, he fails.

I am grateful to Professor W.W. Robson for his constant encouragement during the writing of this book, and to my husband Dennis McDonnell for all his support. I am also extremely grateful for all the assistance given to me by the staff of the National Library of Scotland, the Central Library in Edinburgh, the Edinburgh University Library, and the Harry Ransom Humanities Research Center at the University of Texas at Austin; and for the British Academy and Carnegie Trust awards which enabled me to study there. I was also helped by many people who were connected with Evelyn

Waugh during his lifetime: but my thanks must go particularly to Lady Diana Cooper for her continued interest.

References to Waugh's novels and diaries, and to Christopher Sykes's biography, are to the Penguin editions unless otherwise stated. I am grateful to A.D. Peters & Co Ltd for permission to quote.

J.McD.

Checklist of heroines and their admirers

Decline and Fall (1928)
    Margot Beste-Chetwynde
        'Chokey' Sebastian Cholmondley
        Paul Pennyfeather
        Otto Silenus
        Humphrey Maltravers (Ld. Metroland)
        Alastair Digby-Vane Trumpington

Vile Bodies (1930)
    Nina Blount
        Adam Fenwick-Symes
        'Ginger' Captain Eddy Littlejohn

Black Mischief (1932)
    Prudence Courteney
        William Bland
        Basil Seal

A Handful of Dust (1934)
    Brenda Last
        Tony Last
        John Beaver
        Jock Grant-Menzies

Scoop (1938)
    Kätchen
        William Boot
        Her 'husband'

Put Out More Flags (1942)
    Angela Lyne
        Cedric Lyne
        Basil Seal

Work Suspended (1942)
    Lucy Simmonds
        Roger Simmonds
        John Plant

Brideshead Revisited (1945)
    Julia Flyte
        Charles Ryder
        Rex Mottram

Scott-King's Modern Europe (1947)   Miss Bombaum
                                        Scott-King
                                        Miss Sveningen
                                        Whitemaid

The Loved One (1948)   Aimée Thanatogenos
      Dennis Barlow
      Mr Joyboy

Helena (1950)   Helena
      Constantius

Men at Arms (1952)   Virginia Troy
      Guy Crouchback
      Hector Troy
      Tommy Blackhouse

Love Among The Ruins (1953)   Clara
      Miles Plastic

Officers and Gentlemen (1955)   Virginia Troy
      Guy Crouchback
      'Trimmer' Major
      McTavish

The Ordeal of Gilbert Pinfold (1957)   Margaret
      Gilbert Pinfold

Unconditional Surrender (1961)   Virginia Troy
      Guy Crouchback

Basil Seal Rides Again (1963)   Barbara Seal
      Charles Albright
      Basil Seal

CHAPTER ONE

Women and Waugh

The women in Waugh's life can be seen at three stages: his childhood and early years; the disastrous end to his first marriage; and his thirty years with Laura.

Early girls

Evelyn Waugh grew up with fond memories of his childhood. He loved his mother and resented the fact that his father had prior claim. Although he lunched with his mother in the dining room, the rest of his meals were taken in the nursery to keep him out of his father's way. He saw Arthur Waugh as an intruder, for once his key turned in the lock his mother's company was lost to him for the evening. An interesting fact about Waugh's early conditioning is that although he preferred his mother's treats out, such as queueing for the pit in the theatre, and tea in Lyons' tea-shops, he observed that the more lavish treats his father arranged were part of a masculine and more luxurious way of life. With his father he sat in the stalls, and lunched before the performance at an interesting restaurant in Soho.

His brother Alec was five years older and his father's favourite. Evelyn once said to his mother, 'Daddy loves Alec more than me. But you love me more than you love Alec'. Her reply, because she did not wish to show favouritism, was 'No, I love you both the same'. Evelyn's response was telling: 'Then I am lacking in love.'[1] He also believed that Alec would inherit everything.

His love for his mother was very special and he invented his own language of love to communicate with her. He would sign his letters 'Evoggles goggles moggles', the word 'goggles' meaning love. He also used her high-backed chair in the dining room as a haven. It was understood that he couldn't be touched if he was sitting in it, and if his father or brother were cross with him he would throw himself into it, shouting 'Sanctuary, sanctuary!' He accepted his mother's criticism and agreed with her that his besetting sin was his quick

---

[1] Alec Waugh, *My Brother Evelyn and Other Profiles* (1967), p.164. It is worth noting the influence of primogeniture in Waugh's work. For example, in *Winner Takes All* the elder son not only inherits the estate but takes his younger brother's fiancée as his wife. In *Brideshead Revisited*, although the estate is finally left to Julia, Bridey as the eldest son with all the responsibilities leaves Sebastian no part to play, therefore helping him to become feckless and irresponsible. Waugh expected that his brother, Alec, would inherit his father's house. As it happened, on his mother's death, it was left to Evelyn.

and unkind tongue. It was, of course, something that was to stay with him all his life, and something he reproached himself with in later years when he felt he did not treat her as gently as he should. 'Why does everyone except me find it so easy to be nice?' Pinfold laments after a painful visit to his mother on the eve of his voyage (*The Ordeal of Gilbert Pinfold*, p.31).

The rivalry for his mother's affection continued in later life, for in 1931 when Arthur Waugh was ill Evelyn was unwell at the same time. He apparently took a violent dislike to the nurse who was looking after him, and Mrs Waugh's time was spent divided between husband and son. Apparently for five days there were practically no entries in Arthur Waugh's diary – an unusual occurrence. Evelyn, having upset the household and his father, made amends by ordering his father a dozen quarter bottles of Perrier-Jouet.

Lady Diana Cooper, who met Evelyn Waugh in 1932, says she had no idea that he was devoted to his mother for he never mentioned her, but Lady Dorothy Lygon who went to Highgate and met his mother thinks he was very fond of her.[2] It would seem, however, that in the 1930s, according to Arthur Waugh's diaries of 1929 to 1942 (held in the Special Collections division of Boston University), Evelyn Waugh was extremely close to his mother, taking her to the cinema and dining out with her.

As a child the other person obviously dear to his heart was his nanny, Lucy Hodges. One only has to read Waugh's autobiography, *A Little Learning*, to see the extent of that affection. Christopher Sykes, in his biography of Waugh, believes that Lucy probably instilled in him his aversion to lying. In his autobiography Waugh describes a hoax that he and his friends played on his nanny (they pretended he had drowned) and tells how she burst into tears, not at the hoax but at the fact that Evelyn deceived her. Obviously Lucy commanded not only respect but a great deal of love. As he says himself, he 'lived in joyous conformity to the law of two adored deities, my nurse and my mother'.[3]

Sykes makes the excellent point that, although Waugh portrays many servants in his books with his normal sharp irony, his nannies only receive the mildest of gibes.[4] He treats them gently and with affection, as will be shown in Chapter Six. In fact it is Waugh's nannies who are faithful to the idea of the family as a functioning unit, not his mothers.

If his mother and Lucy were his 'two adored deities', on a slightly lower plane was his relationship with his aunts on his father's side – Connie, Trissie and Elsie. Their dark cluttered house full of 'curiosities' and 'interesting smells' at Midsomer Norton captivated him far more than his own home, and he was once heard to say that he preferred it because people died there. Later he was inclined to believe it was because he was drawn to the mid-Victorian style of the house – a style that was to become prevalent in his own home. When his aunts began to remove their stuffed birds and mounted butterflies to make way for twentieth-century items, the place lost a lot of its charm for

[2] Interview with Lady Diana Cooper (16 November 1981) and with Lady Dorothy Lygon (14 February 1983).

[3] Evelyn Waugh, *A Little Learning* (1964), p.29.

[4] Christopher Sykes, *Evelyn Waugh: a Biography* (1977), p.27.

him. His morbidity, however, had already expressed itself in his fascination for the cellar in his own home. He explains: 'All my life I have sought dark and musty seclusions, like an animal preparing to whelp.'[5]

The aunts, like Lucy, were devout Christians. All three of them held bible classes on Sunday afternoons at home. (Lucy read her bible faithfully from beginning to end without deviating from any section; this would take her six months, and then she would return to Genesis and start again.) When Evelyn started to make a shrine, the aunts immediately offered to make him a frontal.

While at Midsomer Norton, Waugh made friends with the children of Dr Bulleid, and Betty Bulleid was to be one of the first girls he took an interest in. Before Betty however there was Luned, the sister of Barbara Jacobs who married his brother Alec. It was Barbara, with whom his relations were entirely platonic, who introduced him to modern painting, and who explored London with him. She was a modern girl with bobbed hair, mildly artistic in dress and, like her mother, a feminist. In her he apparently found the kind of friend he had lacked at school at Lancing, a fact that hurt Dudley Carew, as one can see in his *Fragment of Friendship*.[6] As a schoolboy Waugh was very lonely, and once confided to Carew: 'I get depressed, Carey, the people I like never like me.'[7]

Waugh obviously enjoyed his relationship with Barbara, but he doesn't seem to have seen her again after her break-up with Alec. They were only married from 1919 to 1921. The subject of their divorce never raises its head either in the diaries or the letters. The nearest Waugh gets to it is a note in the diary of 22 August 1921 which records that they were held up as an example by an older man, giving advice to a younger one, of the tragedy of people marrying young. Perhaps Waugh at this early stage in his life was already hurt by the failure of his brother's marriage to a girl whom he personally admired.

Luned Jacobs, like Betty Bulleid, was a minor romantic attachment. It is possible however to see some of Waugh's attitudes towards women even at this early stage. In his autobiography he records that at parties, while other youngsters grappled on the floor, squealing in the excitement of a game in the dark, he and Luned would 'silently cling and roll together'. It was always he or she who proposed 'the dark game'. This was 1917, and he would have been fourteen. In 1919 he records that he hopes 'the ridiculous affair is at an end'; but in 1920 he is still taking Luned to dances and theatres, though he notes that Betty, on a visit to Midsomer Norton, was looking prettier than Luned. In January 1921 the diary reads: 'However, I have shut down, I think finally, the Luned affair. She wrote me a rather touching, but hysterical and, I fear, rather a self-conscious letter, asking me in almost as many words to go on kissing her. I wrote her a long letter back in which I explained my share in the

[5] *A Little Learning*, p.44.
[6] Dudley Carew, *A Fragment of Friendship: a Memory of Evelyn Waugh When Young* (1974), p.67. The quotation is: 'In *A Little Learning* he gives the impression that he explored London solely in the company of Alec's first wife. This was not so.'
[7] Ibid., p.37.

whole thing and told her it was over.'[8] More telling is the next entry, which reads: 'A letter arrived from Luned – very pathetic: "what a fool is a fond wench." '[9]

It is interesting that even as an adolescent Waugh recorded the self-consciousness of the letter; the style. Luned apparently was not a good letter-writer; and that, strangely enough, also applied to later female friends such as Olivia Plunket Greene and his second wife, Laura Herbert.

Many critics have assumed that Waugh was not interested in girls during adolescence. Dudley Carew questioned his attitude to sex at this time of his life, mentioning Waugh in connection with Ursula Kendall, whom Waugh had met just before he terminated his relationship with Luned Jacobs. Waugh records that Ursula was 'beautiful and gracious and womanly'.[10] The relationship did not amount to much, and Ursula fell in love with Bobbie Shaw.

Carew made a note in his diary of going to church with the Waughs while Ursula and Bobbie were present. He then comments:

> Ursula Kendall was the daughter of Guy Kendall who was, I believe Headmaster of University College School. The interest of this extract however, lies in the fact that there is the mention of a girl in it; and this is something rare. I cannot remember Evelyn and I ever talking much about girls, first, because it was not 'the thing to do', as we understood the phrase, and secondly because, so far as I knew, it was not a subject that attracted Evelyn. He was equivocal and uncertain in his attitude towards sex at this time – his normal, positive forcefulness refused to operate in this particular field.[11]

From this statement it would seem that Waugh was more of a dark horse than Carew realised. Luned Jacobs, Betty Bulleid, Ursula Kendall – Waugh seems to have had the same kind of adolescent relationships as most young men. Christopher Sykes makes no mention of these early relationships either. Waugh's sexual orientation veered from heterosexuality to homosexuality and back again. It is known that he had various relationships at Oxford and that after Richard Pares, Alastair Graham was 'the friend of my heart'.[12] In 1924 Waugh recorded that Christmas Day 'makes one feel a little sad; for one reason because strangely enough my few romances have always culminated in Christmas week – Luned, Richard, Alastair'.[13] The word 'romance' is important, for as Waugh said to Christopher Hollis during his undergraduate days, 'My affections are much more romantic than carnal.'[14]

---

[8] *The Diaries of Evelyn Waugh*, edited by Michael Davie (1979), p.109.

[9] Ibid., p.110.

[10] Ibid., p.109.

[11] Carew, *A Fragment of Friendship*. p.44.

[12] Richard Pares was featured in a short story by Evelyn Waugh, 'Portrait of Young Man with Career', *Isis*, 30 May 1923, p.xxii. And Alastair Graham appears in *A Little Learning* under the pseudonym of 'Hamish Lennox'. Graham's mother, known as the 'Queen Mother', was the model for Lady Circumference in *Decline and Fall*.

[13] *Diaries*, p.194

[14] Christopher Hollis, *Oxford in the Twenties: Recollections of Five Friends* (1976), p.79.

In 1924 Waugh met Olivia Plunket Greene who was to become his next, and first serious, romantic attachment. By 1925 he was believing himself in love with her as well as her family, to whom he had taken an immediate liking. Gwen, her mother, and Richard and David, her two brothers, were all to become friends. Harold Acton described her as having 'minute pursed lips and great goo-goo eyes',[15] a description that Waugh found inadequate. Of Olivia, Waugh said:

> She died unmarried in early middle age, having spent the last twenty years of her life in a remote cottage with her mother, seeing practically no one else. At the age of eighteen she combined the elegance of David with the concentration of Richard; her interests were narrower than his but more intense. A book, a play, a film, a ballet, a new, and usually deleterious friend, a public injustice, generally known and accepted, but suddenly discovered by Olivia, would totally engage her for a time; these crazes were mitigated by a peculiar fastidiousness, which did not prevent her from saying and doing outrageous things, but preserved her essential delicacy quite intact; also by shyness which made her unwilling to make any friends save those who were attracted by her and forced their way into her confidence. She nagged and bullied at times, she suffered from morbid self-consciousness, she was incapable of the ordinary arts and efforts of pleasing and was generally incapable of any kind of ostentation; a little crazy; truth-loving and in the end holy.[16]

The important word in this description is 'holy'. Olivia, though a Bright Young Person, yearned for a quiet religious life and was capable at the rowdiest party of suddenly becoming remote and withdrawn. Evelyn wanted to marry her, but for her it was out of the question. It was the religious aspect under her superficial gaiety that sometimes made her dislike her own life and also abhor Waugh's light-hearted approach to sex; according to Sykes, she also found Waugh physically repulsive.

It was a tortured relationship, and in Alec Waugh's eyes she was the last person to bring his brother happiness. He believed she had no understanding of the creative force that drove Evelyn, and also no comprehension of any personal ambition. She did little for Waugh's confidence as a writer, or lover. She was also a depressive, and after coming up to London to see her Waugh would often return to his job as a schoolmaster in even deeper gloom. He thought however that he expected too much of her because she was a symbol of everything in London he was cut off from. His family however did not like her; they believed she turned him against them, by persuading him that they were dull and bourgeois.

The relationship with Olivia petered out when Waugh met Evelyn Gardner, though they remained friends; but her religious influence, along with her mother's, started him on the road to Catholicism. It is generally thought that Olivia did not make up his mind for him about the Church, but Sykes recalls that on Olivia's death he wrote to a friend: 'She bullied me into

[15] Harold Acton, *Memoirs of an Aesthete* (1948), p.146.
[16] *A Little Learning*, p.218.

the Church.'[17] Certainly it is recorded in the diaries that Waugh asked Olivia in 1930 to find a Jesuit to instruct him.[18]

(Auberon Waugh, since the televising of *Brideshead Revisited*, has squashed the idea that Julia and Cordelia were based on Hugh Lygon's sisters, Mary and Dorothy, and sees Julia as drawn from Waugh's unhappy love affair with Olivia.[19] Sykes believes that Waugh's characterisation of Julia failed because she was not drawn from life – 'no one has yet discerned or suggested a model for Julia.'[20] Auberon Waugh may be right that Olivia played a part because the insubstantial lineaments of the heroine may be due to the fact that Waugh never got to grips with Olivia in real life and could do no better with his fictitious heroine. In the diaries in April 1925 he reveals that he is 'still sad and uneasy and awkward whenever I am with Olivia'. Sykes, however, could be mistaken in saying that Julia was not 'drawn from life', since there is a discernible model in the form of Teresa Jungman, as will be shown later in this chapter.)

One aspect of Olivia that would not have been palatable to Waugh was her interest in negroes. Olivia had a close relationship with Paul Robeson, the negro singer, and had many friends among the cast of the fashionable London negro revue, *The Blackbirds*. Like Nancy Cunard, she mixed openly with blacks, throwing parties for them with her brother David, and talked about black men constantly to Waugh. She also, for a time, supported Communism and, after one discussion with Waugh, wrote and defended Paul Robeson's views, saying that he was 'a *highly* intelligent man and *yet* he holds *my* point of view. *And* he is not an invalid maiden lady living in a remote forest. He has spent years of his life in Russia & all over the continent & I think his son was brought up in Russia.'[21]

In *Decline and Fall* Margot Beste-Chetwynde flaunts her black lover, Chokey, at the school's Sports Day. Through Chokey, Waugh was able to portray what he saw as the determined culture-hunting and defensiveness of the American negro in London. There is also the running sexual innuendo about the attractions that the black man has for the white woman. Waugh was satirising the Mayfair hostesses of the time who took up blacks hoping, as he put it in 'Let us Return to the Nineties', to gain modernity.[22]

Sykes says that there seems to be no model for Margot Beste-Chetwynde,[23] though Terence Greenridge has stated that ' ... of the many facets of various Mayfair hostesses that went into the composition of Margot Beste-Chetwynde – the recognisable feature of the Hon. Nancy

[17] Sykes, p.156.

[18] *Diaries*, p.319. Also interesting is the fact that Alastair Graham joined the Roman Catholic Church in 1924. *Diaries*, p.178.

[19] Auberon Waugh, 'Brideshead: Who Really Was Who', *Daily Mail* 13 October 1981, pp.20-21.

[20] Sykes, p.349.

[21] Ibid., p.435. Waugh's annoyance with Olivia can be seen in the diaries (p.281) where he said: 'Olivia could talk of nothing but black men.'

[22] Evelyn Waugh, 'Let Us Return to the Nineties but Not to Oscar Wilde', in *Essays, Articles and Reviews of Evelyn Waugh*, edited by Donat Gallagher (1983), p.123.

[23] Sykes, p.128.

Cunard with a negro companion was enough for all who had the social intimacy which this aspect of identification required'.[24] However, Margot is likely to be based partly on Olivia, for Margot's companion, Chokey, has a 'fine singing voice' as Robeson had. Moreover in his diaries on 16 October 1925 Waugh records that Olivia arrived, with other friends, at the school that he was teaching at in an 'enormous Rolls-Royce'. Margot Beste-Chetwynde arrives at Paul Pennyfeather's school in an 'enormous limousine of dove-grey and silver'. Again, Harold Acton has observed that 'Nancy Cunard lived in Paris at that time and Waugh did not know her; Olivia Plunket Greene was his closest model'.[25]

The car that Olivia arrived in at the school at which Waugh was teaching belonged to Mrs Arthur Bendir, the mother of Babe McGustie who married Olivia's brother David Plunket Greene. They were later divorced, but both were involved in the negro craze and Babe was rumoured, as were other society women, to have had an affair with Leslie Hutchinson, the black musician. Nancy Cunard was not the only lady of the time who favoured negroes.

Lord Molson has thrown light on Margot's surname: 'I knew a Reggie Best and a Randolph Chetwynd and Evelyn quite unfairly used their names.'[26]

Olivia was then one of the Bright Young People. They first received this name in 1924 when a young journalist coined the phrase in the *Daily Mail*: 'Chasing Clues, New Society Game, Midnight Chase in London, 50 motor cars, The Bright Young People' (26 July 1924). It still applied as late as 1930 (Diana Mosley says it was a description that always made her laugh – 'Evelyn used it of our particularly serious friends, Bright Young Roy Harrod, or Bright Young Henry Yorke'),[27] but by then the treasure hunts, the masquerades, the wild parties had lost their spontaneity. Once the Press gave them their name, the Bright Young People had to live up to their image: the more wicked they were said to be, the more wicked they had to become. As Patrick Balfour said: 'Their attitude, from being a plea for social and intellectual freedom, now appeared as an unabashed crusade for moral abnormality. And so the Bright Young People destroyed themselves, degenerating into a slough of dope and other excesses.'[28]

---

[24] Unpublished letter from Terence Greenridge to Charles E. Linck in the Evelyn Waugh collection held at the Harry Ransom Humanities Research Center at the University of Texas at Austin (HRHRC) at Austin.

[25] Letter from Sir Harold Acton to J. McDonnell, 11 February 1984.

[26] Letter from Lord Molson to J. McDonnell, 7 February 1984. The name 'Margot' is likely to have come from Margot, Lady Oxford. David Lennox, the photographer in *Decline and Fall*, was unmistakable as Cecil Beaton. In *Decline and Fall*, Lennox takes a photograph of the back of Margot Beste-Chetwynde's head just as Cecil Beaton had 'taken a well-known photograph of Margot, Lady Oxford from the same angle', Sykes. p.129.

[27] Diana Mosley, *A Life of Contrasts* (1977), p.78.

[28] Patrick Balfour (Lord Kinross), *Society Racket: a Critical Survey of Modern Social Life* (1933), p.172.

Was Evelyn Waugh a Bright Young Person? Like Nancy Mitford,[29] he seems to have been only on the sidelines, accepted by the group but distancing himself from it and observing the activities and attitudes of his companions. The distancing was partly due to lack of money – the glittering world of London was far away, both socially and financially, from his job as a schoolmaster in Wales. His friends prospered, while he was comparatively penniless.

Waugh resigned his position at the school believing he was to be employed as a secretary to C.K. Scott-Moncrieff in Florence. Unfortunately in July he heard that Scott-Moncrieff did not wish to employ him. This was one blow. He had already suffered another by realising that his position with Olivia was hopeless: 'Olivia scolded me for wasting my time as a schoolmaster instead of becoming an artist, but it was clear in our walks across the windy island and in our long sessions in the lamp-lit parlour – conversations which often lasted literally until dawn – that my infatuation had become a matter of only mild interest to her.'[30] Finally, Harold Acton told him that the opening chapters he had sent him of *The Temple at Thatch* were rubbish. He had no money, no success with Olivia and now, it seemed, no success with his writing. It was a combination of circumstances that led him to attempt suicide by drowning – only stepping back because there were jellyfish in the sea. By the second sting he thought it was: 'An Omen? A sharp recall to good sense such as Olivia would have administered.'[31]

She-Evelyn

Evelyn Gardner, like her closest friends, Nancy Mitford and Pansy Pakenham (with whom she shared a flat), was not a Bright Young Person. Waugh records in his diary for 7 April 1927: 'I met such a nice girl called Evelyn Gardner.'

Sykes says the diaries at this point have more references to Inez Holden than to She-Evelyn, and that at this stage the courtship was 'rudimentary and tepid'.[32] He seems to have overlooked the fact that the entry for Friday 1 July 1927, apart from recording the trip to the cinema with Inez, also records that about a week later Waugh spent a Whitsun weekend at Evelyn Gardner's sister's house, when Evelyn was present. Inez in fact played less part in his life than Olivia, for in August Waugh says that he is still spending a lot of time with Olivia, and it is only on 29 November that we read: 'I see Evelyn a lot and a certain amount of Olivia.' It is interesting that after his proposal to Evelyn, Waugh went directly to tell Olivia, for whom he obviously still had a great deal of affection.

[29] Like her character Sophie in *Pigeon Pie*, 'she was not shy and she had high spirits, but she was never a romper and therefore never attained much popularity with the very young'. Harold Acton, *Nancy Mitford: a Memoir* (1975), p.23. And Lady Dorothy Lygon (interview) has said that Waugh was more of a 'recorder than a doer, certainly in *Decline and Fall* and *Vile Bodies*'.

[30] For a recollection of the Easter holidays of 1925 spent with the Plunket Greene family, see *A Little Learning*, p.226.

[31] Ibid., p.230.

[32] Sykes, p.113.

Evelyn Gardner was a refreshing change from the other girls he knew. As Harold Acton wrote to him: 'I hear she is very pretty and quite different from all the other girls in London.'[33] Anthony Powell met her shortly after Waugh told him that he was going to marry her, and she became a life-long friend. He first heard of her from Alec Waugh, but not in connection with Evelyn. Alec, whom he met by chance near Sloane Square, said:

> Do you know two delightful girls who live just round the corner from here called Evelyn Gardner and Pansy Pakenham? We're always reading newspaper articles about the Modern Girl putting on too much make-up, drinking too many cocktails, being brassy, bad-mannered, gold-digging, but these two couldn't be nicer, prettier, quieter, more intelligent.[34]

After meeting her, Anthony Powell had this to say of Evelyn Gardner:

> The warmth and charm of Evelyn Gardner – who remains a friend to this day – were, on the one hand, in direct contrast with the supposedly brassy traits of that ominous figure, The Modern Girl, while at the same time she seemed in her person to exemplify all that is thought of as most 'modern'. She possessed the looks and figure of the moment, slight, boyish, an Eton crop; that simplicity of style more often to be found breaking hearts at the rackety parties outlined earlier [*Messengers of Day*, pp. 32-5], than in the ballrooms of Mayfair and Belgravia, however pretty the debs; and (Pansy Pakenham among these) some debs were very pretty indeed.[35]

After some opposition from She-Evelyn's family (the two of them became to be known as She-Evelyn and He-Evelyn) they were finally married on 27 June 1928. By September they had a maisonette in Canonbury Square, and as Harold Acton remembers:

> The atmosphere was that of a sparkling nursery. Blake's *Songs of Innocence* belonged there, and *Alice in Wonderland* and a cage of twittering canaries. One hoped to see cradles full of little Evelyns in the near future, baby fauns blowing through reeds, falling off rocking horses, pulling each other's pointed ears and piddling on the rug. I could see myself writing a romance entitled: *Islingtonian Family Waugh*.[36]

Acton paints an idyllic picture but it was one that was not to last.

Decline and Fall came out in the September of 1928, when the two Evelyns were happily ensconced in Canonbury, and was an immediate success. In the early part of January 1929 Waugh left with his wife for a Mediterranean cruise, as she had been unwell. During this cruise he was commissioned to write travel articles for various magazines, and these were later edited for his first travel book *Labels* (published, ironically, in USA as *A Bachelor Abroad*). By

---

[33] Ibid., p.118.

[34] Anthony Powell, *To Keep The Ball Rolling: the Memoirs of Anthony Powell*, Vol.2, *Messengers of Day* (1978), p.64.

[35] Ibid., p.66.

[36] Acton, *Memoirs of an Aesthete*, p.204.

the time they reached Palestine, She-Evelyn was ill again. At Port Said she was suffering from pneumonia and was taken to the British Hospital. When she was out of danger Waugh left her to meet Alastair Graham in Cyprus. Many critics have thought this odd. According to Sykes[37] however, the two had planned to go to Cyprus with Alastair to help her recuperate, but she was not well enough to make the journey.

Labels is very revealing. In the revised version, 'A Pleasure Cruise in 1929' in *When The Going Was Good*, we are first introduced to Geoffrey (Waugh's *alter ego*) and Juliet (Evelyn Gardner) when he meets them on board the ship, the *Stella*. The 1930 edition is entirely different. He meets Geoffrey and Juliet on the train at Monte Carlo, and there is a vivid description of how he saw himself and his wife; a description which was later deleted:

> ... and a rather sweet-looking young English couple – presumably, from the endearments of their conversation and marked solicitude for each other's comfort, on their honeymoon, or at any rate recently married. The young man was small and pleasantly dressed and wore a slight, curly moustache; he was reading a particularly good detective story with apparent intelligence. His wife was huddled in a fur coat in the corner, clearly far from well ...
>
> Every quarter of an hour or so they said to each other, 'Are you quite sure you're all right, darling?' And replied, 'Perfectly, really I am. Are *you*, my precious?'[38]

This passage says a lot about the character of Evelyn Waugh. We know what he looked like; the way he saw himself; the kind of book he liked to read, and the way he liked to be seen to read it. Waugh's ego is extremely strong here, and it is clear that *The Ordeal of Gilbert Pinfold* was not his first excursion into some kind of analysis of himself. Very little however is revealed about Evelyn Gardner, except her illness.

Sykes has pointed out that Geoffrey's anxieties about Juliet's condition obviously reflected Waugh's own feelings;[39] but if one reads the original version of *Labels* carefully it is clear that Waugh was as anxious for himself as he was for She-Evelyn. Consider the following sentences which were deleted from 'A Pleasure Cruise in 1929':

> ... I must admit that I, too, felt profound repugnance towards this unfortunate young couple. I began to visualise myself stranded alone in a Riviera nursing-home.
>
> Juliet and the Frenchman and I sat in our corners in an atmosphere of very intense fear and hostility.

In the light of these remarks, Waugh's visit to Alastair Graham does not

---

[37] Sykes, p.137. Alastair Graham was obviously a good friend to both of them, for Waugh wrote to his father: 'Alastair has given us another £50 so we can struggle along for another week or two.' *Letters*, p.31.

[38] Evelyn Waugh, *Labels* (Duckworth 1930), p.30.

[39] Sykes, p.151.

seem so strange. He appears not to have been too happy at the thought of being alone; and in his diaries for the time when She-Evelyn was ill at Canonbury Square in 1928 it is clear that he spent a lot of time visiting his friends rather than staying with her. He was unable to cope with illness. One must admit that he does not seem to have had a very caring attitude – particularly in the light of an enigmatic postcard he sent to a mutual friend saying that when the card arrived 'She-Evelyn would probably be dead'.[40]

When they came came home at the end of May 1929, She-Evelyn stayed in London while Waugh went to the Abingdon Arms in Beckley, Oxfordshire to write *Vile Bodies*. He was not worried about leaving his wife, for they had arranged for Nancy Mitford to stay at the Canonbury flat to keep She-Evelyn company.

The arrangement seemed a happy one, but while Waugh was away, though he saw his wife at weekends, the marriage between the two Evelyns was threatened; for John Heygate, a friend of both of them, became something more to her, and She-Evelyn told her husband that she was in love with Heygate[41] and that they had had an affair. There was a short reconciliation, but Waugh who could not live with 'anyone who is avowedly in love with someone else'[42] decided to divorce her.

Nancy Mitford, being very fond of Waugh, was shocked and disappointed in her friend. She left the Canonbury house immediately and never got in touch with her again. On Waugh's death, she wrote to Sykes:

> Oh Evil! When has one been so sad? *Daily Telegraph* obituary vile. I'm so sick of hearing that he was a sort of lower class milk deliverer who got on in society by pushing – such rot if one knew his family ... I haven't sent my piece (in French) to Auberon because I never think they care for the other Evelyn being mentioned, but I was obliged to do so as she was the reason why I knew him almost before any of us did – and of course she is the clue to so *much* ... [43]

It is worth looking at a conversation She-Evelyn had with Alec, who had always thought her charming. Alec, arriving at Underhill, his parents' home, and believing that Evelyn was away writing *Vile Bodies* was surprised to hear from his mother that Evelyn was back. He telephoned immediately, and She-Evelyn answered. She was crying and obviously upset. She told him she couldn't talk on the telephone and would like to meet him, and they had supper at the Gargoyle.

[40] *Diaries*, p.305.

[41] Lady Diana says that when Waugh told her about his first marriage and Heygate she was highly amused, the reason for this being that her mother had belonged to a set called 'The Souls' and they had an expression 'Oh how Heygate' meaning something over-conventional, prim or dreary (Interview with Lady Diana). According to Anthony Powell, it was Heygate's father who, because of his 'oppressive social correctness of demeanour and dress', had caused 'The Souls' to coin the verb 'to heygate' or 'do a heygate'. Powell, *Messengers of Day*, p.99.

[42] *Letters of Evelyn Waugh*, edited by Mark Amory (1981), p.39.

[43] Acton, *Nancy Mitford*, pp.174-5.

When she told Alec that she was in love with Heygate, they spent two hours discussing the situation. All we know of this conversation is what Alec Waugh has written:

> 'How is Evelyn taking it?' I asked.
> 'It's terrible. He's drinking too much. It makes him feel ill. And he thinks I'm trying to poison him.'
> Poor, poor Evelyn, racked by a 'Belladonna' hallucination.
> 'You always seemed so happy together,' I said.
> 'Yes, I suppose I was,' then after a pause, 'but never as happy as I've been with my sisters.'
> That seemed an extraordinary thing for a wife to say about a husband.
> 'What are you going to do?' I asked.
> 'That's what we've not decided yet.'[44]

Alec Waugh goes on to say that within a week of his conversation with She-Evelyn his brother came to see him to tell him that he was going to divorce her and asked him to tell their parents. When Alec said it would upset them, Evelyn's reply was 'What about me?' At the end of their meeting he said: 'The trouble about the world today is that there's not enough religion in it. There's nothing to stop young people doing whatever they feel like doing at the moment.'[45]

Most of Waugh's friends were in full sympathy with him, regarding She-Evelyn as utterly heartless. Harold Acton revealed that Waugh was shattered by her desertion: 'He howled with despair.'[46] According to Sykes, Acton also thought that She-Evelyn's long illness had produced some psychological effect and that her love for Evelyn had vanished.[47] It all sounds very plausible, but no one appears to have taken into account that she was seriously in love with Heygate. Heygate is recorded by Alec as being a perfectly pleasant but ordinary young man, and Sykes merely points out that he was a friend of them both. In fact he was a good friend. According to Anthony Powell, he spent a good deal of time at the Waughs' flat, and Waugh liked him a lot in the early days.

When Waugh went away to write *Vile Bodies*, She-Evelyn spent a good deal of time with Heygate and Powell. Powell recalls that at a cocktail party which he gave with a friend at Tavistock Square in June the Waughs turned up separately, and both left early, She-Evelyn having had an exchange of words with Heygate. This was the first public occasion, he contends, at which people were aware that something was adrift in the relationship. About two weeks later Heygate and Powell left for a holiday in Germany. Waugh sent

[44] Alec Waugh, *My Brother Evelyn*, p.191.
[45] Waugh moved fast, as far as the divorce was concerned, and rather viciously. At that time it was still customary to allow wives, even if they were the guilty party, to divorce their husbands. Not so with Waugh. He very clearly saw She-Evelyn as the guilty party. He first filed for divorce on 4 August 1929, but the final petition was dated 3 September; and on 9 September Waugh, his wife and Heygate appeared at E.S.P. Haynes' offices for the unsavoury formality of the serving of the petition on the guilty parties.
[46] *Observer*, Review Section, 25 March 1973, front page.
[47] Sykes, p.140.

Anthony Powell a telegram which read: 'Instruct Heygate return immediately.'[48]

Heygate, who was a BBC news announcer at the time, was more interesting than has been made out. He was a popular host, and during the summer of 1929 was famed for his parties at which he produced a constant flow of sandwiches and salads: he became known as Heygate of 'Party without End' fame. Harold Acton described him later as 'the ebullient author of *Decent Fellows* a naughty novel about Eton',[49] which became a best-seller. Unlike Waugh, he was tall, good-looking and well-dressed; unlike Waugh he was successful with women; unlike Waugh he was heir to a baronetcy. No wonder Waugh's pride was hurt. Apparently he was appalled by the ease with which his wife had rejected him.

Alec Waugh suggests that She-Evelyn may well have realised subconsciously that the marriage would not work for another reason, and that that was why she did not draw back from her affair with Heygate. He believed that after the success of *Decline and Fall* she realised that her role had changed: it was no longer a matter of being He-Evelyn and She-Evelyn and playing house; now she was expected to be the wife and companion of a man of letters. This would mean accepting his weeks away from her when writing and generally arranging their lives around him – a role which Laura Herbert seemed to fill gladly but which, Alec Waugh believed, She-Evelyn's instincts told her she would not be able to. She wanted to write as well, and had already published quite a few articles.

One article by her in the *Evening Standard* for 9 January 1930 provides an interesting insight into the marriage from her point of view. The title was 'The Modern Mother: A Young Wife's Challenging Plea', and the subtitle 'Last Generation Blamed for their Children's Failures and Suffering'. In it she reveals a lot about her own home life as a child, how fears of the dark and spiders were the result of nurses shutting one in dark cupboards and youthful governesses putting spiders down one's back. Because of this cruel upbringing, she believed, her generation would have a better understanding of their children. More important is her revelation about sex:

> Occasionally, they mumbled a few incoherent and to us, incomprehensible sentences which were invariably preceded by the formula, 'You are now old enough to be told about the facts of life' but we did not understand.
>
> They were prudish and veiled their prudery with sentiment. 'Children must be kept innocent,' they said. And the result was that some of us suffered.

Her sex life with Evelyn, it would appear, was not all that she had expected.

[48] See Powell, *Messengers of Day*, pp.123-6. There are two facts that are incorrect in Anthony Powell's account. Waugh did not go to the West country to write *Labels* but to Oxfordshire to the Abingdon Arms at Beckley to write *Vile Bodies*. And the Waughs did not spend the weekend, following their public row, at Salt Grass. That weekend took place earlier in the marriage according to the Hon. Mrs Nightingale ('She-Evelyn'). Letter from the Hon. Mrs Evelyn Nightingale to J. McDonnell, 17 September 1984.

[49] Acton, *Nancy Mitford*, p.27.

In some editions of *Vile Bodies* there is a sentence that reads: 'The truth is that like so many people of their age and class, Adam and Nina were suffering from being sophisticated about sex, before they were at all widely experienced.'[50] Another interesting observation on the Waughs' marriage, perhaps.

It is also intriguing that, in 1930, Waugh in conversation with Nancy Mitford, who was worried about her relationship with Hamish Erskine, who had told her that he didn't believe he would ever feel up to sleeping with a woman, tried to explain to her 'a lot about sexual shyness in men'.[51]

Whatever Evelyn Gardner's reasons, there is no doubt that Waugh was shattered by the event and that all his friends were aware of his feelings. Alec however believed that without Evelyn Gardner he might never have produced *Decline and Fall*, and that his travels after the marriage had broken up gave him the material he needed for his other books. He suggested that, if the marriage had been a success, Waugh might have concentrated on social satires that would have been superficial and brittle. Strangely, he said that in *Vile Bodies* there was no sign of the unhappiness his brother went through – 'There is no change of tempo or temper between the later grief-shadowed chapters and those earlier ones which he had written in expectation of a return to Canonbury Square as soon as he had earned his right to be there. There is no undercurrent of gloom.'[52]

Waugh himself however disputes this. In the 1965 preface to a new edition of *Vile Bodies* he refers to the fact that: 'The composition of *Vile Bodies* was interrupted by a sharp disturbance in my private life and was finished in a very different mood from that in which it was begun. The reader may, perhaps, notice the transition from gaiety to bitterness.'[53]

Bitterness is apparent in Waugh's letters of the time. Both to his parents and to Harold Acton he wrote that there had been no quarrel of any kind. To Henry Yorke he suggested that She-Evelyn's defection was some kind of 'hereditary *tic*';[54] the cause being that two of her sisters had already been divorced. As far as concerned Heygate – whom he called the 'basement boy', because of the unhappy party in Anthony Powell's basement flat – he had only respect for Heygate's parents, who had cut their son out of their will and said that they didn't wish to see him again. (In fact, by the time Heygate and She-Evelyn were married in August 1930, Heygate was once again on friendly terms with his family.) By the end of 1929 Waugh was able to write

[50] This sentence appears in American editions ranging from the 1930 Cape and Smith edition of *Vile Bodies* to the 1960 Dell Laurel edition of *Vile Bodies* and *Black Mischief*. It appears in the Chapman and Hall 1930 first edition, and the Chapman and Hall Modern Library edition, 1935. In 1937 *Vile Bodies* was reset and reprinted and the sentence was deleted. It is not in the uniform edition of 1947 or in the second uniform edition of 1965. It should also be noted that within the same section of *Vile Bodies* Nina admits that 'perhaps love was a thing one could grow to be fond of after a time, like smoking a pipe'. In the diaries there is a comment after Waugh spent a weekend with Evelyn Gardner – 'Gave EG a pipe!' *Diaries*, p.285.

[51] Ibid., p.316.

[52] Alec Waugh, *My Brother Evelyn*, p.194.

[53] Evelyn Waugh, *Vile Bodies* (1965), p.7.

[54] *Letters*, p.40.

to Henry Yorke that he did 'not like Evelyn & that really Heygate is about her cup of tea'.[55]

Sykes believes that the two Evelyns never met again after the divorce, but Michael Davie reveals in his edition of the diaries that at Waugh's instigation they lunched together after he had joined the Roman Catholic Church to discuss She-Evelyn's evidence as a witness in the procedure to annul the marriage in an ecclesiastical court. At this lunch Waugh apparently informed his ex-wife that his father would never see her again, but that his mother did not take such a stern view and she put part of the blame on him for leaving She-Evelyn alone so much.[56] Davie probably has a better understanding of Evelyn Gardner's role than Sykes, as he met her, whereas Sykes saw no reason to do so.[57]

Catholicism was of course to play an immediate and difficult part in Waugh's life. In 1930 he had converted, and in the same year he visited Greece with Christopher Hollis. There he made sure of getting an English paper every day, and when asked why replied: 'Oh, just to see if there is any good news which I might otherwise have missed, such as, for instance the death of Mrs Heygate.'[58] Hollis points out that Waugh didn't expect to be taken too seriously. Nevertheless Waugh knew by this time that if he wanted to marry again it would be impossible as far as the Church was concerned since he was a divorced man, though, as it happened, a declaration of nullity was finally given by the Church.

Vile Bodies was published in 1930, and as a result Waugh found himself thrown out of the Cavendish Hotel by Rosa Lewis, who resented the characterisation of her as the notorious Lottie Crump of Shepheard's Hotel. In 1930, in 'People Who Want to Sue Me', Waugh wrote:

> Not long ago I published a novel in which a few pages were devoted to the description of an hotel. In order to avoid trouble I made it the most fantastic hotel I could devise. I filled it with impossible clientèle, I invented an impossible proprietress. I gave it a fictitious address. I described its management as so eccentric and incompetent that no hotel could be run on their lines for a week without coming into the police or bankruptcy court. Here at least, I thought, I was safely in the realm of pure imagination.[59]

In 1964, in a preface to *The Duchess of Jermyn Street*, Waugh admitted that he had been introduced to the Cavendish by Alastair Graham and was one of the many moneyless young men who were welcomed by Rosa Lewis. He went on to say: 'I was seldom in London and the character I drew from her in my second novel was mostly derived at second hand from the anecdotes and

[55] Ibid., p.41.

[56] *Diaries*, p.306.

[57] Christopher Sykes writes: 'I saw no need to see Evelyn Gardner, whom I had met once, as I found all the relevant material concerning the divorce covered by the documents in the case. I was able to convey a message to that effect to Evelyn Gardner while writing the book.' Letter from Christopher Sykes to J. McDonnell, 4 August 1982.

[58] Hollis, *Oxford in the Twenties*, p.84.

[59] Evelyn Waugh, 'People Who Want to Sue Me', *Essays*, p.73.

imitations of my friends.'[60] In the 1965 preface to *Vile Bodies* he said: 'There was also a pretty accurate description of Mrs Rosa Lewis and her Cavendish Hotel.' He also admitted there that he had been on the fringe, rather than in the centre, of the Bright Young People: he was a voyeur.

Vile Bodies ends with people dispersed, or dead, foretelling the fate of the Bright Young People who had gathered at the Cavendish. Olivia Greene, a near-alcoholic, died of cancer at the age of 48; her brother David committed suicide by drowning after taking drugs; Brian Howard committed suicide; Elizabeth Ponsonby died from alcoholism; Sir Francis Laking from drinking too much yellow chartreuse, aged 26; Hugh Lygon was killed during a motor tour of Germany.

If they didn't die, many of the Bright Young People, like Waugh, suffered broken marriages. Evelyn Gardner's to Heygate didn't last, and she married again, only to have that marriage fail as well. Heygate himself married three times. Diana Mitford, who had married Bryan Guinness and was an extremely close friend of Waugh's, divorced and married Sir Oswald Mosley. David Greene was divorced from Babe McGustie and she married Count Bosdari, Prince Vsevolode deserted Lady Mary Lygon, and Teresa Jungman's marriage to Graham Cuthbertson also failed.

After the break-up of his marriage, Waugh became friends with Bryan and Diana Guinness (*née* Mitford), the rest of the Mitford family, the Pakenhams, the Lygons, the Lambs and many other notable people; and he was lionised by such famous hostesses as Lady Maud ('Emerald') Cunard, whom he satirised as 'Old Ruby' in *Unconditional Surrender*. 'Old Ruby' lived at the Dorchester during the war and threw parties there, just as Lady 'Emerald' Cunard did in real life. The Guinnesses were particularly good friends, and during 1929-30 Waugh often stayed with them at Pool Place in Sussex, and in London and Paris. When Diana Guinness was pregnant he visited her every day. 'She seems to me the one encouraging figure in this generation', he wrote to Henry Yorke, 'particularly now she is pregnant – a great germinating vat of potentiality like the vats I saw at their brewery.'[61]

It has often been suggested that Diana was the model for Lucy in *Work Suspended*. Waugh himself denies it in one of his last letters to Diana, by then Lady Mosley:

> But I must not leave you with the delusion that *Work Suspended* was a cruel portrait of you. It was perhaps to some extent a portrait of me in love with you, but there is not a single point in common between you and the heroine except pregnancy. Yours was the first pregnancy I observed.[62]

Diana Mosley has corroborated this statement. She says that after Waugh's death Laura wrote to her to say that he had been terribly worried in

[60] Evelyn Waugh, 'Preface' in Daphne Fielding, *The Duchess of Jermyn Street: the Life and Good Times of Rosa Lewis of the Cavendish Hotel* (1964), p.5.
[61] *Letters*, p.40.
[62] Ibid., p.639.

case she did.[63] Apparently she didn't. She believes that the only analogy was her pregnancy, and perhaps the fact that they did dine in her room and once went to the zoo together. She writes: 'Lucy was a prime bore as far as I can remember.'[64] Diana certainly was not.

Her pregnancy was not in fact the first that Waugh observed. In his diaries for 15 September 1924 he wrote: 'I went to tea at Jane Marston's. She was looking more beautiful than I had seen her since her first pregnancy; the babies are like all others except that the girl is bald. The midwife who took tea with us was beastly.'

Waugh's relationship with Diana Guinness came to an end abruptly, though apparently she never understood quite why. In the summer of 1930, after the birth of her son Jonathan, they went to many balls and parties, which Waugh did not enjoy. He preferred to sit and talk; she preferred to dance. At one point she tried to mix her two worlds, taking a dinner party of Bright Young People to a conventional ball. Robert Byron was one of her guests. Byron had a habit of playing Queen Victoria, a turn which amused his friends but not the old guard who were present on this occasion. Waugh hated the evening, and it seems to have been the last time she saw him. When she asked what had happened to their relationship, he wrote as follows:

> You ask why our friendship petered out. The explanation is very discreditable to me. Pure jealousy. You (and Bryan) were immensely kind to me at a time when I greatly needed kindness, after my desertion by my first wife. I was infatuated with you. Not of course that I aspired to your bed but I wanted you to myself as especial confidante and comrade. After Jonathan's birth you began to enlarge your circle. I felt lower in your affections than Harold Acton and Robert Byron and I couldn't compete or take a humbler place. That is the sad and sordid truth.[65]

After his parting of the ways with Diana Guinness, Waugh started to see more of the Lygon family. He had known both Hugh Lygon and Lord Elmley at Oxford while Dorothy and Mary Lygon (the two of the four daughters with whom he was to become most friendly) were still in the schoolroom. By 1931 they had grown up, and they became close friends. Waugh was one of the people who stood by the family during the unhappy days when their father, Lord Beauchamp, was revealed by his brother-in-law, the Duke of Westminster, to be a homosexual. The Duke reported his misdeeds not only to the King but also to his sister, Lady Beauchamp, who had no idea what 'homosexual' meant, and the shock was so great that she had a nervous breakdown. Her husband was about to commit suicide but was talked out of

---

[63] Laura Waugh wrote to Lady Mosley in 1966 saying: 'Thank you very much for your letter. Evelyn had been talking so much about you these few weeks – And I know how fond he was of you even tho' you had met so rarely of late years – He was most distressed that you should have in any way connected yourself with Lucy Simmonds & said there had never been any connection between you at all.'

[64] Letter from Lady Mosley to J. McDonnell, 8 November 1981.

[65] *Letters*, p.638.

it by his son. Finally, after resigning his various official appointments to the King, he went abroad.

Waugh had always loved the family and now spent much of his time at Madresfield. The family and the house have often been quoted as the models for *Brideshead Revisited*, but Waugh told Lady Dorothy Lygon before the book was published: 'It's all about a family whose father lives abroad, as it might be Boom – but it's not Boom – and a younger son; people will say he's like Hughie, but you'll see he's not really Hughie – and there's a house as it might be Mad, but it isn't really Mad.'[66]

The Lygon family were not Catholic; Waugh never met Lady Beauchamp and he only met Lord Beauchamp years later in Rome. But although the matrimonial separation of Lord and Lady Beauchamp caused by the Duke of Westminster's revelations cannot be equated with the marital problems of Lord and Lady Marchmain, there is no doubt that, as Alec Waugh has said, the 'situation was suggested to Evelyn' by the events that took place in the Beauchamp family, and Alec Waugh, though he does not mention the peer by name, says that in real life 'Lady Marchmain was the sister of a prominent Duke'.[67]

Lady Dorothy Lygon believes that the resemblance between the two families has been much exaggerated and that Waugh only used a situation, not the characters concerned. 'I am quite sure,' she says, that my sister was not Julia'; and when asked if she thought Cordelia was based on her she replied: 'It hadn't occurred to me, and I don't think it occurred to Evelyn.'[68] There are however some architectural similarities between Brideshead and Madresfield, as we shall see in Chapter Eight.

Waugh insisted that the Lygon sisters should have nicknames. During their nursery days Lady Mary had been called 'Maimie' and Lady Dorothy 'Coote'. Waugh took it a step further. Maimie became 'Blondie', and Coote 'Poll' or 'Little Poll'. He was known to them as 'Boaz' or 'Bo'. Childish names seem to have delighted him because they recalled happy childhood memories.

Waugh never talked to the Lygon sisters of his first marriage, but unfortunately it was not to be the last of his failures in love. In the early 1930s, according to Sykes:

> He was in the awkward position of being involved in two affairs of the heart. In London he had fallen in love with a girl whom he hoped to marry if his former marriage were to be pronounced invalid. Inevitably, even if a plea of nullity succeeded (and he had as yet taken no steps towards it), he would have to wait a long time. Concurrently with this nerve-racking situation, he was being pursued by a married woman with whom he had enjoyed a liaison, and who had fallen deeply in love with him.[69]

[66] Lady Dorothy Lygon, 'Madresfield and Brideshead', in *Evelyn Waugh and His World*, edited by David Pryce-Jones (1973), p.53.

[67] Alec Waugh, *A Year to Remember: a Reminiscence of 1931* (1975), p.106.

[68] Interview with Lady Dorothy Lygon.

[69] Sykes, pp. 182-3.

The married woman was Audrey Lucas, whom Waugh had seen often in the mid-twenties. She had become engaged to, and finally married, Harold Scott, who ran the Cave of Harmony club with the actress Elsa Lanchester. Waugh reported in his diary that he was afraid he was to blame for her engagement, and one presumes from this that she realised that he himself had no thoughts of marrying her. After his wife deserted him, he again saw a good deal of her, quite often in the company of Bryan and Diana Guinness. Why Sykes suppresses her name is a mystery. Alec Waugh revealed that E.V. Lucas's 'daughter Audrey had been a close friend of the family. In 1930 she had had an affair with Evelyn. This was generally well known in London.'[70]

The affair is recorded in the diaries. At one point Audrey thought she was going to have a baby. Waugh's reaction was: 'I don't care much either way really so long as it is a boy.' It turned out that she was not pregnant, at which point he wrote: ' ... so all that is bogus.'[71]

The early 1930s seem to have been a busy time for Waugh. If he wasn't chasing ladies, they were chasing him. The trouble appears to have been that the ones who did the chasing were the ones he was never really interested in. One of his many admirers was Hazel Lavery, the second wife of Sir John Lavery the portrait painter. He records in 1932 before leaving London for Georgetown that he had received several telephone messages from Hazel and found her waiting for him in the vestibule of the Savile. In the letters he informs Henry Yorke when he returns from Georgetown in May, 1933: 'Don't tell Hazel I am back.'[72]

One reason why Lady Lavery is of interest to us is that as late as 1951/2 he writes to Clarissa Churchill apologising for the Christmas present he sent her. He goes on to say: 'I remember long ago when I had no home & spent my life globe-trotting, being furious with Hazel Lavery for giving me a glass swan, thinking (rightly) that it is better to be forgotten than so little remembered.'[73]

The glass swan rankled: the Chief Purser in *Brideshead Revisited* sends Celia Ryder, for her party, a life-size effigy of a swan, moulded in ice.

(William Gerhardi says that of the friends he and Waugh had in common two women stood out by their beauty: Hazel Lavery and Wanda Baillie-Hamilton.[74] The latter was, along with Tallulah Bankhead, the

---

[70] Alec Waugh, *The Best Wine Last: an Autobiography through the Years 1932-1969* (1978), p.45. Also, the *Tatler* on 19 June 1929 (p.538) reported that Audrey Scott was the authoress of an arresting play entitled *Why Drag in Marriage?* which was playing at the Strand Theatre. A reflection perhaps on her relationship with Waugh.

[71] *Diaries*, pp.312, 316.

[72] *Letters*, p.72.

[73] Ibid., p.363. Also, Audrey Morris writes: 'I have written a life of Lady Lavery. She certainly encouraged and was interested in young writers, among them Evelyn Waugh. I know that he dedicated one of his early novels to her ... I think they were just good friends and the association never went further than that. I was told that letters between them existed, but I never ran them to earth and have none in my book. About the swan you mention – It may well be the model for the ice swan in *Brideshead Revisited*.' Letter from Lady Morris to J. McDonnell, 12 October 1982. Lady Morris's book is not yet published.

[74] William Gerhardi, 'The Ordeal of Evelyn Waugh', *Times Literary Supplement*, 12 October 1967, p.961.

model for Waugh's Sonia Trumpington who gives young men black velvet in her bathroom while taking a bath.)

In 1935 Lady Lavery died, aged 38. For years she had been a source of endless gossip – largely because of her involvement with so many young men. On hearing of her death, Waugh wrote to Lady Mary Lygon: ' ... I feel sad at Hazel being dead on account of having been very Dutch to her and so I feel a shit.'[75] 'Dutch' in Waugh terms meant inconvenient, awkward or not encouraging. It derives from the fact that the young lady with whom he fell in love and wanted to marry in the early 1930s was Dutch and was unco-operative. Her name was Teresa Jungman, better known as Baby Jungman.

Teresa Jungman was a Bright Young Person, having led the original group with her sister, Zita, and Elizabeth Ponsonby. She was renowned for pulling stunts, and one of them which she carried out with Maureen Guinness while canvassing for the election in 1929 was reported as follows in the *Tatler*: 'One day they kidnapped a bevy of "Red" women and took them to one of Lord Knebworth's meetings, where they were so moved that they finally left the hall staunch Conservatives with pictures of the "boxing Viscount" in their hats!'[76] This was the stunt perhaps that prompted Julia Flyte's speech to the 'Conservative Women' in *Brideshead Revisited*.

Though Teresa Jungman was a Bright Young Person, she was described by Godfrey Winn as rather different from some of the young ladies in her set: he wrote ' ... there is a world of difference in her attitude in regard to her social duty to the community. She does not make a song and dance about it – though she is on the Committee of a party that is being given at Pinewood on June 14th to help the Invalid Kitchens carry on – but she just goes off every week and does voluntary work to help those who are doing their best to live the lives of decent citizens against overwhelming odds.'[77]

Teresa Jungman was not strikingly beautiful, but she had the fashionable kind of prettiness that was associated with the late Edna Best, as indeed did She-Evelyn. According to Christopher Sykes, they were both of a type that particularly appealed to Waugh.[78] She was once described in the *Tatler* as 'Miss Baby Jungman, minus her hat, and looking more than ever like Edna Best';[79] and on another occasion when she attended the boxing at the Albert Hall the *Tatler* wrote: 'Miss Teresa Jungman was very conspicuous in a ring-side seat, her golden hair seemed to shine out of the smoky atmosphere.'[80]

Lady Betjeman says of her:

She, Baby, and her sister, Zita, were a tremendous pair in London. They came out the year before I did. I remember we were always selling programmes at

[75] *Letters*, p.92.
[76] *Tatler*, 29 May 1929, p.431. For other of Teresa Jungman's stunts, see *Diaries*, p.801.
[77] Godfrey Winn, *A Month of Sundays* (1938), p.84.
[78] Sykes, pp.119, 198.
[79] *Tatler*, 12 December 1928, p.504.
[80] *Tatler*, 1 January 1930, p.3.

charity shows – they were always so much more successful than I was. Everybody was mad about them. Frank Pakenham had a tremendous walkout with Baby, and my brother, Roger Chetwode, had a walkout with her. I don't know how much of a walkout Evelyn had. Teresa was a very attractive blonde as a girl, not strikingly beautiful, but very feminine and demure, and the young men fell before her like hot cakes.[81]

Waugh met Lady Diana Cooper at this time. Of his relationship with 'Baby' she says:

He had a passion for someone called Baby Jungman – he wanted to marry her. She wouldn't. He went on and she was so cold. He'd get a little pink glow for a minute but then she didn't respond. She was very attractive – and strange – and he did love her. But it didn't work. He just wasn't her ticket. Then I think he was pleased with his wife.[82]

Waugh met a 'white mouse named Laura' when he stayed with the Herberts at Portofino in September 1933. In what is thought to be October of the same year he wrote to Lady Mary Lygon:

Just heard yesterday that my divorce comes on today so was elated and popped question to Dutch girl and got raspberry. So that is that, eh. Stiff upper lip and dropped cock. Now I must go. How sad, how sad.[83]

It was indeed: his pride had suffered yet another blow. He continued to court Teresa Jungman but without success. Jeffrey Heath has said that Waugh 'proposed marriage to her, but they were both Roman Catholics and his previous marriage interfered'.[84] But Waugh proposed when he was informed that his annulment was to be heard by the ecclesiastical court and he knew that there was some chance of marriage to Teresa Jungman. Their religion was not her reason for turning him down. Lady Betjeman, who has been in touch with Teresa (now Cuthbertson), reports her as saying that she did not wish to talk about Evelyn to anyone because he was in love with her but she was never in love with him and she had some very sweet letters from him but she preferred to keep the whole affair private.[85]

Nobody has ever suggested that Teresa Jungman was the model for Julia Flyte in *Brideshead*, but it is a distinct possibility. In the original manuscript Julia Flyte had fair hair, which Waugh later changed to dark (Chapter Three n.4). Olivia Plunket Greene was dark and a Catholic; Lady Mary Lygon was fair but not a Catholic; Teresa Jungman was fair and a very strict Catholic. In *Brideshead*, Julia's religion is held against her:

One subject eclipsed all others in importance for the ladies along the wall;

[81] Interview with Lady Betjeman (16 September 1982).
[82] Interview with Lady Diana.
[83] *Letters*, p.81.
[84] Jeffrey Heath, *The Picturesque Prison: Evelyn Waugh and his Writing* (1982), p.117.
[85] Letter from Lady Betjeman to J. McDonnell, 26 September 1982.

who would the young princes marry? They could not hope for purer lineage or a more gracious presence than Julia's; but there was this faint shadow on her that unfitted her for the highest honours; there was also her religion.

Nothing could have been further from Julia's ambitions than a royal marriage. She knew, or thought she knew, what she wanted and it was not that. But wherever she turned, it seemed, her religion stood as a barrier between her and her natural goal. (pp.174-5)

Julia has the problem that of the 'dozen or so rich and noble Catholic families, none at that time had an heir of the right age. Foreigners – there were many among her mother's family – were tricky about money, odd in their ways, and a sure mark of failure in the English girl who wed them' (p.175).

Lady Mary Lygon married a Russian prince, Prince Vsevolode, and the marriage ended in divorce. More important, Teresa Jungman married a Scot in a Canadian regiment, Graham Cuthbertson, and, of course, Julia Flyte married a Canadian, Rex Mottram. 'Foreigners – there were many among her mother's family' must apply to Teresa Jungman, for her mother, Mrs Richard Guinness, had first been married to Nico Jungman, a Dutchman. If we look at Waugh's letters and his description of Rex Mottram we will see the Canadian connection with Teresa Jungman's husband:

> Rex Mottram exerted himself to make an impression. He was a handsome fellow with dark hair growing low on his forehead and heavy black eyebrows. He spoke with an engaging Canadian accent. (*Brideshead*, p.107)

> His life, so far as he made it known, began in the war, where he had got a good M.C. serving with the Canadians and had ended as A.D.C. to a popular general.
> He cannot have been more than thirty at the time we met him, but he seemed very old to us in Oxford. Julia treated him, as she seemed to treat all the world, with mild disdain, but with an air of possession. During luncheon she sent him to the car for her cigarettes, and once or twice when he was talking very big, she apologized for him, saying: 'Remember he's a colonial,' to which he replied with boisterous laughter. (p.108)

> At length Julia arrived, unhurried, exquisite, unrepentant. 'You shouldn't have let him wait,' she said, 'It's his Canadian courtesy.' (p.109)

> He was married in Montreal in 1915 to a Miss Sarah Evangeline Cutler, who is still living there. (p.188)

Waugh wrote of Teresa Jungman:

> The Dutch girl, like so many other people, has got a new youth out of the war ... She dances with Canadian soldiers at night clubs three nights a week and sits up in an A.R.P. post the other four. (*Letters*, p.133)

> Baby Jungman has come to London with a vast baby solely in her

charge ... She has changed a great deal with contact with rough Canadians and loss of virginity and is now frank in thought, coarse in speech and likes a stiff whisky. Very surprising. (p.166)

Lord Longford (then Frank Pakenham) courted Teresa Jungman and in an interview with me (February 20, 1984) he said the following:

Baby Jungman had countless admirers of varying ages. Among the older generation Lord Margesson, the Conservative Chief Whip and Lord Ebury; among my contemporaries, David Cecil, Evelyn Waugh and myself. Charlie Brocklehurst was the most valuable of her admirers; he left her a fortune when he died. Baby was very chaste and virginal. Yet she had all these men at her feet. She had a fascination all her own, in which a sense of humour was prominent. Her father was a Dutch artist, her mother, Beatrice Guinness, who left Jungman and went off with Dick Guinness, came from a highly respected Catholic family in Birmingham.

You would not have said that Baby had the starting point to become a great social figure, but she was sought after everywhere. She stayed with the Salisburys at Hatfield and the Desboroughs at Taplow. Baby was very strict about her Catholic faith. She could not have married Evelyn in the early thirties, because he had not got his ecclesiastical annulment. Anyway, she did not seem to want to marry any of us. No one ever got anywhere with her sexually. Nothing happened with me in that respect and Evelyn and all the others got, I feel sure, the same treatment.

She was very personal and affectionate. But she was more like a nun, like a very friendly and fascinating nun.

Her coolness or reserve, or whatever you like to call it was only broken down by a much-resented man called Cuthbertson, whom she eventually married. Cuthbertson was regarded by all of us as a bounder. You can see how the old bitterness comes back. He was a gentleman by birth, educated at Wellington, but had gone to Canada and joined the Canadian forces. He reappeared as a sergeant-major with a walrus moustache. He obviously had plenty of sexuality. Perhaps it needed someone like that to overcome Baby's chasteness, which possibly he did not even notice.

I have always assumed that Rex Mottram in *Brideshead Revisited* was based on Brendan Bracken. But the Canadian aspect and the fact that Evelyn, like all of us, was jealous of Cuthbertson may have played a part.

I asked Lord Longford whether he thought that Teresa Jungman could have helped to inspire the character of Julia Flyte:

I think it makes sense that she was the model for her rather than Olivia Plunket Greene. They were both Catholics but Olivia Greene was never popular or a success like Baby was. I supose there's always a special girl like that in an era.

Teresa Jungman then was rather 'like a nun', and at the beginning of *Brideshead Revisited* Nanny Hawkins talks about Julia's hair being cut. She thinks it is a pity and comments to Father Phipps that it's 'not natural'. He replies 'Nuns do it', to which she says 'Well, surely, Father, you aren't going

to make a nun out of Lady Julia? The very idea!' (p.38). Julia does not
become a nun, but she does turn back to the Church and renounce both Rex
and Charles. She becomes, as Nanny's allusion foretells, nun-like although
not a nun.

Christopher Sykes has said that Rex Mottram was 'closely modelled on
Brendan Bracken'. He adds: 'Evelyn frequently denied this, but I once
cornered him, telling him that he had rather spoilt the portrait by giving
Mottram black hair instead of Brendan's red hair, and if he thought this was
not a picture of Brendan he was most unobservant. He capitulated and
admitted that Mottram was indeed Bracken. I fancy I was one of very few to
have received this admission.'[86] The main characteristics were clearly based
on Bracken, but one cannot believe that Graham Cuthbertson did not play a
part, particularly as Bracken was Irish and Cuthbertson served in a Canadian
regiment.

In 1946 Waugh wrote in his diaries: 'Baby Jungman is on her way home
with her children, repudiated.'[87] Teresa Jungman's marriage lasted from
1940 to 1945, and Lady Betjeman said the following of it in relation to Evelyn
Waugh:

> She would have been much better off marrying him than the man she did. He
> was a Canadian – he just went off back to Canada and married somebody
> else ... and she is such a strict Catholic which is why she's never married
> anyone else.[88]

Teresa Jungman used to stay with the Lygon family at Madresfield, and
Waugh courted her there as he did elsewhere. It is not surprising that Lady
Dorothy Lygon believes that her sister was not the model for Julia Flyte.

Waugh once told Christopher Sykes, jokingly, that he modelled all his
characters in *Unconditional Surrender* on Teresa Jungman.[89] Sykes says it was
'a complete joke and should not be taken with any seriousness at all'.[90] One
doesn't want to stretch the point, but the fair Virginia Troy married an
American who deserted her, and an American in Waugh's terms was not far
removed from a Canadian.

It is also possible that Thérèse de Vitré in *A Handful of Dust* was lightly
based on Teresa Jungman, for Waugh sometimes spelt Teresa's name as
'Therese'; and in his letters he once referred to her as follows: ' ... Therese
wouldn't look at me because she was fancying a South African gink called
Sonny.'[91]

Thérèse de Vitré is a Catholic and says to Tony, 'No, I am not yet engaged,
but you see there are so few young men I can marry. They must be
Catholic ... ', which sounds most reminiscent of Teresa Jungman's and Julia

[86] Sykes, p.343.
[87] *Diaries*, p.657.
[88] Interview with Lady Betjeman.
[89] *Letters*, p.578.
[90] Christopher Sykes has written: 'I have known Teresa Jungman for many years, but did not
see her while I was writing the biography.' Letter to J. McDonnell, 4 August 1982.
[91] *Letters*, p.66.

Flyte's situation, remembering that Teresa Jungman had a 'brilliant season' just as Julia did.

Again, in *A Handful of Dust* Thérèse is returning to Trinidad, and this situation could well have been prompted by the fact that in December 1932 Waugh visited Trinidad on his journey to South America; and the first entry in his diary while aboard ship was concerned mainly with Teresa Jungman, who had seen him off and given him a gold St Christopher medal. The relationship was not very satisfactory at this point, for although Waugh had discussed the possibility of an ecclesiastical annulment as early as 1930 he did nothing about it until 1933, and when he left for South America he believed that there was little hope of marrying Teresa Jungman and departed with a 'heart of lead'.[92] In Trinidad he was to meet a man called Bartlett who told him that he was 'Teresa's first cousin'.[93]

There is one final source, I believe, for Julia Flyte, and that is Julia Strachey. Waugh referred to her in his diaries, and there is one entry which reads 'dined with Julia Strachey who has cut off all her hair and looks like Hugh Lygon'.[94] Hugh Lygon was one of the models for Sebastian Flyte, and Julia and Sebastian look like each other. Again, in one of Carrington's letters to Julia Strachey in 1929 she said: 'I am sending you your Chinese present. Rather late and rather chilly. But you might wear it sometimes to dazzle the rats.'[95] It was a Chinese robe, and of course Julia Flyte has one in *Brideshead Revisited*. Waugh could well have seen the robe since Julia Strachey spent time with Diana and Bryan Guinness, as he did.

As far as the name 'Julia Flyte' is concerned, the Christian name might have come from Julia Strachey; and the name 'Flyte' would have been known in society circles, for the *Tatler* used to carry amusing drawings by Fish and one of his characters was Lady Flyte. One double page in 1928 was entitled 'Lady Flyte Does Her Christmas Shopping'.[96]

Before we move on to Waugh's second marriage, to Laura Herbert, his relationship with Lady Diana Cooper needs to be discussed. They first met in 1932 at a luncheon party given by Lady Lavery when Lady Diana was playing in *The Miracle* in London. She took to Evelyn immediately, as he did to her, and they became extremely close friends. It is said that she had more control over him than any one except Laura. Nancy Mitford, for instance, was told by Lady Diana that she was far too weak-minded with Waugh. Nancy apparently thought that this was the only way to keep his friendship. It was not an attitude that Lady Diana believed in: if Waugh needed scolding, she scolded him.

It has been suggested that there was more to the relationship than friendship. Waugh might have hoped for more, but on her part there was no attraction. As many admirers as Lady Diana had, she was in love with her husband, Duff Cooper. Although there were many chances for Waugh and

[92] *Diaries*, p.356.
[93] Ibid., p.359.
[94] Ibid., p.243.
[95] *Carrington: Letters and Extracts From Her Diaries*, edited by David Garnett (1979), p.426.
[96] *Tatler*, 30 November 1928.

her to have an affair, since he travelled with her a lot during her tour of the provinces with *The Miracle*, she said, while being interviewed, that nothing ever happened, or more precisely:

> Oh God, no – I don't think he ever courted me in that way – never physically, no – we had every opportunity – he used to come motoring with me – but no, he wasn't a lascivious type.[97]

Lady Diana did not find Waugh physically attractive any more, sadly, than had either Olivia Plunket Greene or Teresa Jungman. She loved him dearly as a friend and kept in close touch with Mr Wu,[98] as she called him until he died, quite often visiting him and Laura, first at Piers Court and later at Combe Florey.

Lady Diana suffered Waugh's black moods[99] throughout the time she knew him. Two years before he died she realised he could no longer enjoy life. He liked being grand and going to the theatre; so she would take a box, and afterwards she would get caviar for supper, but at this point nothing worked. He was just desperately melancholic. After his death she wrote a letter of condolence to Laura, and to his favourite daughter, Margaret. Both replied in the same vein, telling her not to grieve, for he was so miserable and would be happy to be out of it.[100]

Diana Cooper believes that Waugh always had an 'unhappy' nature. Youth, success and his social life kept it at bay for a while. But when those things began to pall, she believes, he reverted to his 'unfortunate' nature. She points out that a couple of years after he married Laura Herbert she asked him whether he was happy and whether there was any fault in the marriage. He said no; the only problem he had was that he loved society and Laura didn't.[101] In later years when melancholia set in, he rarely left Coombe Florey. When she visited him there he was nearly always sad, and if he came to London it was no different.

Waugh would have liked her to become a Catholic, particularly in later years when she was losing faith. She has never joined the Church, but says her prayers in accordance with a structure that he taught her: A for Adoration, C for Contrition, T for Thanksgiving, and S for Supplication. She feels about his attitude towards his religion that he had been a tremendously enthusiastic convert, but that as the war went on his faith began to fail him. She sums the matter up as follows, in comparison with another author: 'I think Graham Greene is a good man possessed of a devil – and that Evelyn is a bad man for whom an angel is struggling.'[102]

[97] Interview with Lady Diana.

[98] Lady Diana says that it was Rudolph Kommer who first coined the name – 'Wooing Mr. Wu I suppose'. Letter to J. McDonnell, 30 October 1981. Also, see Appendix One.

[99] Lady Diana called Waugh her 'dear malignancy'. Philip Ziegler, *Diana Cooper* (1981), p.150.

[100] Interview with Lady Diana.

[101] Ibid.

[102] Ziegler, *Diana Cooper*, p.267.

Diana Cooper believes that Waugh, except in his Oxford days, preferred the company of women. Certainly in later life his friends were mainly female. They had however to be women of rank, wit or beauty – or preferably all three. As Nancy Mitford pointed out when she was talking of Waugh's dreadful behaviour: 'But I find that he is quite all right with Duchesses, so *that* in future will be my clue.'[103]

There are many stories about the beautiful, eccentric Diana Cooper and the irascible Evelyn Waugh, but her main interest for us is that she is the one lady on whom a character was based entirely. Julia Stitch is an exceptional woman, and for that reason I have devoted Chapter Nine entirely to her.

Waugh married 'well' for a second time. Evelyn Gardner was a daughter of Lady Burghclere; Laura Herbert was a daughter of Aubrey Herbert, a half-brother of the Earl of Carnarvon. Strangely, Laura and Evelyn Gardner were first cousins, since Lady Burghclere was Lord Carnarvon's sister. Even stranger is that Olivia Greene was also a cousin of Laura Herbert. (In 1945 Waugh worked out Laura's descent from six or seven Dukes.)

Waugh married Laura Herbert in 1937, after his first marriage was finally annulled. His first full description of her is early in 1935:

> I have taken a *great* fancy to a young lady named Laura. What is she like? Well fair, very pretty, plays peggoty beautifully. We met on a house party in Somerset.
>
> She has rather a long thin nose and skin as thin as bromo as she is very thin and might be dying of consumption to look at her and she has her hair in a little bun at the back of her neck but it is not very tidy and she is only 18 years old, virgin, Catholic, quiet & astute. So it is difficult. I have not made much progress yet except to pinch her twice in a charade and lean against her thigh in pretending to help her at peggoty.[104]

A little later he writes:

> The young lady of whom I spoke to you named Laura came to London with me yesterday but it was not a success for I had a hangover & could only eat 3 oysters and some soda water and I was sick a good deal on the table so perhaps that romance is shattered.[105]

Surprisingly, the romance survived. In the spring of 1936 Waugh wrote to Laura asking her to think about marrying him. That letter reveals Waugh's understanding of his troubled personality, and for that reason I quote a large part of it here:

> I am restless & moody & misanthropic & lazy & have no money except what I earn and if I got ill you would starve. In fact its a lousy proposition. On the other

---

[103] Acton, *Nancy Mitford*, p.82. And in my interview with Lady Dorothy Lygon she said: 'Waugh enjoyed the company of women enormously but the most important thing was that he shouldn't be bored by them; if he was he lost interest.'

[104] *Letters*, p.92.

[105] Ibid., p.93.

hand I think I could do a Grant and reform & become quite strict about not getting drunk and I am pretty sure I should be faithful. Also there is always a fair chance that there will be another bigger economic crash in which case if you had married a nobleman with a great house you might find yourself starving, while I am very clever and could probably earn a living of some sort somewhere. Also though you would be taking on an elderly buffer, I am one without fixed habits. You wouldn't find yourself confined to any particular place or group. Also I have practically no living relatives except one brother whom I scarcely know. [His parents, Arthur and Catherine Waugh were still alive.] You would not find yourself involved in a large family & all their rows & you would not be patronized & interfered with by odious sisters in law & aunts as often happens. All these are very small advantages compared with the awfulness of my character. I have always tried to be nice to you and you may have got it into your head that I am nice really, but that is all rot. It is only to you & for you. I am jealous & impatient – but there is no point in going into a whole list of my vices. You are a critical girl and I've no doubt you know them all and a great many I don't know myself. But the point I wanted to make is that if you marry most people, you are marrying a great number of objects & other people as well, well if you marry me there is nothing else involved, and that is an advantage as well as a disadvantage. My only tie of any kind is my work. That means for several months each year we shall have to separate or you would have to share some very lonely place with me. But apart from that we could do what we liked & go where we liked – and if you married a soldier or stockbroker or member of parliament or master of hounds you would be more tied. When I tell my friends that I am in love with a girl of 19 they look shocked and say 'wretched child' but I dont look on you as very young even in your beauty and I dont think there is any sense in the line that you cannot possibly commit yourself to a decision that affects your whole life for years yet. But anyway there is no point in your deciding or even answering. I may never get free of your cousin Evelyn. Above all things, darling, don't fret at all. But just turn the matter over in your dear head.[106]

Laura married him. At 19 she knew what she was taking on, and it shows a distinct strength of character on her part. She preferred country to town life, and with her Waugh settled down to the domesticity he had longed for, interspersed with social trips away from home in the early days of the marriage.

He wrote many letters to his wife, and since they have been published, a common reaction, as with the diaries, has been to say what an unpleasant husband and father he must have been. It is true that he quite often scolds Laura. At other times he treats her distantly with remarks like 'Give my regards to your children'. It is a curious way to write to a wife.

Lady Diana, like most of his friends, believes that he loved Laura. The Herbert family did not think so. Bridget Grant, his sister-in-law, thought he was unkind to her. Lady Diana once said to Mrs Grant: 'But he loves her, I know he loves her. He's always saying I must get back to poor little Laura.' Bridget Grant's reply was to snort: 'Typical, poor little Laura, why should she be poor little Laura?'[107]

---

[106] Ibid., p.104.
[107] Interview with Lady Diana.

One suspects that she wasn't 'poor little Laura' at all. Frances Donaldson, in *Portrait of a Country Neighbour*, reveals that Laura had a mind of her own. Waugh could not browbeat her, as is so often thought. During one winter, beautifully served meals arrived to the accompaniment of thuds from the floor beneath and a rather unpleasant smell. Laura had her hens in the cellar under the dining room, as she was running out of space on the farm. Waugh's snobbery meant that there was an Italian manservant who, properly dressed, served dinner. Once Laura found that he was good with cows, the man would sometimes come in grey flannel trousers and pullover.

Lady Betjeman disagrees about the beautifully served meals:

> Laura wasn't interested in food, and we always had frightfully dull food, and it pained Evelyn. He would have loved to have had nice food for his friends. One used to have in those days – well, you never see it now – it used to be called 'nursery food' – potatoes without much butter or milk forced through a sieve so that it came out in little worms. I remember we had that one day, and Evelyn rampaged at Laura because it was so dreadful; and I was so sorry for Laura because she was so meek and never argued back. She was the most incredible wife to him; nobody else that he had proposed to would have put up with him – but she was wonderful. She loved him very much.[108]

Whether he browbeat Laura or not, with her Waugh kept alive his sense of fun. His letter to her in 1942, describing at length the efforts of a team of commandos to blow up a tree stump on Lord Glasgow's estate, is as funny as anything he wrote.[109] Sykes misses this warmer and more relaxed aspect of Waugh, which must have been important to Laura, particularly as his public, and then private, behaviour gave way to melancholy.

Whatever his in-laws may have thought, Laura appears to have loved Evelyn. She protected him. There are entries in the diaries which reveal that in her absence he was quite often befogged with drink and suffering from insomnia. Ann Fleming, another good friend, used to try to take him out of himself in the last years, as did Diana Cooper. She remembers one occasion at the Hyde Park Hotel when he would not venture out to dine and kept asking for Laura, who had taken the children to the cinema. She was sad to find him so melancholic and stayed with him until Laura returned. Laura was his companion, his confidante, his supporter – all the things that Evelyn Gardner had not been. The pain of that marriage is reflected in his work. What Laura gave to his writing was something completely different. She understood that he had to be alone to write. When he was at home and wanted peace and quiet, she kept the children out of his way. She seems to have supported him in every way without denying her own personality.

Although Waugh appears to have been rather scathing about his children, he was obviously fond of them, particularly his daughter Margaret, for whom his affection was considerable. She has written a loving memoir of her father, which is printed at the end of Sykes's biography.

---

[108] Interview with Lady Betjeman.
[109] *Letters* p.160.

In an article in 1929, Waugh wrote about the mothers of the new age saying that the modern mother 'aims at a very small family kept well in the background of a hygienic nursery', and that she will see just as much of her children 'as she finds amusing and they will thus learn the excellent principle that they must make themselves agreeable if they want attention'.[110] There were in fact definite rules for children in the Waugh home. As a nursery child you had all your meals in the nursery. Once at boarding school you were allowed when home to have lunch in the dining room. Dinner with the grown-ups didn't happen until you were ten or eleven. Harriet Waugh, who says she had a happy childhood, also points out that they were expected to make conversation at these meals. Their father saw no reason why they should not learn to be entertaining. There was also a game they used to play: having to bring sentences into the conversation when people came to lunch. Waugh would give them sentences and they would give him one. When she was about ten she was given 'Architecture is pure beauty'. Apparently she hadn't spoken during most of the meal and finally said this single sentence. His response was 'What do you mean by that, Hatty?"[111]

For the last twenty years of his life Waugh was essentially a family man, albeit sometimes a reluctant one. The later diaries and letters reveal that most of his days were spent at his country house, where he kept up a large correspondence with his friends. In the letters he rather high-handedly tells Laura off for being a bad correspondent, pointing out that correspondence should be like conversation. Laura, like Olivia and Lady Diana, was a poor letter writer. The friend he found most satisfactory in that respect was Nancy Mitford. Waugh liked gossip and a lurid piece of news would fill him with delight. Most of his gossip came from his female friends. Frances Donaldson points out that 'three-parts misanthropic, one part gregarious and highly curious, he was inclined to like women better than men because they prattle easily'.[112] Nancy Mitford had a talent for letter-writing and sent him all the gossip about London society he loved to hear. When in London he used to visit her at the Heywood Hill bookshop, where she worked, to listen to the latest and juiciest details. She was always surrounded there by fashionable and intellectual friends.

Nancy was one of the many friends whom he encouraged in their writing and his hand can be seen at work in her books. He suggested the title *Pursuit of Love* and also helped her to revise some parts of the book before publication. The entrenching tool 'with which in 1915, Uncle Matthew had whacked to death eight Germans one by one as they crawled out of a dug-out' smacks of Waugh; and the passage describing Uncle Matthew's house with its 'theme of death' was written by him. He also, of course, contributed to the heated discussion of 'U and Non-U' which ended up in *Noblesse Oblige*.

Nancy was beautiful and vivacious and like Waugh had a tendency to

[110] Evelyn Waugh, 'Matter-of-Fact Mothers of the New Age', *Evening Standard* 8 April 1929, p.7.

[111] 'Harriet Waugh is in control of the moon but admits she finds it rather suburban. Perhaps she should have listened to father … ' Maureen Cleave, *Evening Standard*, 17 April 1969, p.11.

[112] Frances Donaldson, *Portrait of a Country Neighbour* (1967), p.20.

shock: a childish quality that Waugh found both endearing and irritating. She once wrote an article in France saying that, as Marie Antoinette was a traitress, the use of the guillotine was justified. It did not go down too well with Prince Pierre of Monaco, who never spoke to her again. Like Lady Diana, her lack of faith worried her as she grew older. She wanted to believe in an after-life and asked Waugh what happened in his faith when people died. Her brief synopsis of his four page reply is as follows:

We die and are judged at once. Saints (?) go straight to Heaven. Sinners straight to Hell. The rest of us get varying sentences in Purgatory. At the Last Trump those still remaining on earth are judged. Those who are serving their sentences have to join up with their bodies (like finding one's coat after a party. I hope the arrangements are efficient). The only bodies who rose again are those of Our Lord's and Our Lady's. The body (the good) is US because we do not, like the Mahomedans, believe that body and spirit are two separate things. I wrote and asked Evelyn why, if the body is us, we are not told to take care of it but on the contrary encouraged to tease it. He said that Cyril Connolly's idea that the body ought to be fed on *foie gras* and covered with kisses is not regular – the body must be mortified. Oh yes – the end of the world is also the end of time. Isn't it interesting? I can hardly wait.'[113]

When Nancy left London to go to Paris Waugh was most upset and appointed Ann Fleming and Lady Pamela Berry, among others, to be his new London gossips. They were both excellent letter-writers.

Waugh had so many female friends that it is impossible to discuss them all at length – the Countess of Avon (Clarissa Churchill), Lady Katherine ('Kitty') Brownlow, Daphne Acton, Daphne Fielding, Elizabeth Ponsonby, Julia Strachey, the Countess of Longford (Elizabeth Harman), Elsa Lanchester, Frances Donaldson, and so it goes on. One favourite who has already been mentioned was Lady Betjeman, and she needs to be discussed in a little more detail for the parts she did, or did not, play in his novels.

Auberon Waugh said in the *Daily Mail* that Lady Betjeman was the model for Cordelia in *Brideshead Revisited*. He also said that his father had had an early passion for her. He added that this had been revealed by Sir Maurice Bowra in his autobiography in revenge against Waugh for portraying him as Samgrass.[114] Her name is not linked directly with Waugh's, however, in Bowra's book. After the chapter on Penelope Chetwode, as she then was, Bowra says: 'Eddie Sackville West met him at a country house where he was about to take a pretty girl for a walk. It was an unusually hot day, and Evelyn was carrying a heavy overcoat. Eddie asked about it and Evelyn answered, 'I hope it may prove useful as a groundsheet.'[115] Auberon Waugh has confirmed that this rather oblique reference is the one he meant and that the young lady was Lady Betjeman, then Penelope Chetwode.'[116]

[113] Harold Acton, *Nancy Mitford*, p.146.

[114] Auberon Waugh, 'Brideshead: Who Really Was Who', *Daily Mail*, 13 October 1981, pp.20-1.

[115] C.M. Bowra, *Memories 1898-1939* (1966), p.174.

[116] Letter from Auberon Waugh to J. McDonnell, 8 December 1982.

Lady Betjeman confirms Waugh's fondness for her but refutes the idea that she was the model for Cordelia:

> The article which you mention by Auberon (and which I never saw as I was in India), is the first intimation that I had that I was supposed to have inspired the character of Cordelia [as you say]. Evelyn did make a few advances from time to time and on one occasion (after I was married to JB) he sent me a copy of *Ninety Two Days* containing only blank pages, presumably because I did not respond. We subsequently used it as a visitor's book. I was very fond of Evelyn and he was always very generous to JB and me and a very loyal friend but I never fancied him![117]

When Waugh was writing *Helena* he wrote to her asking her advice about the riding scenes because she was passionately fond of horses; and also to her husband saying that he was writing her life under the disguise of St Helena's:

> She is 16, sexy, full of horse fantasies. I want to get this right. Will you tell her to write to me fully about adolescent sex reveries connected with riding. I have no experience of such things, nor has Laura. I make her always the horse & the consummation when the rider subdues her. Is this correct? Please make her explain. And is riding enough or must she be driven? Are spurs important or only leather-work.[118]

In a later letter he tells Lady Betjeman that his article on *Helena* for the *Tablet* had the 'fruits of his unaided invention'. He goes on: 'I should welcome detailed criticism. The Empress loses her interest in such things when she is married. I describe her as hunting in the morning after her wedding night feeling the saddle as comforting her wounded maidenhead. Is that O.K.? After that she has no interest in sex.'[119]

Lady Betjeman confirms that she never answered Waugh's questions:

> No, I don't mind talking about it. Well, it was all bosh really. I mean I never had any riding fantasies. I can only think that – there was a sex magazine – it was after I met John and we all used to read it. It was called *London Life* and it was full of sex fantasies – I mean black mackintoshes were the great thing and human ponies and all that sort of thing – and it was just a joke – we didn't indulge in those fantasies. Doesn't he made me ride the pony naked at one time? Well I know he makes me very excited riding on the saddle or something – and I suppose I didn't answer because I didn't want to get involved in that kind of thing – I mean I always liked riding all sorts but in a straightforward way. I didn't want to get involved in any *London Life* thing he might attribute to me that I never did in my life.[120]

[117] Letter from Lady Betjeman to J. McDonnell, 27 January 1982.
[118] *Letters*, p.207.
[119] Ibid., p.218.
[120] Interview with Lady Betjeman. *London Life* was a penny illustrated paper. Although Waugh told Nancy Mitford that he was having 'an interesting correspondence with Mrs Betjeman about horses & sex. Half of it gets confiscated in the post by the socialists' (*Letters*, p.221), Lady Betjeman is quite sure she never answered his questions.

Certainly the riding fantasies are not connected with Lady Betjeman, but Waugh obviously drew on certain aspects of her character for both Cordelia and Helena. Both characters like riding, and as will be seen in the next chapter they share a similar kind of schoolgirl language – 'beastly', 'bosh', 'rot', and 'nonsense', are just a few of the words in their vocabulary. One of Cordelia's favourite expressions is 'Oh, pray not'. At the end of Book One of *Brideshead Revisited*, Charles Ryder says to Cordelia 'You'll fall in love', to which she replies 'Oh, I pray not. I say, do you think I could have another of those scrumptious meringues?' (p.214). In my interview with her, over lunch, Lady Betjeman said to the waitress, 'Oh yes, I'd love some pudding, I love pudding, pray give me a little more cream', and later 'Oh, how lovely, I'm terribly greedy'; and when she was talking about Laura's cooking ability, she said: 'She wasn't in the least bit greedy like me.' Her conversation was also peppered with the odd 'rot', 'bosh', and 'beastly'.[121] Cordelia is described as 'voracious' in her eating habits and she tackles her dinner with 'renewed relish'; and Helena when she has eaten the succulent dishes laid out before her says 'What a spread ... What a blow-out!' Lady Betjeman loves food and writes the occasional cookery article. In 1946 Waugh recorded a visit to her home and made the comment 'Harness everywhere ... Delicious food cooked by Penelope'.[122]

Apart from Julia Stitch, Waugh's female characters are not based on a single individual. There is much about Cordelia and Helena that is like Lady Betjeman, and there is a lot that is not. Waugh's imagination obviously seized on various characteristics of his female friends, and he used some of these characteristics as seeds from which to grow his fictional characters.

To Henry Yorke ('Henry Green') about his autobiography *Pack My Bag* (1940) he wrote 'I never tire of hearing you talk about women & I wish there had been very much more indeed about them and the extraordinary things they say'.[123]

Evelyn Waugh enjoyed socialising with women. And from their company he gained an immaculate ear for their language.

[121] Interview with Lady Betjeman.
[122] *Diaries*, p.660.
[123] *Letters*, p.144.

CHAPTER TWO

An Immaculate Ear for Language

No innuendo of conversation or infelicity of grammar or vocabulary escaped him, and his articulacy was total. Whenever he spoke, it was in perfectly constructed sentences – not through any contrivance, but because that was how his mind arranged itself. In many respects his conversation was like one of those machines for fielding practice at cricket, called I think a slip-catcher, where a ball thrown in can come out at any speed or angle, sometimes with a vicious spin on it, sometimes in a graceful dolly drop. (Auberon Waugh, *Books and Bookmen*, 19 October 1973, p.11)

Evelyn Waugh never used two words where one was enough. A skilled user of the English language, he had a faultless ear for dialogue.

Ronald Firbank is one writer who clearly influenced Evelyn Waugh's early work. James Carens has covered this ground,[1] and the association is also to be found in fragmentary and fugitive writings. Waugh himself published an essay on Firbank,[2] and perhaps took him more seriously than other people had done before him. He admired the man as a technical innovator, and it is worth quoting part of Waugh's essay here, using the same examples he gives from Firbank, and examples from his own works which obviously owe a debt to Firbank.

> His later novels are almost wholly devoid of any attributions of cause to effect; there is the barest minimum of direct description; his compositions are built up, intricately and with a balanced alternation of the wildest extravagance and the most austere economy, with conversational *nuances*. They may be compared to cinema films in which the relation of caption and photograph is directly reversed; occasionally a brief, visual image flashes out to illumine and explain the flickering succession of spoken words.[3]

Waugh quotes from *Valmouth*:

> One sunny May Day morning, full of unrest, Lady Parvula de Panzoust left the Hotel for a turn on the promenade. It was a morning of pure delight. Great clouds, breaking into dream, swept slowly across the sky, rolling down from the

[1] James F. Carens, *The Satiric Art of Evelyn Waugh* (1966), pp.5-10.
[2] Evelyn Waugh, 'Ronald Firbank', *Essays*, pp.56-9.
[3] Ibid., pp.57-8.

uplands behind Hare Hatch House, above whose crumbling pleasances one single sable streak, in the guise of a coal-black negress, prognosticated rain.

'Life would be perfect,' she mused ...

Here is a comparable passage from Waugh's *Decline and Fall* (p.77):

On one side stood the Circumferences, Tangent, the Vicar, Colonel Sidebotham, and the Hope-Brownes; on the other the seven Clutterbucks, Philbrick, Flossie, and two or three parents who had been snubbed already that afternoon by Lady Circumference. No one spoke of the race, but outraged sportsmanship glinted perilously in every eye. Several parents, intent on their tea, crowded round Dingy and the table. Eminently aloof from all these stood Chokey and Mrs Beste-Chetwynde. Clearly the social balance was delicately poised, and the issue depended upon them. With or without her nigger, Mrs Beste-Chetwynde was a woman of vital importance.

'Why, Dr Fagan,' she was saying ...

In *Valmouth* it is the visual image of 'in the guise of a coal black negress' that springs out at us; in the *Decline and Fall* example it is the visual image of 'with or without her nigger' that illumines the cinematic scene that has just flashed in front of our eyes. Mrs Yajnavalkya is the first and probably the most ebullient in a long line of negroes who feature in Firbank's works. Chokey is also the first of Waugh's negro characters.

Waugh says that in Firbank's dialogue 'there is no exchange of opinion. His art is purely selective. From the fashionable chatter of his period, vapid and interminable, he has plucked, like tiny brilliant feathers from the breast of a bird, the particles of his design.'[4] Here he quotes from *The Flower Beneath The Foot*:

'I would give all my soul to him, Rara ... my chances of heaven!'

'Your chances, Olga – ', Mademoiselle de Nazianzi murmured, avoiding some bird-droppings with her skirt.

'How I envy *the men*, Rara, in his platoon!'

'Take away his uniform, Olga, and what does he become?'

'Ah *what –* '

Now an example from *Vile Bodies* (p.12):

'They say that only *one* person has any influence with Mr Outrage ... '

'At the Japanese Embassy ... '

'Of course, dear, not so loud. But tell me, Fanny, seriously, do you really and truly think Mr Outrage has IT?'[5]

'He has a very nice figure for a man of his age.'

'Yes, but *his* age, and the bull-like type is so often disappointing. Another glass? ... '

[4] Ibid., p.58.

[5] The literary reference 'IT' is probably to Elinor Glyn's use of the expression to describe the magnetic charm of the hero, John Gaunt, in her story *IT*. See *IT and Other Stories* (Duckworth, 1927). She was not however the first to use the expression. Rudyard Kipling used it of the central character in his story 'Mrs Bathurst', which can be found in *Traffics and Discoveries* (1904). 'Mrs Bathurst' was first published in 1904.

Fanny Throbbing and Kitty Blackwater of *Vile Bodies* have much in common with Firbank's Rara and Olga; but there is a difference between the two authors. This kind of empty and fashionable small talk is used by Firbank throughout his work. Waugh uses it seldom, if at all, after *Vile Bodies*; only in the conversation of the few 'silly' or 'young' girls in the later books. Even the fashionable ladies in *A Handful of Dust* offer some opinions, however silly those opinions may be; and even those Bright Young People who specialised in saying nothing interestingly become serious. And where Firbank has a delightful but irresponsible grasshopping mind, Waugh hops as effectively but with more responsibility. Very often he points a social moral, which Firbank does not. For example, in *Vile Bodies*, after the customs scene, where the Younger Set talk in the carriage about their goings-on and Archie Schwert's party, he stands aside from his tale to say 'Oh, Bright Young People!' In those four sad little words he points out the futility of their lives. Also, the customs scene with its barbed reference to Sir William Joynson-Hicks, the reactionary Home Secretary of the time, has a sting to it which is absent in Firbank's work.

Waugh then goes on to say that although Firbank's delicate, fashionable dialogue seems to go on without any purpose, 'quite gradually, the reader is aware that a casual reference on one page links up with some particular inflexion of phrase on another until there emerges a plot; usually a plot so outrageous that he distrusts his own inferences'.[6] His example here is from *The Flower Beneath The Foot*, where the King at a dinner party uses the following expression:

> 'I could not be more astonished if you told me there were fleas at the Ritz', a part of which assertion Lady Something, who was blandly listening, imperfectly chanced to hear. (p.32)

Lady Something's hearing puts her under the misapprehension that fleas have been found at the Ritz. But the tale doesn't rest there. Later a young man says he would have not gone to the Ritz if he had known he was going to be so ill. Lady Something informs him that he would have been bitten all over. Farther on, we hear that the Ritz is being sued, and finally we learn that the hotel is empty, apart from one guest.

An example of Firbank's direct influence can be seen in the pages relating to John Andrew's death in *A Handful of Dust*. On page 93 Tony and Brenda talk about John going out with the hunt. Brenda asks, 'Is it quite safe?' to which Tony's reply is, 'Oh, yes, surely?' Brenda has already produced some doubt in us. On page 94 John Andrew says, 'Please God make me see the kill.' On page 100, when he is talking to Nanny about the hunt, she says, 'You won't see any death.' On page 102, we learn that the horse, Thunderclap, is fresh, and on page 103, when the hounds are called off and John has to go home, he cries, 'But there mayn't *be* another day.' On page 105 John dies, the whole thing having been set up by a series of verbal allusions with the two female characters playing a major part. Brenda establishes the situation by

[6] Evelyn Waugh, 'Ronald Firbank', *Essays*, p.58.

posing the doubt that John should hunt (she is also irresponsible enough to let him) and Nanny positively tells us that the child will die; although her remark 'You won't see any death' is obviously more ironic in retrospect. It is also, of course, the nice Miss Ripon who knocks John down.

This allusive conversation is Firbankian in idea, but while Firbank's is a narrative patterning of unconnected details which combine to form a comic effect, Waugh's patterning by this time is more concerned with the thematic effect than the narrative one. Waugh's solely narrative patterning is more obvious in the earlier books such as *Decline and Fall*, which contains the gradual build up to little Lord Tangent's death, and in *Black Mischief* where a game of consequences results in the misapprehension throughout the book that Madame Ballon and General Connolly are having an affair. The difference is that, in *A Handful of Dust*, John Andrew's death is necessary to the theme of the book (unlike the death of little Lord Tangent) because it gives Brenda a reason not to return to Tony. She would not have wanted to break up the family, but without John she feels that there is nothing to break up. Waugh has extended the Firbankian technique so that behind the surface conversation the main development of the theme of the book is happening almost imperceptibly.

Firbank influenced Waugh in the art of counterpoint in the novel, in impressionistic brushstrokes, in cinematic technique (though only to a minor extent as Waugh was always fascinated by the cinema), in the use of innuendo, in the use of italics and ellipses, and possibly in the choice of names. Firbank's Mrs Thoroughfare has a name entirely suited to her character, as does Waugh's Lady Circumference. Waugh has admitted the influence of Firbank in his early work in an interview with Julian Jebb while talking about *Vile Bodies*: 'It was second-hand too. I cribbed much of the scene at the customs from Firbank.' And he also mentioned that he no longer read Firbank, saying that he thought there would be 'something wrong with an elderly man who could enjoy Firbank'.[7] And in the 1965 preface to *Vile Bodies* he said: 'I began under the brief influence of Ronald Firbank but struck out for myself.'[8]

Frederick Stopp, who does not mention Firbank as a literary influence, says that Wodehouse, 'Saki', Fitzgerald and Hemingway were among Waugh's early influences. It is true that Waugh was a great admirer of P.G. Wodehouse and in the same interview with Julian Jebb he said that P.G. Wodehouse affected his style directly.[9] One can see the influence of Wodehouse, particularly in *Decline and Fall* where the conversations between Grimes and Paul have a Bertie Wooster overtone. Also, like Waugh, Wodehouse used the English public school, the English Church and Hollywood as important themes throughout his work. The art of allusive

[7] Julian Jebb, 'The Art of Fiction: Evelyn Waugh', *Paris Review* 30 (1963), pp.77, 80.

[8] Evelyn Waugh, 'Preface', *Vile Bodies* (1965), p.7.

[9] Jebb, *Paris Review*, p.80. Waugh also told Frances Donaldson that he admired P.G. Wodehouse because: 'One has to regard a man as a Master who can produce on average three uniquely brilliant and extremely original similes to every page.' Frances Donaldson, *Portrait of a Country Neighbour* (1967), p.73.

conversation was another feature. Wodehouse's most direct influence was in *Scoop* where we note that William Boot's two uncles, Roderick and Theodore, bear a distinct resemblance to the relatives of Galahad Threepwood of Blandings Castle. And in *Scoop* it is by a clear piece of Waugh/Wodehouse manipulation that Uncle Theodore takes his place at the final banquet rather than John, or William Boot; and Waugh, whose name had been jokingly used by Wodehouse for one of his characters – Waugh-Bonner – reveals his debt to Wodehouse, and continues the joke, in this section of the book:

> Uncle Theodore, after touching infelicitously on a variety of topics, had found common ground with the distinguished guest on his right; they had both, in another age, known a man named Bertie Wodehouse-Bonner. (pp.217-18)

Wodehouse's influence does not extend so deeply in the case of his female characters. Wodehouse had bright young things as Waugh did – and Waugh said when writing *Vile Bodies* that it was 'rather like P.G. Wodehouse all about bright young people'.[10] Wodehouse's bright young girls however did not sleep around, drink and take drugs. They were clean-living, jolly nice types. Also, Wodehouse's upper-class society women were not so fast-moving and fashionable as those of Waugh's Mayfair set. The exception perhaps is the jewel-loving Veronica Wedge whom Richard Usborne describes as 'that lovely dumb blonde who might have come out of an Evelyn Waugh novel'.[11] Finally, Wodehouse, unlike Waugh, had no satire or irony in his work, and he kept the sexual ethic in his books firmly Victorian. He would never have allowed Margot Beste-Chetwynde to sleep with Paul Pennyfeather before marriage.

There is nothing of the morbid quality in Wodehouse that is found in 'Saki', who stands in the line of literary dandies between Oscar Wilde[12] and Ronald Firbank. Certainly Waugh had an affinity with Saki's taste for violence, but he had his own way of making such violence funny. As far as Fitzgerald is concerned, Waugh professed not to have read him until much later in life, so this influence seems unlikely. We know that he admired Hemingway's gift for the language of drunks, but again the influence is small.[13]

Another influence is likely to have been 'Beachcomber' (J.B. Morton). Evelyn Waugh said he thought that 'he showed the greatest comic fertility of any Englishman'.[14] Waugh has a reference to one of Morton's characters in *Brideshead Revisited*. Celia Ryder tells an American Senator that the little

[10] *Letters*, p.36.

[11] Richard Usborne, *Wodehouse at Work* (1961), p.103.

[12] The 'great booby' as Waugh called him may have had some influence. Oscar Wilde was renowned for telling stories, and one of his anecdotes was about his Aunt Jane who threw a party where no one turned up. It is not unlike Waugh's short story 'Bella Fleace Gave a Party', and Wilde's anecdote can be read in W. Graham Robertson, *Time Was* (1931), pp.133-4.

[13] Jebb, *Paris Review*, p.80. Waugh said: 'I think that Hemingway made real discoveries about the use of language in his first novel, *The Sun Also Rises*. I admired the way he made drunk people talk.'

[14] J.B. Morton, *Beachcomber: the Works of J.B. Morton*, edited by Richard Ingrams (1974), p.22.

red-headed man who came uninvited to her party was 'Captain Foulenough in person' (p.234). The Senator takes what she says literally. The allusive conversation carries on to the extent that the little red-headed man is taken off the ship by two plain-clothes policemen. Morton's Captain Foulenough obviously took Waugh's fancy. One of Foulenough's adventures is interesting. 'Captain Foulenough in the Fur Trade' is about the Captain stealing cats from widows and unfortunate ladies to turn them into ermine furs for Maison Katzphur. One lady, a beauty to whom he becomes atttracted, Lavinia Gratcham, purrs when he strokes her cheek. A lot of Waugh's ladies act like cats, as we shall note in Chapter Three.

Foulenough was an excellent name, and Morton like Firbank was fascinated by names. (Peacock also used descriptive names – such as Mr Listless and Mr Larynx in *Nightmare Abbey*; but Peacock does not give such descriptive and ironical names to his female characters.) Morton has women like Lady Screaming, Lady Bursting, Lady Flogge, Mrs Wretch and Mrs Roustabout; Waugh has Lady Circumference, Lady Cockpurse, Lady Throbbing, Miss Mouse and Mrs Melrose Ape. In Waugh's public school in *Decline and Fall* there is a Dr Fagan; in Morton's Narkover School there is a Dr Smart-Allick. Colonel Blount, the eccentric father in *Vile Bodies* has a film made, while in Morton's work there is an eccentric Lord Shortcake who has a film made about his goldfish. Morton, Wodehouse and Waugh all had an obsession with the film world of Hollywood. One of the most striking similarities between Morton and Waugh is their description of Bright Young People. Morton's young things are not nice like Wodehouse's: they have wild parties like Waugh's characters, and they are tired of life. Iris Tennyson, 'alias Woofie, alias Bibbins, alias Foo Foo, alias Mopsy, alias Toots, alias heaven knows what else' is a bright young person who leads her admirer Mr Thake up the garden path, finally marrying her rich American, Adolf Brasch. She, like Nina Blount in *Vile Bodies*, is sick of life, even commenting on a fine night that the stars 'make her sick because they were so putridly smug up there in the revolting sky'.[15]

While he thought highly of Firbank, Wodehouse and Morton, Waugh also admired E.M. Forster, Max Beerbohm, William Gerhardi and Hilaire Belloc. He read Dickens throughout his life, and also detective stories, particularly those of Erle Stanley Gardner.[16] The clues in a detective novel are not unlike the clues that Evelyn Waugh threads throughout his plots.

He admired the *Beggar's Opera*, and in *Brideshead Revisited* one remembers that at Oxford there was a statuette of Polly Peachum on Charles Ryder's mantleshelf. He had obviously read Aldous Huxley, Michael Arlen, Ivy

[15] Ibid., p.43.
[16] In 1966, a memoir 'The Beauty of his Malice', *Time Magazine*, 22 March 1966, p.61 stated that 'Waugh took savage pleasure in annoying Americans – "Erle Stanley Gardner," he announced sweetly to one visitor, "is the finest living American author"'. But Waugh was impressed by Gardner, as can be seen from the correspondence published by Alfred Borrello between Borrello and Gardner and Gardner and Waugh. Gardner, after some investigation, came to the conclusion that Waugh 'really meant what he said', and Waugh admitted to Gardner that he was 'one of the keenest admirers' of his work. *Evelyn Waugh Newsletter*, edited by Paul Doyle vol.4, no.3 (Winter, 1970), p.1.

Compton-Burnett; and he saw popular stage shows such as those of Noel Coward. One suspects that Coward's short witty dialogue also played its part.

The point is, however, that Evelyn Waugh struck out on his own. To see how he did so, let us now look at his feminine language in detail.

Economical and filmic dialogue

Waugh's dialogue is a dialogue of pure economy. In the short story 'Cruise', a particular postcard sums up his style.

> Post-Card
> This is the Sphinx. Goodness how Sad. (p.20)

or in *Black Mischief*:

> No news train. Wired Legation again. Unhelpful answer. Fed doggies in market-place. Children tried to take food from doggies. Greedy little wretches. Sarah still headache. (p.157)

This kind of telegrammatic crispness is reflected throughout Waugh's work. It is a technique which is particularly suited to record the inane chatter of society, the smallest of small talk, or to sum up a philosophy (such as that of Dame Mildred Porch) in the fewest words possible. Certain sections of some of the books seem more like prose poems than anything else:

> She was lying on the dais with her head deep back in the pillow; her face was shining with the grease she used for cleaning it; one bare arm on the quilted eiderdown, left there from turning the switch. 'Why, Tony,' she said, 'I was almost asleep.'
> 'Very tired?'
> 'Mm.'
> 'Want to be left alone?'
> 'So tired … and I've just drunk a lot of that stuff of Polly's.'
> 'I see … well, good night.'
> 'Good night … don't mind, do you? … so tired.'
> He crossed to the bed and kissed her; she lay quite still, with closed eyes. Then he turned out the light and went back to the dressing-room. (*A Handful of Dust*, pp.80-1)

Not a word is excessive. Indeed Waugh uses omission to achieve his effects.

Waugh's economy of dialogue depends to some extent on his filmic technique. *Vile Bodies*, for example, depends on such, for it has no continuity of narrative and hardly any plot. Filmic in form, it shifts rapidly from scene to scene, and the dialogue moves at the same pace.

In *A Little Learning* Waugh revealed that his first visual memory was of a *camera obscura* on the pier at Weston-Super-Mare. He recalled the 'luminous, circular table-top in the dark hut, over which there mysteriously moved the reflections of passing holiday-makers' (p.28). He advised Dudley Carew early in life to go to the cinema if he wished to improve his writing style.

An early story, 'The Balance: a Yarn of the Good Old Days of Broad Trousers' (1926)[17] is interesting. The story unfolds on the cinema screen watched by a cinema audience. In this work he clearly brings filmic technique into his fictional technique. Cuts, close-ups, fast- and slow-action shots, juxtapositions – he uses them all. The story is divided into scenes, such as 'One of Life's Unfortunates', or 'Twelve O'Clock', or 'Paddington Station'. The two housemaids who are watching the film give us their interpretation:

> After several shiftings of perspective, the focus becomes suddenly and stereoscopically clear. The girl is seated at a table leaning towards a young man who is lighting her cigarette for her. Three or four others join them at the table and sit down. They are all in evening dress.
> '*No, it isn't comic, Ada – it's Society.*'
> '*Society's sometimes comic. You see.*'
> The girl is protesting that she must go.
> '*Adam, I must. Mother thinks I went out to a theatre with you and your mother. I don't know what will happen if she finds I'm not in.*'
> There is a general leave-taking and paying of bills.
> '*I say, Gladys, 'e's 'ad a drop too much, ain't 'e?*' (p.256)

In this small scene Waugh writes the film directions in; note too how he captures the dialogue of the housemaids, dropping their aitches, for example. In an early part of the story entitled 'Circumstances' he wrote the following note: 'No attempt, beyond the omission of some of the aspirates, has been made at a phonetic rendering of the speech of Gladys and Ada; they are the cook and house parlourmaid from a small house in Earls Court, and it is to be supposed that they speak as such.'[18]

In the 'Introduction' to the story the following conversation happens after a paper-game has been played which describes Adam, the hero of the story.

> 'Basil, *do* read it please.'
> 'Well, then, if you promise you won't hate me' – and he smoothed out the piece of paper.
> 'Flower – Cactus.
> 'Drink – Rum.
> 'Stuff – Baize.
> 'Furniture – Rocking Horse.
> 'Food – Venison.
> 'Address – Dublin.
> 'And Animal – Boa Constrictor.'
> 'Oh Basil, how marvellous.'
> 'Poor Adam, I never thought of him as Dublin, of course it's perfect.'
> 'Why Cactus?'
> 'So phallic, my dear, and prickly.' (p.253)

It sounds just like the language of the Bright Young People in *Vile Bodies*.

[17] Evelyn Waugh, 'The Balance: A Yarn of the Good Old Days of Broad Trousers', in *Georgian Stories* (1926).
[18] Ibid., p.254.

In 'The Balance', then, Evelyn Waugh experimented with filmic scenes and directions, and with the language of servants and of upper-class young people. By *Vile Bodies* the techniques had been refined. There are no film directions in *Vile Bodies*, although there is a film being made within the story by the Wonderfilm Company with Effie La Touche, but he uses a technique of disconnected and seemingly irrelevant scenes to portray a world that is out of synchronisation with itself. The characters and their dialogue shift as wildly as the scenes. This language appears within the first few pages of the book:

'Creative Endeavour lost her wings, Mrs Ape. She got talking to a gentleman in the train ... Oh, there she is.' (p.10)

'If you have peace in your hearts your stomach will look after itself, and remember if you *do* feel queer – *sing*!' (p.10)

'I don't think one finds quite the same class as Prime Minister nowadays, do you think?' (p.12).

'They say that only *one* person has any influence with Mr Outrage ... ' (p.12)

'Too, too sick-making,' said Miss Runcible, with one of her rare flashes of accuracy. (p.14)

The obedient angel speaks like a schoolgirl being quizzed by her teacher; Mrs Melrose Ape speaks in the language of the evangelist, Aimée Semple McPherson; Kitty Blackwater and Fanny Throbbing specialise in the idle chat of foolish, elderly upper-class ladies; and Miss Runcible is quite obviously an 'in' Bright Young Person.

Filmic dialogue is also used elsewhere. In *Brideshead Revisited* our introduction to Celia Ryder comes in the form of her bird-like chatter ... the sentences flashing before us like a series of fast film takes. In *Scoop*, Kätchen, a 'Garbo', has the kind of dialogue that an actress would have; and the poor quality of her acting and the delivery of her lines make her both amusing and pathetic. In this scene in *Scoop*, Waugh catches both the humorous and the serious in a conversational exchange:

... She unwrapped the speckled foil from the bottle of champagne. 'He is not a good husband to me,' she admitted, 'to go away for so long.' She held the foil to her face and carefully modelled it round her nose.
'Dear Kätchen, will you marry me?'
She held the false nose up to William's.
'Too long,' she said.
'Too long to wait?'
'Too long for your nose.'
'Damn!' said William.
'Now you are upset.'
'Won't you ever be serious?' (pp.142-3)

This little scene, as with many others in Waugh, could have been portrayed beautifully on the cinema screen.

How dialogue carries the burden of meaning

Waugh often uses dialogue to convey the burden of meaning. Here is an excellent example. It is Mrs Beaver's speech at the beginning of *A Handful of Dust*:

> 'Was anyone hurt?'
> 'No one, I am thankful to say,' said Mrs Beaver, 'except two housemaids who lost their heads and jumped through a glass roof into the paved court. They were in no danger. The fire never reached the bedrooms, I am afraid. Still, they are bound to need doing up, everything black with smoke and drenched in water and luckily they had that old-fashioned sort of extinguisher that ruins *everything*. One really cannot complain. The chief rooms were *completely* gutted and everything was insured. Sylvia Newport knows the people. I must get on to them this morning before that ghoul Mrs Shutter snaps them up.' (p.7)

Mrs Beaver's attitude to the fire reveals much about her character and her values. She relishes what has happened to the house because as an interior decorator it means work for her, which in turn means money, which is what she is most interested in. Unfortunately for her the fire didn't reach the bedrooms – unfortunately, because then there would have been a lot of costly structural work to be done, not just redecoration. However, she cannot complain and, fortunately for her, the fire extinguisher was an old one. If it had been modern, less damage would have been caused. Ironically, she refers to Mrs Shutter as a ghoul without realising that that is exactly what she is herself.

In this one paragraph Mrs Beaver sets the tone for the whole of the book, bringing the values of the society of the day into question. She also prepares us for the ironic vein of cruelty that runs throughout the novel. The housemaids jumped to save themselves from the fire. They did the right thing, but then Waugh turns the sentence on its head because Mrs Beaver reveals that the fire never reached the bedrooms. They needn't have jumped.[19] In this piece of conversation Waugh has distilled through Mrs Beaver the values of modern society, and the streak of greed and coldness in her character.

If we compare Waugh's introduction with the opening of Aldous Huxley's *Point Counter Point*, there is a distinct difference. This passage is about Marjorie Carling:

> 'Half-past twelve,' she implored, though she knew that her importunity would

[19] Ann Pasternak Slater has written an interesting essay on this displacement technique of Waugh's. See 'Waugh's *A Handful of Dust*: Right Things in Wrong Places', *Essays in Criticism*, (1982), pp.48-68. Waugh's idea of the two housemaids jumping is likely to be based on an incident that occurred in real life. Bryan Guinness (Lord Moyne) writes: 'At a dance of my parents in 1928, two young maids climbed out on to a glass skylight between one floor and another to watch the guests sitting out below. The glass gave way and they fell through. One was killed and the other badly hurt though she recovered.' *Potpourri from the Thirties* (1982), p.11.

only annoy him, only make him love her the less. But she could not prevent
herself from speaking; she loved him too much, she was too agonizingly jealous.
The words broke out in spite of her principles. It would have been better for her,
and perhaps for Walter too, if she had fewer principles and given her feelings the
violent expression they demanded. (pp.1-2)

The important difference is that Huxley has to tell us about the character of
Marjorie Carling, whereas Waugh's Mrs Beaver tells us all about herself,
without spelling out that she is hard, cold and greedy. Waugh's dialogue is
immediate; it is visual, economical, ironic; it sums up the values of society; it
sets the tone for the book; and it lets the reader fill in the gaps.

Manipulation of dialogue

In *A Tourist to Africa* Waugh was asked at a school to give some advice to the
students who were learning English. He told them that English was
'incomparably the richest language in the world. There are two or three quite
distinct words to express every concept and each has a subtle difference of
nuance'.[20] The students became rather concerned, and the nun in charge of
the class saved the situation by saying that what their illustrious visitor
meant was that, although there were a lot of words, you only needed a few to
be able to make your meaning clear. Evelyn Waugh left it at that, but the
point of the story is the kind of insight he had into his language. He would
pore over the dictionary for hours finding exactly the right word, and quite
often those words were odd or archaic. His knowledge of the language meant
that he was able to manipulate his dialogue most effectively.

The housemaids jumping when they didn't need to is just one example of
how Waugh uses a later sentence to throw a different light on a previous one.
He also quite often shifts the meaning of a word or phrase. In *A Handful of Dust*
the expression 'love and trust' is used in two different ways. At the beginning
of the book they are common words that we understand, and when we are
told on page 125 that Tony had 'got into the habit of loving and trusting
Brenda' it is only what we expect. But on page 152 Waugh turns the
expression on its head, for after Brenda has heard that Tony will not pay her
any alimony Jenny Abdul Akbar sympathises with her friends, and says, 'It's
so like Brenda to trust everyone.'

Waugh often shifts the meaning of a sentence by one single word. Brenda
Last says: 'I never was one for making myself expensive' (p.191). We expect
the word 'cheap', for that is what Brenda is, not 'expensive'. In *The Loved One*
the mortician Aimée, meeting Dennis on the Lake Island of Innisfree, fails to
recognise him immediately and excuses herself by saying, 'My memory's
very bad for live faces' (p.70). In *Vile Bodies*: 'Kitty Blackwater and Fanny
Throbbing lay one above the other in their bunks rigid from wig to toe'
(p.14). Our expectations are jolted. We expect 'head to toe', and by changing
one word Waugh draws a completely different picture.

The *double entendre* is yet another device. Mrs Beaver in *A Handful of Dust*

[20] Evelyn Waugh, *A Tourist to Africa* (1960), p.103.

says that she will have to look for another 'suitable house to split up' (p.53). Although she means to split up into flats, the word also conveys the sense of finding another marriage to split up for financial gain. The *double entendre* is also used in a violent sense: in *Vile Bodies* Adam is told, of Effie La Touche, that 'when they did shoot her they made a complete mess of her ... you never saw such rotten little scraps – quite unrecognisable half of them' (p.42). In fact she was 'shot' with a film camera. And also in *Vile Bodies*, Lottie Crump and the ex-King of Ruritania talk about his wife being locked up in a 'looney house' because she imagines that 'everyone is a bomb'. Many of her relatives have had bombs thrown at them, and when her maid tells her that the chef has 'made one big bomb' she thinks of an explosive device rather than an ice-cream one – and 'since then always her poor brains has was all nohow' (p.39).

Another way Waugh shifts our perspective is by changing the tone of the dialogue. In *The Loved One*, after keeping up her businesslike language, the first mortician throws us by relapsing into such colloquial expressions as 'They fixed that stiff', or 'I'll say it is', or 'Pass the buck'. In *Decline and Fall* Margot Beste-Chetwynde takes the opposite approach. She drops her 'divine' manner and becomes utterly professional when interviewing potential prostitutes.

A phrase can also be the theme of the whole book. In *Scoop*, when Julia Stitch says, 'It's simply a case of mistaken identity' (p.40), she is referring to the gentleman whom she followed in her car into the gentlemen's lavatory; but it is mistaken identity that sends William Boot to Ishmaelia and later promotes Uncle Theodore to a place of honour next to Lord Copper at the celebration banquet.

Waugh also manipulates his dialogue by a heightening of the language, as in the use of French by his female characters:

'Oh, just another boring family *potin.*' (Julia Flyte, *Brideshead Revisited*, p.149)

'There was a certain amount of *gêne* with relatives.' (Brenda Last, *A Handful of Dust*, p.126)

'Well, perhaps a little *mal soignée*, darling.' (Margot Beste-Chetwynde, *Decline and Fall*, p.193)

'My dear, he looks very *tapette.*' (Fanny Throbbing, *Vile Bodies*, p.27)

Figuratively, '*potin*' means to stir things up, or a fuss or rumpus – quite acceptable in the *Brideshead* family situation. '*Gêne*' means discomfort and again is applicable to Brenda's situation. '*Mal soignée*' contrasts the situation between Margot's and Paul's life style. She is impeccably groomed and moving in rich circles in the outside world, while Paul is badly groomed because he is in prison. '*Tapette*' is an interesting word, for the rather obscure meaning in French is 'homosexual' and in the 1920s it was a word that was used by society. Douglas Goldring writes of how young women 'flattened their chests and cropped their hair in the effort to compete with "pansies" and "tapettes" '.[21]

---

[21] Douglas Goldring, *The Nineteen-Twenties* (1945), p.226.

French vocabulary is only used by Waugh's upper-class ladies, not by any females lower down the rungs of the class ladder. In those days it was still part of a lady's education to speak French. Waugh does, however, make fun of his aristocratic ladies, for in *Vile Bodies* Lady Throbbing and Mrs Blackwater drink champagne which Mrs Blackwater calls '*champagne*' and she pronounces it 'as though it were French', while Lady Throbbing with 'late Victorian *chic*' calls it 'a bottle of pop' (p.12). Also, on page 130 the world-weariness of the old ladies becomes apparent through their use of French. Talking about the bright young people, at a party at Anchorage House, they wonder if they appreciate how easy it is for them to be bad:

> ' ... young people take things so much for granted.
> *Si la jeunesse savait.*'
> '*Si la vieillesse pouvait*, Kitty.'

Waugh is actually using the modern French forms of *savait* and *pouvait* here, for the epigram comes from the obsolete French epigram '*si jeunesse savoit, si viellesse pouvoit*' meaning 'if youth had the knowledge, if old age had the strength'.[22]

Childish language

In *Brideshead Revisited*, Cara says: 'Sebastian is in love with his own childhood. That will make him very unhappy. His teddy-bear, his nanny ... and he is nineteen years old ... ' (p.100).

Waugh, like Sebastian, was always in love with his childhood; and consequently childish language recurs in his work. Stephen Spender, in his discussion 'The World of Evelyn Waugh', says: 'Evelyn Waugh and many of his characters belong to a generation old enough to have passed their childhoods before the First World War, though not old enough to have fought in it.'[23] Waugh's memories of childhood, like those of his characters, are the memories of a society where nannies and governesses played a major part in bringing up the children. Waugh likes to remember that childish world where innocent games were played, but in his books it is mixed with cynicism, sophistication and sometimes even a hint of incest. Let us look at some examples.

The first relationship for discussion is that between Basil Seal and Barbara Sothill who are brother and sister. They appear together first in *Black Mischief*, then in *Put Out More Flags* and finally in *Basil Seal Rides Again*. The tone is different in each of the books. In *Black Mischief* (1932) Barbara appears not to think very much of Basil and there is no childish conversation between them. If anything she regards him as a tiresome brother who is constantly getting into hot water, and always scrounging on her. On page 74 Waugh actually says that she doesn't regard him with the same hero-worship as she did

[22] This is Epigram 191 from H. Estienne's *Les Premices* (1594).

[23] Stephen Spender, 'The World of Evelyn Waugh', in *The Creative Element: a Study of Vision, Despair and Orthodoxy among Some Modern Writers* (1953), p.159.

twenty years before. In fact there is a lack of continuity in tone here, for in *Put Out More Flags* (1942) Barbara obviously adores her brother. Consider the scene where Barbara starts by crying because of the problems of the evacuees and ends up on the sofa wrestling with Basil, giving Doris, one of the evacuees, the impression that something else is going on:

> 'I'm cleverer than Freddy. Babs, say I'm cleverer than Freddy.'
> 'I'm cleverer than Freddy. Sucks to you.'
> 'Babs, say you love me more than Freddy.'
> 'You love me more than Freddy. Double sucks.'
> 'Say, I Barbara, love you Basil, more than him, Freddy.'
> 'I won't. I don't ... Beast, you're hurting.'
> 'Say it.'
> 'Basil, stop at once or I shall call Miss Penfold.'
> They were back twenty years, in the schoolroom again.
> 'Miss Penfold, Miss Penfold, Basil's pulling my hair.' (pp.84-5)

Childish language in a childish language game is something that we have probably all played at some time in our lives. By this technique Waugh lets Basil acquire a certain innocence which makes his normal character as rogue and con-artist more sympathetic. It also brings a fresh light to Barbara Sothill, who has just been seen in the previous pages as the lady of the manor whom people come to for advice. The effect of her crying and joining in such childish repartees makes her a warmer person. On page 102 another kind of understanding is reached:

> 'Basil, you're up to something. I wish I knew what it was.'
> Basil turned on her his innocent blue eyes, as blue as hers and as innocent; they held no hint of mischief. 'Just war work, Babs,' he said.
> 'Slimy snake.'
> 'I'm not.'
> 'Crawly spider.' They were back in the schoolroom, in the world where once they had played pirates. 'Artful monkey,' said Barbara, very fondly.

Spender, in the same article, believes this childish conversation has sinister overtones.[24] Yet Barbara knows that Basil is not innocent. She knows he is capable of acting in a toadying manner and that he lives by his wits. His innocent blue eyes do not deceive her. Her knowledge, put into childish 'call you names' language, only serves to heighten our awareness of how well she knows him; and how she accepts his failings because she is so fond of him. Remember how on page 16 she chuckles when she recalls Basil's stealing her mother's emeralds so that he could go to Azania. She knows he is incorrigible.[25]

---

[24] Ibid., p.160.

[25] Barbara and Basil have much in common with Kate and Anthony, the twins, in Graham Greene's *England Made Me*. Both relationships have unmistakably incestuous overtones, although in Greene's book Kate's love for her brother is a tragic emotion. It is significant that her only good sexual experience with her lover, Krogh, is prompted by a visitor who reminds her of Anthony. Waugh's Barbara does not have the same problems.

In *Basil Seal Rides Again* Basil and Barbara are both a lot older. The conversation between them about Basil's daughter Barbara still has some childish overtones. The words 'chump' and 'rot' are used, but Barbara, instead of being a schoolroom miss, has now become the schoolmistress. When Basil suggests she might not like it if young Barbara runs off, her reply is, 'She'd never think of such a thing. Don't put ideas into the child's head for God's sake. Give her a dose of castor oil' (p.269). And later, 'Well, keep her under lock and key ... '

Although Barbara and Basil do not relapse into childish conversation in *Black Mischief*, Sonia Trumpington does. When Basil visits her, she and Alastair are in bed with their dogs:

> Alastair said, 'We can't have dinner with these infernal dogs all over the place.'
> Sonia: 'You're a cheerful chap to be in bed with, aren't you?' and to the dog, 'Was oo called infernal woggie by owid man? Oh God, he's made a mess again.' (p.78)

This kind of childish talk does not make Sonia a warmer person as Barbara's childish conversation did; if anything it rubs us up the wrong way. It is irritating. Note too, how Sonia thinks what fun it would be if she and Alastair were to go to Azania too. She sees Basil's trip as an adventure. After having dinner in bed they all play 'Happy Families', a card game which, like 'Animal Farm', recurs in Waugh's books. However, when Basil returns from Azania and wants to tell Sonia about his experiences, including cannibalism and the fact that Prudence has been eaten, she doesn't want to hear. It's suddenly not 'fun' any more:

> '*Basil*. Once and for all, we don't want to hear travel experiences. Do try and remember.'
> So they played Happy Families till ten ... (p.232)

In *A Handful of Dust* Mrs Rattery joins Tony in 'Animal Snap', which isn't her cup of tea at all, to help keep his mind off John Andrew's death and how Brenda is going to take the news. The irony is that Albert comes in to draw the curtains, and repeats to the other servants that Tony was sitting there clucking like a hen while his son lay dead upstairs.

In *Vile Bodies* there is not much childish conversation, but the effect of a shared childhood is much more serious. Nine marries Ginger because she played with him when young. When she introduces him to Adam, she explains that he 'used to play with her as a child' (p.118). Later Adam tells Agatha Runcible: 'She used to play with him when they were children. So she's going to marry him' (p.187). After deciding to marry Ginger, Adam wants Nina to change her mind, but she says: 'Darling, don't *bully*. Besides, I used to play with Ginger as a child. His hair was a very pretty colour then' (p.190). She finally passes off Adam as Ginger, to the extent that the neighbours admit that they wouldn't have recognised him, but then remind him 'with relish of many embarrassing episodes in Ginger's childhood, chiefly acts of destruction and cruelty to cats' (p.214).

What Waugh is getting at in *Vile Bodies* is a serious underlying philosophy, and one that comes from his own snobbery: people should not marry outside their own class. Nina and Ginger understand each other because they used to play together as children; they come from the same background. Adam is a nobody. Put simply, Ginger has money and Adam doesn't.

Helena takes yet another approach to childish language. Once again Waugh brings to the novel the particular style needed for it. *Helena* is full of slang, colloquialisms and childish language. Why doesn't Helena talk like an Empress? Waugh possibly believed that a modern idiom was needed to carry the Roman Catholic history. A modern idiom would make the views of the book more acceptable to the modern reader.

Helena's childish conversation ranged from such schoolgirl expressions as 'what a lark', 'what a sell-out', 'what sucks', 'beano', 'blow-out', 'chum', 'bosh', 'rot', and 'beastly' (a word that many of Waugh's heroines use) to the kind of inquisitive challenging conversation that schoolgirls engage in; except that Helena does it when she is very old:

> 'But how do you know He *doesn't* want us to have it – the cross, I mean? I bet He's just waiting for one of us to go and find it – just at this moment when it's most needed. Just at this moment when everyone is forgetting it and chattering about the hypostatic union, there's a solid chunk of wood waiting for them to have their silly heads knocked against. I'm going off to find it,' said Helena.
>
> The Empress Dowager was an old woman, almost of an age with Pope Sylvester, but he regarded her fondly as though she were a child, an impetuous young princess who went well to hounds, and he said with the gentlest irony: 'You'll tell me won't you? – if you are successful.'
>
> 'I'll tell the world,' said Helena. (p.128)

Waugh said of Helena, ' ... she I represented as being a simple English girl thrown greatly to her disgust into the imperial life, not the least enjoying the high position, and putting her finger at once on what was wrong with Imperial Rome at that time which was they were losing the sense of actuality.'[26]

In Helena there is also the nursery rhyme based on 'Old King Cole was a merry old soul'. Helena's father King Coel has music played for him by 'three strings and a wayward pipe'. A traditional legendary nursery rhyme has been reshaped here for satirical effect.

Special group languages

Frederick Stopp has said of Waugh: 'Group languages are his especial forte; it

---

[26] Evelyn Waugh in an interview with John Freeman, 'Face to Face', BBC TV, 26 June 1960. And his 'Notes on Translating Helena' (HRHRC) said that Helena 'speaks the slang of a slightly old-fashioned aristocratic school-girl' and that '"Bosh" = nonsense. But a difficult word to translate as it is only used by old fashioned schoolgirls. It is highly proper and juvenile.' And he also said that 'Fausta speaks ultra-fashionable 1930 slang' and that: 'The Wandering Jew talks lower middle-class slightly Americanized slang. A sharp contrast must be kept between his speech & Helena's.'

is astonishing what a wide range of specialised and professional jargon he has
at his command: criminals, drunks, Bright Young People, newspaper men,
undergraduates, officers and other ranks, schoolgirls'.[27]

Let us now look briefly at some of these group languages:

Mannered society ladies

Margot Beste-Chetwynde, Brenda Last, Julia Stitch, Julia Flyte, Celia
Ryder, Sonia Trumpington and Virginia Troy all have the following words
and expressions in common:

> darling
> beast/beastly
> sweet/sweety/poor sweet/the sweet/my sweet
> heaven/heavenly/heavens/rather heaven
> old boy/poor boy
> bless
> bores/bore/bored/boring
> tired/tired of
> fun
> angel/the angel/poor angel

Underneath their mannered exterior the ladies are very different people, as we
shall see below, pp.60-72, but there is one who stands completely apart from
the rest and that is Virginia Troy.

Virginia has a 'high, fine candour' that none of the other heroines
possesses. She is completely frank and direct in her conversation. As she says
to Guy, in *Unconditional Surrender*, when she realises that she is making no
headway with him about a future for them together again, 'You must know
me well enough to know I was never one for dirty tricks, was I?', and then she
informs him that she is 'with child by Trimmer'. Virginia's 'candour' also
allows her to use 'obscenities', and yet they always sound 'attractive on her
lips'. When she perceives that Uncle Peregrine thought that she had designs
on him, she says, 'You thought perhaps I might provide your third —'. The
obscenity does not make Uncle Peregrine 'wince', he even finds it rather
'attractive'. Later, she uses the same word to Guy, for she tells him that he is,
like the rest of the Crouchbacks, 'over-bred and under-sexed', and when she
says that they are 'dying out as a family' she also questions: 'Why do you
Crouchbacks do so little —ing?' That 'then unprintable word' is again used
'without offence' (p.146). Virginia's use of rude words is a likeable facet of her
personality, unlike Mrs Leonard who, in *Men at Arms*, has a 'cheeky' forward
manner and tries to be one of the boys. She is reprimanded by her husband
and told to 'Keep it clean, Daisy, for heaven's sake' (p.64). Virginia's
lady-like obscenities are acceptable, whereas Mrs Leonard's smutty remarks
are not.

---

[27] Frederick J. Stopp, *Portrait of an Artist* (1958), p.182.

Schoolgirls

The two main characters who fall into this category are Cordelia Flyte and
Helena. They both have 'beastly' in common like the mannered ladies, but
they use such other expressions as 'bosh', 'rot', 'chump', and 'nonsense'.
Barbara Sothill, whom one would classify as a virtuous woman, also has
some of this language in common with them when she lapses into her nursery
conversation with Basil, and uses words like 'chump' and 'sucks'.

The angels in *Vile Bodies* also fall into the schoolgirl category. On page 94
the other angels question Chastity about her outing with Mrs Panrast, a
lesbian, and they do it in a typical schoolroom manner: pinching and teasing
her. Chastity's language reverts to girlish expressions such as: '*Ooh, ow, ow.
Please*, beast, swine, cads ... please ... ooh ... ' Waiting to perform at Lady
Metroland's house they even have supper in 'what was still called the
schoolroom' (p.92).

Nurses and nannies

Waugh's female characters are also treated as though they are children by
the various nurse figures in the novels.

The nurse in *Vile Bodies* talks to Agatha Runcible in childish language:

> She took the flowers from Adam's hand, said, 'Look, what lovelies. Aren't
> you a lucky girl?' and left the room with them. She returned a moment later
> carrying them in a jug of water. 'There, the thirsties,' she said. 'Don't they love
> to get back to the nice cool water?' (p.186)

And on page 189:

> 'Have a chocolate sister?'
> '*Ooh, chocs!*'

The nurse reverts to the kind of baby talk she would use if a child was sick.
This is a technique that Waugh uses elsewhere. In *Work Suspended* Lucy
Simmonds calls the sister 'Kempy'. When asked why by John Plant, her reply
is, 'She asked me to' ... 'and she's really very sweet' (p.192). In *Brideshead
Revisited* Celia Ryder calls the stewardess who is nursing her 'Mrs Clark' and
tells Charles that she is 'being so sweet'. In turn Mrs Clark treats her like a
child, as 'Kempy' does Lucy: 'Now, now, dear ... the less we are disturbed
today the better' (p.239). In *Unconditional Surrender* Virginia Troy calls Sister
Jennings 'Jenny' when Gervase is born; but once she has recovered from the
birth she reverts to 'Sister Jennings'.

Being ill or having a baby in Waugh's terms is a reason for reversion to
baby talk. People like to be cossetted when they are ill, and his language aptly
and ironically reflects this. The reaction to the Sister after the birth of the
child is also natural. A certain bonding has taken place between the two
females which displaces their social classes for a short period of time. Waugh's

irony however is not lost on us; his male characters are not in favour of these starched misses who control the sick room. Adam would like to get Agatha's nurse drunk by giving her more cocktails; Charles Ryder notes of his wife that 'she was always quick to get servants' names' and that the 'stewardess had the air of a midwife, standing by the bed, a pillar of starched linen and composure'; and John Plant, who resents the inanities that pour out of the maternal Lucy's mouth, mocks at 'sweet' and 'Kempy'.

If nurses are of a different social class so are nannies, and their language reveals their class. In *Brideshead Revisited* Charles Ryder notices that Nanny Hawkins's speech, 'sharpened by years of gentle conversation, had reverted now to the soft, peasant tones of its origin' (p.328). It is not only the tone but the phrases that she uses that reveal her social background, as can be seen from those that appear in her long monologue at the end of the book:

> his nerves something shocking
> I ought by rights
> it doesn't come natural
> nor they hadn't been in the house not a month
> I said to the girl Effie who does for me
> I said to Mr Wilcox who comes to see me regular. (pp.328-9)

Nanny Hawkins also uses this kind of lower-class language earlier in the book, but not nearly to the same extent. Like Nanny Hawkins, Nannie Price in *Scoop* keeps up 'a more or less continuous monologue' while playing cards with William, Uncle Theodore and Mr Salter. Her class is revealed by such phrases as 'There, there dearie' (p.211). In *A Handful of Dust* the social difference between the Lasts and Nanny is shown mainly by the way that Nanny repeatedly calls Brenda 'my lady', as well as using such expressions as 'I'm sure I don't know' and 'There's been no doing anything with him'.

By writing down the speech of his nanny figures Waugh sets them apart, making them almost another species. (The social status of Waugh's nannies is also discussed in Chapter Six.)

Waugh also uses the language of his nannies to contrast characters. In *A Handful of Dust*, the groom, Ben Hacket, and John Andrew's nanny are worlds apart. John Andrew's bad language, picked up from Hacket – 'I just opened my bloody legs and cut an arser' (p.23) – is a far cry from Nanny's prim and evasive speech. Nanny uses such expressions as 'We'll see' and 'That's asking', whereas Ben makes 'decisive and pungent judgments' (p.21). When John Andrew asks to have his milk in his mother's room the conversation goes:

> 'That depends.'
> …
> 'What does it depend on?'
> 'Lots of things.'
> 'Tell me one of them.'
> 'On your not asking a lot of silly questions.'
> 'Silly old tart.' (p.21)

Nanny's evasions and Ben Hacket's influence result here in John Andrew calling his nanny names, and deriving so much pleasure from her discomfort that he dances in front of her chanting 'Silly old tart, silly old tart' over and over again. Nanny's grim expression finally sobers him up, and when she tells him 'I am going to speak to your mother about you' he tries to explain that he doesn't know what the word means.

Waugh then uses the expression 'silly old tart' thematically for the next few pages to highlight the different responses of the different characters. Whereas Nanny is shocked, Brenda is amused and chokes 'slightly into her face towel' (p.22). Brenda, herself, does not correct John Andrew; she tells Nanny that she will talk to her husband about it. She and Tony then share the joke, with their laughter culminating in her saying 'Darling ... *you* must speak to him. You're so much better at being serious than I am' (p.22).

Most of the nanny language in *A Handful of Dust* is corrective language, for nanny is constantly trying to overcome the influence of Hacket and it is not a job that Brenda will be responsible for. In fact, when John Andrew informs John Beaver that he can tell that the grey horse has got worms by its dung, Brenda says, 'Oh dear ... what would nanny say if she heard you talking like that' (p.28). When John Andrew tells Miss Tendril how Peppermint hadn't been able to 'cat the rum up', Nanny says, 'How many times have I told you not to go repeating whatever Ben Hacket tells you?' (p.34) Nanny's constant correction pays off, for when John Andrew refuses to visit the kennels with Tony, Hacket tells him that he's an 'ungrateful little bastard' to which John Andrew retorts, 'And you ought not to say bastard or lousy in front of me, Nanny says not' (p.78).

Tones of voice

There are a number of tones of voice which all of Waugh's nannies use, and they can be defined as the imperative tone, the reproachful or 'I told you so' tone, the concerned tone, and the indulgent tone.

The imperative tone: this consists mainly of orders:

'Just you stay where you sit ... ' (*Scoop*, p.205)

'Wash your hands ... and brush your hair nicely.' (*Scoop*, p.206)

'Sit down. Cut the cards, Mr Theodore.' (*Scoop*, p.211)

'Go straight to the nursery.' (*A Handful of Dust*, p.21)

'And that shirt needs darning. Bring it to me before it goes to the wash.' (*Brideshead Revisited*, p.147)

The reproachful tone:

' ... though she ought to wait for the tea, I told her, it's what the Conservative Women come for.' (*Brideshead Revisited*, p.37)

'And miss Julia? She *will* be upset when she hears. It would have been *such* a surprise for her.' (*Brideshead Revisited*, p.38)

'He always sends to me at Christmas, but it's not the same as having him home. Why you must all always be going abroad I never did understand.' (*Brideshead Revisited*, p.287)

'Gallivanting about all over Africa with a lot of heathens, and now you *are* home you don't want to spend a few minutes with your old Nannie! (*Scoop*, p.205)

'I don't know what your mother will say at you going down to dinner in your flannels.' (*Scoop*, p.206)

'There,' said the officer more in the tones of a nanny than a sea-dog, 'just see what you've gone and done now.' (*The Ordeal of Gilbert Pinfold*, p.47)

The concerned tone: this is nearly always to do with health:

'Well,' she said, 'you *are* looking peaky. I expect it's all that foreign food doesn't agree with you. You must fatten up now you're back. Looks as though you'd been having some late nights, too, by the look of your eyes ... ' (*Brideshead Revisited*, p.147)

'Oh, what's happened, Mr Hacket, is he hurt?' (*A Handful of Dust*, p.20)

The indulgent tone: this comes to light mainly when the nanny's charges revert to childhood in some way:

Sebastian hobbling with a pantomime of difficulty to the old nurseries, sitting beside me on the threadbare flowered carpet with the toy-cupboard empty about us and Nanny Hawkins stitching complacently in the corner, saying, 'You're one as bad as the other; a pair of children the two of you. Is that what they teach you at College?' (*Brideshead Revisited*, p.78)

Figurative speech: more than other characters in his work, Waugh's nannies speak figuratively:

'There's many a young heart that beats in an old body ...
The harder the wooing the sweeter the winning ...
There's many a happy marriage between April and December.' (*Scoop*, p.211)

'It would never do if baby came knocking at the door and found Sister unable to lift the latch.' (*Work Suspended*, p.178)

'Those that ask no questions hear no lies ... ' (*A Handful of Dust*, p.21)

'Isn't he a fine big man?' (*Work Suspended*, p.193)

'Swallowed your tongue, have you?' Nannie would ask. (*Men at Arms*, p.227)

Bright Young People

Here we have the most original group language. When Alec Waugh read the manuscript of *Vile Bodies* he asked if the slang of 'drunk-making' and 'shy-making' was Evelyn Waugh's own invention. 'No,' replied his brother, 'the young Guinness set was using it.' 'A month later, a few days before publication of the book, I noticed that its use had spread beyond the narrow radius of that set. In another two months it would have reached the fringes of the fashionable world. Within six months it would have been "old hat". Evelyn caught the tide at its flood. Ten days after publication, every conversation was peppered with "poor-makings", "drunk-makings", "rich-makings"; Evelyn had set a vogue.'[28]

In *Vile Bodies*, Agatha Runcible is the main mouthpiece for the language and she uses the following expressions:

    too, too sick-making
    too, too shaming
    too, too awful
    shy-making
    better-making
    sad-making
    rich-making
    drunk-making
    how too divine
    too bogus

The jargon that the Bright Young People were using and that Agatha uses in *Vile Bodies* so captivated many critics that they used it frequently in articles. As Waugh said in the preface to the second uniform edition of the book, it 'so captivated one prominent dramatic critic that for weeks he introduced into articles week after week: "Too sick-making, as Mr Waugh would say." '[29]

Interestingly, Agatha Runcible really is the only communicator of such language. Nina Blount is rather as Waugh was, a Bright Young Person on the edge of things. Complacent as she is, she views the rounds of parties with some distaste and genuine boredom. Her language consists mainly of 'I've got rather a pain' which is used five times plus other versions of the same thought. 'Bore' and 'boring' are also part of her standard vocabulary. In fact the only time that she uses the Bright Young People's language is when she is telling Adam about her honeymoon with Ginger and says of it that it was 'too

[28] Alec Waugh, *My Brother Evelyn and Other Profiles* (1967), p.195. The *OED* does not credit Waugh with inventing the language. In the supplement 'shy-making' is credited to W. Somerset Maugham's *Cakes and Ale or The Skeleton in the Cupboard* which was published in September 1930 while Waugh's *Vile Bodies* was published in January. Maugham does not use the adjectives in his work. They are only mentioned in passing: 'The wise always use a number of ready-made phrases (at the moment I write 'nobody's business' is the most common), popular adjectives (like 'divine' or 'shy-making'), verbs that you only know the meaning of if you live in the right set (like 'dunch'), which give a homely sparkle to small talk and avoid the necessity of thought' (p.23). Eric Partridge does credit Waugh with recording the language first and says that it was slang rather than colloquial and that it was restricted 'almost wholly to the educated and/or the cultured, especially in Society and near-Society'.   [29] Evelyn Waugh, 'Preface', *Vile Bodies*.

spirit-crushing, as poor Agatha used to say' (p.206).

Nina and Agatha do have one aspect of language in common, however. They both use Cockney. On page 58 Agatha comes down to breakfast in the Prime Minister's house. 'Good morning, all,' she says, 'in Cockney'. On page 80 when Adam asks Nina if she minds if he seduces her, she says, 'Not as much as all that', and then adds 'in Cockney' ... 'Charmed, I'm sure.' Taking off an East End accent was obviously fashionable, as were such expressions as 'shy-making'.

Waugh contrasts the different sets of young people by his language. Miss Brown, like Miss Mouse, would like to be 'in' with the younger set. After inviting Agatha to stay, Miss Brown when asked by her mother if she had a good time the previous night, replies, 'It was just too divine.' Her mother questions what she means, and she relapses into 'I mean it was lovely'.

Housewives

> They were both wearing hats like nothing on earth, which bobbed as they spoke. (*Vile Bodies*, p.67)

So Waugh describes two ladies on the train to Aylesbury who are commenting on the gossip column in the morning paper. Later, on page 137, there are two different housewives gossiping. Waugh differentiates between the two classes of housewives, not by pseudo-phonetic transcription (none of the housewives drop their aitches), but by the idiom they use. The first two ladies are members of the Conservative Association and their dialogue is peppered with such phrases as 'That's our member; such a nice stamp of man' or 'It is clearly a case in which a mandate from the constituencies is required. I'll talk to our chairwoman ... ', or metaphorical speech such as 'It was not a moment to spoil the ship for a ha'p'orth of tar'. These ladies are discussing the terrible example that Sir James Brown has set by letting his daughter have a Bright Young Persons' party at his house. They see it in relation to their own children: 'There's our Agnes, now. How can I stop her having young men in the kitchen when ... '

The second set of ladies are also discussing the Younger Generation, but not in relation to the goings-on of the Bright Young People. They are of a lower class and are worrying about the future of their children. Again, they do not drop their aitches but speak in a certain idiom. The conversation is sprinkled with 'a very good position', 'you ought to think yourself lucky', 'can't expect *work* to be interesting', 'throwing up a good job', 'nothing to fall back on'. Then the lady turns to the bad influence of her son's posh new friends: 'earning more money than he is', 'more to throw about', etc. She then turns to the subject of her daughter. To begin with it is again about work – 'in a very nice job', 'treat her very fair' – and then she moves to the subject of the girl's latest escort. Apart from the obsession with work, the only thing to tell us what class the lady comes from is the slight slipping of grammar every now and again. For example: 'all right for them that have influence' or 'people remarked how much they were about'.

Interestingly, whereas Waugh's housewives do not drop their letters or syllables, certain members of the old-guard aristocracy do, particularly when they are, like Lady Circumference, a member of the hunting, shooting and fishing set. Her speech is full of 'ain't' and ''em' and she drops the final 'g' on many of her words: 'shockin'', and 'maddenin'' for example.

The rhetoric of revivalism

Waugh often uses parody to mock at some of his characters, and one of his weapons is the rhetoric of revivalism. This is exemplified in *Decline and Fall* by Chokey's impassioned speech.[30] And the technique is used particularly to illustrate the character of Mrs Melrose Ape in *Vile Bodies*, who was apparently based on the American revivalist Aimée Semple McPherson:[31]

> 'I'm sick ashamed of you,' repeated Mrs Ape, 'and you've made Chastity cry again, just before the big act. If you must bully someone, *why* choose Chastity? You all know by this time that crying always gives her a red nose. How do I look, I should like to know, standing up in front of a lot of angels with red noses? You don't ever think of nothing but your own pleasures, do you? *Sluts.*' This last word was spoken with a depth of expression that set the angels trembling. 'There'll be no champagne for anyone to-night, see. And if you don't sing perfectly, I'll give the whole lot of you a good hiding, see. Now, come on, now, and for the love of the Lamb, Chastity, *do something to your nose.* They'll think it's a temperance meeting to see you like that.' (*Vile Bodies*, p.95)

This passage has been chosen because apart from the language of revivalism it illustrates the true character of Mrs Melrose Ape. (There are more obvious revivalist passages in the book: for example, on the boat where she addresses her fellow passengers with all her magnetic power and as many religious words as possible.) The ironic passage above shows, however, just how little love and consideration Mrs Melrose Ape possesses; she only has her own self-interest at heart.

Note too that Waugh often uses another character to put such language in its place. Later, on page 100, when Mrs Melrose Ape addresses her audience with 'Brothers and Sisters ... *just you look at yourselves*', it is Lady Circumference who puts her in her place with a snort of disapproval and the comment, 'What a damned impudent woman.'

A similar technique is used in *The Loved One*. Aimée informs us that her father lost his money in religion and, apparently, and ironically, that is why she is called Aimée, after Aimée McPherson. She then tells Dennis her life's story, saying, 'It's really rather a poetic story'. It is, as we know, not in the

---

[30] Chokey's enthusiasm in *Decline and Fall* has something in common with that of Ronald Firbank's Marchesa Pitti-Conti in *The Princess Zoubaroff*, who gets carried away with the cultural things she has achieved – 'I have been in Oxford and in Cambridge. [*Beginning to gesticulate*] And into the Hebrides even – yes! I have seen the modern Athens! But no! [*With a grimace*] Also Abbotsford I was at. [*Ecstatic, cultured*] Sir Valter Scott! [*Recollecting herself*] But Salisbury on a summer morning – Salisbury!' See *The Works of Ronald Firbank*, vol.3 (Duckworth, 1929), p.180.

[31] See Sykes, p.147.

least poetic and Waugh parodies an attitude which he finds absurd; and does so with a monologue which is tinged with the rhetoric of revivalism. This time however it doesn't need another character to show up the absurdity of the language; Aimée does it herself:

> 'Well, I didn't know quite what to think. I'd never seen a dead person before because Dad left Mother before he died, if he is dead, and Mother went East to look for him when I left College, and died there. And I had never been inside Whispering Glades as after we lost our money Mother took to New Thought and wouldn't have it that there was such a thing as death. So I felt quite nervous coming here the first time. And then everything was so different from what I expected. Well, you've seen it and you know. Colonel Komstock shook hands and said: "Young lady, you are doing a truly fine and beautiful action" and gave me fifty bucks.' (p.75)

A 'truly fine and beautiful action', is repaid in a materialistic society by the reward of 'fifty bucks'.

Telephone talk

In the Preface to *Vile Bodies*, Evelyn Waugh wrote: 'I think I can claim that this was the first English novel in which dialogue on the telephone plays a large part.'[32]

Certainly Waugh used telephone conversation throughout the novel, as he did indeed in *A Handful of Dust*. However, it was not entirely new. Katherine Mansfield used it in *The Garden Party* (1922) briefly; Michael Arlen used it in *The Green Hat* (1924), and used it extensively for four pages of conversation between the narrator of the story and the heroine Iris Storm; and in 1926 Beverley Nichols used a great deal of telephone conversation in *Crazy Pavements*.

However, there are distinct differences. By the time we get to Waugh, the technique of the telephone conversation has been refined. Beverley Nichols is full of such comments as 'Hence the telephonic conversation, which must now be recorded'. The language itself, however, when used on the telephone is not so different from Waugh's language:

> 'Is that you, Don?'
> 'Yes, Julia.'
> 'I want you to ask Brian Elme to lunch.'
> 'I have already done so!'
> 'Liar.'
> 'If you insist … ' (*Crazy Pavements*, p.93)

Michael Arlen's telephone conversations in *The Green Hat* are very full, and consist of quite a few explanations about the way people talk on the telephone: 'They shout on the telephone, people do … ' (p.283), 'Iris, you are shocking the girl at the exchange' (p.286), 'Can you stand there with your lips to the

---

[32] Evelyn Waugh, 'Preface', *Vile Bodies*.

receiver, which I hope your servants clean for you, and tell me you are not my friend?' (p.286).

The difference with Waugh is that he used the telephone to help create the theme of the book. As Stephen Spender has pointed out about *Vile Bodies*, when Adam remembers that he is engaged to be married to Nina Blount and telephones her, the following conversation ensues:

> 'Oh, I say. Nina there's one thing – I don't think I shall be able to marry you after all.'
> 'Oh, *Adam*, you are a bore. Why not?'

As Spender has said, this 'sets the tone of their relationship, which is spent in Adam getting, and throwing away, the financial opportunity for marriage'.[33] The conversations come and go as the money comes and goes. Chapter 11, which is just two pages long and consists only of telephone conversation, is interesting because of its repetition of language, which in a few well-chosen words conveys a depth of meaning. For that reason I quote it in full:

> Adam rang up Nina.
> 'Darling, I've been so happy about your telegram. Is it really true?'
> 'No, I'm afraid not.'
> 'The Major *is* bogus?'
> 'Yes.'
> 'You haven't got any money?'
> 'No.'
> 'We aren't going to be married to-day?'
> 'No.'
> '*I see.*'
> '*Well?*'
> '*I said, I see.*'
> '*Is that all?*'
> '*Yes, that's all, Adam.*'
> 'I'm sorry.'
> 'I'm sorry, too. Good-bye.'
> Later Nina rang up Adam.
> 'Darling, is that you? I've got something rather awful to tell you.'
> 'Yes?'
> 'You'll be furious.'
> 'Well?'
> 'I'm engaged to be married.'
> 'Who to?'
> 'I hardly think I can tell you.'
> 'Who?'
> 'Adam, you won't be beastly about it, will you?'
> 'Who is it?'
> 'Ginger.'
> 'I don't believe it.'

---

[33] Stephen Spender, *The Creative Element*, pp.164-5.

> 'Well, I am. That's all there is to it.'
> 'You're going to marry Ginger?'
> 'Yes.'
> '*I see.*'
> '*Well?*'
> '*I said, I see.*'
> '*Is that all?*'
> '*Yes, that's all, Nina.*'
> 'When shall I see you?'
> 'I don't ever want to see you again.'
> '*I see.*'
> '*Well?*'
> '*I said, I see.*'
> 'Well, good-bye.'
> 'Good-bye ... I'm sorry, Adam.' (pp.183-4; italics added except 'is' in line 4)

The repetition of the phrases 'Well? ... I said, I see' conveys both the impersonality of the whole transaction, and hurt and retaliation. Earlier telephone conversations in the book are peppered with such phrases as 'angel', 'sweet', and 'darling'.

In *A Handful of Dust* telephone conversation is used in much the same way to illustrate the turn of the tide in the relationship between Brenda and Tony. At the beginning, Brenda gets impatient with Tony for calling her at the flat when he is drunk, because she doesn't want him to come around; but although she prevents him from doing so, her language is affable and affectionate. She treats her drunk husband rather like an errant child. Later when it gets to the stage of talking about alimony payments she accuses him of bullying her, and making her feel a beast. There is no warmth left – everything is reduced to financial terms, and Tony, making sure that she understands that he would have to sell Hetton, finally realises that she doesn't give a damn about the place. Like Nina and Adam, they become, over the telephone, cold impersonal strangers. This use of a distancing effect is the strongest way in which Waugh uses telephone dialogue.

How language reflects character

Frederick Stopp has seen Waugh's heroines as falling into the category of those with Life Force and those who are waifs; with some hovering in between.[34] However, there is one characteristic that most of the female characters have in common: their obsession with money. If one takes the heroines and lists the financial words and phrases that they use, a definite pattern emerges. (To distinguish the words, I have put them in italics.)

Margot Beste-Chetwynde, *Decline and Fall*

I still *manage* a great deal of father's *business*.

---

[34] Frederick Stopp, *Portrait of an Artist*, pp.198-200.

I could find you a *job*.

D'you want any *money in advance*?

You *pay* for them out of your *salary* in *instalments*.

Probably only a matter of giving the right man *a few hundred francs*.

People talk a great deal of nonsense about being *rich*. Of course it is a bore in some ways, and it means endless work, but I wouldn't be *poor*, or even *moderately well-off*, for all the ease in the world.

Margot Beste-Chetwynde, *Vile Bodies*

I feel my *full income*.

Kätchen, *Scoop*

Will you give me *twenty pounds* for them?

Will you give me the *money* now?

Will you think it very *greedy* if I ask for a *hundred dollars* now?

She would sell them for *sixty American dollars*.

Will you please send us the *money* there.

We look forward very much to getting the *money*.

Lady Circumference, *Decline and Fall*

What d'you *pay* your head men?

That boy's doing no good for himself. Got *fined twenty pounds* the other day, his mother told me. Seemed proud of it. If my brother had been alive he'd have licked all that out of the young cub.

We all *feel the wind* a bit since the war.

Dingy, *Decline and Fall*

Not *supplied* with soap or boot polish.

The butter *has to do* for three loaves.

Cut the crusts *as thin as possible.*

Don't *waste* it.

Sinful to *buy* Mr Prendergast a tie.

Dame Mildred Porch, *Black Mischief*

The coal *bill* seemed surprisingly heavy.

Not letting the servants become *extravagant.*

No need for the dining room fire to be lit before luncheon at this time of year.

Saved me a visit to the *bank.*

No trouble about *currency.*

Sonia Trumpington, *Black Mischief*

We haven't any servants, we got very *poor* suddenly.

Everyone's got very *poor* and it makes them duller.

She's the only one who doesn't seem to have lost *money.*

A crisis – something about *gold standard.*

Barbara Sothill, *Put Out More Flags*

I remember last time you stayed here I had to pay him over *ten pounds* that you'd borrowed.

I suppose you'll want some *money.*

Angela Lyne, *Put Out More Flags*

I don't want *five and nines.* I want one *three and sixpenny.*

It isn't the *price.* The *five and nines* are too far away. I want to be near, in the *three and sixpennies.*

I can't see if I'm far away. I said *three and sixpence.*

Too far away to recognise anyway in the *five and ninepennies.*

Father's friends were all hard-boiled and *rich* – men like Metroland and

Copper ... then I met Cedric who was *poor* and very soft-boiled ...

I *bought* him an octopus once and we had a case made for its tank, carved with dolphins and covered with *silver leaf.*

I'll offer them *fifteen thousand.*

You'd like to be *rich* wouldn't you?

If anyone is [rich after the war] I shall be.

If no one is, I don't suppose it matters so much being *poor.*

Nina Blount, *Vile Bodies*

How much *money* have you?

Just ask him for some *money.*

Have you got any *money?*

When will you next have some *money?*

We shan't be any *poorer* than we are now.

You haven't got any *money.*

If only you were as *rich* as Ginger, Adam, or only *half as rich.* Or if only you had any *money* at all.

Lottie Crump, *Vile Bodies*

I drove the King down ... I won't have him travelling *third class.*

He's got *pots of money* ... *a thousand pounds* is nothing to him.

It's not so much the *price* of the chandelier ...what *money* can make, *money* can mend.

Doge, have you got any *money?*

Judge What's-your-name, got any *money?*

What about my little *bill?*

We get a bit muddled with the *books* now and then.

Here's a blank *cheque book*.

And *twopence* for the *cheque*.

Aimée, *The Loved One*

Dad lost his *money* in religion so I had to learn a trade.

She never *tipped* me more than a *quarter*.

She still only gave me a *quarter*.

After we lost our *money* Mother took to New Thought.

'Young lady, you are doing a truly fine and beautiful action' … and gave me *fifty bucks*.

– Yes, a little. But then you see Loved Ones can't *tip* so that it works out nearly the same. But it isn't for the *money* I work. I'd gladly come for nothing only one has to eat and the Dreamer insists on our being turned out nicely.

He has not very much *money*.

An American man would despise himself for *living on* his wife.

I was offered a Big Chance to improve my *position* and now no more is said of that.

As often as not it was *I took you out*.

First Mortician, *The Loved One*

Zones of course vary in *price*.

We have single sites as low as *fifty dollars*.

They range about 1,000 *dollars*.

We have double plots there at 750 *dollars* the pair.

Your signature to the *order* and a *deposit*.

The *benefits* of the *plan* are twofold.

Now approaching your *optimum earning phase*.

– *investments, insurance policies* and so forth.

Pay for it while you are best able to do so.

Brenda Last, *A Handful of Dust*

Might be fun to *eat someone else's food* for a bit.

Pointless *keeping up* a house this size.

I suppose we're lucky to be able to *afford* to keep it up at all.

Do you know how much it *costs* just to live here?

We should be *quite rich* if it wasn't for that.

We *support* fifteen servants indoors ... while Tony and I have to fuss about whether it's *cheaper* to take a car up to London for the night or *buy* an excursion ticket.

An old married woman and *quite rich* ... so I'm going to *pay*.

Let's ask for the *bill*.

How much do I *tip* him? ... Are you sure that's enough? I should have given *twice as much*.

They couldn't get married because of *money*.

I'll *sock* you a movie.

I've spent heaps of *money*.

They are *three pounds* a week, no *rates* and *taxes*.

What's *three pounds* a week? Less than *nine bob* a night. Where could one stay for less than *nine bob* a night ...

I'm sure we spend much more than *three pounds* a week through not having a flat.

Bimetallism,[35] you know.

[35] Brenda Last studies 'Bimetallism'. Roger T. Burbridge says that Brenda took very little effort to cover up her affair with Beaver, 'not even taking the time to learn a few terms in economics (bimetallism has nothing to do with that subject) ... ' See 'The Function of Gossip, Rumor and Public Opinion in Evelyn Waugh's *A Handful of Dust*', *Evelyn Waugh Newsletter*, vol.4, no.2 (Autumn, 1970). As 'Bimetallism' is 'the system of allowing the unrestricted currency of two metals (e.g. *gold and silver*) at a fixed ratio to each other, as coined money' (*OED*), Burbridge's point is worthless.

The *lawyers* are doing everything.

I know it sounds a *lot* but ...

I have to *feed him* a bit of high-life every week or so, and I suppose that'll all stop if there's a divorce.

The Ritz isn't cosy at lunch-time and it *costs eight and six*. I daren't *cash a cheque* for three weeks ...

It might occur to her to *sock* a girl a meal once in a way.

I never was one for making myself *expensive*.

I've got to have some *more money*.

They never seem to *pay dividends* nowadays. Besides it's very difficult to *live on so little*.

Haven't I got any rights under the *marriage settlement* or anything?

Can you tell me whether Mr Last made another *will*?

Thérèse de Vitré, *A Handful of Dust*

My father has one of the *best* houses in Trinidad.

There are two or three other *rich* families and I shall marry into one of them.

She had a ring with a *big diamond*.

There's one called Mendoza who's *very rich*.

Mrs Beaver, *A Handful of Dust*

One really cannot complain. The chief rooms were *completely* gutted and everything was *insured*.

She *hasn't paid* for the *toile-de-jouy* covers we made her last April.

Didn't hold a card all the evening and came away *four pounds ten* to the bad.

But that's so *expensive*.

It's very difficult for you ... and you're wonderful about *money*. I ought to be grateful that I haven't a son always coming to me with *debts*.

I wonder if that would be running you in for more than you meant to *spend*.

Any time you are *buying* cuttings or seeds do get them through me. I've made quite a little *business* of it ...

Virginia Troy, *Men at Arms*

I hope you got a big *price*.

Money gone, me gone, all in one go.

How wretched you make it sound. No work. No *money*.

Virginia Troy, *Officers and Gentlemen*

It's very *expensive*.

I couldn't possibly let you *spend your money* on me. I was just wondering whether I could *afford to stand you* dinner.

Something to do with Mr Troy and the war and *foreign investments* and *exchange control*. Anyway my London *bank* manager has suddenly become very shifty.

We're not having any tonight. Always read the menu from *left to right*.

Virginia Troy, *Unconditional Surrender*

Money ... I've never known what it was like to have *no money* ... Tim made a *will* leaving all he had to some girl. Papa never left me anything. He thought I was well *provided* for.

At first they thought it was just some difficulty of *exchange control*.

Not only no *alimony* but an *overdraft* and a *huge lawyer's bill*. I did the only thing I could and *sold jewels*.

They aren't going to the police or anything but I've got to *refund the money* – £250.

I've been *hawking* furs around.

All I *possess* in the world is downstairs in your hall.

I think I'd prefer your man. Not *expensive*?

I might *afford* that.

It's awfully sweet of you to take me in *free*.

I couldn't possibly *afford* to.

Explain to him that I'm *broke*.

Really broke.

The *hundred pounds* will have to wait.

I'm dead *broke*.

Cards and gin. You won't mind having to *pay* for them, will you?

What does all that mean in *income*?

Not beyond the dreams of *avarice*.

But better than a slap with a wet fish. And you had a *pittance* before. How about Uncle Peregrine? He must have a *bit*. Is that *left* to you?

Kerstie Kilbannock, *Officers and Gentlemen*

Darling, don't breathe a word to Brenda and Zita that you aren't *paying* … Not a word, darling, that you're being *paid*.

Kerstie Kilbannock, *Unconditional Surrender*

Mr Troy will have to *cough up* eventually. Americans are great ones for *alimony*.

What's the best *offer* you've got?

I happen to have a little *money* in the *bank* … I could go a bit higher than that.

I'm sure we can find enough to make up to £250.

She's not *costing* us much.

She was awfully decent to us when she was *rich*.

A *guinea* a visit I think.

Virginia talking of *money*: you remember Brenda and Zita used to *pay rent* when they lived here?

Wondered if you wouldn't feel more comfortable if you *paid* something.

Would I go to my *bank manager* and suggest he *embezzled money* for me?

He's never been in the house except to charge a *guinea* a time.

Yes and *quarter the price.*

From these statements about money we can see which financial categories the female characters fall into.

Relaxed about money
Margot Beste-Chetwynde
Angela Lyne
Sonia Trumpington
Kerstie Kilbannock
Lottie Crump

Worried about money
Socially
Nina Blount
Thérèse de Vitré
Lady Circumference

To be able to live
Brenda Last
Virginia Troy

Thrifty
Dingy Fagan
Dame Mildred Porch

Mercenary
Kätchen
Mrs Beaver

Materialistic
Aimée
First Mortician

Margot Beste-Chetwynde is South American, *nouveau riche* and a procuress. She has plenty of money and, in her terms, works hard for it. When we first meet her she is single again, the rumour being that she poisoned her first husband. As Sir Humphrey Maltravers says, 'Damned awkward position to be in – a rich woman without a husband ... What Margot ought to do is to marry – someone who would stabilize her position, someone ... with a position in public life' (p.130). As we know, Margot marries him, and does so, not because of any financial reasons but to regain respectability with the old guard after Paul is sent to prison. Her remark in *Vile Bodies*, 'I feel my full income', confirms that she now has both income and position.

Angela Lyne has plenty of money and is entirely relaxed about it, accepting that it is part of her attraction for Basil Seal; as indeed it was for her husband Cedric, who was poor and the opposite of her father in every way, which is why she chose him. She will sit in cheaper seats in the cinema because she can see better. She can also afford to be relaxed as she will be one of the few people who are still rich after the war.

Sonia Trumpington gets steadily poorer throughout the novels but is relaxed about it, moving from home to home and coping with each new situation as it comes along.

Kerstie Kilbannock, although very relaxed about money, is also very conscious of it. She allows people who have lost their money to work for her in her canteen and she pays them. But if they still have money, like Virginia Troy, she charges them for the privilege. By *Unconditional Surrender* she is one of the few who still have money and she relaxes far more for she is able to buy Virginia Troy's fur coat when Virginia is at her lowest point.

Lottie Crump is entirely relaxed, borrowing money from one person to lend to another, and putting poor young men's expenses on rich men's bills, though the poor young men usually end up by having to pay something in the end. She also of course likes to have a little bet as well as a little drink.

In the 'Worried About Money' category there are two divisions. Nina Blount is worried about money socially. She cannot marry Adam and live in the style she is accustomed to, so she marries Ginger, and has Adam on the side. Thérèse de Vitré is obsessed with marrying a man from a rich family, and once she learns that Tony is married doesn't speak to him again. There is no financial future there for her. Lady Circumference falls into this category as well. She is very aware about money and what things cost, and as we are told in *Decline and Fall*: 'she never felt quite at ease with people richer than herself' (p.79).

The heroines who are worried about living are Brenda Last and Virginia Troy. Both of them have been used to a good income while married, but once those marriages split up they find that life becomes difficult. In the end Brenda marries Jock Grant-Menzies, whom people thought she should have married in the first place, and Virginia remarries Guy Crouchback because he is rich again, and because she is pregnant.

The thrifty category includes Dingy Fagan and Dame Mildred Porch, both of whom are extremely careful with their money. In the mercenary category comes Kätchen who has a certain charm in the way she asks for money, and the greedy Mrs Beaver who has no charm at all. Aimée and the First Mortician fall into the materialistic category, and with them Waugh is mocking the whole of American materialistic society.

Who then are the exceptions to the monetary rule? Money does not come into Agatha Runcible's vocabulary. As one of the Bright Young People who have money, she is living life to the death. Money is not mentioned by Julia Stitch, Prudence Courteney or Helena. All three of these characters obviously have money, which we can tell by their social standing, but they have other things to occupy their minds. Julia Stitch is a literary lady. She corrects her daughter's Latin homework, does crosswords and talks about E.M. Forster. Prudence is obsessed with sex and her 'Panorama of Life'. Helena is preoccupied with her marriage and religion. Barbara Sothill and Lucy Simmonds in *Work Suspended* are both virtuous women, and both are rich. Money only comes into Barbara's vocabulary when Basil wants to borrow some from her; and Lucy makes only one comment herself about money, and that is to do with a girlfriend's parents whom she describes as 'separated and terribly poor'. Lucy, who fights for the rights of the workers, goes into the cheap cinema sets with Miss Meikeljohn because her friend insists on paying her share, although she is poor, and Lucy respects her friend's integrity. However, when Lucy is heavily pregnant, Miss Meikeljohn allows her to buy good seats as comfort is clearly necessary. Lucy is rich, but she is responsible about money, and we learn, not from her language but from the narrator, that she likes to see her money being put to good use.

Brideshead Revisited seems on the surface to be the complete exception to the rule. There is the question of whom the estate will be left to, but there is no haggling over that. Lord Marchmain's will is accepted. The obsession in *Brideshead* is obviously more with religion, but there is one passage which sums up Lady Marchmain's attitude to both religion and money:

> 'When I was a girl we were comparatively poor, but still much richer than most of the world, and when I married I became very rich. It used to worry me, and I thought it wrong to have so many beautiful things when others had nothing. Now I realise that it is possible for the rich to sin by coveting the privileges of the poor. The poor have always been the favourites of God and his saints, but I believe that it is one of the special achievements of Grace to sanctify the whole of life, riches included.' (p.122)

Lady Marchmain is considered to be a 'saint' by some people, but this is hardly a saintly attitude, as can be seen from the contortions that she goes through to justify her position. Cordelia who goes off to do good works and Sebastian who gives up all his wordly goods are the two saintly people in the family, not Lady Marchmain.

Lady Marchmain is not generous with her wealth, as can be seen by the way that she controls the purse-strings as far as Sebastian is concerned. His finances are 'perpetually, vaguely distressed'. He tells Charles that he could always ask his mother for money, and when Charles says why doesn't he ask Lady Marchmain for 'a proper allowance' his answer is, 'Oh, mummy likes everything to be a present.' Lady Marchmain likes her son to be indebted to her.[36] There is one other passage connected with money which is a brilliant

---

[36] Lady Marchmain has something in common with Brian Howard's mother. Howard was a Bright Young Person. 'The other significant impression I get is that Mrs Howard must have been one of the supreme Vampire mothers of all time. Her habit of stringing Brian along with money doled out in driblets instead of either giving him a fixed allowance or telling him that he must be totally independent and earn his own living, might have been cunningly calculated to keep him in subjection. She reminds me at times of the atrocious 'Lady Marchmain' in *Brideshead Revisited* who used the same sort of tactics in trying to control Sebastian's drinking.' See *Brian Howard: Portrait of a Failure*, edited by Marie Jacqueline Lancaster (1968), p.xx.

revelation of Lady Marchmain's character; and that is when she discovers that Charles has been supplying Sebastian with money with which to buy alcohol:

> '*I don't understand*,' she said. '*I simply don't understand* how anyone can be so callously wicked.'
> She paused, but I do not think she expected any answer; there was nothing I could say unless I were to start again on that familiar, endless argument.
> 'I'm not going to reproach you,' she said. 'God knows it's not for me to reproach anyone. Any failure in my children is my failure. But *I don't understand* it. *I don't understand* how you can have been so nice in so many ways, and then do something so wantonly cruel. *I don't understand* how we all liked you so much. Did you hate us all the time? *I don't understand* how we deserved it.' (p.163, italics added)

Unlike Julia's outburst on mortal sin, the language of which has been heavily criticised and justly so, this passage puts one in mind of the telephone conversation between Nina Blount and Adam Fenwick-Symes. Like the repetition of their phrase 'Well? ... I said, I see', Lady Marchmain's 'I don't understand' repeated six times within the nine sentences of her speech reflects her hurt and her complete lack of understanding of Charles Ryder's action. The speech reveals much about Lady Marchmain, for ironically she sees Charles as being 'callously wicked' and 'wantonly cruel', and she does not understand how he could have seemed so 'nice' or why they all 'liked' him so much. Lady Marchmain is, without realising it, talking about herself. To the outside world, apart from Anthony Blanche, she appears a good, saintly, woman – and yet her children quite often see her as a destructive human being, a killing influence in their lives.

Was Waugh on Lady Marchmain's side? No, he was not. He wrote to Nancy Mitford in reply to the same question: 'Lady Marchmain, no, I am not on her side; but God is, who suffers fools gladly; and the book is about God.'[37]

Waugh specialised in the language of fashionable ladies. Although he could draw other female characters successfully, he wasn't so interested in lower-class language. 'Society' was his forte. As mentioned at the end of Chapter One, he admired Henry Green's use of feminine vocabulary in *Pack My Bag*. But in 1950 he wrote to Nancy Mitford that he thought nothing of *Nothing*. His criticism was that Green had not defined his characters' social position, and that he 'had lost his ear through spending so much time with low-class women'.[38] It was certainly something that didn't happen to Waugh.

[37] *Letters*, p.196.
[38] Ibid., p.328.

CHAPTER THREE

Description of Women

The conscientious novelists of today convey their narrative, atmosphere and characterisation by means of innuendo rather than direct description.[1]

In the first three novels Waugh was indeed 'the conscientious novelist'. The reader is told almost nothing, directly or indirectly, about the physical attributes of the female characters. Margot Beste-Chetwynde in *Decline and Fall* is 'like the first breath of spring'; Nina Blount in *Vile Bodies* looks like something out of *La Vie Parisienne* and Prudence Courteney in *Black Mischief* has a 'gramophone voice', a 'sophisticated voice' and a 'vibrant-with-passion voice'. The books achieve the dazzling distinction that their heroines exist only in terms of their actions, and how they impinge on the other characters.

From *A Handful of Dust* onwards, and until the *Sword of Honour* trilogy, Waugh is less rigorous. Women are described more conventionally. These descriptions are often illuminated by skilful flashes of manic wit:

> Her face was oval, her profile pure and classical and light. Her eyes greenish and remote, with a rich glint of lunacy. (of Aimée, *The Loved One*, p.46)

> Her features were as regular as marble and her eyes wide and splendid and mad. (of Kate Carmichael, *Officers and Gentlemen*, p.63)

But they are conventional descriptions none the less, and some of them – particularly the favourable and enthusiastic ones – convey little. (Julia Flyte in *Brideshead Revisited* is probably described more fully than any other female character in Waugh, but she hardly comes to life.)

Waugh's descriptions may conveniently be divided into the direct and the allusive. At their best the direct descriptions are near parody, deliberately restrained in preparation for some outrageous fact:

> One feature only broke the canon of pure beauty; a long, silken, corn-gold beard. (of Clara, *Love Among the Ruins*, p.198)

> ... and on the balcony, modestly robed in bath towels, sat Miss Sveningen eating beefsteak. (*Scott-King's Modern Europe*, p.226)

> ... a resolute little Negress in a magenta tea-gown who darted across the hall

[1] Evelyn Waugh, 'Tess – As a Modern Sees It', *Evening Standard*, 17 January 1930, p.7.

and barred her way to the drawing-room.

'I am Black Bitch,' she had explained simply. (*Black Mischief*, p.52)

Waugh's allusive descriptions derive, predictably, from the cultural areas he admired:

Like Helen of Troy. A very striking woman. (of Virginia Troy, *Unconditional Surrender*, p.132)

Helen of the white arms, fair among women. (of Helena, *Helena*, p.22)

... fresh and exquisite as a seventeenth-century lyric. (of Margot Beste-Chetwynde, *Decline and Fall*, p.133)

a nereid emerging from fathomless depths of clear water. (of Brenda Last, *A Handful of Dust*, p.16)

'... my mother used to sit in front of a Flaxman bas-relief so as to give me ideal beauty'. (of Lucy Simmonds, *Work Suspended*, p.179)

A face of flawless Quattrocento beauty ... (of Julia Flyte, *Brideshead Revisited*, p.54)

So might have smiled some carefree deacon in the colonnaded schools of fifth-century Alexandria and struck dumb the heresiarchs. (of Clara, *Love Among The Ruins*, p.200)

A Valkyrie. Something from the heroic age. (of Miss Sveningen, *Scott King's Modern Europe*, p.218)

The classical image might have been sober fact, so swift and silent and piercing was the dart of pleasure. (of Susie, *Put Out More Flags*, p.146)

... a more civilised age would have found her admirably proportioned; Boucher would have painted her half clothed in a flutter of blue and pink draperies, a butterfly hovering over a breast of white and rose.[2] (of Mary Nichols' friend, *Put Out More Flags*, p.122)

Some pejorative descriptions draw on equally predictable sources:

... her make-up was haphazard and rather garish, like a later Utrillo. (of Angela Lyne, *Put Out More Flags*, p.159)

Her make-up ... was sploshy, like the John portrait. (of Angela Lyne, *Put Out More Flags*, p.171)

[2] In *The Ordeal of Gilbert Pinfold* while Pinfold is waiting for Margaret to arrive in his cabin he wonders whether he will be able to sustain his interest in the forthcoming event. But as he gazes at the bunk he imagines it 'filled with delicate, shrinking, yielding, yearning nudity, with a nymph by Boucher or Fragonard, and his mood changed again. Let her come' (p.116).

Little that is new will be learned from an analysis of Waugh's allusions, but it is worth examining some of the themes which recur when he describes women more directly.

That so many of his heroines should be fair, and blue-eyed, or be like cats, tells us something about Waugh's tastes and ideals, as well as about the fashion of the time. Rather more significant is the abiding image of the mask. As a symbol of contemporary anxiety, of appearance as opposed to reality, the mask was favoured by a number of writers about women; but Waugh's use of it prompts the thought that he may have been more at home, as a writer, with the slipping mask than with the real woman beneath.

Fair ladies

Waugh's heroines are nearly always fair. Brenda Last has a 'very fair, underwater look'. Kätchen has golden hair. Helena has hair that is sometimes 'golden in the sunlight' or 'more often dull copper in her cloudy home'.

Clara in *Love Among The Ruins* has a golden beard and golden hair, and comes from Browning's poem of the same name – she represents 'the girl with eager eyes and yellow hair'.[3] Angela Lyne is referred to as that 'golden daughter of fortune'. The friend of Mary Nichols in *Put Out More Flags* has 'fair curly hair' and 'a fair skin'. Mrs Rattery is known as 'The Shameless Blonde'. Elfreda Grits in *Excursion in Reality* has a 'platinum-blonde wind-swept head'. Gladys Crutwell in *Winner Takes All* has 'fluffy yellow hair' and Bessie, in the same story, is 'fair'.

If Waugh's heroines have dark hair they still have very fair skin.

Julia Flyte, who had fair hair in the original manuscript,[4] was finally given dark hair but has 'white skin', and her hair is 'silk and jewelled'. Aimée's hair is 'dark and straight' but her skin is 'transparent and untarnished by sun'.[5]

We have seen that Waugh admired Edna Best's fair kind of beauty, and apart from Olivia Plunket Greene and Evelyn Gardner, who had dark hair and eyes but fair skin, most of the women in Waugh's life were fair. Teresa Jungman had hair that was 'spun of the flimsiest canary-bird silkiness';[6] Lady Mosley, Lady Mary Lygon and Lady Diana Cooper were all fair, as was Waugh's second wife, Laura Herbert, whom he described as 'fair' and 'very pretty'.[7] We should also remember that from his mother's side Waugh inherited the blood of Lord Cockburn who was of Saxon-Norman origin. He

[3] Evelyn Waugh wrote: 'The beard was designed for Mrs Eden.' *Letters*, p.407. Clarissa Eden was another close female friend.
[4] 'Julia received most attention in the carbon typescript. For one thing, Waugh had to decide whether her hair was to be dark, as in the first half of the manuscript, or golden, as in the lushly romantic scenes aboard ship. He curbed his usual preference – at least in fiction – and chose dark.' Robert Murray Davis, *Evelyn Waugh, Writer* (1981), p.164.
[5] In his essay 'This Sun-Bathing Business' Waugh stated that after a day's sun-bathing 'if you have fair hair you look ludicrous, if you are dark you are a tolerable imitation of a Spanish donkey-boy'. *Essays*, p.86.
[6] Cecil Beaton, *The Book of Beauty* (Duckworth 1950), p.35.
[7] *Letters*, p.92.

tells us in *A Little Learning* that Cockburn's portrait by Raeburn 'was regarded as so typical of his race that it was lately used on the bank-notes of the Commercial Bank of Scotland.[8] Like her great-grandfather, Catherine Waugh was fair, but Waugh said of her that there 'was nothing Pre-Raphaelite about my mother'.[9]

In the short story 'On Guard' and in *Work Suspended* the clue can be found to Waugh's fair heroines. Millicent Blade in 'On Guard' has a notable head of 'naturally fair hair' but what endears her to 'sentimental Anglo-Saxon manhood' is her nose.[10] In *Work Suspended*, Julia has the kind of 'succulent charm – bright, dotty, soft, eager, acquiescent, flattering, impudent – that is specially, it seems, produced for the delight of Anglo-Saxon manhood'. Anglo-Saxon is the clue. Waugh himself admitted that he believed in nationality – 'not in terms of race or of divine commissions for world conquest, but simply this: mankind inevitably organises itself into communities according to its geographical distribution; these communities by sharing a common history develop common characteristics and inspire a local loyalty; the individual family develops most happily and fully when it accepts those natural limits.'[11]

Waugh's heroines share common characteristics. They are drawn from the aristocracy. They are white. They are fair. They are beautiful. They are Anglo-Saxon.

Blue eyes

As far as eyes are concerned it is evident that the novelists of the day used the beauties of the day for their inspiration. Nancy Cunard was described by Daphne Fielding as having remarkable blue eyes – 'lances of Egyptian blue, water-light, luminous eyes that shone like a wild animal's as they witnessed the unjust ways of the world from the dark loneliness of childhood'.[12] Paula Gellibrand had enormous blue eyes, the lids of which she glossed with Vaseline. Lady Diana Cooper, the model for the blue-eyed Julia Stitch, was the proprietor of the 'blind, blue stare'.[13] All three of these beauties and many others peered out from the pages of glossy magazines. Many of Waugh's friends also had blue eyes. Richard Pares, his first great friend at

---

[8] *A Little Learning*, p.10. Waugh's Scottish background can also be seen in the many tartan references in his work. Lady Circumference in *Vile Bodies* wears 'galoshes and a high fender of diamonds under a tartan umbrella'. Miss Sveningen in *Scott King's Modern Europe* wears a 'tartan fillet in her hair' with her chocolate-brown evening dress. Kate Carmichael's curls in *Officers and Gentlemen* are also 'bound with tartan ribbon'. She is a Scottish nationalist. Margot Beste-Chetwynde in *Decline and Fall* sits at a table covered with 'Balmoral tartan'.

[9] *A Little Learning*, p.31.

[10] Millicent Blade could have been lightly based on Teresa Jungman, who was fair like Millicent and had an endearing nose which was described by Cecil Beaton in *The Book of Beauty* (p.35) as a 'waxen buttony nose'. Millicent Blade's dog who bites her delectable nose was according to Waugh 'rather like Grainger [Lady Mary Lygon's dog] only not so intellectual perhaps more like Wincey' [Teresa Jungman's Blenheim spaniel]. *Letters*, p.91.

[11] Evelyn Waugh, *Robbery Under Law: The Mexican Object-Lesson* (1939), p.17.

[12] Daphne Fielding, *Emerald & Nancy: Lady Cunard and her Daughter* (1968), p.17.

[13] Philip Ziegler, *Diana Cooper* (1981), p.24.

Oxford, was described by Waugh as having 'blank blue eyes',[14] and John Sutro, a lifelong friend, he remembered as having 'large innocent blue eyes, taken one might think, from one of the Mitford sisters'.[15]

If we take Michael Arlen, Aldous Huxley, Henry Green and Evelyn Waugh, we will see that all four specialise in blue-eyed beauties. Arlen's Iris Storm (partly based on Nancy Cunard) has eyes that are 'blazing blue, like two spoonfuls of the Mediterranean in the early morning of a brilliant day'. They also glow like an animal's. During a nightclub scene in *The Green Hat* a Prince rises to dance with the girl 'of the blind blue eyes', and Arlen's other female character, Venice, has eyes that are 'blue, mad blue'. Aldous Huxley's Anne in *Crome Yellow* has 'pale blue eyes'; another character, Mary, has 'china blue eyes' and the anti-hero Denis, while looking at himself critically in the mirror, thinks wishfully that 'his eyes might have been blue and not green'. Mrs Viveash in *Antic Hay* has eyes that are like 'the pale blue eyes which peer out of the Siamese cat's black-velvet mask'. Henry Green, writing of 1931-38 in *Party Going* (1938), describes his heroine, Amabel, as having that 'azure glance of fame'. Amabel, with her blue eyes, is always being seen in photographs in the weekly papers. (The mythologising of Amabel is like that of Julia Flyte – both girls have a mythical status because they are seen from afar by the people who read the popular press. Their names are household names like those of film stars.)

Many of Waugh's heroines, then, have blue eyes, and his descriptions of them are somewhat lacking in originality. Julia Stitch in *Unconditional Surrender* becomes another Iris Storm. Her eyes are described first as 'her true blue, portable and compendious oceans'; and later as 'her eyes were one immense sea, full of flying galleys'.[16] In *Put Out More Flags* Basil Seal has eyes like those of his sister, Barbara Sothill – 'as blue as hers and as innocent'. Also, the girl who is a friend of Mary Nichols whom he meets while looking for a home for the Connolly children has 'huge, pale blue eyes' and those 'great eyes' later hold him 'dazzled, like a rabbit before the headlights of a car'. In *Basil Seal Rides Again* his daughter Barbara has blue eyes – 'star-sapphire eyes in the child-like face under black tousselled hair gazed deep into star-sapphire eyes sunk in empty pouches' (p.274).

Julia Flyte has the 'blank stare and gaze of the period', and although Waugh never says that her eyes are blue he gives an impression of blueness by describing how, when she is asleep, her 'blue lids' fall over her eyes. (Blue eyeshadow normally goes with blue eyes.) Lady Marchmain is 'huge-eyed' and Anthony Blanche comments of her: 'It is extraordinary how large those eyes look and how the lids are veined blue where anyone else would have

[14] *A Little Learning*, p.191.

[15] Ibid., p.194.

[16] Frederick J. Stopp points out that the allusion is to Hérédia's sonnet on Cleopatra, 'whose eyes were "*toute une mer immense où fuyaient des galères*"'. *Evelyn Waugh, Portrait of an Artist* (1958), p.177. And Waugh wrote of J.F. Roxburgh's influence at Lancing: 'To hear him declaiming: "*Nox est perpetua, una, dormienda*" or "*Toute une mer immense où fuyaient des galères*" ... not as my father read poetry with a subtle cadence, but like a great negro stamping out a tribal rhythm – was to set up reverberations in the adolescent head which a lifetime does not suffice to silence.' *A Little Learning*, p.158.

touched them with a finger-tip of paint.' Lady Marchmain's eyes are obviously so blue that she doesn't need eye-shadow.

Although Michael Arlen made his character Venice have 'mad blue eyes', madness was not, as with Waugh, a normal feature of his work. In Waugh's novels madness abounds, and it is quite often to be noted in the eyes of the aristocracy. This can be seen very clearly in the short story 'Bella Fleace Gave a Party'. The first description of Bella tells us that her eyes are 'pale blue, blank and mad'. While she is waiting for her guests to arrive she sits on a chair at the head of the stairs gazing out with her 'blank, blue eyes'. None of her invited guests arrive (she forgot to send the invitations) and when four people do, who were not invited, she draws herself up and fixes them with her 'blank, blue eyes'. The Morstocks and the Gordons, the uninvited guests, stand transfixed by the 'mad blue eyes of their hostess'.

In *Officers and Gentlemen* the mad laird of Mugg has 'fine, old blue blank eyes' and his niece Kate Carmichael has eyes that are 'wide and splendid and mad'. Aimée in *The Loved One* has eyes that contain 'a rich glint of lunacy'. We must not forget that Waugh himself was fair with blue eyes – eyes that were often described as 'bulging', 'popping' or 'blazing'.

Cat-like

The idea of a woman looking or acting like a cat is not unusual in literature but in the 1920s and 1930s the feline image was particularly strong.

Elinor Glyn's *Three Weeks* was published in 1906 and banned in 1907. It was made into a sensational film in 1924 – sensational because of a passionate love scene on a couch covered in tiger skin. The hero of the novel sees the heroine as his 'Tiger-Queen'. She purrs, and is described as having a 'gliding feline movement' and being full of 'cat-like grace'. She is also, however, described as a snake. Her figure 'so subtle in its lines' makes him 'think of a snake'. She has a 'strange, snake look' and her eyes 'fascinated him and paralysed him, like those of a snake'. She quivers with the 'movements of a snake' and the drapery of her dress flows in graceful lines like 'a serpent's tail'. Elinor Glyn used the imagery of the tiger-skin to convey passion, but she combined it with snake imagery to give a feeling of sinuousness and spellbinding power. Freud might well have said that such use of snake symbolism reflected her own obsession with sexuality, since in Freudian terms the snake represents the penis.

The effect of Elinor Glyn's 'tiger-skin' lead to a craze for fur, and society beauties like Nancy Cunard dressed in leopard skin and set a fashion.

In 1929 Betty May wrote *Tiger Woman*, an autobiography, in which she described a fight between herself and a girl in Paris. She recounts how she blacked the lady's eyes and 'beat her lips against her teeth, till her mouth was full of blood'. After biting the man who pulled her off, she was called '*Tigre*' and given the name of 'Tiger Woman'.

Rosamond Lehmann in *Dusty Answer* (1927) describes the heroine's mother as 'something in the triangular outline, in the set of the eyes, the expression of the lips, made you think of a cat'; and when the mother meets one of her daughter's friends the comment is made: 'If to her cat-deep self she said: "So that's the one!" her diamond-like eyes did not betray her.' But Rosamond Lehmann also gives her male characters cat-like qualities. Charlie, who is as beautiful as a girl, is thought of in such terms as 'Charlie undoubtedly lapped up music as a kitten lapped milk', while Roddy is imagined as jumping and 'landing in a soft relaxed cat-like crouch' and Martin is a 'tiger for raw vegetables'.

Michael Arlen has Venice in *The Green Hat* compare herself to a mouse when she nearly drowns, but she also states that she could only let out a 'miaow'. And Iris Storm, the heroine of that same book, has hair that flames 'tiger-tawny' and she says that she has killed 'lions and tigers too, in twelve years' wanderings through hell'.

Some male authors used the cat as an unflattering image. Aldous Huxley in *Crome Yellow* gives Anne a 'cat's smile' which is later referred to as her 'tight cat's smile'. In Henry Green's *Party Going* the females watch Max like 'cats over offal', and Julia sees Amabel, her rival and the heroine of the novel, as 'a cat that has just had its mouse coming among other cats who had only the smell'.

Waugh also uses cat imagery a great deal to describe and reflect on human behaviour. Julia Flyte has a scene in *Brideshead* where she shows her claws. In her argument with Charles her face is seen as 'cat-like but unlike a cat'. She hysterically spits out her anger at Ryder. First she acts like a cat biting him, and then she changes the bite to a 'lick of her tongue', and Charles sees her as both 'cat on the roof-top' and 'cat in the moonlight'. Julia has all the instincts of a cat but not those of a pet one. As we learn early on the 'cat-and-mouse pastimes of the hearth rug' are not for her. Julia is 'no Penelope'. Like a big cat, a tigress, she has to hunt in the modern jungle of the town for her mate. Her first catch is Rex Mottram, her second Charles Ryder.

In *Black Mischief*, Prudence Courteney uses the expression 'Lovey dovey, cat's eyes' which William tells her she got out of a book, one that had 'been all round the compound'; and she agrees that she did. Waugh was probably referring here to William Gerhardi's *The Polyglots* where the heroine, Sylvia, uses the same expression. Sylvia also acts like a cat: 'She was warm; she lay there all in a bundle, purring "Mrr-mrr-mrr ... " '

A Handful of Dust contains plenty of cat imagery. Brenda Last is described as rubbing her cheek against Tony 'like a cat'. We are told that 'it was a way she had'. It is also a way that she has with John Beaver. When he kisses her, as with Tony, she rubs against his cheek 'in the way she had'. After being with Beaver, Brenda returns home to curl up kittenishly next to Tony on the sofa. Note that when she returns from London she always becomes a 'waif' and has a cup of bread and milk. Like a cat who has been out on the tiles she comes home for her creature comforts.

Tony also sees his wife as a cat. In one of his dreams, when the Indians have been frightened by Dr Messinger's toy mice, he says to her: '*You* wouldn't be frightened of a toy mouse.' Brenda, the cat, doesn't reply: she sits huddled over her bowl of bread and milk as she used to do when she came back from London.

If Brenda acts like a cat, so does Jenny Abdul Akbar, the lady provided for Tony. She, however, is far more obvious. Brenda curls up like a kitten next to Tony but Jenny tells him: 'I like just to curl up like a cat in front of the fire, and if you're nice to me I'll purr, and if you're cruel I shall pretend not to notice – just like a cat ... Shall I purr, Teddy?'

John Andrew, Brenda and Tony's son, uses the word 'cat' in its sense of 'to be sick', and although his Nanny tells him that Miss Tendril, the Vicar's sister doesn't want to hear that rude word, that rude word is what *A Handful of Dust* is all about – sick relationships. Note too how Brenda talks about John Beaver in cat terms. She thinks that he is likely to be 'as cold as a fish' and she also sees him as a 'cub'.

If Julia Flyte and Brenda Last are big cats, tigresses, so is Miss Sveningen in *Scott-King's Modern Europe*, who is first seen as moving 'cat-like towards the soldiers' and later is described as a 'giant carnivore' when she eats beefsteak on Whitemaid's balcony.

Clara in *Love Among The Ruins* creates a cat image for herself when she applies her stage make-up and gives herself eyebrows that are 'extended and turned up catwise'.

In *Put Out More Flags*, Molly Meadows tells Peter Pastmaster, when she virtually proposes to him, that 'Sarah and Betty' will be 'as sick as cats'. Molly, another huntress, has caught the big fish first.

Julia Stitch is never described as a cat, but in *Officers and Gentlemen* she is not about to let Guy let the cat out of the bag; Ivor Claire's secret is safe with her. Ironically, when she gives Guy his bedroom, which is below ground level with a concrete floor and cockroaches, she asks him if he's 'fond of cats'. Without waiting for a reply she throws in 'two tiger-like animals' and shuts the door. Guy is Mrs Stitch's prisoner, and she is playing cat-and-mouse with him. Her final unkindness is to drop the envelope that he gives her, with the identity disc in it, into the waste-paper basket.

Kätchen in *Scoop* is never described as a kitten either, but Kätchen, apart from a girl's name, is also the German for kitten. And Kätchen is not unlike a kitten. She's playful, easily hurt, but tough. Cat-like, she comes in out of the rain, shelters, feeds and grooms herself (at William's expense) and then goes on her way.

To return to Elinor Glyn, as late as 1952 in *Men at Arms* (p.125), Waugh wrote of Virginia Troy being at a party where an air-marshal remarks that the polar-bear rug before the fire reminds him of a rhyme:

Would you like to sin
With Eleanor Glyn
On a tiger skin?
Or would you prefer
To err
With her
On some other fur?

When Virginia asks who Eleanor (sic) Glyn is, she gets the reply, 'Oh, just a name, you know. Put in to make it rhyme, I expect. Neat isn't it?' Waugh does not state the obvious, which is that Virginia's sexual adventures have something in common with that of the lady on the tiger-skin.

Like Rosamond Lehmann, Waugh also describes some of his male characters as cats, but he always does so in an inflattering light. In *Men at Arms*, Guy is rejected by Virginia when he tries to sleep with her and afterwards is described as 'a stray cat, slinking back mauled from the rooftops, to a dark corner among the dustbins where he could lick his wounds' (p.135). Guy cannot win in an encounter with a stronger cat.

The feline quality was not one that appealed to Waugh. Again, in *Men at Arms*, he writes of a physical training instructor who is a 'sleek young man with pomaded hair' who has 'unnaturally glittering eyes' and who performs 'his great feats of strength and agility with a feline and, to Guy, most offensive air of sang-froid' (p.51).

Cats have always been seen as aloof, independent, promiscuous and, unlike a faithful dog, capricious in their affection. The fact that Waugh's women have so many feline characteristics says a lot about Waugh's view of the female sex.

Masks, or ladies not quite revealed

The obscuring of the face is an important element in the physical description of women in the novels of the 1920s and 1930s, and it is an element that Waugh had in common with other writers of the period.

The most popular way of obscuring the face was to see it as a mask. Michael Arlen in *The Green Hat* (1924) describes the face of his heroine, Iris Storm, as though it were 'turned to a mask of white stone with two amethysts for eyes. It was a mask that face, and those were the eyes of a mask'. Aldous Huxley's Anne Wimbush has a face which, when it is expressing nothing, is 'no more than a lazy mask of wax' (*Crome Yellow*, 1921); while Mrs Viveash in *Antic Hay* (1923) smiles 'like a tragic mask', and Lucy Tantamount's face in *Point Counter Point* (1928) is 'a pale mask that had seen everything before'. Graham Greene's Minty in *England Made Me* (1935) sees Garbo's face as 'the unreal loveliness and the unreal tragedy of a mask like Dante's known too well'.

If faces are not described as masks they are often obscured by other means. In *Valmouth* (1919) Firbank's Mrs Hurstpierpoint actually covers her face completely with a 'jet-black visard' so that her white face does not frighten a black child. William Gerhardi in *The Polyglots* (1925) has his heroine, Sylvia, wearing a 'hideous hat' which wholly covers 'the upper portion of her face'; while Michael Arlen adds mystery to Iris Storm by concealing her face with the brim of her famous green hat. Arlen is echoed in *Brideshead Revisited*, for Julia 'like most women then, wore a green hat pulled down to her eyes' (p.117).

D.H. Lawrence in *The First Lady Chatterley* (1928) describes Constance, Lady Chatterley, as follows: 'She put a thick veil over her face, like a Mohammedan woman, leaving only her eyes. And thus she stood naked before her mirror and looked at her slow, golden-skinned, silent body.' Lady

Chatterley wonders why one only ever sees the face of a person when it is probably the worst part of one. Her husband suggests that it is by the face that the personality is revealed. Lawrence with his interest in female sexuality has Constance question this, suggesting to her husband that there might be something more than personality, that the body might have a life of its own. She recalls how lovely a torso is, in sculpture, without its head. Lawrence is, of course, preparing us for her affair with the gamekeeper, but it is interesting that Lawrence has Constance mask herself and question the power of the body over the face.

The mask was not a new phenomenon. In 1897, Max Beerbohm in *The Happy Hypocrite* had as his hero an aging rake, Lord George Hell, who wears a youthful mask to disguise himself while pursuing a young girl. When the mask is torn off the signs of age and decadence have disappeared because his true and innocent love has made him the man of the mask, rather than the man behind the mask. This is the opposite of Wilde's *The Picture of Dorian Gray* (1890), where the portrait of Dorian becomes the 'mask of his shame' and 'the face of his soul' while he, Dorian, keeps his beauty.

Masked balls played an important part in society life in the 1890s, but by 1900, and with the fall of Wilde, that decade came to its end and the idea of the mask was not to re-assert itself until the twenties when its image was used by journalists as well as novelists.

Virginia Woolf was described thus in *Vogue* in 1926 by Victoria Ocampo: 'Try to imagine a mask that even without life, without intelligence would be beautiful. Then imagine this mask so impregnated with life and intelligence that it would seem to have been modelled by them. Imagine all this, and you will still have only a faint idea of the charm of Virginia Woolf's face, a charm that is the result of the most felicitious encounter of matter and soul in the face of a woman.[17]

The image of the mask was a strong one. This was partly because of make-up which gave the female face an entirely different look, and partly because of the life mask which was popular at the time. (An advance on the death mask used in the 1890s.) As far as make-up was concerned, J.B. Priestley had the following to say of the girls at the Nottingham Fair in 1933: 'The girls, whose thickly powdered faces were little white masks without lines but daubed with red and black, looked like dolls out of some infernal toyshop, and the appearance of them all was fascinating and frightening.'[18] And Barbara Cartland wrote of Waugh's girl friend Olivia Plunket Greene as having 'a dead-white expressionless face made up like a mask'.[19] The life mask played its part in *Crazy Pavements* where Lord William Motley's secret hobby is that of making life masks of his friends. In Waugh's own diaries in May 1930 he recorded that he had gone with Diana Guinness to see the life mask she was having made of herself. He says: 'It is lovely and very accurate. She has promised me a copy in white and gold plaster.' In July 1936 he also

[17] Victoria Ocampo of Virginia Woolf in *In Vogue: Sixty Years of Celebrities and Fashions from British Vogue* (1975), p.61.

[18] J.B. Priestley, *English Journey* (1933), p.139.

[19] Dudley Carew, 'He-Evelyn and She-Evelyn', in *Evelyn Waugh and His World*, p.40.

recorded that he called on Lady Diana Cooper and 'found her with face expressionless in mud mask'.

Lady Diana Cooper was of course the model for Julia Stitch. In October 1936, Waugh says in the diaries that he made 'a very good start with the first page of a novel describing Diana's early morning'. This was *Scoop*, and when we first meet Julia Stitch she is in bed and 'her normally mobile face encased in clay was rigid and menacing as an Aztec mask'. It would seem that Waugh's heroines, like the heroines of the other novelists of the day, had to have some mystery about them, for most of them have this obscuring of the face in common – whether their faces be masked, in shadow or veiled in some other way.

Angela Lyne in *Put Out More Flags* has a face that is 'mute. It might have been carved in jade.' Her face is also described as a 'calm and pensive mask'; and her mouth which is beginning to droop a little is seen as 'the droop you sometimes saw in death masks'. (Mr Joyboy in *The Loved One* is of course the expert on the death mask.) Angela's face gives nothing away. Waugh says of her: 'A stranger might have watched her for mile after mile, as a spy or a lover or a newspaper reporter will loiter in the street before a closed house, and see no chink of light, hear no whisper of movement behind the shuttered facade ... ' To disguise her appearance because of her drinking she also takes to wearing 'spectacles of smoked glass', and when she appears in public it is behind 'dark glasses'. Interestingly, even Dame Mildred Porch and Miss Sarah Tin in *Black Mischief* wear smoked spectacles.

In *Put Out More Flags* even Susie, one of Basil's 'silly girls', is first seen thus: 'A figure approaching appeared in silhouette, and in somewhat indistinct silhouette.' Virginia Troy in *Officers and Gentlemen* is seen sitting 'as it were, in a faint corroding mist'. When Miles first meets Clara in *Love Among The Ruins* he is conscious only of 'a shadow which stirred at the sound of the latch and turned, still a shadow but of exquisite grace to meet him'. Then 'the shadow took form', and we learn that 'the full vision was all that the first glance had hinted; more than all, for every slight movement revealed perfection.' Clara's beard does not quite 'obscure her delicate ovoid of cheek and chin' and Miles sees her as though she 'might have been peeping at him over ripe heads of barley'. At the hospital, after the operation, Miles finds Clara sleeping, 'the sheet pulled up to her eyes'. When she wakes she pulls the sheet higher, and finally Miles realises that her eyes and brows are all that are left of the face he loved. Below them is 'something quite inhuman, a tight, slippery mask, salmon pink'. And Clara manages to achieve a double mask, for on top of the new substance of her face she gives herself, with the use of make-up, a 'full mask as though for the lights of the stage'.

Brenda Last in *A Handful of Dust*, when she comes down the stairs to meet John Beaver, is seen as carrying 'a vast disordered sheaf of Sunday newspapers, above which only her eyes and forehead appeared as though over a yashmak'. She is also a 'legendary, almost ghostly name, the imprisoned princess of fairy story'. When Tony Last meets the native woman Rosa we are informed that 'the shadow of her high cheekbones hid her eyes'. Our first image of Julia Flyte in *Brideshead Revisited* is that of 'a vague, girlish figure' in the back of a car; and towards the end of the novel – 'in the gloom of that room she seemed like a ghost'. Her rival, Mrs Champion, is described as having 'cold eyes watching behind her sunglasses'; and her mother, Lady Marchmain 'that Reinhardt nun' is seen at parties in Venice in 'a cocoon of gossamer ... part of some Celtic play or a heroine from Maeterlinck'.

Minor characters have their faces obscured as well. In *Unconditional Surrender*, Everard Spruce's secretaries are known as 'Spruce's veiled ladies' because of the long hair which envelops them.[20] They are described as speaking 'through a curtain of hair' or 'the hair through which she spoke was black' or there is one particular secretary who, like a nun, keeps 'custody of her eyes'.

In *Vile Bodies* the heroines hide their faces with make-up. Nina Blount makes Adam Fenwick-Symes turn his back, while she puts on her face, until she is ready to present a mask to him: 'She invariably made him turn his back until it was over, having a keen sense of modesty about this part of her toilet, in curious contrast to some girls, who would die rather than be seen in their underclothes, and yet flaunt unpainted faces in front of everyone.' The moralities are ironically reversed here. Nina doesn't worry about being seen nude, or in her underclothes, as long as her face is painted, because her painted face means that she is representing someone other than herself to Adam and he is not to be let in on the secret of her artifice. Agatha Runcible also uses make-up to create another self. After her experience at the customs she is seen to be 'working hard with lipstick and compact'. Her make-up is so extreme that she is taken for a 'tart'. As Lottie Crump says, 'You look so like one, got up like that'.

Vile Bodies is of course about the Bright Young People and one must remember the parties they went to: 'Masked parties. Savage parties. Victorian parties, Greek parties, Wild West parties, Russian parties, Circus parties, parties where one had to dress as somebody else ... ' Lady Marchmain's image, that of the 'Reinhardt nun', reflects the craze of the time for dressing up in pageants and *tableaux vivants* as nuns, saints or the Madonna – a craze helped by Lady Diana Cooper's appearance as the Madonna in Max Reinhardt's play *The Miracle*. Habits, drapes and wrapped heads were the fashion. Waugh himself played the game. As he says in *The Ordeal of Gilbert Pinfold*, 'the part for which he cast himself was a combination of eccentric don and testy colonel and he acted it strenuously ... until it came to dominate his whole outward personality'.

Sean O'Faolain has said that in Waugh's work the mask of virtue, and other masks, are ripped away. He mentions how Waugh's Basil Seal 'would watch in the asparagus season a dribble of melted butter on a woman's chin, marring her beauty and making her look ridiculous, while she would still talk and smile and turn her head, not knowing how she appeared to him'. He also

[20] Frances Donaldson writes: 'In *Unconditional Surrender* the character called Everard Spruce has two secretaries. One is called Frankie, the other is called Coney, the nickname by which Mrs Ralph Jervis is known to her friends. She is someone of whom I see a great deal – enough for people often to say: "Coney and Frankie", or "Frankie and Coney" ' (*Portrait of a Country Neighbour* (1967), pp.113-14).

mentions Angela Lyne's make-up, which Waugh describes as follows: 'Her make-up was haphazard and garish, rather like a later Utrillo.' O'Faolain says that Waugh says somebody else's make-up is 'sploshy, like a John portrait'. (In fact it is again Angela Lyne's make-up towards the end of *Put Out More Flags*.) He believes that 'there is no venom in the unmasking, no bitter hate'.[21] These are strong words and one would love to agree with him, but on the other hand there is no doubt that Waugh derived some perverse satisfaction from seeing women at a disadvantage. In *A Handful of Dust*, Jenny Abdul Akbar eats muffins for tea:

> She ate heartily; often she ran her tongue over her lips, collecting crumbs that had become embedded there and melted butter from the muffin. One drop of butter fell on her chin and glittered there unobserved except by Tony. It was a relief to him when John Andrew was brought in. (p.85)

It is John Andrew who points out to Jenny that she has butter on her chin, and she laughingly reaches for her bag exclaiming that Tony '*might*' have told her. There are differences, however, between Tony Last and Basil Seal. Basil delights in the butter on the chin; Tony is embarrassed by it.

In *The Death of the Heart* Elizabeth Bowen has a passage in which her male character, Eddie, while having tea with the young heroine, Portia, tells her that she is beautiful:

> ... 'You said I was beautiful.'
> 'Did I? Turn round and let me look.'
> She turned an at once proud and shrinking face. But he giggled: 'Darling, you've got salt stuck all over the butter on your chin, like real snow on one of those Christmas cards. Let me wipe it off – stay still.'
> 'But I had been going to eat another crumpet.'
> 'Oh, in that case it would be rather a waste –'[22]

The difference between Elizabeth Bowen's Eddie and Evelyn Waugh's male characters is striking, and says quite a lot about Waugh's maturity as compared with hers.

Other female characters also suffer at Waugh's hands. Kate Carmichael in *Officers and Gentlemen* is thought by Guy to have skin that is either 'freckled' or has been 'splashed with peaty water' which she hasn't washed off, or otherwise it is a 'hereditary stain'. He continues to describe her 'brown blotches'. Ludovic in *Unconditional Surrender* sees The Smart Woman, Lady Perdita, with 'smudges of soot on her face'. In *Tactical Exercise* Elizabeth Verney's husband looks at her while she is sleeping: 'Unlike her normal habit, she was snoring. He stood for a minute, fascinated by this new and unlovely aspect of her, her head thrown back, her mouth open and slightly dribbling at the corner' (p.167). In *The Loved One* Dennis Barlow sees the courting couples and notes how 'one girl blew bubbles of gum like a rutting

[21] Sean O'Faolain, *The Vanishing Hero: Studies in Novelists of the Twenties* (1956), p.58.
[22] Elizabeth Bowen, *The Death of the Heart* (1938), p.138.

camel' (p.67). Charles Ryder's father in *Brideshead Revisited* asks him if he liked the young lady, Gloria Orme-Herrick, whom he had invited to dinner. When Charles replies 'no' he questions him as to whether it was 'her little moustache' that he 'objected to or her very large feet' (p.70). Also in *Brideshead*, Sebastian and Charles go to 'Ma Mayfield's' and meet up with two girls: 'One had the face of a skull, the other of a sickly child' (p.112). They become known as 'Death's Head' and 'Sickly Child' and Julia is most impressed when she hears about their 'skulls and consumptives' (p.118). And as late as 1960, in *A Tourist to Africa*, Waugh recorded 'the thighs of middle-aged women quiver horribly at the library steward's table ... the three Arabs ... wear the light cotton robes of their people and always look cool and elegant and clean' (p.38).

Edmund Wilson has said that 'Evelyn Waugh is perhaps the only male writer of his generation in England who is able to make his women attractive'.[23] This is a strange comment if we consider how often Waugh sees women at a disadvantage. One of Waugh's best descriptive passages about women still shows them in an unattractive light: the passage in *Put Out More Flags* where Peter Pastmaster is trying to decide which girl he will marry:

> He really could see very little difference between the three girls; in fact he sometimes caused offence by addressing them absent-mindedly by the wrong names. None of them carried a pound of superfluous flesh; they all had an enthusiasm for the works of Mr Ernest Hemingway; all had pet dogs of rather similar peculiarities. (p.152)

Waugh was not the only male author who saw women at a disadvantage. Michael Arlen in *The Green Hat* when describing Iris Storm's even regiment of white teeth remarked: 'On a middle one was wedged a small string of tobacco; it lay coiled there like a brown maggot, and when I told her about that she removed it with the nail of her finger and regarded it' (p.16). He also explains that when Iris is asleep he touches up her make-up: 'Her mouth drooped like a flower, and there was a little shiny bit in the valley between her cheek and her nose. To this I applied a little *Quelques Fleurs* talc powder on a handkerchief, that when she awoke she should not think so ill of herself as I did' (p.42). Aldous Huxley in *Point Counter Point* has Philip Quarles suddenly see Lucy Tantamount at a disadvantage when she laughs. Lucy opens her painted mouth – 'and her tongue and gums were so much paler than the paint of her lips tht they seemed (it gave me a queer creepy shock of astonished horror) quite bloodless and white by contrast'. This image reminds Quarles of the sacred crocodiles in India with the white insides of their mouths. The image so stirs him that he considers it a good opening for his novel:

> I shall begin the book with it. My Walterish hero makes his Lucyish siren laugh and immediately (to his horror; but he goes on longing for her, with an added touch of perversity, all the same and perhaps all the more) sees those disgusting crocodiles he had been looking at in India a month before. (p.407)

[23] Edmund Wilson, ' "Never Apologize, Never Explain": The Art of Evelyn Waugh', *Classics and Commercials* (1951).

Arlen seems to have had some sympathy for his heroine in the way that he makes his narrator touch up her make-up so that she will be unaware of how she looked to him and, more important, won't be disappointed in herself. Huxley enters a world of Freudian fantasy where the beautiful Lucy becomes a preying crocodile. And what about Waugh? Interestingly, this unattractive viewing of the female is not confined to his male characters. Helena, for example, sees Fausta as glittering and pouting 'like a great gold-fish'; but Fausta, who has been worked on by the beauty specialists, is unaware of the impression she is creating. It would seem simply that Waugh preferred his women unpainted, and there are such examples to be found in his work. Clara, when Miles first falls in love with her in *Love Among The Ruins*, is described thus: 'Her lips under the golden moustachios were unpainted.' Aimée in *The Loved One* has lips that are 'artificially tinctured, no doubt, but not coated like her sisters' and clogged in all their delicate pores with crimson grease'.

If we look at Waugh's diaries there are some definite clues to his personal preferences. In 1925 he records: 'Next day to everyone's surprise Olivia came down dressed and having finished her Elizabeth Arden in time for breakfast.' In 1930 he reveals that Lady Cranborne was disconcerted by 'Olivia's urban clothes and make-up' and goes on to say that Olivia's make-up also had 'a sad effect on Pansy's cook who has in emulation bought a great quantity of cosmetics and goes off to Salisbury every afternoon looking like Lady Lavery'. In 1936 he takes Laura to Paganis and states rather disapprovingly 'she with paint on her face'. (Both Evelyn Gardner and Laura Herbert used little in the way of cosmetics, which again tells us something about the type of natural beauty that he preferred.) As late as 1947 he states about a trip to Stockholm: 'Girls very pretty and not disfigured by paint and hairdressing.' The most important entry however is in 1934 when, talking of having tea at Gerald Berner's, he tells us that he sat next to a lady for some time and then proceeded 'to tell her that she had lipstick all over her face'. He comments: 'It made her look as though she were smiling.'

Waugh obviously abhorred any kind of make-up and liked women to be scrubbed clean of any artifice. His views on the cleanliness of women did not change much over the years. In *Scoop* (1938) Nanny Price tells Mr Salter that Priscilla is 'a good girl at heart, though she does forget her neck sometimes ... comes out of the bath as black as she went in' (p.211). This low opinion was echoed in 1962 in an article for the *Daily Mail* where Waugh attacked both sexes for having 'dirty necks and finger-nails' and stated: 'A few girls who work as mannequins are professionally clean; countless others should be sent to bed supperless.'[24]

In *The Ordeal of Gilbert Pinfold* (pp.105-6) Waugh writes of the time when he was young and used to frequent a house of 'bright, cruel girls who spoke

[24] Evelyn Waugh, 'Manners and Morals – 2', *Essays*, p.591.

their own thieves' slang' and played cruel games:[25]

> When a stranger came among them, they would all – if the mood took them – put their tongues out at him or her; all, that is to say, except those in his immediate line of sight. As he turned his head, one group of tongues popped in, another popped out. Those girls were adept in dialogue. They had rigid self-control. They never giggled. Those who spoke to the stranger assumed an unnatural sweetness. The aim was to make him catch another with her tongue out. It was a comic performance – the turning head, the flickering, crimson stabs, the tender smiles turning to sudden grimaces, the artificiality of the conversation which soon engendered an unidentifiable discomfort in the most insensitive visitor, made him feel that somehow he was making a fool of himself, made him look at his trouser buttons, at his face in the glass to see whether there was something ridiculous in his appearance.

Waugh obviously found this game disturbing, and it would seem that in his writings, without necessarily being aware of it, he retaliated by playing a cruel game on his female characters.

Masked, veiled, in shadow or made-up – the obscuring of the face is an important feature of Waugh's work. Henry Green, in his autobiography *Pack My Bag* (1939), gives us a clue as to the attitude of the male toward the female in the early part of the century: 'But we, a year or two past puberty ... imagined women as one dreams at one's desk of a far country unvisited with all its mystery of latitude and place' (p.116).

Waugh's Margot Beste-Chetwynde appears to be 'like the creature of a different species'; and Dennis Barlow in *The Loved One* perhaps sums up Waugh's attitudes best ... 'but Dennis came of an earlier civilisation with sharper needs. He sought the intangible, the veiled face in the fog, the silhouette at the lighted doorway, the secret graces of a body which hid itself under formal velvet.'

---

[25] The 'bright, cruel girls who spoke their own thieves' slang', who were 'adept in dialogue' and whose smiles turned to 'sudden grimaces' were probably lightly based on the Mitford sisters. Unity and Decca had a private language called 'Boudledidge'. Jonathan Guinness in *The House of Mitford* (1984, p.292) explains that 'it had to be uttered while making a miserable, frowning, and rather costive-looking grimace ... the language itself was English with the vowels distorted, the consonants softened and extra syllables inserted'. Also see below, Chapter Eight, n.38.

CHAPTER FOUR

The Intelligence of Women

Lunched Resident but women were present so could not talk of anything interesting. (*Diaries*, p.344)

Christopher Sykes has said that, apart from Mrs Stitch, all Waugh's 'attractive women had been bitches or idiots or both'.[1] None of them are complete idiots, but Waugh makes it quite clear that the female mind is inadequate. Women are fine for gossip and social chit-chat (he enjoyed the more intelligent ones for that himself), but for serious conversation and intellectual thought one needs the company of men. Even Mrs Stitch, who is an exception to the rule, as we shall see in Chapter Nine, is not allowed to be her normal intelligent self when she is with Lord Copper. She has to use her charm to get him to send Boot to Ishmaelia; and, of course, it turns out to be the wrong Boot.

Waugh said in a radio talk, 'Up to London', about the coming-out season of debutantes: 'If she starts with older brothers and sisters and popular parents, little need be done for her beyond buying her some clothes, having her photographed by the right photographers who are on good terms with the illustrated papers, and teaching her three simple topics of conversation – one high brow, one high spirited, and one flirtatious.[2]

Waugh was not alone in his thinking. Women authors such as Virginia Woolf, Anita Loos, Rosamond Lehmann and Nancy Mitford acknowledged the picture even if they didn't agree with it.

Virginia Woolf deliberately avoided writing at a conscious level about what it meant to be a woman living in the society of her time. In *A Room of One's Own* (1929) she called for her fellow women writers not to lash out on the subject of injustice to women, and the oppression of women, as women writers had done in the past, but 'to use writing as an art, not as a method of self-expression', and she said: 'It is fatal for anyone who writes to think of their sex ... It is fatal for a woman to lay the least stress on any grievance; to plead even with justice any cause; in any way to speak consciously as a woman ... anything written with that conscious bias is doomed to death ... it cannot grow in the minds of others' (pp.156-7). Virginia Woolf was never able

---

[1] Sykes, p.286.

[2] Evelyn Waugh, '*Up to London – 111*', BBC Radio, 21 June 1938, Transcript. Waugh also said that the English debutante with her 'senseless prattle' was 'fit only for the schoolroom'. 'Why Glorify Youth?', *Essays*, p.127.

to reconcile her feminist and her artistic ideals. Feminine sexuality does not dominate her female characters' lives, but they still act out those daily and, quite often, boring lives in a female way based on perceptions and sensitivities which are quite different in kind to those of the male characters. This 'female' consciousness cuts them off from any kind of positive action, for their inner experiences are more significant to them than any real contact with the male world outside themselves.

Anita Loos in *Gentlemen Prefer Blondes* (1926) makes the comment: 'So the gentleman said a girl with brains ought to do something else with them besides think' (ch.1). Waugh in *Brideshead Revisited* talks about the 'intruders' who penetrated Oxford in Eights Week – 'a rabble of womankind ... twittering and fluttering'. Even female undergraduates were not really taken seriously.[3]

Rosamond Lehmann in *Dusty Answer*[4] (1927) has a heroine, Judith, who is very bright and goes to Cambridge, but whose mother says to her at one point: 'If you were a little more stupid you might make a success of a London season even at this late date. You've got the looks. You *are* stupid – stupid enough, I should think, to ruin all your own chances.' And throughout the book Judith is criticised by various young men for, as they cynically put it, wanting to 'become a young woman with *really* intellectual interests'.

Judith is unrepresentative of the woman of the 1920s. She has been coached in music and taught Latin and Greek by her father, a man who, like Nancy Mitford's 'Uncle Matthew', doesn't believe in girls going to school. In 'Literary style in England and America' Waugh pointed out how English boys learnt Latin and Greek while English girls learnt French. As he went on to say, the girls who were praised for their 'idiomatic volubility' wrote, when they grew up, 'as though they were babbling down the telephone – often very prettily, like Miss Nancy Mitford'.[5]

Nancy Mitford, in fact, was described by Brian Howard, who was known to think little of the feminine intellect, as 'a delicious creature, quite pyrotechnical, my dear, and sometimes even profound'.[6] Harold Acton thought that that was quite a compliment from Howard. A compliment maybe; a double-edged one certainly.

If the female authors of the time were aware of the problem, Waugh and his contemporaries treated the intellect of women with great condescension.

[3] And Waugh makes the point in *A Little Learning* that at Oxford 'undergraduettes lived in purdah' and the proctors retained 'their right to expel beyond the university limits, independent women who were thought to be a temptation' (p.168). And while Classical Mods and Greats were 'still pre-eminent in esteem', followed by Modern History, Law and Theology, 'English Literature was for women and foreigners' (p.173).

[4] Waugh did not approve of such novels as *Dusty Answer*. In 'Why Glorify Youth' he wrote: 'The whole Glorious Youth Legend was invented by the elderly and middle-aged ... There was the Beauty of Youth Legend. This assured the success of such works as *Dusty Answer* and *Young Woodley*. Oh, lovely youths and maidens! Oh, bodies of classic grace and splendour! Rapturous calf love! Important doubts and disillusionments! Oh, grand apotheosis of pimply adolescence! The novels in their tens of thousands swirled and eddied like flood water through the circulating libraries ... ' *Essays*, p.126.

[5] Ibid., p.480.

[6] Harold Acton, *Nancy Mitford: a Memoir* (1975), p.23.

Ronald Firbank in *The Flower Beneath The Foot* (1923) has the Countess admiring Shakespeare's 'Julia *sees* Her' and the English Ambassadress says: ' "Friends, Comrades, Countrymen ... I used to know it myself." ' Firbank's women were all ladies who specialised in fashionable small talk; highly mannered, extremely precious, with rarely a brain in sight.

Anthony Powell in *Afternoon Men* (1931) has two women, Susan and Lola (whose appearance is 'oafish'), whose intelligence he comments on indirectly. Lola when she feels 'hopeless' reads Bertrand Russell and tells the hero, Atwater, that when she reads Russell on mental adventure she is 'reinspired'. When asked reinspired to what, she has no answer except 'just reinspired'. When Atwater takes her to his flat he hopes that 'she won't begin on Bertrand Russell again' and when she asks him about his first editions he decides that he cannot 'do all the stuff about the books' that night. Sleeping with him another time, Lola comments as he draws the curtains: 'In modern sculpture I think the influence of Archipenko is paramount.' With this kind of pretentiousness, Powell denigrates his female character. The other girl, Susan Nunnery has a fresh mind which is free from cliché; she seems 'separate' always from the room of people she is in. The difference between Lola and Susan is expressed by their responses to the fact that Atwater works in a museum. Lola says: 'That must be very interesting work, isn't it', while Susan says: 'May I visit you there?' Powell, however, still never tells us that Susan is intelligent. She is different from the other girls in the book in that she doesn't get handed on from man to man; she has 'individual chic', but like the others she still needs a man to fulfil her life, which is why she goes to America with Verelst.

Aldous Huxley in *Crome Yellow* (1921) also has his male characters acting intelligently while the women live out their lives through them. (Peacock did this a century earlier.) Denis Stone is a poet; Henry Wimbush is writing a history of his house; Gombauld is a painter; Ivor Lombard has an extraordinary number of accomplishments; and Mr Scogan is the archetype of the erudite, worldy-wise men who stroll in and out of Huxley's novels. The women are only interested in the men. Anne Wimbush professes some attraction to both Denis and Gombauld. Mary Bracegirdle who has had some training in art is attracted to Gombauld, but is defeated by him when, after trying to have what she thinks is a serious discussion with him about painting, and thinking that he is about to make love to her – 'The moment might have come, but she would not cease to be intellectual, serious' – he smacks her gently on the backside and sends her packing. Mary has large 'blue china eyes whose expression was one of ingenuous and often puzzled earnestness'. Denis Stone asks Jenny Mullion at one point whether she is a '*femme supérieure*' to which she replies 'Certainly not. Has anyone been suggesting that I am?' Mr Scogan has gently, but cynically, flattered Mary Bracegirdle by telling her that she is a '*femme supérieure*' after one of her earnest offerings to the conversation. She is not a superior lady. Jenny Mullion, however, is, but doesn't recognise it in herself. Because of her deafness she misinterprets the remarks of others and takes her revenge by drawing wonderfully talented, but unflattering, caricatures of her fellow guests.

In *The Polyglots* (1925), William Gerhardi has his hero, Alexander, reading
Wilde's *Dorian Gray* to the heroine, Sylvia. Alexander notes that 'while I read
aloud Sylvia "prepared" an expression of wonderment on her face, to show
that she was sensitive to what I read. But she began to fret as I read on,
absorbed, and then nestled to me closely.' Sylvia is only interested in kissing
and cuddling. *Dorian Gray* is too 'highbrow' for her, and she admits to
preferring something more 'fruity'.

Wyndham Lewis in *Tarr* (1919) also had his hero, like Powell's Atwater,
being disgusted with the clichéd mind of the female. In his case it is his
fiancée, Bertha (whom he refers to as a 'dolt'), who has a plaster-cast of
Beethoven in her apartment and a photograph of the Mona Lisa – 'Tarr hated
the Mona Lisa' (p.38). Lewis is an interesting author because he has the
other female character in the novel, Anastasya, recognise the immaturity of
Tarr's attitude towards women. After telling him that he is 'absurd about
women' and that he is like a 'schoolboy', she goes on to say: 'I set out
thinking of you in this way – "Nothing but a female booby will please that
man!" I wanted to please you, but I couldn't do it on those lines. I'm going to
make an effort along my own lines. You are like a youngster who hasn't got
used to the taste of liquor; you don't like it. You haven't grown up yet. I want
to make you drunk and see what happens!' (p.291). Although Tarr eventually
becomes Anastasya's 'slave', rather than she being his, and lives with her, he
still has a woman on the side – a mistress called Rose Fawcett who bears him
three children. Tarr always sees sex as something separate from intelligence.

Michael Arlen's narrator asks when he first meets Iris Storm in *The Green
Hat*: 'Why, was she intelligent too?' Unfortunately no more than the heroines
of the other authors mentioned; Iris is a 'house of men' and her sexuality is
her strength. Her intelligence was 'that random, uninformed but severely
discriminating taste which maddens you ... she put up a gallant, insincere
defence for the Imagistes but it turned out that she had never read any, and
wasn't at all sure what they were ... ' (pp.23-4). But perhaps Arlen's Iris
Storm hits the nerve when she pours scorn on the satirist. She says: 'Has ever
any even fairly human-looking person ever been a "satirist"? But I suppose if
they weren't so plain they wouldn't have so much time to be obscene on paper'
(p.25). Arlen has his narrator reply: 'You don't allow to all men one common
failing, which shows particularly when the men are satirical writers: they
must always write about women rather in the spirit of unclean-minded
undergraduates who are very upset at not having physically enjoyed their first
woman as much as was to be expected. It is from such things that satirical
genius is made' (p.25).

It sounds to be a description that might well suit Evelyn Waugh, but there
is, however, still a difference between Waugh and his contemporaries.
Powell, Huxley and Arlen create women characters in their novels who,
quite often, read widely ... and yet they appear to take pleasure in showing up
the superficiality of their heroines' knowledge. Waugh does not need his
heroines to be widely read to disparage them. The heroines of Waugh's novels
are, on the whole, well-off and independent in their social activities, but their
personal resources are 'feminine' ones, and so their success in life depends on

how well they attract and manipulate the affections of their men.

Though often sophisticated and aware, Waugh's women are not, in the feminist sense, emancipated. Margot Beste-Chetwynde may sit 'upright at the table ... the very embodiment of the Feminist movement', but she cannot function in her social world without a suitable husband. Waugh's women, then, define themselves too much in the traditional terms of what is expected of them as women. The only time they step outside the traditional role is to exercise their new sexual freedom. Waugh gives his heroines stereotyped roles to play; and those roles may be divided into three categories, some of which overlap with each other: heroines who use sex-appeal for security, heroines whose intelligence is subordinated in favour of the stereotyped role, and the few heroines who enjoy sex and are 'moderns'.

Heroines who use sex-appeal for security

Nina Blount

Nina Blount wants marriage, while Adam Fenwick-Symes wants, and needs, a successful career. When we first meet Adam, his book, which was to be published and the proceeds used to marry Nina, has been confiscated and burnt by Customs. During his getting of, and throwing away of, his financial opportunities for marriage, he at one point becomes Mr Chatterbox, the society gossip-writer. Stephen A. Jervis has called Adam 'an ordinary fellow, thoroughly unspectacular',[7] but Adam has more imagination and spark than most critics give him credit for. He invents people and occasions to fill up his column, making it highly original.

Unfortunately for him, Adam's creative ability culminates in his invention of the 'green bowler': unfortunately, because after being told by Lord Monomark that green bowlers were not to be mentioned again, Adam leaves Nina and Ginger to write his column while he visits Colonel Blount. The result of this is that Nina mentions a green bowler, and Adam loses his job. Waugh does not make Nina unintelligent, she manages to write the column, but the news that she puts in about Edward Throbbing's engagement is true and the imaginary piece about the green bowler is borrowed from Adam. Her powers of invention are limited, compared with those of Adam, and Waugh makes her incompetent at the job.

Throughout *Vile Bodies* there are allusions that suggest that Adam, the son of a Professor, is quite clever. When his book is confiscated at Customs he is also carrying books on architecture, history, economics, a dictionary and a copy of Dante's *Purgatorio*. Literary allusions also feature in Adam's thoughts. At Berkhamsted a man gets into the train and spends his time doing sums in a notebook which never seem to come right; and Adam thinks of Lear: 'Has he given all to his daughters?' At lunch with Nina's father he reads *Punch*. Ginger, having found out that Adam writes things in the papers says,

---

[7] Stephen A. Jervis, 'Evelyn Waugh, *Vile Bodies* and the Younger Generation', *South Atlantic Quarterly* LXVI (Summer, 1967), p.446.

'You must be frightfully brainy.'

Nina throughout the book either has 'a pain' or is bored. A facet of her personality is that she expects her man to keep her entertained. She says to Adam, 'Do be amusing, Adam, I can't bear you when you're not amusing'; so Adam tells her stories about people being whipped (p.90). Nina's one attempt at a literary allusion is inept. She corrects Ginger about 'This sceptr'd isle ... ', saying that it doesn't come out of a poetry book, that it is a play[8] because she's acted in it. Even her father, Colonel Blount, when he thinks Adam is asking him about Nina being in his film, says, 'To tell you the truth, I very much doubt whether she has any real talent' (p.149).

Nina's main concern throughout the book is marriage – sex actually gives her 'a pain' although she does admit that perhaps making love is 'a thing one could grow fond of after a time, like smoking a pipe' (p.91). Although she is sympathetic enough to sleep with Adam before marriage, knowing that her father has signed Adam's cheque as 'Charlie Chaplin', she still believes that they will marry in the future. Nina's role in life is to exchange sex for the financial comforts of marriage, while Adam's is to make enough money, by writing or other means, to keep her. Once he fails, the wealthy Ginger moves in, for, as Ginger says, 'Nina's a girl who likes nice clothes and things, you know, comfort and all that' (p.195).

Nina gets engaged to Ginger when, once again, Adam says he hasn't any money after all and can't marry her. When Agatha Runcible mentions the engagement, Nina's response is: 'Yes, it's very lucky. My papa has just put all his money into a cinema film and lost it' (p.188). While engaged, she agrees to dine, and to sleep, with Adam, but says: 'If only you were as rich as Ginger, Adam, or only half as rich. Or if only you had any money at all' (p.191). After this particular night with Adam, Nina, the next morning, begins to wonder whether she can 'bear Ginger', but on hearing that Adam has sold her to his rival she marries Ginger immediately, and will not break her honeymoon with him as Adam suggests but tells Adam that she hopes they can fix something up over Christmas.

Nina puts up with sex with Ginger for the sake of security but admits to Adam that the 'honeymoon was hell' (p.206). Sex is obviously more enjoyable with Adam, and this is where Nina's role overlaps with that of the 'heroines who enjoy sex', for she 'happily' commits adultery with Adam even though she accepts that she will return to Ginger because Adam is still unlikely to get any money.

Brenda Last

The reason for Brenda's desertion is boredom. As Mrs Beaver says early on in *A Handful of Dust*, 'Wasted on Tony Last, he's a prig. I should say it was time she began to be bored' (p.9).

Brenda's relationship with Tony was fine when she first married him because he had plenty of money and they used to go to plenty of parties. After

---

[8] William Shakespeare, *Richard II*, Act 2, Sc.1.

his father died, Tony became responsible for Hetton Abbey, a house that eats up all their money. Brenda is bored with not being able to spend as she used to, and she is bored with her husband because he no longer thinks of anything except Hetton. Their monotonous lives are only relieved by trips to the local cinema and Woolworths, and by experimenting with various diets. Brenda is also sexually bored with Tony.

Brenda reads the romantic serial aloud to Tony, but he doesn't listen to it. When Beaver visits Hetton, he and Tony take out the 'more remarkable folios' in the Hetton library and examine them; and after dinner Tony reads the papers while Brenda and Beaver play games – an omen for the future. After Beaver has left, Tony says of him: 'I must say he took a very intelligent interest when we went round the house.'

If Brenda ever goes to London it is to shop, have her hair cut or go to her bone-setter, a recreation she particularly enjoys; and when her sister, Marjorie, tells her about the new treatment that Mr Crutwell is giving her, Brenda is envious. The sexual implication here is obvious, and when Brenda later lies on the osteopath's table having her vertebrae snapped and feeling his 'strong fingers', she thinks about Beaver.[9]

Part of Brenda's attraction to Beaver, a '*dreary*' young man, is that he needs to be taught 'a whole lot of things'; and again, the implication is a sexual one. She can't teach the old dog, Tony, new sexual tricks, but she can teach the young one. The affair fascinates the 'gang of gossips' for this particular reason. Beaver has always been considered a joke; even his mother says that he's always had a 'Lack of Something' and supposes that an 'experienced woman like Brenda' will be able to help him. If Brenda had run off with Robin Beardsley or Jock Grant-Menzies whom 'nearly everyone had had a crack at one time or another', it would have been a commonplace affair. Brenda could not have taught Robin Beardsley or Jock Grant-Menzies anything; but by teaching Beaver she makes him suddenly interesting to the society crowd. No one likes Beaver except Brenda and even she accepts that it's 'very odd' that she should.

Brenda uses her sex-appeal to get Tony to agree to her taking a flat in town. She wears 'pyjamas at dinner' and afterwards snuggles up 'close to Tony on the sofa'. Tony is not stupid. He recognises her seduction techniques and says 'I suppose all this means that you're going to start again about your flat?' (p.55) Brenda gets her way, and for a while Tony supports both her and Beaver, for Brenda, being rich compared with Beaver, is always 'socking' him a meal or a movie. Like Nina Blount, Brenda steps outside her 'sex-appeal for security' role to enjoy herself with another man, but as soon as her financial support is threatened, she panics. She expects Tony to sell Hetton to keep her in the style she is accustomed to; and she needs him to do so, so that in turn she can support the penniless Beaver. As soon as Tony refuses to divorce her, or pay her any alimony, all is lost. Beaver leaves her. After Tony makes his decision to go abroad, he visits the Greville Club, which is a club of

[9] There is an interesting link here with Beverley Nichols' *Crazy Pavements* (1925), p.91., where Lady Julia Cressey gives up osteopathy after one treatment as it is the 'old maid's romance' and is 'rather too tame'.

'intellectual flavour, composed of dons, a few writers and the officials of museums and learned societies', and it is here that he meets Dr Messinger and arranges to join his expedition. Finally, Tony ends up by reading Dickens to Mr Todd. This is an ironic twist, because Tony used to read aloud to Brenda (as Alexander did to Sylvia in Gerhardi's *The Polyglots*) during the first year of their marriage until she told him that 'it was torture to her'.

In *A Handful of Dust* none of the men are amazingly bright, but they are more intelligent than Brenda. Tony has been to private school and university, runs his estate and has thought of standing for Parliament. (One of Brenda's explanations to Tony of the sense of her non-existent economics course is that she might be able to help him with the financial side of the estate in the future, but of course she doesn't attend university.) Jock Grant-Menzies is a Member of Parliament, though his joke politics only extend to the matters of pigs and pork pies. John Beaver is wet but has been to Oxford and worked in an advertising agency until the slump. He also tells jokes with 'good effect'. Brenda, without Beaver, and financially embarrassed at the end of the novel, has no skills which would enable her to get a job. She cannot survive without a man. Her adventure with Beaver has cost her dearly, and her only answer is to marry the rich Jock Grant-Menzies. Brenda Last, in the end, like Nina Blount, uses her charms to secure her future.

Kätchen

Kätchen is another heroine who uses her sex-appeal for security. After her pseudo-husband has disappeared, she is left without any money and turns to William. She charms him constantly into giving her money so that she can buy new clothes, lingerie and make-up. A kind of modern Mata Hari, she is also able to use her charms (and William's money) to secure information about what is going on in Jacksonville. But Kätchen is not a very clever spy because, while talking to most of her informers, she forgets that she is there to get information; she spends so much time talking about the things that she is buying that she doesn't talk about politics; except to the Austrian, whose sister is governess to the President's children, who tells her that the President has been locked up for four days. Even after getting that information Kätchen is more concerned with going out, as it is a nice day, than with William sending her news to *The Beast*.

Kätchen is not intelligent enough to interpret the knowledge she obtains; and her secretarial acumen only extends to being ready with William's cheque book when he agrees to pay her two hundred pounds to be his informant. Kätchen's mind is only razor-sharp when it comes to money. Cast opposite Kätchen, we have William, another product of a private school. His command of French is only just adequate; his general knowledge is poor as he rarely reads the newspapers, and consequently he has no idea of who is fighting whom in Ishmaelia. Also, his job as the writer of 'Lush Places' has been passed on to him by the widow of he man who held it before him, the Rector at Boot Magna. However, William does write his column well; he knows his poets; and he is not stupid – unlike the other journalists he will not go to Laku, a place that doesn't exist. Compared with Kätchen, his intelligence is well above the ordinary. Kätchen's reason for sleeping with William is that she is afraid. As she says, 'But now I am thinking, what is to become of me? A few weeks and you will go away. I have waited so long for my husband; perhaps he will not come' (*Scoop*, p.142). In case her husband does not return she secures a passage to England, for herself, by giving herself to William.

Aimée Thanatogenos

The intellectual difference between Dennis Barlow and Aimée Thanatogenos is easily apparent. Dennis in fact explains the relationship to Mr Schultz as a Jamesian one – 'American innocence and European experience'. (Waugh said that the tale should not be read as a satire on morticians but as a study of the Anglo-American cultural impasse with the mortuary as a jolly setting.)[10]

Dennis, a poet with a 'high reputation', who represents the jaded, degenerate European, has come to write the life of Shelley for Megalopolitan Studios but hasn't had his contract renewed, and spends his night shift at the pets' cemetery reading poems from the *Oxford Book of English Verse* to which he has become an addict. He gets a reliable fix from 'certain trite passages of poetry which from a diverse multitude of associations never failed to yield the sensations he craved; he never experimented; these were the branded drug, the sure specific, big magic. He opened the anthology as a woman opens her familiar pack of cigarettes' (p.17).

Against Dennis is placed Aimée, a 'decadent' whose lips are not clogged with make-up but seem 'to promise instead an unmeasured range of sensual converse'.[11] Aimées lips never fulfil their promise. Aimée is only interested in marriage, and the first clue to this is when we learn that 'Mr Joyboy was unmarried and every girl in Whispering Glades gloated on him' (p.56).

The intellectual differences between Aimée and Dennis are summed up when they meet on the Lake Island of Innisfree. Dennis tells Aimée that he is only there to write a poem; and she exclaims '*A poem?*' Poetry to Aimée means such persons as Sophie Dalmeyer Krump, whom she couldn't work on because she was only a novice cosmetician but whom she studied and who had, she learned, 'Soul'. Dennis teases her about having a 'poetic occupation', but she doesn't see the joke and proceeds to tell him the 'poetic' story of her life. She tells him that she's always been artistic and how, apart from taking art at college, she took Psychology and Chinese for 'Cultural Background'. When Dennis first quotes Keats at her she doesn't recognise the ode, but thinks it beautiful, and that encourages Dennis to lie. To be fair he never says he wrote it; in answer to her first 'Did you write that?' he replies 'You like

---

[10] *Letters*, p.248.

[11] In the second draft of the manuscript Waugh described Aimée's lips as giving promise of 'exquisite tactile communication'. See Robert Murray Davis, *Evelyn Waugh, Writer* (1981), p.202. It is interesting that Waugh should change to the word 'converse' which in modern English means to engage in conversation, or more interestingly, to commune spiritually with someone; while in obsolete terms it means to have sexual intercourse. Aimée certainly engages in conversation, and later she communes with higher spirits, but she never has sexual intercourse.

it?'; and when she asks 'Did you write it after you came here first?' he says 'It was written long before' – but the seed of plagiary has been sown, and Dennis starts to use the English poets to further his courtship of Aimée.

As it turns out the English poets are not all that helpful in a Californian courtship – 'nearly all were too casual, too despondent, too ceremonious, or too exacting; they scolded, they pleaded, they extolled' (p.84). The only poem that hits the mark is a song within Tennyson's *The Princess*;[12] a song that draws on Eastern sources, on the standard images of Persian love poetry:

> Now sleeps the crimson petal, now the white;
> Nor waves the cypress in the palace walk;
> Nor winks the gold fin in the porphyry font;
> The fire-fly wakens; waken thou with me. (first stanza of lines 161-74)

Dennis knows few poems so 'high and rich and voluptuous' as this, but whereas the films and the crooners can fulfil Aimée's ideas of love, the English poets cannot.

While Dennis searches for poetry to help his conquest, Aimée writes to the Guru Brahmin with her hopes and fears. Aimée is not concerned with the workings of her mind but with the reaction of her body. She knows that Joyboy loves her 'honourably', but she questions the fact that she does not have the same response when she is with him '*as other girls say they have when they are with their boys and what one sees in the movies*' (p.81). She thinks she has those feelings about Dennis, but she does not like him being unethical because she is ethical and has no intention of sleeping with him before marriage. As she says in a later letter to the Guru – '*often he wants unethical things and is so cynical when I say no we must wait*' (p.101).

When Dennis's true nature is revealed, Aimée has no difficulty in choosing where her future security lies. 'She held in her person a valuable concession to bestow; she had been scrupulous in choosing justly between rival claimants. There was no room now for further hesitation' (p.105-6). She gets engaged to Joyboy.

Facing Dennis with the fact that she is upset to think that she learnt poems by heart that were written by people hundreds of years ago, and that he meant her to think they were his, Dennis enlightens her:

> 'There, Aimée, you misjudge me. It is I who should be disillusioned when I think that I have been squandering my affections on a girl ignorant of the commonest treasures of literature. But I realise that you have different educational standards from those that I am used to. No doubt you know more than I about psychology and Chinese. But in the dying world I come from quotation is a national vice.'

Paul Doyle has made the point that the satire on Aimée's skimpy education is reduced by the fact that the love poem Dennis sends her beginning 'God set her brave eyes wide apart' is by a minor English poet, Richard Middleton,

---

[12] The song is called 'Summer Night'.

and there is no reason why she should know it. His view however is questionable, as Middleton was respected in his day and had had a play *The District Visitor* performed in America in 1921.[13]

The difference between Dennis and his 'vestal virgin' of Whispering Glades is summed up when Dennis says, reminding Aimée of the vow that she took at the Lover's Seat: ' "I will luve –" ' You can't fail to understand those words, surely? It's just the way the crooners pronounced them' (p.110). At this, 'intellectual processes' start to work in Aimée's 'exquisite dim head'. And Aimée's dilemma is complete when Dennis tells her that, having taken the most sacred oath that there has ever been in the religion of Whispering Glades, 'if it isn't sacred to kiss me through the heart of the Burns or Bruce,[14] it isn't sacred to go to bed with old Joyboy' (p.111). The impasse is complete. The puritanical Aimée is lost.

Julia Flyte

Julia Flyte, like the previous heroines, uses her sexual attraction in the first part of *Brideshead Revisited*, to obtain a husband. The débutante of the year, she is apparently 'witty as well as ornamental' but is little interested in anything but marriage, which she sees as the beginning of life: 'To be married, soon and splendidly was the aim of all her friends. If she looked further than the wedding, it was to see marriage as the beginning of individual existence; the skirmish where one gained one's spurs, from which one set out on the true quest of life' (p.174).

Because of the scandal that surrounded her father, and her religion, there are difficulties for Julia in finding the right man. Her Protestant friends can marry elder sons who would not consider marrying her; and of the rich Catholic families there are no heirs available of marriageable age when she is on the market. There are other men around, but 'the shame' for Julia is that she has to 'seek them'. During these days she has no eyes for Charles Ryder, who is utterly unsuitable. She builds in her imagination the kind of husband she wants; someone like a wealthy Catholic widower, an English diplomat who would like to bring some new life into his Embassy in Paris; someone who shared her 'mild agnosticism' but was prepared to bring his children up as Catholics, and to want only a small family, not the yearly Catholic pregnancy; and of course, to be financially well-off. Charles Ryder does not fit the picture (for when Julia first met him she was in search of her future husband) – 'I was not her man. She told me as much, without a word, when she took the cigarette from my lips' (p.176).

By the time Julia meets her imaginary 'Eustace', a 'wistful Major in the Life Guards' who matches her criteria, it is already too late, for she has fallen in love with Rex Mottram and is determined to have him. Rex too is looking for a 'Eustace', and Julia being a 'top débutante' with a dowry is the catch he is after. Julia needs to be married, and so will offer Rex her body and her

---

[13] Paul Doyle, *Evelyn Waugh Newsletter*, vol.15, no.3 (Winter, 1981), p.7. Also, see below, Appendix Two.

[14] Dennis is being ironic here. Also, see Appendix Two.

social assets, while Rex in turn will offer her his social position which has a certain amount of mystery and spice that her friends will envy. The fact that he is Brenda Champion's lover also sharpens Julia's appetite for him.

Rex Mottram is a gambler and a Member of Parliament, plays golf with the Prince of Wales and is on 'easy terms', it would seem, with everyone. He didn't go to University and has the opinion that it means 'you start life three years behind the other fellow'. Rex is about to convert to Catholicism, though Father Mowbray doesn't think that he has the slightest 'intellectual curiosity'; and Cordelia hoodwinks him with bizarre tales of Catholicism which he believes.

Both Rex and Charles are ambitious. Charles gave up his degree at Oxford after Sebastian was sent down and over the years has become a successful architectural painter, spurred on by the even more ambitious Celia. *Ryder's Country Seats, Ryder's English Homes, Ryder's Village and Provincial Architecture*, and finally, *Ryder's Latin America* make him wealthy, but Charles, deep down, still has the urge to recover the inspiration that he had known at Brideshead, where it had been an 'aesthetic education' for him to dwell.

When Charles meets Julia again, she is unhappily married to Rex, has lost her baby, and has also had an affair with someone else. Her 'good upbringing' kept her faithful for a long time. Julia has only filled her empty life by having an affair, whereas Charles, after Celia is unfaithful to him, pours himself into his work. When they meet, Charles is no longer the 'pretty boy' who was Sebastian's friend; now he is 'lean and grim' – qualities which appeal to Julia, a sad, unfulfilled lady. Julia steps outside her 'sex for security' role, but because of her guilt she can never abandon herself like Margot Beste-Chetwynde or Virginia Troy. 'Sin' is always in the way.

Heroines whose intelligence is subordinated
in favour of the stereotyped role

Angela Lyne

Angela Lyne is the wife of Cedric Lyne, a 'dilettante architect', and since her affair with Basil Seal she is described as having been for seven years on a 'desert island'. Fashion has become a 'hobby and distraction' for Angela, just as her husband, Cedric, has his grottoes to keep him occupied. Waugh creates in Angela a lady who has a mind but hardly ever uses it. We are told throughout *Put Out More Flags* that she has a 'swift and orderly mind', that she is capable of giving 'precise, prudent directions' to her brokers for 'the disposition of her fortune' and, more important, that she 'talks like a man' – a phrase that Waugh uses more than once:

> At dinner she drank Vichy water and talked like a man. (p.120)

> She danced and drank her Vichy water and talked sharply and well like a very clever man. (p.120)

> Mrs Lyne whose conversation was that of a highly intelligent man. (p.159)

Her own coterie formed round her and she talked like a highly intelligent man. (p.162)

It would be interesting to know how Waugh thought a 'highly intelligent man' talked; and whether Olivia Plunket Greene's comment about Paul Robeson being a 'highly intelligent man', as mentioned in Chapter One, had anything to do with this barbed description; but obviously, in Waugh's mind, they talk more intelligently than a highly intelligent woman. He never tells us what Angela says, for Angela is a mask, who had accepted her husband as a young officer with artistic leanings 'as being like herself a stranger in these parts'.

Angela's intelligence is repressed because of her stereotyped dependence on a man, Basil Seal. Her drinking gets out of hand until Basil, hearing about her plight outside the cinema, comes in like a knight on a charger to save her. In the scene where Angela and he decide what to do about her drinking habits she tells him that she was in love with him. When Basil queries the 'was' – she admits that she still is. In the end Angela is not much better than Basil's silly girls'. They, like Susie, might not 'understand a word of any language', whereas Angela talks like an 'intelligent man', but like Angela they are soppy about Basil. Basil is Angela's emotional weakness, while Angela is Basil's strength.

Helena

'Helena, red-haired, youngest daughter of Coel, Paramount Chief of the Trinovantes, gazed into the rain while her tutor read the *Iliad* of Homer in a Latin paraphrase' – and so we are introduced to Helena.

Helena is a very intelligent girl, but like Angela Lyne her intelligence is repressed by the roles she has to play. Helena, who is determined when she has been educated to go and find Troy, doesn't fulfil her quest until she is an old lady. First she is sidetracked by falling in love with Constantius, the man who fulfills her sexual riding fantasies. When Constantius asks her what else she does apart from hanging around the stables, she says she is still being educated, for 'we Britons think a lot of education'. Her father, having been asked for her hand in marriage, tells her that he never expected such a thing, because she is not like her sisters – 'fine, plump girls, who know all about cooking and sewing'. Helena not only looks, and rides, like a boy, but her tutor Marcias has told her father that she has 'a masculine mind'.

Once married to Constantius, Helena is told by the Governor's wife that she must study to make herself a fit wife for him, and when she tells the lady that she spent her days in Britain reading poetry, being educated and hunting, she is informed that she 'won't be able to do that now'. Gradually her admiration for Constantius cools; something dies in her when she learns of his betrayals, his lies and his butchery, which he carries out for his own personal glory. The death of the great philosopher Longinus also strikes 'another wound in Helena's heart' – with this it seems somehow that 'her education had come to its end'. Constantius is only interested in his career, and when they move to Dalmatia to further it Helena travels forward 'without hope'. She is right to, for it is here that her husband takes a mistress, a woman much older than herself. Her only surprise is the woman's age. She had expected that when she was old her husband would want someone younger – 'Men always do. Papa did.' Helena is intelligent enough to know that her life is not a full one, but at this point she does nothing for herself; she simply lives through her son Constantine and his education. Helena's questioning intelligence only comes back into play when Constantius joins the cult of Mithras. Constantius calls her questioning 'childish', but she is only trying to get at the truth.

Apart from taking a mistress, who is later murdered, Constantius, again for the sake of his career, divorces Helena and remarries. Helena lives alone for the next thirteen years, and her intelligence, repressed because of her unsatisfactory marriage, in which her only role was to fulfil Constantius' demands sexually, and as a 'career wife', stays dormant. She makes her new home a place that will be 'very nice' for her son and his wife to come home to; for now Constantine is the 'focus of all her plans'. She plants olive trees, but her planting doesn't bear fruit, for Constantine comes to take her and his wife away; now to follow *his* career. When Constantine talks to her about the Christians and mentions their books, she exclaims 'Oh books', for she has lost interest in such matters; even going as far to suggest to Minervina, Constantine's divorced wife (her son has followed in his father's footsteps), that she should take an interest in her garden to help fulfil her life, as Helena has done; the same Helena who once thought that that wasn't enough, when Calpurnia did so.

Helena has a 'salon', but she treats Lactantius, her grandson's tutor, as a 'pet'. It is not until her old tutor, Marcias, arrives that she starts to think again; to feel something 'unsuitable to the occasion take shape deep within herself and irresistibly rise; something native to her, inalienable, long overlaid, foreign to her position, to marriage and motherhood ... foreign to the schooling of thirty years, to the puzzled, matronly heads in the stuffy, steamy hall' – the curious, questing, young red-head Helena is born again. Her 'clear, schoolroom tone' rings out; Helena wants her questions answered. She tells Lactantius when they talk about religion that she has the feeling that 'somehow the answer was there all the time if we had only taken a little more trouble to find it'. She considers herself too old for change, too old to do anything about anything; but she is not, for her education is not finished until she finds the cross.

Until she is elderly, Helena represses her intelligence to the stereotyped roles of wife, mother, deserted wife and Empress. Her role is subservient. First she does as she is told by her husband, and then by her son. Not until Constantine gives her the 'old Rome' does she make her move to find the True Cross, and so to make Rome a holy city. Pope Sylvester regards her 'as though she were a child, an impetuous young princess who went well to hounds' – and so she is; for in old age Helena recovers that curiosity of spirit that leads her to discover her one true love.

Lucy Simmonds

Lucy Simmonds, again, is a very intelligent lady, but in her case both her intelligence and her sexuality are repressed because of her maternal instincts. As Roger Simmonds says to John Plant, his play *Internal Combustion* may be put on if Lucy finds the money, but she is not too keen as 'she's having a baby, and that seems to keep her interested at the moment'.

John Plant and Roger Simmonds were both at Oxford together and edited an undergraduate magazine; both are writers. Plant writes detective fiction, and Simmonds has published some 'genuinely funny novels on the strength of which he filled a succession of jobs with newspapers and film companies'. Lucy, the young, grave, rather Jamesian heroine has a straightforward intelligence. She thinks that her husband Roger is a 'great writer', and Plant finds this disconcerting as he and his friends decry their work, an attitude which Lucy, being 'a serious girl', finds quite unintelligible. The more flippant they are about their work, the less she thinks of it, and them. She expects the best from Roger, which is why he dresses in artistic clothes and talks intellectually; and Roger has not just married Lucy for her money, because he has some of his own. In fact 'money alone would not have been worth the pains he had taken for her; the artistic clothes and the intellectual talk were measures of the respect in which he held Lucy.' So although Basil Seal feels that poor Roger 'has had to become a highbrow again', Roger doesn't object; and even Basil realises that Lucy is a 'critical' girl.

Lucy is interested in politics, and Roger becomes so as well. Plant tries to suggest that it is a novel thing for Roger, to which Lucy replies that her husband probably doesn't talk about politics to people unless he knows that they have a genuine interest. Plant rudely suggests that she should 'keep him to that' and is surprised when his bad manners cause no reaction. Roger's friends are like his family to her – she doesn't expect to reform their manners or their attitudes. Lucy still calls Plant by his Christian name, whereas a more 'commonplace girl' might have rebuked him with a 'Mr Plant'. Lucy in Plant's eyes is 'faultless', a Madonna-like character.

Lucy is not silly or girlish, and she makes no pretences. When John Plant says that his father's painting is very 'fashionable', she is astonished and tells him that that wasn't what had been in her mind at all. She goes on to explain about the two soldiers who had been seen in front of a window in Duke Street reconstructing one of his battle pictures – 'I think that's worth a dozen columns of praise in the weekly papers.' She also admits that she has never read any Kipling. Lucy doesn't talk like a man, but she writes like one. When she sends Plant a formal acceptance to his invitation he studies her writing – 'She wrote like a man'. Lucy signs herself 'Yours sincerely' not 'Yours ever' or 'Yours with a non-committal squiggle'. Again she is not an ordinary girl.

Plant wants to be recognised for himself not, like Basil, as one of Roger's friends. This acceptance of him by Lucy becomes apparent when she tells him that Roger is writing a detective story. Lucy who had said to Julia that Plant wrote '*thrillers*' in a disparaging tone of voice has now, like Julia, become a fan – 'You were perfectly right. They *are* works of art.' Lucy's reason, however, for taking Plant up is that she is lonely, and cut off from her husband by her pregnancy. Waugh writes:

> He did not, as some husbands do, resent his wife's pregnancy. It was as though he had bought a hunter at the end of the season and turned him out; discerning friends, he knew, would appreciate the fine lines under the rough coat; but he would sooner have shown something glossy in the stable. He had summer business to do moreover; the horse must wait till the late autumn. That, at least, was one way in which he saw the situation but the analogy was incomplete. It was rather *he* that had been acquired and put out to grass, and he was conscious of that aspect, too. Roger was hobbled and prevented from taking the full stride required of him, by the habit, long settled, of regarding sex relationships in terms of ownership and use. Confronted with the new fact of pregnancy, of joint ownership, his terms failed him. As a result he was restless and no longer master of the situation; the practical business of getting through the day was becoming onerous, so that my adhesion was agreeable to him. Grossly, it confirmed his opinion of Lucy's value and at the same time took her off his hands. (p.173)

Roger Simmonds leaves John Plant to look after his wife while he gets on with his detective story and his Spanish aid committee meetings, rather as Waugh left Laura's family to look after her while he got on with his writing.[15]

In *Work Suspended* Lucy's sexuality and intelligence are repressed to the stereotyped role of motherhood. As the pregnancy progresses Lucy becomes 'concerned only with the single, physical fact of her own exhaustion', not willing to join in Roger's discussions of the snobbery among nurses and how it is 'like something out of Thackeray'. Lucy spends hours at the zoo with Plant, wanting to watch nothing but Humboldt's Gibbon which draws her, hypnotically, to its cage. The baby whom, as it drained her of her physical energy and her mental resources, she thought she would hate, becomes after the birth, 'such a *person*', and she loves him. While the men flounder, Lucy basks in the contentment of motherhood.

The few heroines who enjoy sex and are 'moderns'

Margot Beste-Chetwynde

Paul Pennyfeather is first a scholar, and then a schoolmaster; then he works briefly for Margot Beste-Chetwynde (not understanding the nature of her business) and finds himself put in prison, where he can meditate on life and read books. Finally he returns to Oxford to continue his theological career.

Paul Pennyfeather only ever appears as a 'shadow' of what he really is. Waugh wrote the following of Paul when he was dining with Arthur Potts in *Decline and Fall*:

> For an evening at least the shadow that has flitted about this narrative under

[15] Mark Amory says that Waugh was 'consistently absent at the birth of his children'. *Letters*, p.331, n.9. Also, see below, Appendix Three.

the name of Paul Pennyfeather materialised into the solid figure of an intelligent, well-educated, well-conducted young man, a man who could be trusted to use his vote at a general election with discretion and proper detachment, whose opinion on a ballet or a critical essay was rather better than most people's, who could order a dinner without embarrassment and in a creditable French accent, who could be trusted to see to luggage at foreign railway-stations and might be expected to acquit himself with decision and decorum in all the emergencies of civilized life. This was the Paul Pennyfeather who had been developing in the placid years which preceded this story. In fact, the whole of this book is really an account of the mysterious disappearance of Paul Pennyfeather, so that readers must not complain if the shadow which took his name does not amply fill the important part of hero for which he was originally cast. (p.122)

Against Paul, the scholar, Waugh places the character of Margot Beste-Chetwynde, a procuress, whose main interests in life are her lovers and her business, the shady Latin-American Entertainment Company. After Paul has first met Margot at the School Sports Day, he asks Grimes what he believes the relationship to be between her and the negro, Chokey. Grimes's reply is that he doesn't think that 'she trots with him just for the uplift of his conversation'; in fact, Grimes believes that it is just a 'simple case of good old sex' (p.85). When Margot invites Paul to King's Thursday, she informs him, through her son, Peter, that she has had a row with Chokey. It is quite obvious that Paul is to be Chokey's replacement. At King's Thursday, Margot offers to find Paul a job in her business. Paul's reaction, on being told that it is mostly to do with South America, is to suggest, quite sensibly, that he ought to know Spanish, a reaction that causes Margot to laugh and tell him that he is 'being difficult'. At dinner, that same evening, Waugh, with great irony, sums up Margot's non-intellectual role – for we learn that Margot 'talked about matters of daily interest' – such matters as her jewels being reset, the wiring of her London house, the cook going off his head and Bobby Pastmaster trying to borrow money from her yet again. When Paul informs her that he would like to marry her, he has to prove himself; not by enlightening her about any aspects of his character, or his business acumen, but by his sexual prowess. Once he has behaved satisfactorily in bed, Margot is willing to announce their engagement.

Before the wedding Paul receives numerous small gifts from Margot – a 'platinum cigarette case'; a 'dressing-gown'; a 'tie-pin or a pair of links'. The money he spends on himself goes on some personal necessities and 'a set of Proust'. Meanwhile at Margot's villa in Corfu the 'great bed, carved with pineapples, that had once belonged to Napoleon III' is being prepared for her with 'fragrant linen and pillows of unexampled softness'.

When Paul is in Egdon Prison the sexual/intellectual dimensions of his relationship with Margot become even more apparent. Margot, using her influence with Sir Humphrey, manages to get small delicacies and books into the prison for him. The Chaplain even gives him the 'new Virginia Woolf' which has only been out for two days. When Margot finally visits Paul she hardly knows what to talk to him about, but on being asked how Alastair is responds with the information that he's 'rather sweet' and 'always at King's Thursday now. I like him.' Apart from her preoccupation with the fact that the old guard are beginning to cut her, she has little to say to Paul, and the gulf between them is clearly shown in the line: 'They talked about some parties Margot had been to and the books Paul was reading' (p.195).

As some of the other heroines break out of their 'sex for security' roles to enjoy sex, Margot does the opposite, and breaks out of her 'sex for enjoyment' role to obtain security. Having been cut by Lady Circumference she decides to marry Sir Humphrey Maltravers in order to secure her social status. She then uses him to help get Paul out of prison. Finally Paul returns to Oxford and is visited by Peter Pastmaster who reports that though married to Maltravers, now Viscount Metroland, Margot is perfectly happy because 'she's got Alastair all the time'. Now secure, Margot has reverted to her 'sex for enjoyment' role. Against this information we learn that Paul is shortly to be ordained. The scholar and the siren are continuing to play their parts.

Prudence Courteney

Prudence's sexual role is extremely simple – her desire to experiment with sex is activated by her sense of boredom with everything else around her. The time she spends with William is spent in trying to amuse him – 'Oh dear, men are so hard to keep amused' – and she uses various styles of voices and kisses to try to keep him occupied. William, for his part, tells Prudence stories – 'I will say one thing for you,' said Prudence. 'You do know a lovely lot of stories. I dare say that's why I like you.' When Basil arrives, William is dropped like a hot brick. Prudence actually persuades him into exercising the ponies while she takes some exercise with Basil with whom her erotic imaginings have finally been fulfilled. She is amazed that she wanted to be in love such a lot that she had 'even practised on William'.

Prudence's role is simply a sexual one against the more intelligent roles of the men. Waugh gives her something to write, but it is a 'Panorama of Life' – written in 'sprawling, schoolroom characters', an adolescent's erotic imaginings, of which the last chapter is one that even Prudence's fertile imagination would have found hard to conceive. Against this, even William Bland, as uninteresting as his name suggests, has some more intelligent role to play in life. Apart from throwing poker dice and serving cocktails, he reads detective stories (always a good thing in Waugh's mind) and plays his part at the Legation when needed – looking after Dame Mildred Porch and Miss Sarah Tin, whom he finally comes to admire – and standing in for Sir Samson at the Coronation, only to return to the Legation with the news of Achon's death. William accepts Prudence's infidelity with Basil because he is actually quite unmoved by it. Prudence's comment that William had had her to himself for six months and wasn't he 'just bored blue with it' gets the response: 'Well I dare say he'll be bored soon.'

Basil, meanwhile, is the entrepreneur, and superior to William and the other Europeans in the community because he is dissatisfied with their dull and trivial lives. Basil, who had been adopted as a candidate in the West Country and had been expected to get in at the next election, but had been stood down because of his wayward behaviour at, and after, the Conservative ball, is obviously intelligent. He has travelled 'all over Europe', speaks 'excellent French' and five other languages, and enjoyed a 'reputation of peculiar brilliance' at Oxford. To his female admirers he is a '*bore*' because he is so '*teaching*' and talks all the time about Indian dialects or gives endless lectures about Asiatic politics; but on the other hand as one of the girls remarks 'he is a corker'.

Prudence obviously finds him a corker, but again all they have in common is sex. Basil, who has combined his forces with Mr Youkoumian, his opposite, the Armenian entrepreneur, finds the strain of the Ministry of Modernisation growing on him, and his brief rides out with Prudence are all that give some relief from his busy day. Looking as ill as he does, and with the problems of being the go-between between Seth and Youkoumian, he gets no sympathy from Prudence, who can only see it in terms of herself – ' "Of course, you wouldn't remember that there's me too, would you?" said Prudence. "Not just to cheer me up, you wouldn't." '

Basil, who thinks Prudence is a 'grand girl' (an expression he also uses of Angela Lyne), can't keep up with Prudence's insatiable appetite and says, 'I'm so tired I could die.' Ironically it is Basil's appetite, later in the book, that is satisfied in a rather unexpected manner.

Virginia Troy

Virginia obviously enjoys sex, and her role in *Men at Arms, Officers and Gentlemen* and *Unconditional Surrender* is acted out through that dimension. While the men are involved in the war effort, Virginia continues to flit from lover to lover.

Virginia is interesting because she is the one heroine for whom Waugh corrects her mispronunciations or wrong use of words. This is most clearly demonstrated in *Unconditional Surrender*. Uncle Peregrine is described as 'well travelled, well read, well informed' and as a 'stranger in the world' for he can only see Virginia as a 'Scarlet Woman'; and just as Trimmer's eye is not sharp enough in *Officers and Gentlemen* to realise that Virginia 'fitted a little too well into her surroundings', so Uncle Peregrine's eye is not sharp enough to read the 'faint, indelible signature of failure, degradation and despair' that is written on her face. But it is Uncle Peregrine who first corrects her. When she says 'You're not homosexual?' he replies: 'Good gracious, no. Besides the "o" is short. It comes from the Greek not the Latin.' Later when Virginia says to Guy, a Balliol man, that the Crouchbacks are 'effete', meaning that they are ineffectual, Guy informs her that the word actually means 'having just given birth'. Virginia tells him that he's just like Peregrine in the way that he corrects her. This kind of cruelly critical remark humiliates Virginia and puts her in her place as an empty-headed tart.

When Virginia leaves the Kilbannocks she leaves a small present for Ian. This is Pyne's *Horace*, which has been given to her by Uncle Peregrine, a bibliophile, as an 'inappropriate and belated Christmas present'. It is inappropriate because Virginia would have no interest in Horace. Again, when Virginia is in London with Uncle Peregrine, her lack of education is shown by the fact that while he reads her Trollope, she makes a *layette* – 'It was a survival of the schoolroom, incongruous to much in her adult life, that she sewed neatly and happily. It was thus that she had spent many evenings in Kenya working a quilt that was never finished' (p.159). And while the 'little Trimmer' grows in Virginia's womb, Waugh also has Major Ludovic's book growing at the rate of 3,000 words a day.

The only time that Virginia changes role is when she discovers that she is pregnant by Trimmer, cannot get an abortion and has no money to live on. To secure financial aid, and status for herself and her child, she asks Guy to marry her. When it comes to the crunch, Virginia, like all the other heroines, needs a man to support her; but she is different in the respect that once she marries Guy she does everything in her power to please him ... 'with gentle, almost tender, agility adopted her endearments to his crippled condition. She was as always lavish with what lay in her gift' (p.197). The cynical tone is obvious here, but one can't get away from the fact that although Virginia is a tart she is a sympathetic one.

In 1911, Max Beerbohm wrote in *Zuleika Dobson* (ch.7) that 'beauty and the lust for learning have yet to be allied'. They were not to be so in Evelyn Waugh's work. His beautiful women have very little to offer in the way of brains, and if they do they are considered to be freaks:

> As a girl, in her first season, an injudicious remark, let slip and overheard, got her the reputation of cleverness. Those who knew her best ruthlessly called her 'deep'.
> Thus condemned to social failure ... (of Elizabeth Verney in 'Tactical Exercise', p.162)

Interestingly, Lady Betjeman was told, as a debutante, that she was too clever and not pretty enough to marry well – she would have to take her chances with the intellectuals. She did, and married John Betjeman.[16]

As we have seen with *Brideshead Revisited*, Waugh mocks at the idea of women attending a university; and it is a theme that occurs in his other works as well. Guy Crouchback, noting that Kate Carmichael can't spell political (she spells it 'pollitical'), asks:

> 'Did you *pass* your exams at Edinburgh, Miss Carmichael?'
> 'Never. I was far too busy with more important things.' (*Officers and Gentlemen*, p.65)

Of Clara's Klugman operation in *Love Among the Ruins*, Waugh writes:

> 'It does go wrong like that every now and then. They had two or three cases at Cambridge.'
> 'I never wanted it done. I never wanted anything done. It was the Head of Ballet. He insists on all the girls being sterilized. Apparently you can never dance really well again after you've had a baby. And I did want to dance really well. Now this is what's happened.'

[16] Interview with Lady Betjeman, 16 September 1982.

'Yes,' said Dr Beamish. 'Yes. They're far too slapdash. They had to put down those girls at Cambridge, too. There was no cure.' (p.199)

'I heard the reason they put down one of the Cambridge girls was that she kept growing fatter and fatter.' (p.206)

and in *Basil Seal Rides Again*:

'How did your girl ever meet a fellow like that?'
'At Oxford. She insisted on going up to read History. She picked up some awfully rum friends.'
'I suppose there were girls there in my time. We never met them.'
'Nor in mine.'
'Stands to reason the sort of fellow who takes up with undergraduettes has something wrong with him.' (pp.259-60)

As late as 1950, Waugh gave the following advice to young people about to leave school – 'MEN: go to the University, read philosophy, history and the classics; ride horses. WOMEN: go to Europe; learn the French and English languages; study architecture and modesty.'[17] He wanted his daughter Harriet to go to a finishing school, which she rebelled against, and he wrote the following of his daughter Teresa when she was in the running for a scholarship at Somerville: 'I was convinced that it was merely from civility to Maurice that she was asked to an interview, but it appears that she is really certain of acceptance.'[18] He later wrote to Ann Fleming, 'I am sending Teresa to Boston for the autumn. She got a second like all girls.'[19]

Waugh obviously believed that some women had brains, but seemed to consider that they were a minority, and when they were intelligent he didn't always relish the fact, saying that 'intelligent women are the sworn enemies of good port'.[20] It is interesting, however, that although Waugh pours scorn on the feminine intellect he gives his heroines the power to control the destinies of his heroes.

[17] Evelyn Waugh, 'These Names Make News', *Daily Express*, 26 May 1950, p.3.
[18] *Diaries*, p.748.
[19] *Letters*, p.526.
[20] Evelyn Waugh, *Wine in Peace and War* (1947), p.67.

CHAPTER FIVE

Heroines in Control

The distance between Waugh and his women can, of course, be looked at in two ways. On the one hand he holds them off with all the crushing condescension of the Junior Common Room; on the other he can be seen as unable to approach them as whole human beings. It comes as no surprise, then, that while excluding women from the 'real' world of men's affairs, he also and invariably makes them the prime movers in the structure of the novels.

This is nothing new. From Hera to the Madonna, men have set women apart and yet acknowledged their primal role. Waugh is no exception. He gives his heroines power while causing his heroes to be powerless in some way; and consequently, the heroes are ruled by the actions of the heroines.

The controlling role of Waugh's heroines is at its strongest when he produces a pivotal point in the novel – a point where a line of dialogue or an event hits a nerve in the heroine and causes her to act differently so that the fortunes of the hero are changed. The controlling role is also at its strongest when the heroines do not explain or apologise for their actions.

> 'Oh, Margot, let's get married at once.'
> 'My dear, I haven't said that I'm going to yet. I'll tell you in the morning.'
> (*Decline and Fall*, p.137)

Margot Beste-Chetwynde in *Decline and Fall* takes Paul Pennyfeather as her lover, gets him involved in her prostitution business, expects him to go to prison for her, uses her contacts to get him released, and then marries someone else and takes another lover. The passive Paul is powerless to do anything about it – and so ends up, where he started out, at Oxford.

Margot moves in and out of the pages of *Decline and Fall* never explaining her actions but always being 'a woman of vital importance'. Her sudden decision, when visiting Paul in Egdon Prison, to marry Sir Humphrey Maltravers is given to Paul as a *fait accompli*: 'It's simply something that's going to happen.' The pivotal point that changed Margot's attitude to Paul is in the letter she had sent to him previously saying that Lady Circumference had cut her and that she was afraid of being socially ostracised. That is her reason for marrying Maltravers. In *Vile Bodies*, Waugh wrote: 'The motives for Margot Metroland's second marriage had been mixed, but entirely worldly; chief among them had been the desire to re-establish her somewhat shaken social position ... ' (p.96).

The pivotal point in *Vile Bodies* is when Nina meets her childhood sweetheart Ginger, described by Adam in his column as 'one of the wealthiest and best-known bachelors in society'. She announces her engagement to Ginger after Adam has once again told her that they can't get married. When Adam says he doesn't believe her, her response is: 'Well, I am. That's all there is to it.'

It seems that Adam is in control when he sells her to Ginger, but he is not really, for when he suggests that he might be able to buy her back Nina has already married his rival; and it is Nina who suggests that they might be able to see each other at Christmas. When Ginger goes to join his regiment Nina takes Adam to Doubting Hall and continues her affair with him. Again Adam seems to be in control when he says that he has sent Ginger a cheque for her, but Nina is fully aware that it is worthless, and when Adam says that he might have to send her back Nina's reply is: 'I expect it will end with that.' Nina knows full well that she has no intention of giving up Ginger and, in fact, manipulates Ginger into forgiving Adam for having an affair with her. Prosperous, with Ginger, in Whitehall, she deprives Adam of his baby by writing and telling him that Ginger has convinced himself that the child is his; again she has no intention of letting him think otherwise. The hapless Adam is left alone on the 'biggest battlefield in the history of the world' with a cheque for £35,000 which will only buy beer and newspapers. Nina never has to offer explanations because the reader knows that her decisions are based on financial security. Her father loses his money in the Wonderfilm company; Adam's fortunes go up and down, but Nina is determined that her income should be stabilised.

Brenda Last, after John Andrew's death, leaves Tony saying: 'I couldn't stay here. It's all over, don't you see, our life down here.' Tony does not see what she means at all. Brenda's response to the death of John Andrew is the most important pivotal point in *A Handful of Dust*. Waugh half prepares us for Brenda's attitude by having her sister Marjorie comment that it will mean 'the end of Mr Beaver', while Polly Cockpurse believes that it will be the 'end of Tony so far as Brenda is concerned'. Lady St Cloud believes that love is 'stronger than sorrow' and that only Tony and Brenda can help each other after such a catastrophe. But for Brenda the consequence of John Andrew dying is that she feels able to leave Tony as there is no longer anything to bind her to him. As she says in her letter to Tony, when she writes to tell him that she wants a divorce so that she can marry John Beaver – 'If John Andrew had not died things might not have happened like this. I can't tell.' Brenda shows no guilt, offers no apologies for her actions and hopes to remain friends with Tony. Understandably, after receiving the letter 'it was several days before Tony fully realised what it meant. He had got into the habit of loving and trusting Brenda.'

Brenda, not by her adultery, but by her financial demands on Tony, is directly responsible for his leaving Hetton Abbey and going abroad, and therefore indirectly responsible for his having to spend the rest of his life reading Dickens aloud to Mr Todd. It is a fate that Tony, perhaps, deserves, for after Brenda leaves him he never once makes any effort to get her back.

On the strength of her brother's saying that she is fed up with Beaver and wants to come back to Hetton, he rings her; but once she informs him that the information is incorrect he gives up. Tony is completely passive about losing Brenda. He only becomes active when her actions threaten him with the loss of Hetton. After he has left, Brenda's financial problems are short-lived because she has it within her power to marry Jock Grant-Menzies; but Tony is powerless to do anything about his situation with Mr Todd.

In *Scoop* the influential Mrs Stitch is indirectly responsible for the innocent William Boot being sent to Ishmaelia and Waugh said that 'Mrs Stitch and the first Boot were invented as a device by which a retiring, bucolic, innocent young man (the second Boot) should find himself thrown into the fantastic world of special correspondents'.[1]

Kätchen's[2] controlling role is weak, and we must question whether Waugh only brought her into the plot feeling that there had to be some love interest. It is even questionable that she is the heroine of the piece, as it is Julia Stitch who is the prime mover. True, Kätchen is instrumental in William's getting his first 'scoop', and consequently in his not getting fired after all; but she is only partly responsible for the second major 'scoop', because it is Bannister's understanding of the situation which makes things clearer to William, and it is Baldwin who writes the main scoop for him.

Of the two pivotal points in *Scoop* that affect William's return to Boot Magna only one is to do with Kätchen. The pivotal point in her controlling role is when her German pseudo-husband returns to her, causing her to leave with him rather than William. With this action, Waugh prepares us for the fact that William will return to Boot Magna. But the far more important pivotal point for him doing so is when on his return to England he sees first his passport photograph blown-up on the front page of *The Beast*, and then in the current issue the amazing story of his journalistic career. Knowing that it was non-existent he is overcome with shame, and retires to the country – not willing to venture away again in case his nannies should see him make a further 'ass' of himself.

Kätchen's concern, once her 'husband' is back, is how to obtain English nationality for them both. If she had found it was possible to do so by marrying William, she would have married him first and then left with her 'husband' afterwards. Once she realises that William cannot help them, she takes his boat, which suddenly becomes '*our* boat', in which she leaves with the German. She still controls William, for she manipulates him into helping her put the boat together while her 'husband' snoozes. Although she discusses throughout, with William, what her plans are – at the end she acts very much in the style of Brenda Last. Brenda wanted to remain friends with Tony; Kätchen tells William that she will send him a postcard to let him know that they are all right. Unlike Paul Pennyfeather who was too naive to know that Margot Beste-Chetwynde was using him, William is fully aware that he is being used by Kätchen; and, unlike Tony Last with Brenda,

---

[1] Evelyn Waugh, 'Memorandum for Messrs Endfield & Fisz on the film scenario for *Scoop*' (HRHRC).

[2] See below, Appendix One for some insight into Kätchen's name.

William never was in the habit of 'loving and trusting' Kätchen. Therefore his emotional reasons for wishing to return to Boot Magna to the secure love of his nannies where his feelings can't get hurt – not in the same way, anyhow – are entirely credible.

Scoop is weakened because the most powerful controlling role is held by the minor character, Mrs Stitch, and not by the heroine, Kätchen, with whom William is involved.

Aimée Thanatogenos, even when dead, indirectly exerts an influence over both Dennis Barlow's and Mr Joyboy's lives; for by committing suicide, 'without design', in Joyboy's workroom she leaves the way open for Dennis to blackmail Joyboy. Her controlling role in *The Loved One* has an extremely strong pivotal point which causes her to kill herself. Mr Joyboy reveals to Aimée that her fiancée is a liar and a cheat, but in a way it simplifies things for her. She disengages herself from Dennis and announces her engagement to Joyboy. The pivotal point occurs not when Mr Slump, the phony Guru Brahmin, tells her to find a high window to jump out of, but when Dennis appeals to her spiritual self and refuses to release her from her vow. Aimée would 'rather die' than be claimed by Dennis, and when she realises that he is not going to release her she is in turmoil. Mr Joyboy doesn't help by telling her that they will talk about it tomorrow and to 'take a good sleep, honey-baby'. Dennis speaks to her as her 'spiritual director'; Joyboy speaks to her as 'Poppa'; and finally Mr Slump, a drunk, now out-of-work, unethical journalist, speaks to her as a mystic; and she takes both his brutal advice and phony wisdom to heart because neither her present nor her past offer any meaningful alternative. Aimée leaves no suicide note – 'no letter of farewell or apology' – because prompted by 'Attic voices' to a 'higher destiny' she injects herself with cyanide, rather than jump out of a window, and considers the matter to be 'between herself and the deity' she serves.

Joyboy is at Dennis's mercy; and for Dennis, Aimée's death is a happy release. Powerless in the society he was in, he was doomed to follow a theological career to satisfy Aimée's requirements of him as a husband. Now he is free to follow higher things. As he says to Joyboy, 'I have work to do, and this is not the place to do it. It was only our young friend who kept me here – she and penury.' Between Sir Ambrose and Joyboy he makes enough money to return to England – 'a favourite of Fortune'.

Prudence Courteney is, without knowing it, very powerful, for she is responsible for Basil Seal's return to England. There is nothing Basil can do about having eaten her and, as tough as he is, he can, quite literally, no longer stomach life in Azania. The pivotal point of Prudence's controlling role in *Black Mischief* is Basil's famous line, 'You're a grand girl, Prudence, and I'd like to eat you', and Prudence's equally telling reply, 'So you shall my sweet, so you shall.' This pivotal point is not, however, like the ones previously mentioned. The line of dialogue might hit a nerve in Prudence – and, indeed, with her response, she forecasts her own future – but it does not cause her to act differently. Unlike Aimée who chooses to commit suicide; Prudence does not choose to be the delicacy of a cannibal feast.

In an 'Open Letter to the Archbishop of Westminster', who was then the owner of the *Tablet* and who had criticised the book for its 'foul invention' of Prudence's death, Waugh said that he had introduced the 'cannibal theme in the first chapter and repeated it in another key in the incident of the soldiers eating their boots, thus hoping to prepare the reader for the sudden tragedy when barbarism at last emerges from the shadows and usurps the stage'. He went on to say: 'It is not unlikely that I failed in this; that the transition was too rapid, the catastrophe too large.'[3]

As Frederick Stopp points out, if Waugh failed it was 'an artistic failure, not a moral one';[4] and part of that artistic failure is that Prudence, although indirectly controlling Basil's future, does not, like the other heroines, control her own.

The same weakness applies in *Put Out More Flags*, in which Angela Lyne, the heroine, is only one of three rich women who dedicate Basil Seal to the war effort. His sister, Barbara Sothill, believes that the war is 'what he's been waiting for all these years' and thinks of him in terms of all the heroes in the war books she has read – seeing him as Siegfried Sassoon, T.E. Lawrence and Rupert Brooke. His mother, Lady Seal, imagines him as a gallant officer joining the ranks of such famous names as Sidney, Wolfe and Nelson – 'Now she had a son to offer her country'; and Angela, tired of her seven-year, lonely affair with Basil, delves deep into her mind and behind the 'calm and pensive mask' of her face thinks 'Till death us do part', and the image of death recurs ... 'Death the macabre paramour in whose embrace all earthly loves were forgotten; Death for Basil, that Angela might live again.' As it happens it is the death of her husband, Cedric Lyne, that is the pivotal point that allows Angela to live again, but with Basil. And Basil has very little choice in the matter. As Angela says, 'Neither of us could ever marry anyone else, you know.' Basil tries such lines as 'What's the sense of marrying with things as they are' and 'I shall be a terrible husband', but Angela accepts that 'one can't expect anything to be perfect now'.

This pivotal point is not, however, a very strong one. Both Lady Seal and Barbara Sothill have more to do with Basil's fortunes throughout the novel than Angela; and Angela's controlling role is also weakened by the fact that she loses control of her actions. Waugh explained the reason for this. In 1946 he said of his major characters that he had 'very little control over them'; that he started 'them off with certain preconceived notions of what they will do and say in certain circumstances' but that he constantly found them 'moving another way'. Of Mrs Lyne he said: 'I had no idea until halfway through the book that she drank secretly. I could not understand why she behaved so oddly. Then when she sat down suddenly on the steps of the cinema I understood all and I had to go back and introduce a series of empty bottles into her flat. I was on board a troopship at the time. There is a young destroyer commander who sat next to me at a table who can bear witness of this. He asked me one day at luncheon how my book was going. I said, "Badly. I can't understand it at all" and then quite suddenly, "I know, Mrs Lyne has been drinking".'[5]

[3] Frederick J. Stopp, *Portrait of An Artist* (1958), p.32.
[4] Ibid.
[5] Evelyn Waugh, 'Fan-Fare', *Essays*, p.303.

Although Waugh had to go back and introduce the empty bottles, Angela's drinking is still out of character with the Angela we met in *Black Mischief* who was very much in control of how much money she gave Basil:

> 'I'm going to give you some money.'
> 'Well, that is nice.'
> 'You see, when you rang up I knew that was what you wanted. And you've been sweet tonight really, though you were boring about that island. So I thought that just for tonight I'd like to have you not asking for money. Before, I've enjoyed making it awkward for you. Did you know? Well I had to have *some* fun, hadn't I? – and I think I used to embarrass even you sometimes. And I used to watch you steering the conversation round. I knew that anxious look in your eye so well … ' (p.87)

And her drinking is also out of character with the constructive Angela, at the beginning of *Put Out More Flags*, who drinks Vichy water and who organises the hospital at Cedric's Folly as well as fitting Basil out for his interview with the Lieutenant-Colonel. Out of character too is Basil's chivalry in dealing with her problem, which is to make sure she drinks in company with him, and not alone, thereby causing her to drink less and him more.

Waugh said (in his dedication, to Randolph Churchill) at the beginning of *Put Out More Flags*, that he was dealing with a 'race of ghosts, the survivors of the world' they had both known ten years previously, and that is precisely the problem. In the first part of the narrative Basil behaves just as he has always done, and in the later part, where he becomes both patriotic, and responsible for Angela (instead of her being responsible for him), it shows a change of heart that is hardly plausible. Much truer to form is the conversation where they both realise that Basil will be an impossible husband, and where Angela is finally in control. Angela's role is still weak, however, because Waugh has her expecting very little from Basil – 'If there's one thing right the day is made' – and yet he expects the reader to see the 'new spirit abroad' in him.

The strength of Lucy Simmonds' controlling role is that she is not fully conscious of the change within herself during her pregnancy while other people are. Sister Kemp knows that when 'The Day' arrives (the pivotal point of Lucy's role) Lucy will have no further need of Roger, John or Miss Meikeljohn. As she says, 'I shall call you Mrs Simmonds until The Day … After that you will be my Lucy'. Both Roger Simmonds and John Plant have a passive part to play in the whole affair, and once labour starts Lucy has no need of either of them.

Lucy's pregnancy prevents John Plant from having an affair with her; and by transferring her affections, after the birth of her child, to the baby and 'Kempy', she leaves Plant impotent, with no further part to play in her life.

Work Suspended saw Waugh's first use of the first-person narrator. This was to be repeated in *Brideshead Revisited*, and Charles Ryder is the same kind of passive character as John Plant. Lucy Simmonds' and Julia Flyte's roles, however, are most interesting to compare. Lucy's maternal instincts are understandable, although not necessarily appreciated, and need no explanations from her. Julia Flyte has spiritual power, for her religion controls Charles Ryder's future; but there is a weakness in Julia's controlling role, for unlike Lucy and the other heroines she feels that she has to explain her actions.

The pivotal point in Julia's role comes when Brideshead tells her that Beryl Muspratt could not accept any invitation from Julia: 'It is a matter of indifference whether you choose to live in sin with Rex or Charles or both – I have always avoided inquiry into the details of your *ménage* – but in no case would Beryl consent to be your guest.'[6] (This minor, social, pivotal snub has much in common with Margot's situation where a social snub from Lady Circumference caused her to act differently.) As Sean O'Faolain has pointed out, 'the result of this bombshell is a harrowing emotional outbreak from Julia in a long speech delivered to Ryder, alone, on the subject of her sin'.[7] What O'Faolain does not point out is that this is the passage in the book where Ryder's expectations of marrying Julia crumble. He says that when her father returns home to die, 'Julia is so affected by seeing him, at the point of his final coma, bless himself that she refuses to marry Ryder, breaks off the proposed marriage, and, we are to understand, returns to the religion of her parents'.[8] But Julia's reasons for not marrying Charles are actually based on the 'sin' she talks about in the previous passage, and she actually says to Charles: 'All the future with you, all the future with or without you, war coming, world ending – sin.' Although Julia, after her outburst and her reconciliation with Brideshead, tells Charles that 'there's no turning back now' and that she wants to put her life in 'some sort of order' and that's why she wants to marry him, Charles realises that there has been both 'estrangement and misunderstanding'. When Julia finally says goodbye to Charles she realises that he knew it was going to happen, and he tells her that he has known 'since this morning; since before this morning, all this year'. The weakness of Julia's role is that she has to explain herself. For the first time Waugh gives his heroine a moral conscience, and her reasons for her actions are tedious beyond belief. A Margot Beste-Chetwynde, a Brenda Last, even a Virginia Troy would have told the world to go to hell. Julia can't because of her 'sin', but if only she had behaved differently, such as going into the chapel and shutting the door behind her, rather than excusing herself to Charles, her controlling role would have been much stronger. Charles knows why she is acting the way she is. Just as one found Basil Seal's new spirit implausible in *Put Out More Flags*, so Julia's conversion based on 'It may be a private bargain between me and God, that if I give up this one thing I want so much, however bad I am, He won't quite despair of me in the end' seems almost unChristian in its attitude.

Helena is baptized after, but not necessarily because, she has learnt that her son Constantine has 'not exactly' turned Christian but has 'put himself under the protection of Christ'. Once baptized, Helena's aim is to save Constantine,

---

[6] Waugh also saw this as the turning point for in his 'Memorandum for the filming of *Brideshead Revisited*', 18 February 1947, he wrote: 'A moment comes when Lord Brideshead employs the conventional term "living in sin" which suddenly strikes Julia's conscience' (HRHRC).

[7] Sean O'Faolain, *The Vanishing Hero: Studies in Novelists of the Twenties* (1956), p.65.

[8] Ibid., p.61.

for 'Power without Grace' is no good. The pivotal point that causes her to go and look for the cross comes when Constantine tells her and Pope Sylvester that Rome will always be heathen, and that he intends to build a new Rome – a 'great *Christian* capital, in the very centre of Christendom; a city built around two great new Churches dedicated to – what do you think? – Wisdom and Peace'. Helena's reaction to the idea of Constantine's soulless Rome, and to the discussions going on about the hypostatic union, is to decide to try and find the cross.

Helena's controlling role, the religious role, is weakened because the religious theme is only one of three. Waugh outlined the themes as 'the story of a woman's life', 'the split between East and West', and the 'themes of conversion'.[9] Waugh also thought that *Helena* was a masterpiece and, when asked why, said: 'It's never been done before. Nearest thing to it is E.M. Forster's sketches of Alexandria. They're unrecognized masterpieces, but they're disconnected and very short.'[10] Forster's *Pharos and Pharillon* is not, indeed, an historical novel, and by using Forster's technique and making the structure of Helena so disconnected, when it has so many themes that need to be held together, Waugh creates an unbalanced form which makes it hard for Helena's controlling role, the religious role, to sustain everything else that is going on.

Virginia Troy's controlling role in the *Sword of Honour* trilogy is strong because there are three pivotal points connected with her which directly affect her actions and consequently Guy Crouchback's spiritual and domestic future. The first is in *Men at Arms* where Guy, after his conversation with Mr Goodall, takes the first opportunity to go to London to see Virginia – intending, after his years of celibacy because of his religion, to sleep with her, understanding (because of what Goodall has told him) that it would not be a sin in the eyes of the Church because their civil divorce does not count.

Virginia's violent reaction to Guy's attempted seduction is quite understandable. She even slightly respects the man who calls her a 'tart'; but the pivotal point comes when, on asking Guy what his priests would think about him 'picking up a notorious divorcée', he informs her that they would say 'Go ahead'.

At this point in the novel, Virginia, in her own way, is far more honourable than Guy. She knows that not only has she not been his wife in name for the last eight years, but also that she has not been his wife in spirit either; and the thought of him claiming her as his rightful property in the eyes of the Church is repellent to her: 'I thought you'd taken a fancy to me again and wanted a bit of fun for the sake of old times. I thought you'd chosen me specially, and by God you had. Because I was the only woman in the whole world your priests would let you go to bed with. That was my attraction. You wet, smug, obscene, pompous, sexless, lunatic pig.' Guy has made a classic Roman Catholic boy's blunder, and he pays for it. Virginia leaves and he is left drained – emptier even than before.

[9] Harvey Breit, *The Writer Observed* (1957), p.148.
[10] Ibid.

In *Officers and Gentlemen* it is the people's hero, Trimmer, who succeeds with Virginia, for against her will she is sent to tour the industrial towns with him as a boost to the morale of the munitions workers. By letting the anti-hero Trimmer enjoy himself with Guy's wife, Waugh creates yet another strand in Guy's disillusionment with his God, his country and his friends. Virginia Troy, like Brenda Last, never apologises to Guy for her sexual misdemeanours. She admits in *Unconditional Surrender* that she has 'designs' on him, and only when she realises that she is not getting anywhere does she inform him 'without any extenuation or plea for compassion, curtly almost' that she is going to have Trimmer's child. This is the pivotal point of Virginia's controlling role in the novel, for by this direct and honest approach Guy changes his mind and marries her; not as he explains to Kerstie Kilbannock 'in spite' of Virginia's condition but 'because of' it. They might laugh at him in Bellamy's, but as far as Guy is concerned there is 'another life to consider' – and for Guy, who understands that he has never in his life performed a 'single positively unselfish action', the saving of that 'soul' becomes important enough to compensate for any 'loss of face'. The third pivotal point is that by staying in London with Uncle Peregrine, and sending the baby to the country with Angela Box-Bender, Virginia leaves the way open for herself to be killed, which she consequently is, as a bomb drops on Uncle Peregrine's flat, and her death ensures Guy's future domestic happiness.

Book Three of *Unconditional Surrender* is called 'The Death Wish'. Major Ludovic gives that same title to his novel, and he knows that Lady Marmaduke who is a 'bitch' must 'die in the last chapter', and so she does, in decline. Virginia also dies, but the important fact is that she wants to die. When she sends Gervase with Angela she recuperates comfortably from the birth of her child in Uncle Peregrine's flat while wondering as she hears the bombs chugging overhead whether that's 'the one that's coming here?' (p.191). Virginia is tired of life; she can't bear having had Trimmer's child; and her action in the end is a generous one, for she knows that Guy will be able to remarry and that she would never have made him happy anyway.

The difference between Virginia's attitude and Eloise Plessington's attitude to the bombs is also pointed out. Eloise, every time she hears an engine cutting out, says that she prays 'Please God don't let it fall on me'; and of Virginia she says:

> ' ... I'd got very fond of her this winter and spring but, you know, I can't regard her death as pure tragedy. There's a special providence in the fall of a bomb. God forgive me for saying so, but I was never quite confident her new disposition would last. She was killed at the one time in her life when she could be sure of heaven – eventually.' (p.201)

Virginia, of course, has become a Catholic, and Uncle Peregrine says that she makes the clergy 'laugh' and 'she's a much jollier sort of convert than people like Eloise Plessington' (p.185). Virginia's soul, as she has become a Catholic and confessed her sins, will, like the soul of her baby, now be saved. Her wish for death is in many ways an unselfish wish. She knows that Guy will be better off without her, whereas Eloise's wish to look after Gervase is prompted by self-interest: for she does see the bomb that has killed Virginia as a 'special providence' for she has an unmarried daughter whom she can now push at Guy. And Domenica Plessington does eventually marry Guy Crouchback.

After Virginia's death, Everard Spruce describes her to Frankie and Coney as: 'Virginia Troy was the last of twenty years' succession of heroines ... The ghosts of romance who walked between the two wars' (p.200). He reads a description out to the two girls, which is not from Michael Arlen's *The Green Hat* and a description of Iris Storm, but a description of Mrs Viveash in Aldous Huxley's *Antic Hay*, and says that Virginia was the last of the type ... 'the last of them – the exquisite, the doomed, and the damning, with expiring voices'. But Virginia, whatever Waugh says, is not one of these heroines. She does not have an 'expiring' voice; rather, she is a jolly sort at heart, for although her 'laughter has seldom been heard in recent years' when she does laugh with, and at, Uncle Peregrine, we are reminded that:

> ... it had once been one of her chief charms. She sat back in her chair and gave full, free tongue; clear, unrestrained, entirely joyous, with a shadow of ridicule, her mirth rang through the quiet little restaurant. Sympathetic and envious faces were turned towards her. She stretched across the table cloth and caught his hand, held it convulsively, unable to speak, laughed until she was breathless and mute, still gripping his bony fingers. (*Unconditional Surrender*, p.136)

This is a warm picture of Virginia, and it is not a picture that could ever have been drawn of Mrs Viveash of whom Waugh said the following:

> She has her classic, dignified bereavement. Promiscuous sexual relations bore her. But she has, we are told, almost limitless power, power which, I must confess, has never much impressed me. She was 25 when I was 20. She seemed then appallingly mature. The girls I knew did not whisper in 'expiring' voices and 'smile agonizingly' from their 'death beds'. They grinned from ear to ear and yelled one's head off. And now thirty years on, when women of 25 seem to me moody children, I still cannot weep for Mrs Viveash's tragic emptiness.[11]

Virginia is not dignified, and she enjoys promiscuous sexual relations. She is sometimes a sad lady, but she cannot be called 'tragic', for Virginia does not have 'regrets' about the life she has led; and at the end of *Unconditional Surrender* she seems to be at peace with herself. In some ways she has been fulfilled, both through her role as a mother and through her conversion to Catholicism. Virginia is no Mrs Viveash; she is far more in the mould of one of those 'girls' whom Waugh knew; and if, by any chance, she was based on a heroine with an 'expiring' voice it is possible that it was neither Mrs Viveash nor Iris Storm but Virginia Tracy, the heroine of Michael Arlen's *Piracy*, published in 1925.[12]

[11] Evelyn Waugh, 'Youth at the Helm and Pleasure at the Prow: *Antic Hay* by Aldous Huxley', *Essays*, pp.471-2.
[12] Mrs Viveash, Iris Storm and Virginia Tracy were all lightly based on Nancy Cunard. Both Michael Arlen and Aldous Huxley were in love with her at one time in their lives.

Virginia Tracy in *Piracy* 'almost got married twice, but finally made a *coup de coeur* by marrying an American' whose name was Hector Sardon and who was a millionaire. She later marries Lord George Tarylon but has an affair with Ivor Marlay. She then returns to Lord Tarylon. There are numerous men in her life. Virginia Troy marries her first two serious beaux, Guy Crouchback and Tommy Blackhouse. Her third marriage is to Bert Troy, a wealthy American. She, too, has numerous affairs but finally remarries Guy Crouchback.

The two Virginias have much in common. They are both fair; they both have a high degree of candour; they are both popular with the opposite sex; they are both generous with money, although Virginia Troy becomes penniless whereas Virginia Tracy does not; they both have a mocking, sharp and slightly antagonistic quality to their personality; and both appear in the popular press and have their names bandied about in a rather unpleasant way. Virginia Tracy's name and face are familiar – 'too familiar – to that increasing part of England that must read its daily and weekly lot of gossip in the papers' (*Piracy*, p.160); while Trimmer, when he sees Virginia Troy's face, is 'struck by a sense of familiarity; somewhere, perhaps in those shabby fashion-magazines, he had seen it before' (*Officers and Gentlemen*, p.74). Virginia Tracy is seen as glamorous, but there is a 'rottenness in that glamour' and 'Quite decent men took faint licence with her name, while lewd men who had never met her, said that they had touched her, they chuckled at the mention of her name' (*Piracy*, p.160). And Virginia Troy is described as:

> ' … Tommy took her from him, then Gussie had her for a bit, then Bert Troy picked her up when she was going spare.'
> 'She's a grand girl. Wouldn't mind having a go myself one of these days.'
> For in this club there were no depressing conventions against the bandying of ladies' names. (*Men at Arms*, p.22)

Both girls are attractive but do not try to attract. Trimmer sees Virginia Troy as 'a woman equipped with all the requisites for attention, who was not trying to attract' (*Officers and Gentlemen*, p.74), while Ivor Marlay sees Virginia Tracy as having 'such queerly little consciousness of her looks that you could take your fill of staring as she sat or walked and not offend' (*Piracy*, p.80). Both girls have acquired a reputation. Both when they are near despair are connected with the likeness of a broken toy – Virginia Tracy lies there 'like a broken Venetian toy' while Virginia Troy, when her 'designs' on Guy are not working, starts to sing a song that they both knew in their youth about 'a little broken doll'. Virginia Tracy is aware that she is a legend, like the book that Ivor Marlay has written called *The Legend of the Last Courtesan*, while Virginia Troy is defined by Everard Spruce as the last of the 'expiring' heroines. Virginia Tracy develops a mysterious gynaecological complaint and undergoes a serious operation; Virginia Troy becomes pregnant but does not have an abortion; Virginia Tracy dies, a rather mysterious and gallant death; and Virginia Troy, like her, also chooses to die.

The power that the two girls have in common is not the 'limitless power' of Mrs Viveash but the power of pleasing. Virginia Tracy pleases the young men of the First World War for she is 'conscious only of liking them immensely. She loved one and then another ... ' (*Piracy*, p.77); while Virginia Troy pleases those of the Second World War, for 'her power of pleasing was to her still part of the natural order which had been capriciously interrupted' (*Unconditional Surrender*, p.147). Virginia Tracy recognises that 'making love to me has become a recognised institution, it was the only careless game that the war didn't make more expensive' and Virginia Troy has that same recognition.

Waugh's war trilogy has often been likened to Ford Madox Ford's Tietjens saga, and the two heroes, Guy Crouchback and Christopher Tietjens, have much in common, but neither Tietjens' wife, Sylvia, nor his mistress, Valentine, have much in common with Virginia Troy. However, although Virginia Troy and Virginia Tracy have similar outlooks and lives, there can be no comparison between the two books. Michael Arlen's *Piracy* is romantic and wildly overwritten, and revolves only around the themes of adultery, social aspiration and death; whereas Waugh's work, apart from being in a different league as far as style is concerned, contains those same themes and the major ones of Catholicism, and a chance of salvation for all.

CHAPTER SIX

The Nanny: Servant or Mother?

And always keep a hold of Nurse
For fear of finding something worse.
(Hilaire Belloc, *Bad Child's Book of Beasts*, 1896)

Having a nanny, in Waugh's mind, was connected with being in the right kind of social class, although he did not argue with the old-fashioned kind of nursery. In 'Matter-of-Fact Mothers of the New Age' he pointed out that the modern mother turned away from the old-fashioned kind of nursery which was a 'teeming and inaccessible warren' at the top of the house 'ruled despotically by a superstitious "nanny", and physicked with curious distillations' to a 'small family kept well in the background of a hygienic nursery'.[1] Waugh himself came from a small family, but the nannies in his books are the kind of nannies who were associated with the 'teeming warrens' at the top of the house. However, unlike Evelyn Gardner who said 'How many of us have suffered from the cruelty of a stern Victorian nurse, who shut us into dark cupboards and thus caused an intense fear of the dark',[2] Waugh's nannies are kind, as was his own nanny, Lucy, of whom he said: 'I think Lucy fully returned my love. She was never cross or neglectful'.[3]

Kind his nannies may be, but they are very definitely given their right social status. Nanny Hawkins in *Brideshead Revisited* reigns supreme over the nurseries at the top of the house, and has her own servants to wait on her:

> Presently nanny said: 'Ring the bell, dear, and we'll have some tea. I usually go down to Mrs Chandler, but we'll have it up here today. My usual girl has gone to London with the others. The new one is just up from the village. She didn't know anything at first, but she's coming along nicely. Ring the bell.'
> (*Brideshead*, p.38)

Nanny Hawkins, like the governess in any aristocratic house, has her own special status, and it is a status that does not change in Waugh's books, even when the fortunes of the family are laid low. Rex Mottram tells Charles

---

[1] Evelyn Waugh, *Evening Standard*, 8 April 1929, p.7. A comprehensive study of the nanny figure in history and literature has been written by Jonathan Gathorne-Hardy. See *The Rise and Fall of the British Nanny* (1972).

[2] Evelyn Gardner, 'The Modern Mother: a Young Wife's Challenging Plea', *Evening Standard*, 9 January 1930, p.7.

[3] *A Little Learning*, p.30.

Ryder that the family are spending far too much money, and points out that apart from running a pack of foxhounds, keeping up both Brideshead and Marchmain House, not raising the rents or sacking anyone, they have 'dozens of old servants doing damn all, being waited on by other servants' (p.168). When Charles visits Brideshead during his army days he finds an old housemaid taking tea up to Nanny Hawkins, and takes it for her. Even though Nanny is now alone at Brideshead with only Father Membling to keep her company as Julia, Cordelia and Brideshead are away at the war, she still has her girl 'Effie' who 'does for' her.

In *Scoop* both Nannie Bloggs and Nannie Price are bedridden, as are William's widowed grandmother, Sister Watts, her first old nurse, and Sister Sampson, her second old nurse. Aunt Annie's old governess, Miss Scope, is also confined to bed. The only nurse who is still on her feet is Nurse Granger, and her duties include looking after all the other nurses as well as the failing butler, Bentinck, and James the first footman who is also confined to his room. The Boots are thought of as being as 'poor as church mice' because they cannot afford to entertain; and the reason that they cannot do so is that they have ten servants who wait 'upon the household and upon one another' and who do so in 'a desultory fashion' as they cannot spare very much time because of the 'five meat meals which tradition daily allowed them' (p.19). In *Scoop* the social order is reversed, for it is the nannies who rule over the house rather than the family.

Nancy Mitford, when she was talking about 'The English Aristocracy' in *Noblesse Oblige*, and their attitude to money, said of her imaginary family, the Fortinbrases, when they were ruined: 'They have two babies, Dominick and Caroline, and a Nanny. Does it occur to either Lord or Lady Fortinbras to get a job and retrieve the family fortune? It does not. First of all they sell everything that is not entailed, thus staving off actual want. They shut up most of the rooms in their house, send away the servants (except, of course, Nanny), and get the Dowager Lady Fortinbras and her sister to come and cook, clean, dust and take trays upstairs to the nursery.'[4]

Once established in an aristocratic family, a nanny cannot be easily removed; and besides, she is such a part of the family, bringing up, quite often, generation after generation, that it is quite unthinkable that she should be thought of as a servant who can be dismissed. When Tony Last leaves Hetton Abbey, and Brenda without any money, he still instructs his lawyer, Mr Graceful, to pay the wage bill at Hetton, and when Richard Last takes over, although he shuts down some of the house he only gets rid of the footmen. In *Unconditional Surrender* Virginia asks Angela Box-Bender, Guy's sister, if she could take the baby, Gervase, back with her – 'Old Nanny would look after it surely?' (p.191). Angela and Guy's nanny has looked after both of them, and after Angela's son, Tony, but she is still in residence, and although Angela is doubtful about her wanting to look after a young baby, she takes up Virginia's suggestion.

[4] Nancy Mitford, 'The English Aristocracy', *Noblesse Oblige*, edited by Nancy Mitford (1956), p.50.

Waugh declares the social position of the nanny in many ways. In *A Handful of Dust* John Andrew's nanny has her position usurped by the groom, Ben Hacket. When her charge, John Andrew, was a small child she had taken him ('panting at the bridle') on his little Shetland pony round the paddock. When John Andrew is older, his riding instruction becomes a 'man's business', and while Ben Hacket teaches him, Nanny sits crocheting and worrying about her charge. When John Andrew is rebuked by his father for calling his nanny a 'silly old tart' he is told to think of all the things that his nanny does for him every day, to which he replies, 'She's paid to.' The young John Andrew already knows that his nanny is his inferior, and his father enforces that awareness by telling him that as a gentleman he must be considerate to people 'less fortunate' than himself, 'particularly women' (p.23). John Andrew, at an early age, puts his nanny firmly in her place. First he goes to meet his father at the station, saying that he '*made*' his nanny let him come; and even nanny has to admit that he made such a nuisance of himself that she gave in to him. Secondly, by John Andrew's 'earnest entreaty', on the day of the hunt, she is 'confined indoors, among the housemaids whose heads obtruded at the upper windows' (p.100). Unlike Waugh's nanny, Lucy, this puts her 'out of temper', and she is thoroughly resentful. The young master has overruled her authority, and denigrated her in front of the other servants.

The social standing between nannies is also noted. In *Work Suspended* Sister Kemp belongs to a 'particularly select and highly priced corps of nurses' (p.178). She can walk in the most desirable areas of the park unlike inferior nurses who, if they try to trespass, do it at the 'risk of cold looks' (p.178). Because of Sister Kemp's standing, Lucy's perambulator will be socially established by the time the permanent nanny takes charge. Sister Kemp admits that 'the snobbery among nurses is terrible. I've seen many a girl go home from Stanhope Gate in tears ... Of course, they ought to have known. There's always Kensington Gardens for them' (p.179). Even Sister Kemp has her social limitations. Although she had attended a house 'in nodding distance of Royalty', she found the gardens there 'dull', by which both John Plant and Roger and Lucy realise that she had come up against a similar kind of treatment as the one she had been previously talking about.

In *Vile Bodies* there is a grave debate in the servant's hall at Lady Metroland's house about what status Mrs Melrose Ape's 'angels' should be given. The butler, Blenkinsop, is quite certain that they aren't guests, and after much discussion it is decided that the angels are 'nurses, and that became the official ruling of the household' (p.93). The second footman, however, thinks that they are just ' "young persons", pure and simple, "and very nice too", for nurses cannot, except in very rare cases, be winked at, and clearly angels could' (p.93).

In *Unconditional Surrender* Virginia mentions that Mrs Corner, the housekeeper, will be 'over the moon to see the last of it', meaning that when the nursery is cleared there will be no more, as Waugh puts it, 'normal, ineradicable hostility between nursing sister and domestic staff' (p.191).

Nannies had a lot more power than domestic staff, as one can see from Arthur Box-Bender's arrangements for the nation, during the war, in *Men at Arms*:

Box-Bender's arrangements were the microcosm of a national movement. Everywhere houses were being closed, furniture stored, children transported, servants dismissed, lawns ploughed, dower-houses and shooting lodges crammed to capacity; mothers-in-law and nannies were everywhere gaining control. (p.22)

The nanny's position also means that she is always rather well-off, because she is secure in her position and has little to spend her money on as everything is found for her. Nanny Hawkins in *Brideshead Revisited* is described as follows:

Long hours of work in her youth, authority in middle life, repose and security in her age, had set their stamp on her lined and serene face. (p.37)

Nanny Hawkins is so secure that when the military take over Brideshead her life is not affected, unlike the new Lady Marchmain who is turned out and ends up in a hotel at the seaside.

In *Scoop* the 'richest member of the household' is Nannie Bloggs, who keeps her savings in a red flannel bag under the bolster on her bed. Her savings grow because of her interest in horse racing[5] and her aptitude for backing a winner. She and Nannie Price play dominoes and cards for money, and their opponents, whether William, Uncle Theodore or Mr Salter suffer at their hands, owing them numbers of shillings. Nannie Bloggs can also afford to be generous, and when William leaves for London she sends him down three golden sovereigns to see him on his way. Nannie Bloggs is conscious of money to the extent that she reminds William, after their game of dominoes, that he owes her thirty-three shillings; and Nannie Price ends her game of cards with Mr Salter losing twenty-two shillings.

In *A Handful of Dust* the only reference to money is John Andrew's remark that his nanny is paid to look after him. But nannies are also people to be looked after. Christopher Sykes has commented that Waugh subscribed to charities who 'looked after such people in old age'.[6] This fact is borne out in his writing: in *Officers and Gentlemen* Guy Crouchback recalls visits with his mother to an old retainer, Mrs Barnet. Asking his mother why they visit the old lady (they always take provisions to her), she says: 'Oh, we have to. She's been like that ever since I came to Broome' (p.227).

Waugh in his response to Nancy Mitford's 'U', 'non-U' debate, disagreed with many of her opinions, and although he never commented on her view of nannies being servants who were always secure, he did make the following distinctions about the nanny:

All nannies and many governesses, when pouring out tea, put the milk in first ... Sharp children notice that this is not normally done in the drawing-room.[7]

---

[5] Waugh's nanny, Lucy, did not appear to have any interest in horse-racing, but Waugh, at the age of seven, wrote 'The Curse of the Horse Race'. The tale was against betting, and Waugh said that 'no doubt the moral was derived from Lucy'. *A Little Learning*, p.62. The story can be found in *Little Innocents: Childhood Reminiscences*. Preface, Alan Pryce-Jones (1932), pp.93-6.

[6] Sykes, p.27.

[7] Evelyn Waugh, 'An Open Letter', in *Noblesse Oblige*, p.75.

Waugh was quite clear about the social standing of his nannies, but he might not have been aware of how often he turned them into mother figures.

The nanny as a mother figure

In *A Little Learning* (p.29) Waugh talked of 'two adored deities, my nurse and my mother'. It is revealing that he puts his nurse before his mother, because the nanny figure is far more important in his works than the mother figure.

In *Brideshead Revisited* Nanny Hawkins likes to watch her visitors' faces and 'think of them as she had known them as small children; their present goings-on did not signify much besides those early illnesses and crimes' (p.146). It is Nanny Hawkins's treatment, rather than Lady Marchmain's, of those 'early crimes' and the way in which she brings the children up that influence them for the rest of their lives. Her main effect is on Julia, and it is the religion that she has instilled in her in childhood, more than that instilled by her mother, that makes Julia revert to her religion at the end of the book. When Julia tells Charles that she has been punished for marrying Rex, she says: 'You see, I can't get all that sort of thing out of my mind, quite – Death, Judgement, Heaven, Hell, Nanny Hawkins, and the catechism. It becomes part of oneself, if they give it one early enough' (p.247).

Julia, although she remembers being with Cordelia, with the catechism, in her mother's room before lunch on Sundays, has most of her memories of religion connected with her nanny and the night nursery. When she talks about 'sin' she connects it with 'a word from so long ago, from Nanny Hawkins stitching by the hearth and the nightlight burning before the Sacred Heart' (p.274). And when Charles tells her that her feelings of guilt stem from all the nonsense that she was taught in the nursery and says 'You do know at least that it's all bosh don't you?', Julia replies: 'How I wish it was!' (p.276). When Charles sees her to bed he doesn't know whether, when her lips move, she's saying good night to him or saying a prayer, and if a prayer he sees it as 'a jingle of the nursery ... some ancient pious rhyme that had come down to Nanny Hawkins from centuries of bedtime whispering ...' (p.278).

Nanny Hawkins could not stop Julia marrying Rex, and physically she cannot stop Julia marrying Charles either. Her response to their news is ' "Well, dear, I hope it's all for the best," for it was not part of her religion to question the propriety of Julia's actions' (p.287).[8] But Nanny's conditioning pays off, for Julia finally gives up Charles.

It is Sebastian who first takes Charles Ryder to Brideshead, not to visit his mother but to see his nanny.[9] When Charles doesn't understand why he can't meet Julia, who nanny has told them is there, Sebastian's answer is that

[8] Robert Murray Davis notes that Waugh changed the text: 'Nanny Hawkins does not presume to judge the actions of the Flyte family, but the proof's version of her reaction to the news of Julia's coming divorce and marriage to Ryder – "Yes, dear, that'll be a nice change" – is flippant and seems to condone adultery, and Nanny is nothing if not pious. The tone and implication are adjusted by the novel's "Well my dear, I hope it's all for the best".' *Evelyn Waugh, Writer* (1981), p.172.

[9] Sebastian was partly based on Alastair Graham and Waugh, when in Scotland with Alastair Graham, visited and had tea with Graham's old nurse. *Diaries*, p.259.

he's not going to let Charles get mixed up with his family. 'They're so madly charming. All my life they've been taking things away from me. If they once got hold of you with their charm, they'd make you their friend not mine, and I won't let them' (p.39). Charles then asks if he can at least see some more of the house to which Sebastian says 'It's all shut up. We came to see Nanny' (p.39). Sebastian is not afraid of Charles's meeting his nanny because he is secure in her love and he knows that she has no reason to threaten his relationship with Charles, whereas he knows that his mother is compelled to use her charms to seduce his friends and anyone else who comes to Brideshead, because she needs to conquer people and have them admire her.

Charles Ryder, because he is a social climber, suggests to Sebastian, when he does a sketch of the fountain at Brideshead, that he should give it to Lady Marchmain ...

> 'Why? You don't know her.'
> 'It seems polite. I'm staying in her house.'
> 'Give it to nanny,' said Sebastian. (p.79)

Nanny, who has heard that the fountain is something to be admired but can't see the beauty of it herself, is pleased with Charles's sketch, which she thinks has 'quite the look of the thing' and puts it among the collection on the top of her chest of drawers. This collection of Nanny Hawkins's is very important, for it sums up an essential difference between her and Lady Marchmain – her deep interest in the children as compared with Lady Marchmain's more superficial one. It is worth quoting two passages in full which describe the rooms of the two women:

> It was a charming room, oddly shaped to conform with the curve of the dome. The walls were papered in a pattern of ribbon and roses. There was a rocking horse in the corner and an oleograph of the Sacred Heart over the mantlepiece; the empty grate was hidden by a bunch of pampas grass and bulrushes; laid out on top of the chest of drawers and carefully dusted, were the collection of small presents which had been brought home to her at various times by her children, carved shell and lava, stamped leather, painted wood, china, bog-oak, damascened silver, blue-john, alabaster, coral, the souvenirs of many holidays. (p.38)

> This room was all her own; she had taken it for herself and changed it so that, entering, one seemed to be in another house. She had lowered the ceiling and the elaborate cornice which, in one form or another, graced every room was lost to view; the walls, one panelled in brocade, were stripped and washed blue and spotted with innumerable little water-colours of fond association; the air was sweet with the fresh scent of flowers and musty potpourri; her library in soft leather covers, well-read works of poetry and piety, filled a small rosewood bookcase; the chimney piece was covered with small personal treasures – an ivory Madonna, a plaster St Joseph, posthumous miniatures of her three soldier brothers. When Sebastian and I lived alone at Brideshead during that brilliant August we had kept out of his mother's room. (p.122)

Nanny's room has not been worked at. It is a haven of peace and love, and has its own natural charm. Cosy and inviting, it sums up the place the children have in her heart with their treasures laid out lovingly for all to see. Lady Marchmain's sitting-room represents the 'intimate modern world'. It should be charming, but to the children it is 'her' room, a place that is suffocating in the extreme, and which is full of 'personal treasures' that have nothing to do with them. Whereas Lady Marchmain has 'posthumous miniatures' of her brothers, Nanny has the 'photographs, and holiday souvenirs' of her children[10] (p.287).

It is Nanny Hawkins in *Brideshead Revisited* who holds the family together; it is she who waits in the empty nursery for her wandering charges to return. Not glamorous or charming like Lady Marchmain, but warm-hearted and understanding, she represents the true values and sentiments of motherhood. When Lady Marchmain dies, Nanny stays on, and the children, with all their problems, still come to her, Brideshead even taking rooms next to her in the old nurseries before he marries another mother figure, Beryl Muspratt.

Waugh also pours scorn on the other mother figure in the book, Celia Ryder. She has a 'motherly heart' which makes her 'cable daily to the nanny at home' (p.223). Celia, an adulteress, has little part to play in her children's lives. It is nanny who makes a 'Welcome'[11] banner with Johnjohn for Charles's return.

In *Scoop* we learn that William Boot has a widowed mother and a widowed grandmother, but they are unimportant compared with Nannie Bloggs and Nannie Price. William has a dream, a secret wish, that he has only confided to one person dear to him; not his mother but his nanny. He wants to go up in an aeroplane, and Nannie Bloggs, his confidante, has promised him a trip in one if she wins the Irish Sweepstake. William's dream is realised with his trip to Ishmaelia, but Nanny Bloggs disapproves of him 'gallivanting about all over Africa with a lot of heathens' (p.205); and Nannie Price also disapproves because she cuts his articles out of the paper so that the other members of the family can't see them. Nannie Price is 'hard as agate about matters of money and theology' (p.211).[12]

When William is worried about his reputation, he is most concerned about what his nannies will think of him, not his mother; and when Mr Salter is sarcastic about the two old ladies it gets him nowhere:

[10] Interestingly, Waugh spent most of his early childhood at home in the day-nursery which was covered with a pictorial wallpaper representing figures in medieval costume. His mother had a small sitting-room where he 'sometimes sat with her'. And although he lunched in the dining-room with his mother, he had all his other meals in the nursery so that he was out of his father's way. *A Little Learning*, p.43.

[11] Alec Waugh recalls: 'When I returned for the school holidays, my father used to paste over the face of the grandfather clock in the hall, "Welcome home to the heir of Underhill." Evelyn's comment on this was – he was then only six – "When Alec has Underhill and all that's in it, what will be left for me?" My father never put the notice up again.' *My Brother Evelyn and Other Profiles* (1967), p.164. The banner obviously rankled, for in *Vile Bodies* (p.201), Florin talks about the 'Welcome Home' banner that the Colonel's mother made for the Colonel and his brother when they were boys.

[12] Religion is important as far as all of Waugh's nannies are concerned; even Ambrose Silk cynically recalls in *Put Put More Flags* how his nanny told him of 'a Heaven that was full of angels playing harps' (p.60). And in *A Handful of Dust*, John Andrew's nanny takes him to church regularly on Sundays.

'These ladies you mention; no doubt they are estimable people, but surely, my dear Boot, you will admit that Lord Copper is a little more important.'

'No,' said William gravely, 'Not down here.' (p.210)

And later Mr Salter explains to his managing editor, 'Mr Boot ... is afraid of losing the esteem of his old nurse', to which the managing editor replies 'Women' (p.213).

A Handful of Dust sums up the difference between the mother and the nanny figure superbly, for when John Andrew dies Brenda cries with relief on hearing that her son has died, rather than her lover, John Beaver, whereas Nanny is genuinely upset ... 'Nanny was there in tears' (p.105). And after the inquest, while Brenda is acting mechanically and thinking about leaving Tony, Nanny is still 'red eyed' and upset. Nanny has the reaction that the mother, Brenda, should have had. All Brenda can say is, 'Poor little boy, poor little boy'; and even says to Tony, 'I suppose there'll have to be a funeral' (pp.21-2). The death of John Andrew means that Brenda can leave Tony and that is what is uppermost in her mind.

Mothers, with the exception of Helena, are insensitive and unaffectionate human beings in Waugh's work. Margot Beste-Chetwynde allows her son, Peter, to mix his own cocktails at an early age, and to procure lovers for her. Lady Seal is only concerned with how her son, Basil, appears to the social world. She also controls the purse strings, as Basil's father disinherited him. Any fond memories that Basil, and his sister Barbara, have of their childhood are connected with the schoolroom and their old governess, Miss Penfold. Lady Circumference is more concerned at what people will think about her not going to Margot's wedding than she is about her son, Lord Tangent's death: 'It's maddenin' Tangent having died just at this time ... People may think that's my reason for refusin.' I can't imagine that *anyone* will go' (*Decline and Fall*, p.149). Simon Balcairn's mother, the ex-Countess of Balcairn, Mrs Panrast, is a Lesbian; while Miles Malpractice's mother, Lady Throbbing, is a mother of such little consequence that her son, a homosexual, never visits her. John Beaver's mother promotes his cause for monetary gain. Adam Fenwick-Symes's mother is not mentioned, his father is dead; Nina Blount only has a father, Colonel Blount. Agatha Runcible's mother, 'poor Viola Chasm', and her father, Lord Chasm, do not appear to visit her in hospital. It is the Bright Young Things who rally round – and who, indirectly, kill her. Angela Lyne's father is a Glasgow millionaire, 'jovial' and 'rascally' and with 'hard-boiled' friends like Lord Copper and Lord Metroland. Angela's mother plays no part in her life; and she, Angela, is a bad mother herself. She finds her son Nigel, whom she hardly ever sees, trying – 'Cedric ... for God's sake don't let him be a bore. Go with Miss Grainger into the next room, darling' (*Put Out More Flags*, p.171). Guy Crouchback's mother died when he was young; Paul Pennyfeather has a guardian; and Charles Ryder, when asked by Julia if he has an 'awful family', when he and Sebastian are put in prison for the night, says: 'Only a father. He'll never hear about it' (p.118). Kätchen's father went away to South America, when she was sixteen, supposedly to look for her mother who had left them, leaving her to work in a dance hall; and Aimée's father 'left Mother before he died, if he is dead, and Mother went East to look for him when I left College and died there' (p.75). Virginia Troy appears to have no relatives of her own to turn to in her time of need, and she talks about her son Gervase as 'it' and hands it over to Guy's family to look after. Lucy Simmonds is an orphan whose Aunt lives on her income, and uses it to help bring her own daughters out.

Nanny and the nursery, not parents, seem to be Waugh's idea of security and love. Maurice Bowra writes of Waugh:

> He longed for some home in which he could regain the blitheness and the security of childhood, and for one deceived year of marriage he thought he had found it. When the dream broke, he still sought it. Despite his hard-boiled attitudes, he was incurably sentimental about this. He wanted warmth, children's games, children's talk, the enclosed universe of the nursery.[13]

Many critics have noticed Waugh's sentimental harking back to the nursery; among them Bernard Bergonzi, D.S. Savage, 'Donat O'Donnell' (Connor Cruise O'Brien), Stephen Spender, Frederick Stopp and James Carens. D.S. Savage has been the harshest in his criticism, saying of Waugh that he 'reveals the predicament of Immaturity. He is the brilliant undergraduate who has difficulty in growing up. As a comic writer he remains at a distance from experience which he views with a premature cynicism; as a serious novelist he endeavours to comprehend experience but is prevented by the mists of sentiment exhaled from a childish or adolescent Innocence which has never, really, been outgrown.'[14]

One has to agree with Savage, but there is yet another criticism to be made. None of the critics mentioned has recorded the fact that Waugh's sentimentality does not, on the whole, apply to his heroines, only to his heroes.

All the heroes in Waugh's novels remember their childhood with an unusual degree of affection. Sebastian Flyte carries his teddy bear, Aloysius,[15] with him wherever he goes; and Sebastian's desire is that life should be 'always summer, always alone, the fruit always ripe, and Aloysius in a good temper ...' (p.77). Sebastian, as Cara says, is 'in love with his own childhood. That will make him very unhappy. His teddy-bear, his nanny ... and he is nineteen years old ...' (p.100).

Charles Ryder feels that by knowing Sebastian he was 'given a brief spell of what I had never known, a happy childhood, and though its toys were silk shirts and liqueurs and cigars, and its naughtiness high in the catalogue of grave sins, there was something of the nursery freshness that fell little short of the joy of innocence' (p.46). But amidst the dissipation Charles is conscious of

---

[13] C.M. Bowra, *Memories 1898-1939* (1966), p.175.

[14] D.S. Savage, 'The Innocence of Evelyn Waugh', in *Focus Four: The Novelist as Thinker*, edited by B. Rajan (1948), p.35.

[15] Sebastian Flyte was not the only young man to have a teddy bear. In real life, John Betjeman had a toy bear called 'Archibald'; Keith Douglas had a giant teddy bear as his constant companion at Oxford; and Beverley Nichols, being different, had a toy rabbit called 'Cuthbert'.

'home-sickness for nursery morality' (p.61).

Tony Last, himself a father, has a room called 'Morgan Le Fay' in which he has slept 'since he left the night nursery' (p.15). Its contents form 'a gallery representative of every phase of his adolescence – the framed picture of a dreadnought (a coloured supplement from *Chums*[16]), all its guns spouting flame and smoke ... (p.16). Like Tony, Alastair Trumpington in *Put Out More Flags* also recalls *Chums*, for to Alastair the war is like an adventure story out of the magazine. Alastair is as 'jealous as a schoolboy' of Peter Pastmaster's military uniform, which he studies with the 'rapt attention of a small boy' and which reminds him of his own cadet corps service at Eton (pp.44-5). Later he talks to Sonia with great excitement of how the troop he wants to join have 'special knives and tommy-guns and knuckle-dusters' and wear 'rope-soled shoes' (p.217). Sonia indulges Alastair in his fantasies just as Molly Meadowes sees Peter Pastmaster, who is thinking of marrying her for dynastic reasons, as 'an adorable little boy'. She has, at first, been bored stiff by him going on about the 'good old days', but when he is unsure about how to handle the drunken Mrs Lyne, she changes her mind about him: 'You looked like a little boy at his private school when his father has come to the sports in the wrong kind of hat' (p.158). In *Put Out More Flags*, Basil Seal who has a 'rather childish mouth' (*Black Mischief*, p.71) plays childish games with his sister, Barbara, which James Carens sees as 'somehow unwholesome, particularly for a man and woman nearing middle age'.[17] It is indeed unwholesome, for the relationship has very definite incestuous overtones. Guy Crouchback also harks back to his childhood. When the Brigadier tells them that tomorrow they will meet the men that they will 'lead in battle', it is a phrase that sets 'swinging' for Guy 'all the chimes of his boyhood's reading' (p.165).

On the whole the heroines seem to have no childhood memories worth recalling. Virginia Troy has found for herself a place in the world of 'coolness, light and peace', whatever trouble she may cause other people: 'She had found that place for herself, calmly recoiling from a disorderly childhood and dismissing it from her thoughts' (*Unconditional Surrender*, p.75). It's hardly surprising that she should do so, for Virginia is a woman who does not indulge much in 'reminiscence or speculation' and time passes without her giving a thought to such matters as her seduction by a friend of her father's who 'had looked her up, looked her over, taken her out, taken her in, from her finishing school in Paris' (*Officers and Gentlemen*, p.77). Virginia's childhood would appear to have been rather an unsavoury one. Interestingly, in *Unconditional Surrender* Virginia also acts as a nurse to Guy 'adapting her endearments to his crippled condition', and when Guy leaves the flat he feels 'as though he were leaving a hospital where he had been skilfully treated' (p.196).

Brenda Last's childhood is never referred to; and Brenda is most uneasy when it comes to playing childish games. Christmas at Hetton is torture for Brenda because Tony and his relatives indulge in charades, and she worries

---

[16] Waugh wrote: 'I was equally and uncritically entranced by the pages of *Chums* ...' *A Little Learning*, p.60. In this section of the book he also recalls all his childhood hobbies – and they all correspond to those of his heroes.

[17] James F. Carens, *The Satiric Art of Evelyn Waugh* (1966), p.40.

that 'any lack of gusto on her part might be construed by the poor Lasts as superiority' (p.61). Brenda, however, like Sonia Trumpington and Mary Meadowes, treats her men as though they were boys. When Tony tries to talk to her about her economics course, she says, 'Now run and put on your coat. They'll all be downstairs waiting for us' (p.80). And John Beaver says, 'You talk to me as if I was an undergraduate having his first walk-out' (p.47).

Aimée in *The Loved One* has no childish memories, but one of her suitors, Mr Joyboy, is tied to his mother's apron strings. In Aimée's hour of need, Mr Joyboy won't leave his mother because her new bird is arriving: 'Why, honey-baby, I couldn't leave Mom the very evening her new bird arrived, could I? How would she feel? It's a big evening for Mom, honey-baby. I have to be here with her' (p.113). Dennis Barlow, when he leaves the Megalopolitan studios for the Happier Hunting Ground, finds that there 'the scars of adolescence healed' and he experiences 'a tranquil joy such as he had known only once before, one glorious early Eastertide when, honourably lamed in a house-match, he had laid in bed and heard below the sanatorium windows the school marching out for a field-day' (p.23). When Dennis asks Aimée whether she was interested in her kind of work as a child, she sidesteps the question and says she has always been artistic.

Kätchen's childhood was obviously not a happy one, with both her parents leaving her, and she obviously misses what she never had, for she happily joins in a game with William of pretending to row the canoe in his room. Kätchen, too, treats her pseudo-husband as a child. She fondly broods over the German saying such things as 'Is he not thin?' and 'How he snores. That is a good sign. Whenever he is well he snores like this ... But he is dirty' (p.161). A mother's attitude rather than a wife's reaction.

Margot Beste-Chetwynde only remembers her younger years with impatience as she thinks how hideous King's Thursday is and remembers how as a 'romantic young heiress' she had walked 'entranced among the cut yews, and had been wooed, how phlegmatically, in the odour of honeysuckle' (p.118). Margot does not recall her childhood years at all. Paul Pennyfeather, on the other hand, spends four weeks of his life in solitary confinement in prison, which are among the happiest weeks he has known, and he puts it down to the fact that 'anyone who has been to an English public school will always feel comparatively at home in prison' (p.188). What Paul is actually experiencing, and enjoying, is a return to the order and discipline of the nursery.

Adam Fenwick-Symes in *Vile Bodies* never refers to his childhood, but he is, interestingly enough, given a past, because when he takes Ginger's place at Doubting Hall with Nina at Christmas the villagers regale him with tales of his childhood, that is Ginger's childhood, which consist mainly of 'acts of destruction and cruelty to cats'. Nina only ever refers to her childhood in connection with the fact that she used to play with Ginger as a child, although Adam does see a cabinet in Colonel Blount's library which contains 'the relics of Nina's various collecting fevers – some butterflies and a beetle or two, some fossils and some birds' eggs and a few postage stamps' (p.72). The collection is far more reminiscent of a boy's collection than a girl's ... as is

Priscilla's collection in *Scoop*. Priscilla has a 'homely, girlish room' and little is done, apart from removing her loofah and nightdress, 'to adapt it for male occupation'. Priscilla collects china animals along with 'slots of deer, brushes of foxes, pads of otters, a horse's hoof, and other animal trophies' (p.203). Again, trophies that would be more at home in a boy's room.

Julia Flyte, Helena and Barbara Sothill (who reverts to childish games with Basil) are exceptions to the rule.

Julia Flyte recalls the happiness of her childhood when she is catching up with Charles Ryder on their lives on board the ship ... 'She told me, as though fondly turning the pages of an old nursery-book, of her childhood, and I lived long, sunny days with her in the meadows, with Nanny Hawkins on her camp stool and Cordelia asleep in the pram, slept quiet nights under the dome with the religious pictures fading round the cot as the nightlight burned low and the embers settled in the grate' (*Brideshead Revisited*, p.244).

Helena plays horses, as she did when she was a child, and we are also told that she makes friends with Calpurnia 'in sudden starts and pauses, as if playing with her affections the nursery game of "grandmother's steps"' (p.59).

Waugh's heroines, then, apart from Helena and Julia Flyte, do not recall their childhood in sentimental terms; and even Julia Flyte doesn't talk about the feminine equivalent of *Chums* magazine. Is it, one wonders, because subconsciously Waugh is using his heroines as replacement mother figures ... Virginia mothering Guy, Brenda instructing Tony and John Beaver, Kätchen doting on her German lover ... or is it simply that he doesn't understand that girls have fond memories of their childhood as well? Either way his heroes are more stunted in growth than his heroines. It would seem that, except where the heroines play the role, the nannies play the part of the mother in Waugh's work.

CHAPTER SEVEN

Jungle Rhythms: The Female as Victim

It's the three-eight rhythm. The Gestapo discovered it independently, you know. They used to play it in the cells. It drove the prisoners mad. (*The Ordeal of Gilbert Pinfold*, p.46)

There are many veins of savagery that run through Evelyn Waugh's work; but what has not been fully appreciated is the recurring theme of music in the novels which anticipates the death or victimisation of the heroines and other female characters. Jungle, jazz and negro rhythms are common, while Indian, oriental and religious music also play a part. Music helps to determine the fate of the following: Agatha Runcible, Fausta, Aimée Thanatogenos, Prudence Courteney, Virginia Troy.

Agatha Runcible

In *Vile Bodies*, although Agatha Runcible[1] is hastened to her death by the sound of music, Waugh marks her down as a victim from the start: she is mistaken for a well-known jewel-smuggler and 'stripped to the skin by two terrific wardresses', which she considers 'too, too shaming'. At Archie Schwert's party, which people have been invited to attend dressed as 'savages', Agatha appears in 'Hawaiian costume' and is described next morning by Sir James Brown, as a 'sort of dancing Hottentot woman half-naked'. Agatha, by tumbling down the steps of the Prime Minister's house in her 'savage' costume, brings down the government, for Sir James gets plenty of adverse criticism from the Press. Meanwhile Flossie Ducane, a friend of Judge Skimp, and a lady of easy virtue, swings from a chandelier in Shepheard's Hotel, falls and later dies. Lottie Crump says that it is not the 'price of the chandelier' that worries her but 'having a death in the house and all the fuss'. The owner of a disreputable hotel, Lottie Crump manages to get a discreet announcement about the death in the papers, while Sir James, a pillar of society, is brought low by Agatha's behaviour. 'Fuss' is an important word in

---

[1] 'Runcible' comes from Edward Lear's *Nonsense Songs* (1871) and was probably used by Waugh because his friend Richard Pares had 'subtle theories about Edward Lear'. See Harold Acton, *Memoirs of an Aesthete* (1948), p.122. In the *Cherwell* 2 February 1924 there was an article by A. Snell, believed to be Pares's pseudonym, 'A Disquisition on the word "Runcible" in Edward Lear', in which there were a number of definitions of the word – one of them being 'liable to crash' and another a woman of 'boisterous or loose manners'. Both were applicable to Agatha. See pp.44, 46.

Agatha's vocabulary as well; when Adam is upset about his book being confiscated and is arguing with the customs men, Agatha simply says, 'Adam, angel, don't fuss or we shall miss the train.' Agatha has no thought for anyone else and is thoroughly disreputable. As Waugh said of his heroine (he obviously thought of Agatha and not Nina as the heroine of *Vile Bodies*): 'She was a young lady of crazy and rather dissolute habits. No one, I should have thought, would see herself in that character without shame. But nearly all the young women of my acquaintance, and many whom I have not had the delight of meeting, claim with apparent gratitude and pride that they were the originals of that sordid character.'[2]

Stephen Marcus has said of Waugh that 'nothing is more patent than that he loved the Hon. Agatha Runcible who disappeared in the company of a racing car and ended in drunken delirium in a nursing home, or that he loved Lady Metroland, proprietress of an international chain of brothels ...'[3] Waugh certainly liked Margot Metroland, and it is obvious in the dashing style and panache he bestows on her, but Agatha is another matter. Seeing her as a 'sordid character' does suggest that Waugh did have a moral message to convey in *Vile Bodies*, for Agatha has no redeeming characteristics and, consequently, is not allowed to live.

Her death is first hinted at when she says to Adam, 'I've been awake all night killing bugs with drops of face lotion, and everything smells, and I feel so low I could die' (p.157). Later, having been warned against smoking in the pits at the race course, she throws her cigarette over her shoulder and it lands, luckily, in one of the water rather than the petrol tanks – 'Had it fallen into the petrol it would probably have been all up with Miss Runcible' (p.166). Having been careless enough to wave the blue flag that will bring No.13 into the pit, and irresponsible enough not to want to face an angry driver, Agatha retires to the refreshment tent for 'another drink', and the barmaid says, offering them champagne, that 'people often feel queer through watching the cars go by so fast – ladies especially' (p.171). The Italian driver, Marino, throws a spanner into No.13's car and injures the driver, whom Archie, a few sentences later, describes as 'murdered'. Agatha is wearing the brassard of 'Spare Driver' and when asked if she is willing to drive says that she is, but admits that it's 'not *absolutely* safe, Adam. Not if they throw spanners.' As she zooms off in the car she says, 'Goodbye ... goodness, how too stiff-scaring' (p.174). The careless and drunken Agatha crashes into Marino, who has to retire. It looks as though she is about to set a new lap record, but she also is retired, for she is last seen off the race course 'proceeding south on the bye-road, apparently out of control'. The car is eventually found 'piled up on the market cross of a large village about fifteen miles away', and Agatha is

[2] Evelyn Waugh, 'People Who Want to Sue Me', *Essays*, p.73. It was a Bright Young Person, Elizabeth Ponsonby, who inspired the character of Agatha. Harold Acton writes: 'Elizabeth Ponsonby was thinly disguised as Agatha Runcible' (Letter to J. McDonnell, 11 February 1984). Lord Molson says: 'I have always understood that Elizabeth Ponsonby was the original of Agatha Runcible' (7 February 1984); and Lady Mosley writes: 'Yes, Agatha Runcible was Elizabeth Ponsonby' (2 February 1984).

[3] Stephen Marcus, 'Evelyn Waugh and the Art of Entertainment', *Partisan Review* XXIII (Summer, 1956), pp.349-50.

later found at Euston Station, whence she is conveyed to a nursing home and kept in a darkened room.

There is a gramophone under Agatha's bed and it is a key point in the lead-up to Agatha's demise, for Miles arrives with some new records and Agatha moves 'her bandaged limbs under the bedclothes in negro rhythm', while the gramophone plays the 'song which the black man sang at the Café de la Paix' (pp.188-9). In Waugh's terms this suggests that the savages have gathered, and the 'negro rhythm' signals the onset of an unpleasant event.

When Matron arrives on the scene she is appalled and says, 'Whoever heard of cocktails and a gramophone in a concussion case? ... Why, I've known cases die with less' (p.191). (The gramophone is an important clue in Waugh because it always heralds his dislike of something and is generally connected with uncivilised behaviour. In *Brideshead Revisited* when Charles Ryder visits Sebastian in Morocco the things he dislikes about Sebastian's house are 'three things, the gramophone for its noise – it was playing a French record of a jazz band – the stove for its smell, and the young man for his wolfish look' (p.203).[4]

Sean O'Faolain has said that Waugh grants the Bright Young People 'virtues, however foolishly applied, as when he allows them to visit the sick – Miss Runcible – though so boisterously that their kindness helps to polish her off'.[5] But the Bright Young People have no virtues and they are not kind. When Agatha first disappears, Miles is more concerned with his stomach: 'I shall die if I don't eat something soon ... let's leave Agatha until we've had a meal' (p.177). Later, when he learns what has happened to the car, he says: 'I suppose we ought to do something about it ... This is the most miserable day I ever spent ... We must go to this beastly village and look for Agatha', to which Adam replies that he can't leave the Major because he might give his fortune away (p.180). When they hear at the railway station that Agatha felt 'odd' but had got a ticket to London, they heave a sigh of relief and go and have a good meal. They learn that Agatha is in the nursing home but don't go and visit her until ten days later. They are warned that she must have no kind of excitement as she has had a 'severe shock', but that doesn't prevent them from feeding her cocktails and playing music. They are thoroughly irresponsible.

Rose Macaulay has made the interesting observation that Agatha 'dies in a nightmare of skidding wheels and crazy speed, crying "*Faster, Faster*". Symbolic but admirable in its reticent realism. Would the later Waugh, the Waugh of *Brideshead*, have been equal to this, or would he have floundered the girl into remorse, bewildered terror of death, change of heart, perhaps introducing Father Rothschild, the priest, into her last hour? There is no such concession here: Agatha dies as she has lived, in a hectic spin.'[6]

The ending, as Rose Macaulay says, is 'admirable', but, although not overt as in *Brideshead*, there is a strongly religious theme in *Vile Bodies* which is

---

[4] The young man is the uncivilised German, Kurt, who plays the music so loudly that Ryder has to shout to make himself heard above the 'dance music'.

[5] Sean O'Faolain, *The Vanishing Hero: Studies in Novelists of the Twenties* (1956), p.53.

[6] Rose Macaulay, 'Evelyn Waugh', *Horizon*, 14 December 1946, p.364.

never allowed to develop. Agatha is quite aware that she and her friends cannot get off the track that they are on:

'How people are disappearing, Adam ... D'you know, all that time when I was dotty I had the most awful dreams. I thought we were all driving round and round in a motor race and none of us could stop, and there was an enormous audience composed of gossip writers and gate crashers and Archie Schwert and people like that, all shouting at us at once to go faster, and car after car kept crashing until I was left all alone driving and driving – and then I used to crash and wake up.' (pp.188-9)

The Bright Young People are doomed and seem to have no hope of salvation because they do not recognise religion when they see it. Agatha first explains that someone had left 'an enormous stone spanner in the middle of the road'. Later she explains that her motor-car would not stop – a spanner had been thrown at her and that 'there had been a stone thing in the way. They shouldn't put up symbols like that in the middle of the road, should they, or should they?' (p.182). The market cross is seen as a symbolic cross by Agatha, but Waugh never develops the religious theme, and Agatha's question about religion is, consequently, never answered. Religious values are brought into question purely for comic effect, as can be clearly seen with the film that the Wonderfilm Company make of the life of John Wesley – 'the most important All-Talkie super-religious film to be produced solely in this country by British artists and management and by British capital' (p.144).

Comic effect is also achieved by the other religious characters in the novel. Father Rothschild is incongruous as the Jesuit priest, and although he analyses the problems of the Bright Young People his religion can offer no solution to their problems; and Mrs Melrose Ape, the 'magnetic' American revivalist, with her tawdry band of travelling angels, offers bogus religion for a price and leaves the country as soon as there is a hint of trouble.

The savagery of Mrs Ape is first highlighted by her arrival at the ship in a 'travel-worn Packard car, bearing the dust of three continents, against the darkening sky' (p.9). Darkness in Waugh, as in Conrad, is most often associated with some primitive idea. The weather is bad and rough seas are promised, so Mrs Melrose Ape tells her 'angels' that if they have 'peace' in their hearts their stomachs will look after themselves and 'Remember, if you *do* feel queer – *sing*. There's nothing like it.' Meanwhile Waugh notes of the other 'prominent people' who are embarking that 'to avert the terrors of sea-sickness they had indulged in every kind of civilised witchcraft but they were lacking in faith' (p.11). While the ship pitches and rolls, the voices of Mrs Ape's angels are heard singing wildly 'as though their hearts would break in the effort ... Mrs Ape's famous hymn, There ain't no flies on the Lamb of God' (p.16). A most appropriate hymn for Mrs Ape, as there are no flies on her at all. While the angels sing, Mrs Ape goes to the smoking room, where Adam and a 'miserable little collection of men' are feeling sea-sick, and leads them in a hymn saying:

'You'll feel better for it body *and* soul. It's a song of Hope. You don't hear much about Hope these days, do you? Plenty about Faith, plenty about Charity. They've forgotten all about Hope. There's only one great evil in the world to-day. Despair. I know all about England, and I tell you straight, boys, I've got the goods for you. Hope's what you want and Hope's what I got.' (p.20)

Mrs Ape would of course sell anything, but other people's reactions to her singing show just how little religion is available to the country at large, not just to the Bright Young People. Father Rothschild turns 'his face to the wall' on hearing it; Mrs Blackwater thinks that a 'hymn' must mean that they are possibly in 'danger'; the Captain says he 'never could stand for missionaries'; Agatha thinks that it is 'so like one's first parties ... being sick with other people singing'; Mrs Hoop thinks that she might give 'the Catholics the once over'; the angel, Divine Discontent, says 'her again'; and Mr Outrage hears nothing, for his mind is filled with dreams of the 'cooing voices' of the Orient.

When the ship comes into Dover, Mrs Ape takes round the hat, for, as she points out, 'salvation doesn't do them the same good if they think it's free' (p.22). Mrs Ape is to make her '*debut*' at Lady Metroland's house, which Chastity describes in a world-weary way as 'nothing to make a song and dance about'. The Bright Young People arrive like a 'litter of pigs', and Lady Metroland tells Chastity that she is 'far too pretty a girl' to waste her time 'singing hymns' and offers her a job in South America. Mrs Ape looks 'like a *procureuse*' in Lady Throbbing's eyes but, as she says, 'perhaps I shouldn't say that *here*, should I?' (p.99).

Mrs Melrose Ape fails because of Lady Circumference's interruption, but Simon Balcairn does not realise that, as he has left the room beforehand when there had been an air of unease. Before he puts his head in the gas oven he telephones his paper and dictates a pack of lies about what happened: '*Scenes of wild religious enthusiasm ... reminiscent of a negro camp-meeting in Southern America ... broke out in the heart of Mayfair yesterday ... The Hon. Agatha Runcible joined Mrs Ape among the orchids and led the singing, tears coursing down her face ...*' (pp.104-5).

Simon Balcairn's 'swan-song' causes more than 'sixty-two writs' for libel, as both the older and the younger generation have been mentioned in his column as having aired their various sins; but, of course, this baring of the breast is all lies and in Agatha's case the clue is in the quotation that Waugh uses at the beginning of *Vile Bodies*:

> 'If I wasn't real,' Alice said – half laughing through her tears, it all seemed so ridiculous – 'I shouldn't be able to cry.'
> 'I hope you don't suppose those are real tears?' Tweedledum interrupted in a tone of great contempt. (*Through the Looking-Glass*)

Agatha's tears are not 'real', but Mrs Melrose Ape, in her normal manner, takes advantage of the situation by giving an interview to the Press in which she confirms Balcairn's story. She also gets her Press agent to send the account to 'all parts of the world' and leaves with her angels (apart from Chastity and Divine Discontent who have gone to work for Lady Metroland) to 'ginger up the religious life of Oberammergau' (p.109). Mrs Melrose Ape is first introduced in the book as a 'very dangerous woman'; and for this reason there is a flaw in Waugh's plot because, after her initial introduction, and the fact of her being put in her place by Lady Circumference, nothing else happens. The change of tone in the novel mentioned by Waugh could be the reason; certainly it seems at the beginning as though she is going to control the destiny of the people in the novel, but, in fact, she peters out.

The experiences of the Bright Young People are 'too shaming' and 'too, too sick-making'. Their lives are futile, and it is Chastity, a 'woebegone fragment of womanhood', who has returned from South America because of the war, who sums up that futility in her monologue, ending the list of her sorry activities with 'There didn't seem anyone anywhere … *My* isn't war awful?' (p.224).

Waugh said in 'The War and the Younger Generation': 'There was nothing left for the younger generation to rebel against, except the widest conceptions of mere decency. Accordingly it was against these that it turned. The result in many cases is the perverse and aimless dissipation chronicled daily by the gossip-writers of the Press.'[7] But he also wrote that 'a small group of young men and women are breaking away from their generation and striving to regain the sense of values that should have been instinctive to them'.[8] One of that group was obviously Waugh himself.

Fausta

In *Helena* King Coel always has dirges sung at his feasts; his favourite piece is 'the lament of his ancestors'. Helena withdraws from the 'death song of her ancestors' and from the 'catalogue of mortality' of brutal deaths to indulge her horsey fantasies. At her wedding the royal bards sing the 'epithalamium' – the nuptial ode that has been handed down from father to son; and when she and Constantius retire for the night the music can still be heard. Revellers with torches make their way round the marriage house singing, and Helena wants her husband to come to the window and join her in watching the minstrels. But Constantius does not join her and Helena stands alone while the song come to its end, and the 'torches dwindle in the darkness, glimmer and expire' and the voices 'die to a murmur and fall at last quite silent'. Helena and Constantius are worlds apart, and the fact that Helena listens to the music alone seems to signal her future loneliness in her marriage to Constantius.

Constantius and Constantine, his son, both sing hymns but for the wrong reasons. Constantius is initiated into the pagan cult of Mithras; and according to Calpurnia, when Helena asks her what they do, 'they dress up. Men love that. And they act sort of plays to each other and sing hymns and have the usual sacrifices, you know' (p.66). Constantine, when he is Emperor, has prayers, a practice that he has 'just instituted'. Amid 'clouds of incense' he is led to the lectern where, after psalm singing, he gives a sermon in 'a special tone of voice which he had lately grown for the occasion' (p.109).

---

[7] Evelyn Waugh, 'The War and the Younger Generation', *Essays*, p.62.
[8] Ibid., p.63.

Both Constantine and Fausta believe in witchcraft and they interview two new witches who have been sent from Egypt, both of whom are black. Fausta, hoping to get rid of Helena, as she has got rid of nearly everyone else, produces the witches for their last performance. The young witch is thrown into a trance by the older one and, after a while, starts 'rhythmically' to sway and thump. Unknown to the three people watching, 'music ... was sounding in the girl's heart, drumming from beyond the pyramids, wailing in the bistro where the jazz disc spun' (p.116). The girl, in 'soft tones, rhythmical as the beat of the tom-toms, sweet and low like a love song', prophesies what Fausta wants her to – the guile of Helena and her possible betrayal of Constantine; and she does it by singing a primitive chant about a chief (based on Napoleon[9]) who has been duped by Helena, and the last verse goes:

Gazing on the ocean, all alone
Saddest chief that ever was known
Nothing but the ocean for mile on mile.
Played for a sucker by British guile,
Tied up tight in durance vile
And left there to rot on Helena's isle.
Ave atque vale! Heil!

The song, however, does not cause Helena's death at Constantine's hands but the death of Fausta, for Constantine recognises what his wife is up to, and will not condone having his mother murdered as his son and friends have been. He realises that the 'guile' is not Helena's, but Fausta's. Fausta, unaware of this, and after making sure, as she thinks, that Constantine has understood the implication of the chant, goes to take her bath ... that bath of which she is so proud, and of which she has previously said 'I could die there quite happily' (p.97).

Ironically Fausta reflects in her bath that 'unprompted' and 'unrehearsed' the 'little negress ... had said the one thing that was so precisely needed'. To Fausta it seems like a miracle, but as she reflects she realises that the bathroom 'was definitely getting too hot ... really getting unpleasantly, intolerably hot'. She rings the bell, but nobody comes and the blood drums in her ears 'the witch's rhythm *The World was her baby but baby got sore*' (p.118).

Fausta, who glitters and pouts 'like a great gold-fish' and has 'terrible fish-eyes' and is 'as cool as a fish', dies sliding and floundering until she finally lies still, 'like a fish on a slab'; and later we learn that there is nothing left of her – 'She had passed with a winking of gold fin and a line of bubbles. Even the two Eusebiuses had struck her name from their prayers' (p.126).

Fausta, an adulteress, who has 'not once been caught in a peccadillo', dies to the sound of jungle rhythms because even for Constantine she has 'gone too far'.

[9] In his 'Notes on Translating Helena' (HRHRC), Waugh wrote: 'These verses, which refer of course to Napoleon, require very careful translation. They are written in the style of the popular songs of the negroes of the British West Indies.' He gave the following definitions: 'chips=gambling counters', 'shake the bonco' (actually written as 'shook the bones')='shake dice'; 'natural'='winning score', 'kitty'= 'total sum of money on table'; 'chop'='food', 'baby'='lover', 'sore'='angry', 'snake's eyes'='bottom score', and 'played for sucker'='duped'.

Virginia Troy

Virginia, of course, dies, and wants to, at the end of *Unconditional Surrender*, but Virginia, rather than being a victim of a falling bomb, is more a victim of the State.

In *Officers and Gentlemen* we learn that for Virginia it has always been not 'age or death' that mattered but 'the present moment and the next five minutes which counted' (p.78); and that is the basis of her meeting with Trimmer in a Glasgow hotel, a meeting which is to change her life. Virginia's availability is, as always, her downfall. The adulteress, sooner or later, has to pay for her sins. 'Gustave ... the guide providentially sent on a gloomy evening to lead her back to the days of sun and sea-spray and wallowing dolphins' is also sent to haunt her with jungle rhythms.

For Virginia 'certain things which had been natural' in Glasgow in the fog in November have 'no existence' in the spring in London; but for Trimmer, Virginia is a 'hallowed memory'. Trimmer is made a national hero as a result of Ian Kilbannock's press release about the successful raid on the French railway (which Trimmer had nothing to do with) and his picture is cut out of the paper by Miss Vavasour and framed, while Virginia is not in the least affected by the news. The 'Demon Barber', as Trimmer comes to be called, 'utterly nauseates' her.

Trimmer, however, can only think of Virginia in terms of crooning 'Night and day ... you are the one ... Only you beneath the moon and under the sun ...' (p.212). Ian Kilbannock is told by Virginia, when he says that Trimmer keeps chanting 'You, you, you', to tell him to 'go to hell'. Unfortunately for Virginia, whom Trimmer describes to the American press as unforgettable – 'There was something about her as well, you know how it is – like music' – Ian realises that something has happened between the two of them; and while he tells her that he has just left Trimmer 'humming horribly' he is working out how he can save Trimmer, for all Trimmer's 'bounce' has gone and he is saddened because of Virginia's lack of interest in him. Ian, who is worried about his 'name', tries to blackmail Virginia – 'As the victim remarked, it's you, you, you. Do I have to remind you that you came to me with tears and made my home life hideous until I got you this job? I expect a little loyalty in return' (p.219).

Virginia is appalled and says that she only left her canteen job to go and work for Ian to be sure of getting away from Trimmer. Ian doesn't understand why, if Glasgow was 'fun', Virginia will not co-operate with him. He tells her that Trimmer now 'thinks he's in love', to which she replies: 'Yes, it's too indecent' (p.219). This inversion of morality is something that Virginia pays for dearly, for with little money or friends to support her she finally has to give way to Kilbannock's demands. On Guy Crouchback's return to England he is told by Kilbannock that he has 'sent poor Virginia to put some ginger' into Trimmer because he was pining, and 'now things are humming again – except for Virginia, of course. She was as sick as mud at having to go –Scunthorpe, Hull, Huddersfield, Halifax ...' (p.248).

'Poor Virginia' gets even poorer in *Unconditional Surrender*; she becomes poorer financially, and poor in the sense of being pitied when she realises that she is with child by the 'Demon Barber'. Trimmer is being sent to the States, without Virginia, as the BBC don't want to renew the 'Voice of Trimmer' programme; but Virginia, who really feels that she has 'done two years' with Trimmer, does not escape his voice so easily. Until she met Trimmer, Virginia had enjoyed a '*douceur de vivre* that was alien to her epoch; seeking nothing, accepting what came and enjoying it without compunction' (p.75). After Trimmer, darkness creeps into her life.

Virginia wants an abortion,[10] and her introduction from Kerstie Kilbannock's charwoman, Mrs Bristow, is to a Dr Akonanga in Blight Street, an apt address in Waugh's terms for an abortionist if one thinks of a blight as something that mars or prevents growth. She learns, however, that the doctor has moved to Brook Street (Brook Street being the 'respectable address' of an abortionist which Dr Puttock had given her earlier but which she had been unable to find). The woman at the address tells her that Dr Akonanga has 'gone up in the world' and is doing 'work of national importance. He's a clever one, black as he may be. What it is, there's things them blacks know what them don't that's civilised' (p.82). When Virginia arrives in Brook Street the following happens:

> From high overhead at the top of the wide staircase came sounds which could only be the beat of a tom-tom. Virginia climbed towards it thinking of Trimmer who had endlessly, unendurably crooned 'Night and Day' to her. The beat of the drum seemed to be saying: 'You, you, you.' She reached the door behind which issued the jungle rhythm. It seemed otiose to add the feeble tap of her knuckles. She tried the handle and found herself locked out. There was a bell with the doctor's name above it. She pressed. The drumming stopped. A key turned. Virginia was greeted by a small, smiling, nattily dressed Negro, not in his first youth; there was grey in his sparse little tangle of beard; he was wrinkled and simian and what should have been the whites of his eyes were the colour of Trimmer's cigarette-stained fingers; from behind him there came a faint air blended of spices and putrefacation. His smile revealed many gold-capped teeth. (pp.82-3)

Trimmer's barbarism is completely connected in Virginia's mind with Dr Akonanga, for the decapitated, sacrificial fowl that she sees pinned down on his table, waiting for him to perform his witchcraft, is the equivalent of Virginia being pinned down sexually by Trimmer and being sacrificed for, and by, the nation. She explains to the doctor with her 'high incorrigible candour' that she is one of those women 'who wants to get rid of babies', but she is unsuccessful in her demand for an abortion because the doctor only committed such barbarous crimes, as Waugh would have seen it, in peace-time; in war-time he is working for the 'government' and 'democracy'; and more important than helping Virginia is his job of giving 'Herr von

---

[10] Waugh wrote of Ann Fleming: 'She gave me some particulars about abortion in wartime for my next volume.' *Diaries*, p.736.

Ribbentrop the most terrible dreams' (p.84). What those dreams were planned to be Virginia doesn't know, but what she does know is that she dreams that 'she was extended on a table, pinioned, headless and covered with blood-streaked feathers, while a voice within her, from the womb itself, kept repeating: "You, you, you" ' (p.84).

Abortion being impossible, Ian and Kerstie Kilbannock try to think of whom Virginia could marry. Guy is suggested by Ian, but Kerstie thinks it a disgusting idea, so she suggests Trimmer. Ian, however, points out that Virginia hates him because he 'fell in love with her' and that 'was what sickened her'. He explains:

> 'He used to sing "Night and Day" about her, to *me*. "Like the beat, beat, beat of the tom-tom, when the jungle shadows fall." It was excruciating.' (p.89)

When Virginia decides that she must remarry Guy she admits to him that the rumours he heard about herself and Trimmer were true, and she shudders at the memory – 'The things that happen to one' (p.130). Trimmer's baby grows in Virginia's womb 'without her conscious collaboration'; and when she becomes a Catholic and confesses 'half a lifetime's mischief' in 'less than five minutes' she kneels to pronounce the 'required penance', and as she does so 'Little Trimmer' stirs in her womb.

When Virginia dies, mass is said for her and Guy constantly remembers her in his prayers. There is a sense that, by converting to Catholicism, Virginia washes away the savagery that has been connected with Trimmer and escapes from the beating of the tom-tom and finds peace. Trimmer, though, disappears and is suspected of jumping ship in 'South Africa'. The jungle rhythms have been silenced for Virginia but not for him.

What is interesting about Trimmer's situation is that it is so different from Hooper's in *Brideshead Revisited*. Both are common men and Waugh has a contempt for their mediocrity which he believes to be characteristic of their class. He sees them as both vulgar and stupid and as representative of the ignorant masses who will destroy the beauty and refinement of civilised life; the life of the aristocracy. *Brideshead* was published in 1945 and *Unconditional Surrender* in 1961. However, in 1960, in the preface to the new edition of *Brideshead*, Waugh wrote that 'the English aristocracy has maintained its identity to a degree that then seemed impossible. The advance of Hooper has been held up at several points.' So, whereas Hooper in Brideshead survives the war to become one of the demanding masses, Trimmer is made a national hero but is dispensed with when he is no longer needed; and what better place to have the barbarian jump ship than South Africa, where he is bound to survive.

Aimée Thanatogenos

When Dennis Barlow first visits Whispering Glades he is aware, in the gardens, of the subdued notes of the 'Hindu Love-Song'. When he enters the door marked 'Inquiries' the same song welcomes him; and when the 'Mortuary Hostess' takes him through a 'soft passage' into a 'chintzy parlour' the song comes to an end and is 'succeeded by the voice of a nightingale'. On his way to the 'Slumber Room' the nightingale is silenced and gives way to the organ and 'strains of Handel'.

Dennis hesitates with his hand on the door of the 'Slumber Room', for he is aware of communication with someone beyond the door. That someone is Aimée, and their meeting is symbolic, for when the doors open and Aimée stands there, the 'low voices of a choir discoursing sacred music' can be heard, and at the moment of their meeting 'a treble voice' of 'poignant sweetness' is heard to break out with 'Oh for the Wings of a Dove' (p.60). The line comes from Psalm 55, line 10 – 'Oh that I had wings like a dove for then would I fly away and be at rest' – which is exactly what Aimée does by the end of *The Loved One*.

Aimée's preparations for her meeting with Mr Joyboy are 'the prescribed rites of an American girl'. She uses a deodorant, a mouthwash, and finally brushes some perfume into her hair. That perfume hints at what is to come, for it is called 'Jungle Venom' and, although Aimée hears no music, the advertising copy of the product states that '*from the depth of the fever-ridden swamp ... where juju drums throb for the human sacrifice, Jeanette's latest exclusive creation JUNGLE VENOM comes to you with the remorseless stealth of the hunting cannibal*' (p.88).

The evening is not a success, and Aimée, when she gets home, immediately writes to the Guru Brahmin and the writing-paper smells of 'Jungle Venom'. Mr Slump is quite right in his observation of Aimée that she is a 'prize bitch', for the venomous tone of her letter denigrating Mr Joyboy for helping his mother in the house and looking undignified in his apron does show that she cannot distinguish between 'glamour and worth'. Mr Joyboy, when he was thought to be a financial success, was a better proposition that Dennis Barlow; but once Aimée comes up against the drab reality of the unromantic and unglamorous life that he leads with his mother and her parrot, her attraction to Dennis reasserts itself. When she learns that Dennis has deceived her, she knows that there is only one choice open to her – and that is Mr Joyboy; the 'voluptuous tempting tones of "Jungle Venom" were silenced' (p.106).

When Dennis won't release her from her vow Aimée returns to her apartment, where she falls 'victim to all the devils of doubt'. Switching on the radio, 'a mindless storm of Teutonic passion possessed her and drove her to the cliff-edge of frenzy' (p.112). The music is interrupted by a commercial for 'Kaiser's Stoneless Peaches', during which time Aimée calls Mr Joyboy, hoping that he will come over and advise her. She can hardly hear him for the 'babel, human and inhuman' that is coming over the telephone caused by Mrs Joyboy trying to teach her new parrot to talk. Mr Joyboy, not the parrot, has the inhuman quality here, for although he keeps calling Aimée his 'honey-baby' (seven times within half a page of dialogue) he will not leave his mother. The 'big evening for Mom' with her new parrot is more important than any questions Aimée wishes to discuss in connection with their marriage. Even Aimée's impassioned 'I must see you' gets the reply 'Now, honey-baby, I'm going to be firm with you. Just you do what Poppa says this minute or Poppa will be real mad at you' (p.113). Aimée again resorts to 'grand opera', but she is 'swept up and stupefied in the gust of sound'. It is too much for her, and her brain only starts working again when there is silence – at which point she calls the Guru Brahmin and is told to 'take a high jump'. Finally, her mind 'free from anxiety' and prompted by 'attic voices' to a 'higher destiny', Aimée takes her own life in Mr Joyboy's silent workroom.

Prudence Courteney

Vernacular hymns in the tin-roofed missions, ancient liturgy in the murky Nestorian sanctuaries; tonsure and turban, hand drums and innumerable jingling bells of debased silver. And beyond the hills on the low Wanda coast where no liners called and the jungle stretched unbroken to the sea, other more ancient rites and another knowledge furtively encompassed; green, sunless paths; forbidden ways unguarded save for a wisp of grass plaited between two stumps, ways of death and initiation, the forbidden places of juju and the masked dancers; the drums of the Wanda throbbing in sunless, forbidden places. (*Black Mischief*, p.117)

Prudence sits writing her 'Panorama of Life' in her Legation home, with its English-style garden which is being cultivated by Lady Courteney, unaware of the real life that is going on all around her. A life where Seth's father, Seyid, is eaten by the Wanda; where Seth himself is poisoned; where Mr Youkoumian ill-treats his wife; where General Connolly thumps Black Bitch[11] on the head and locks her in a cupboard; and where the boots ordered for the army by Basil Seal are eaten at a special feast – 'hand drums beating; bare feet shuffling unforgotten tribal rhythms'.

White or black – both races feel the lash of Waugh's scorn, for each is as bad as the other. Seth with his childlike attitude to modernising everything possible and his acceptance of the fact that his father has been eaten – his main concern then being that 'as yet the Wanda are totally out of touch with modern thought ... We might start them on Montessori methods' is no worse, perhaps better, than Dame Mildred Porch and Miss Sarah Tin[12] who have come to investigate the conditions in Azania as far as cruelty to animals

[11] General Connolly's name was based on that of Cyril Connolly. 'Jean Connolly was dark, and by an inimical blond-preferrer could conceivably be hideously described as "Black Bitch".' Sykes, p.173. Cyril Connolly wrote of his wife: 'I have really enjoyed nothing except sleeping with my negress again'; and Virginia Woolf described the couple as 'baboon Connolly' and 'his gollywog slug wife Jean' and also as 'a less appetising pair I have never seen out of the Zoo, and the apes are considerably preferable to Cyril. She has the face of a gollywog and they brought the reek of Chelsea with them'. See *Cyril Connolly: Journal and Memoir*, edited by David Pryce-Jones (1983), pp.196, 255 n.2.

[12] Dame Mildred Porch and Miss Sarah Tin were based on the two ladies whom Waugh met in Addis Ababa: 'Two formidable ladies in knitted suits and topees; although unrelated by blood, long companionship had made them almost indistinguishable, square-jawed, tight-lipped, with hard, discontented eyes. For them the whole coronation was a profound disappointment. What did it matter that they were witnesses of a unique stage of the interpenetration of two cultures? They were out for Vice ... Prostitution and drug traffic comprised their modest interests, and they were too dense to find evidence of either.' *Remote People* (Duckworth, 1931), p.44.

is concerned and who are blind to the human suffering surrounding them. They do not wear 'smoked spectacles' for nothing.

Against this background Prudence starts her affair with Basil, and what an uncivilised affair. Sordid and furtive, it is conducted in Basil's room which is above Mr Youkoumian's store. The 'rank smell of tobacco smoke' pervades the place; the butt of Basil's cigar floats, a soggy mess, in the tin hip-bath into which he has thrown it; and Basil himself is unshaven. The room is very little different from Sonia's and Alastair Trumpington's in London, which is not fouled by smoke but by dogs – 'Oh God, he's made a mess again' – and even Basil comments 'How dirty the bed is, Sonia'[13] (p.78). Other girls in London take a delight in Basil's appearance – 'It's nice him being so dirty' (p.70). Life is as uncivilised in London as it is in Azania.

When the time comes for Prudence to leave by aeroplane for London she reflects that she 'ought to get some new ideas for the *Panorama*', for sexually she has used up both William and Basil. A.E. Dyson has said that Waugh shows tenderness in his final picture of Prudence's reflections as she sets out for home.[14] This seems a strange opinion, for Waugh shows up Prudence's superficiality in his cynical account of the life she expects to lead as part of her 'natural heritage'. Prudence has not learnt anything in Azania, apart from a few sexual tricks, and her one desire is to show off to the friends who were at school with her because they will seem 'so young and innocent'.

The not-so-innocent Prudence is to have her last experience not among the savages in London, but among the savages in Azania; and Basil is partly to blame, for when escorting Seth's body to Moshu he sends a message ahead to the Chief, saying: 'Assemble your people, kill your best meat and prepare a feast in the manner of your people' (p.226). Prudence, their captive since her plane crashed, is obviously their best and most delicate meat, and Basil, without realising it, signs her death warrant. Conducted by 'music' to Moshu, Basil attends Seth's funeral. The tribesmen join in the 'dance of the witches'; there is chanting and the 'hand-drums' throb and pulse; and Basil draws 'back a little from the heat of the fire, his senses dazed by the crude spirit and the insistence of the music', which for the natives becomes an orgiastic experience. And finally, when he learns that he and the 'big chiefs' have eaten Prudence, it is against the background of circling dancers, 'ochre and blood and sweat glistening in the firelight' and 'tireless hands drumming out the rhythm' (p.230).

The cannibalism in *Black Mischief* was thought to be distasteful (the pun is intended) by some critics (see above, pp. 113-14); but the eating of

---

[13] Wanda Baillie-Hamilton, along with Tallulah Bankhead, inspired the character of Sonia Trumpington (see *Diaries*, p.794). Her name could also have inspired that of the 'Wanda' in *Black Mischief*, for in Waugh's terms she was rather a savage, and was treated savagely. She threw a bun at the Mayor in her husband's constituency after which he abandoned his political career; and Randolph Churchill once threw a cocktail in her face (ibid., p.315). The mess that Sonia's dog makes could have had its origin in Waugh's comment after taking tea with Olivia Plunket Greene: 'The house was very much disorganized by her bitch's parturition' (ibid., p.311).

[14] A.E. Dyson, 'Evelyn Waugh and the Mysteriously Disappearing Hero', *Critical Quarterly* 2 (Spring, 1960), p.75.

Prudence is not nearly as cruelly drawn as the episode where Mr Youkoumian offers Basil his wife's place on the train:

> 'Look, you give me hundred and fifty rupees I put Mme Youkoumian with the mules. You don't understand what that will be like. They are the General's mules. Very savage stinking animals. All day they will stamp at her. No air in the truck. 'Orrible, unhealthy place. Very like she die or is kicked. She is good wife, work 'ard, very loving. If you are not Englishmans I would not put Mme Youkoumian with the mules for less than five hundred. I fix it for you, O.K.?'
> 'O.K.,' said Basil. 'You know, you seem to me a good chap.' (p.98).

Youkoumian's barbarity is worse than that of the cannibal tribes of the Wanda. They have eaten human flesh all their lives and can see no wrong in it, whereas Youkoumian must know that it is wrong to suggest that his wife should travel with the mules. All he is concerned about is the amount of money that he can obtain from Basil. He stresses the degree of discomfort for his wife, and what a 'good' and 'loving' wife she is, to make the business proposition more credible. His inhumanity shows itself first in the way that he presumes that she will likely 'die' or be 'kicked' – the word 'die' comes first; and secondly in the fact that he gives her a 'little jar of preserved cherries' to take with her on the journey to compensate her for her change of accommodation ... a gesture that seems to say that Youkoumian recognises that his wife will be displeased by the turn of events; and a gesture that, in fact, makes him even more unsympathetic in our eyes.

What is extremely ironic is that Youkoumian is not dealing with the kind of Englishman who would be shocked by such a proposal. He is dealing with Basil Seal, a man who later terrifies the women at the Legation with stories of 'Sakuyu savagery ... shaved all the hair off her head and covered it with butter. White ants ate straight through into her skull ...' (p.210). When it is suggested to Basil by the Minister that the 'ladies should be kept in ignorance of such facts', Basil's telling reply is 'Oh, I like to see them scared' (p.210). Basil, when approached by Youkoumian, is delighted by his proposal and the irony is that after hearing the catalogue of horrors that could befall the man's wife he responds with 'You know, you seem a good chap to me'. This whole episode is revealing, for Basil and Youkoumian are both entrepreneurs and both are survivors in an uncivilised world, whether it be Azania or England.

*

These, then, have been the major female characters whose death or victimisation have been connected with jungle music. The only heroes whose fates are connected with such music are Tony Last and Gibert Pinfold, Waugh himself.

Tony Last, when he is drugged by Mr Todd[15] so that he will not meet the party who are searching for him, goes to sleep to the Pie-wie Indians' song

---

[15] Mr Todd was based on Mr Christie whom Waugh met on his travels to Boa Vista. See *Diaries*, p.366.

which they sing in an 'apathetic and monotonous manner'; the 'cadence of song rose and fell interminably, liturgically' and as the Pie-wies begin to dance Tony falls asleep thinking of England and Hetton.

(Waugh said of *A Handful of Dust* that 'it grew into a study of other sorts of savage at home and the civilised man's helpless plight among them' and that it 'dealt entirely with behaviour. It was humanist and contained all I had to say about humanism.'[16] Waugh puts over this theme superbly by intercutting Tony's experiences in the jungle with news of what is happening in London, showing that savages exist there as well as in the bush. For example, when Tony and Dr Messinger meet Rosa,[17] a Machushi Indian, and they want to go to Pie-wie Indian country, they are told that the men are out hunting 'bush-pig'. Ironically, at the same time in London Jock Grant-Menzies is pushing a bill through Parliament about the modification of the size of a pig's belly for use in the manufacture of pork pies; and while Tony is having to bribe Rosa with cigarettes so that she will help them with their expedition, Brenda is having to bribe John Beaver with promises of trying to get him into certain exclusive clubs. The savage, Rosa, and Brenda become one in Tony's mind, which is hardly surprising as they both demand things from him. In Brenda's case it is money; in Rosa's it is cigarettes. As Brenda's language is peppered with financial terms, Rosa's is peppered with two phrases – 'You give me cigarette' and 'Give me' which occur eleven times within the few pages of her appearance. Like Brenda, Rosa leaves Tony, but ironically she, and the other Indians, are terrified by the supposedly civilised, musical and mechanical toy mice produced by Dr Messinger as a bribe ... 'a high wail of terror' is heard from the womenfolk. While Tony feels isolated in the jungle, Brenda fares no better in London, for all her friends, if they can be called that, leave her, as it is the summer and they have better things to do – such as her sister, Marjorie, who goes cruising round Spain stopping off for the bull-fights. Savagery abounds at home and abroad.)

Much more interesting is the fate of Mr Pinfold ... for in this autobiographical novel is is the girls, and the Bright Young People generally, who play jungle rhythms to torture Mr Pinfold.

Martin Green has said that Waugh 'seems to have appreciated jazz and black music, at least to begin with ...',[18] and this is absolutely right, for in 1919, at the age of sixteen, he recorded in his diaries that he had been to a dance and there was 'an excellent jazz band'.[19] In 1920 he went to an 'At Home at the Rhys' in the afternoon, where 'one Solomon, an appalling little Jew and great musician, played but did not convey anything to me. It is rather awful to be such a barbarian at music. I miss an awful lot by it. There I was sitting bored to distraction with Stella trembling and swaying in ecstasies.'[20] In 1925 Waugh

[16] Evelyn Waugh, 'Fan-Fare', *Essays*, pp.303-4.

[17] In 1933 on his journey to Boa Vista, Waugh met a 'pretty Indian girl named Rosa'. *Diaries*, p.365.

[18] Martin Green, *Children of the Sun: a Narrative of Decadence in England after 1918* (1977), p.331.

[19] *Diaries*, p.46.

[20] Ibid., p.66. The music would have been classical music as the reference is to Solomon Cutner (his professional name was Solomon) who was recognised for his excellent performances of Beethoven and Brahms.

records seeing Layton and Johnstone at the Alhambra, black American 'duettists' and 'syncopated singers'.[21] In 1926 he goes to the 'Blackbirds' revue where the cast are all 'negroes and negresses'.[22] The clue to Waugh's changing attitude is in the entry of 1927 which reads: 'Olivia could talk of nothing except black men ... We went later to the Blackbirds and called on Florence Mills and other niggers and negresses in their dressing rooms. Then to a night club called Victor's to see another nigger – Leslie Hutchinson.'[23] The next few entries are full of references to the Blackbirds and various parties, of one which Waugh records: 'Olivia and I both felt more than a little lonely.'[24] The tide was turning: in July 1927 Waugh went to 'help Olivia out' with Rudolph Dunbar, a black man who was visiting her, and wrote: 'Noisy gramophone all the time made my head ache.'[25]

By the time he published *The Ordeal of Gilbert Pinfold*, Waugh was ready to write of himself: 'His strongest tastes were negative. He abhorred plastics, Picasso, sunbathing, and jazz – everything in fact that had happened in his own lifetime' (p.14). As far as jazz was concerned one can't help but think that Olivia and her relationship with Paul Robeson, and other black musicians, played its part in Waugh's growing distaste for such music.

The rhythm that is used in *Pinfold* is the 'three-eight rhythm' used by the Pocuputa Indians and picked up by the Germans, Russians and Hungarians to torture people with; and it is this rhythm that makes Mr Pinfold's cabin suddenly turn into a 'prison cell' (p.46). The music is torture for him because he 'was not one who thought and talked easily to a musical accompaniment. Even in early youth he had sought the night-clubs where there was a bar out of hearing of the band'[26] (p.46). While Pinfold's friends need jazz as 'a necessary drug', Pinfold prefers 'silence'.

At first, Pinfold hears someone else being tortured, and the torture seems to be being conducted by the Bright Young People. Their leader is a woman whose harsh voice caused Mr Pinfold 'peculiar pain', 'makes his hair stand on end' and 'sets his teeth on edge' (p.50). For Pinfold the tone of the voice is 'excruciating', and he nicknames the owner of it Goneril.

Against the grating voice of Goneril is placed the 'honey-tongue' of Margaret, the Cordelia of the scene, who seems to be sorry for the victim concerned, and who later in Pinfold's imagination wants to have an affair[27]

[21] *Diaries*, p.199.
[22] Ibid., p.264.
[23] Ibid., p.281.
[24] Ibid., p.282.
[25] Ibid., p.286.
[26] In *Brideshead Revisited*, Anthony Blanche, at a party given for the 'Black Birds' says: 'Let me talk to *you*, Charles', and the two of them find 'a corner in another room' where they can hear themselves speak (p.195).
[27] Margaret could have been lightly based on Waugh's own daughter, Margaret, for whom he had an 'unhealthy affection' (*Letters*, p.423). When she got engaged he wrote to Lady Diana: 'I would forbid the marriage if I had any other cause than jealousy and snobbery. As it is I pretend to be complaisant. Little Meg is ripe for the kind of love I can't give her' (*Letters*, p.593). And Lady Diana said: 'When Margaret got engaged I was terrified of how he'd bear it. He adored this girl. However, thank God, she married a Catholic. He took it very well indeed, very well.' Interview, 16 November 1981.

with him. The victim is tried and found guilty, and Pinfold listens to the punishment that is dealt out, which results in 'the moans and sobs of the victim and the more horrific, ecstatic, orgiastic cries of Goneril' (p.59). The victim dies, but the next morning Pinfold in the bright light of day can hardly credit that it happened, and questions himself as to whether, among other things, it could be a 'charade of the bright young people' (p.61).

As it turns out it is no charade, for in Pinfold's mind his turn is next, and the first hint of trouble is when the BBC Third Programme appears to be giving a talk by Clutton-Cornforth on the hackneyed work of Gilbert Pinfold during which Clutton-Cornforth is interrupted by a female singer who sings a raucous music-hall song about 'Gilbert the filbert, The knut with the K' which disturbs Pinfold and later, when he has gone to bed, it starts up again. The cry is for 'Music. Music' ... and the voices want him out of his cabin so that their owners can whip him. Mr Pinfold does not move. Margaret, who thinks they are being 'rather beastly' to him, tries to soothe him with her sweet singing, but to no avail – Mr Pinfold sits up all night with his stick ready to ward off any intruders.

Mr Pinfold decides that the constant chatter that he hears aboard the *Caliban*[28] accusing him of homosexuality, anti-semitism, fascism, communism and numerous other things is a game devised 'by the passengers in the *Caliban* for their amusement and his discomfort'; and he equates the game with the one that was played by the 'bright, cruel girls' of his youth.

Margaret makes sexual advances, and Mr Pinfold listens to the preparations that are made for her wooing of him – an 'epithalamium' is chanted, and as Mr Pinfold waits in his cabin the 'folk-ritual of Margaret's preparations' fills it with 'music'. Everything is in Mr Pinfold's imagination, so Margaret never comes, and finally, overcome with 'weariness and boredom', he says 'I'm sorry Margaret ... I'm too old to start playing hide and seek with schoolgirls' and he goes to bed (p.118).

By page 121 Mr Pinfold thinks that the Bright Young People have 'gone too far', for on top of their hoaxes they are now reading his messages. He complains to the Captain and arranges to get his cabin changed and at this point Goneril tells him that he's a 'dirty little sneak ... We'll get even with you. Have you forgotten the three-eight rhythm?' (p.125). Mr Pinfold finally determines that 'Angel' the man from the BBC who had interviewed him at Lychpole is the villain of the piece, and his change of cabin seems for a while to disconcert 'Angel and his staff (there were about half a dozen of them, male and female, all young, basically identical with the three-eight orchestra)' (p.128).

Having realised that Mr Pinfold is not getting enough sleep, which is why he's not responding to their treatment, Angel and his friends play records to send him off. The first has been devised by Swiss scientists for 'neurotic industrial workers' and the supposedly 'soporific noises' are those of factory machinery. Understandably he can't sleep ... and tells them that they are

---

[28] *Caliban* was the name of Shakespeare's 'savage and deformed slave' in *The Tempest* and is a word that is now used to describe a 'brutish' or 'brutalized' man.

'bloody fools ... *I'm* not a factory worker' (p.134). Angel sees the sense of this and tells them to 'turn off that record. Give him something rural' and Mr Pinfold is treated to the sound of nightingales for a long time.

Finally Pinfold writes to his wife explaining to her that Angel has a 'Box'[29] which is 'able to speak and to hear ... They are trying to psycho-analyse me ... They first break the patient's nerve by acting all sorts of violent scenes which he thinks are really happening. They confuse him until he doesn't distinguish between natural sounds and those they induce ... Anyway they have had no success with me ... All they have done is to stop my working. So I am leaving them' (pp.136-7).

Mr Pinfold now manages to reverse the situations. The Bright Young People babble on, but he doesn't let it affect him; and what is most ironic is that he finally torments them by reading aloud to them, for it seems that they cannot disconnect their box and have to listen to everything he says. He reads *Westward Ho!* 'very slowly hour by hour', and when they plead with him to stop he torments them 'in his turn by making gibberish of the text, reading alternate lines, alternate words, reading backwards, until they pleaded for a respite. Hour after hour Mr Pinfold remorselessly read on' (p.139). As Tony Last read remorselessly to Brenda, so Pinfold/Waugh reads to Angel and his friends; but whereas Tony does not survive the jungle, Pinfold/Waugh does. The voices are finally silenced. Once home with his wife, and having seen the doctor, he is told that it was all because of the mixture of his prescribed grey pills combined with the bromide and chloral that he was taking without his doctor's knowledge – a 'simple case of poisoning' (p.156).

Waugh said to Frances Donaldson of *The Ordeal of Gilbert Pinfold*:

> It is a great piece of luck for a middle-aged writer to be presented with an entirely new theme.[30]

The theme of his own personal hallucinations was new, but the theme of music in *Pinfold* was, once again, as in the other novels, used to indicate some form of barbarity.

*

There is one other incident in the novels which is connected with music, though not jungle rhythms, which is worth mentioning, and that is where, in *Love Among The Ruins*, Miles visits Clara in the hospital at 'SANTA-CLAUS-TIDE' (p.208). As Clara draws the sheet down to show Miles her new 'inhuman ... tight, slippery mask, salmon pink' of a face, the television by the bedside delivers a song – 'an old forgotten ditty: "O tidings of comfort and joy, comfort and joy, O tidings of comfort and joy" ' (p.214). Miles feels sick

---

[29] Waugh wrote 'Laura was taken by Diana Oldridge to Uley to consult a witch about the health of a cow. This witch not only diagnoses but treats all forms of disease, human and animal, by means of an object called "the Box" – an apparatus like a wireless set, electrified, and fitted with dials.' *Diaries*, p.754.

[30] Frances Donaldson, *Portrait of a Country Neighbour* (1967), p.75.

and has to leave. The carol is, of course, entirely appropriate. There can be no 'comfort and joy' in a world where Clara has just had an abortion to get rid of their child so that she can continue her dancing career; and in Waugh's eyes Clara deserves that 'inhuman' face.

Waugh once said in true Swiftian style to a prospective dinner guest, during war-time, that they would be unable to honour her in their usual style because of rationing – 'But we could boil the baby.'[31] Waugh's indictment of humanity does show a certain affinity with Swift, and Waugh himself said of a book that he had read about Swift in 1965: 'I found many affinities with the temperament (not of course the talent) of the master.'[32] Certainly there are affinities, for the King of Brobdingnag's verdict on Gulliver's fellow-Europeans as 'the most pernicious Race of little odious Vermin that Nature ever suffered to crawl upon the Surface of the Earth' is followed by Waugh in *Black Mischief* with his description of the masked ball where savage and civilised become one:

> Paper hats were resumed: bonnets of liberty, conical dunce's hats, jockey caps, Napoleonic casques, hats for pierrots and harlequins, postmen, highlanders, old Mothers Hubbard and little Misses Muffet over faces of every complexion, brown as boots, chalk white, dun and the fresh boiled pink of Northern Europe. False noses again: brilliant sheaths of pigmented cardboard attached to noses of every anthropological type, the high arch of the Semite, freckled Nordic snouts, broad black nostrils from swamp villages of the mainland, the pulpy inflamed flesh of the alcoholic, and unlovely syphilitic voids. (p.111)

This is not the harsh raging of Swift, but Waugh's revulsion is clearly apparent, as it is in *Remote People*, where in the 'Third Nightmare' he returns to London and dines at a new supper restaurant (p.240):

> I was back in the centre of the Empire, and in the spot where, at the moment, 'everyone' was going. Next day the gossip-writers would chronicle the young M.P.s, peers, and financial magnates who were assembled in that rowdy cellar, hotter than Zanzibar, noisier than the market at Harar, more reckless of the decencies of hospitality than the taverns of Kabalo or Tabora. And a month later the wives of English officials would read about it, and stare out across the bush or jungle or desert or forest or golf links, and envy their sisters at home, and wish they had the money to marry rich men.
> Why go abroad?
> See England first.
> Just watch London knock spots off the Dark Continent.[33]

Waugh constantly compared the civilised world with that of the dark continent and constantly found the civilised world wanting. In *Brideshead Revisited* jungle rhythms do not actually occur, but the parallel of London

[31] Ibid., p.6.
[32] *Letters*, p.634.
[33] Evelyn Waugh, *Remote People* (Duckworth, 1931), p.240.

with the jungle is only too apparent. Anthony Blanche, who has returned from Tangier and meeting Sebastian's 'clod of a German' friend, Kurt, says ' "It was *too* macabre. So back I came, my dear, to good old England – *Good old England.*" he repeated, embracing with a flourish of his hand the Negroes gambling at our feet, Mulcaster staring blankly before him, and our hostess who, in pyjamas, now introduced herself to us' (p.197). The hostess asks them who all the 'white trash' are – a nice inversion; and Mulcaster's girl goes off with a 'black fellow'.

(In *Brideshead Revisited*, the theme of the civilised aristocracy being threatened by such outside forces as the 'primitive savage', Rex Mottram, and the common man, Hooper, is a muddled one, for there is not a clear enough distinction between the attitudes of the aristocracy and the people. The press release given out by Celia Ryder at Charles's viewing states: '*That the snakes and vampires of the jungle have nothing on Mayfair is the opinion of socialite artist Ryder*' (p.254); and Ryder is absolutely right. The vampire is Lady Marchmain, who is described by Anthony Blanche as such when he says that she keeps a 'small gang of enslaved and emaciated prisoners for her exclusive enjoyment. *She sucks their blood* ... They never escape once she's had her teeth into them. It is witchcraft' (p.56). Sebastian describes his mother as a '*femme fatale* ... She killed at a touch' (p.206). And Sebastian's desire, later on, is 'to go to the bush, as faraway as he could get, amongst the simplest people, to the cannibals' (p.290). In Sebastian's mind the cannibals are simple in their outlook; they kill quickly and for a reason, to eat – they do not torture, killing a person slowly, as his mother does.

If Lady Marchmain is a 'savage', so in some ways is Julia, who in the 1945 edition was described as 'renaissance tragedy ... a *fiend* – a passionless, acquisitive, intriguing, ruthless *killer*' (p.49). Robert Murray Davis says that Waugh deleted this passage from the 1960 edition to make Julia 'look less ridiculous in anticipation of her role as Charles's lover'.[34] More probably he deleted it to make Julia seem more civilised in her context of seeing Rex as a 'primitive savage'. Even the portrayal of Cordelia is confused. She is described by Blanche as a girl whose 'governess went mad and drowned herself' (p.54). In fair typescript, Waugh added Cordelia's memory of the drowning in the scene where she stands on the stone bridge at Brideshead looking down into the water with Charles Ryder. When she tells him that her governess drowned there, he tells her that it was the first thing that he had heard about her; to which she replies 'How very odd ...' (p.293). Robert Murray Davis believes that Waugh inserted the memory sequence 'of her governess's suicide to contrast the actual Cordelia with the monster whom Blanche posited'.[35] Waugh should have deleted both references for, apart from Sebastian, it is quite obvious that Cordelia is the only saintly one of the family, and such red herrings only confuse the picture. Against such portraits of Lady Marchmain and Julia, Hooper and Rex Mottram seem relatively harmless.)

[34] Robert Murray Davis, *Evelyn Waugh, Writer* (1981), p.134.
[35] Ibid.

Waugh's dislike of humanity, and his tolerance of humanity, are clearly apparent in his works, but the question must arise whether there is more dislike and less tolerance directed towards the female sex than the male. The heroes of Waugh's novels may be weak and ineffectual, but he never feels the need to exterminate them as he does many of his heroines ... who, on the whole, he portrays as dissolute characters. It would seem that, in the manner of Juvenal and Swift, he reflects traditional views, showing womankind as the embodiment of vice, hypocrisy, deception, and generally not living up to the fair face that she presents to the world.

Waugh said that he was not a satirist[36] and in this he was right to some extent, for the society that he portrays has no standards of common decency; but he was a moralist, and the moral that he most often points seems to be that the world would be better off without women like these. He admitted, for example, that there was a 'moral purpose' to the *Sword of Honour* trilogy, and that Guy's solution is to decide to make himself 'responsible for the upbringing of Trimmer's child, to see that he is not brought up by his dissolute mother'.[37] This is not to say that Waugh sees the lives of his heroes as anything but futile, but they are portrayed as romantic and idealistic – qualities which the heroines do not share.

There is no hope, on earth, for example, for the dissolute Virginia, although Waugh does show a surprising amount of tolerance and sympathy for this character as he grants her the saving of her soul – something that does not happen to the other heroines; but there is hope for Guy Crouchback, on earth, for apart from marrying Virginia he makes redemptive, although unsuccessful, efforts to save Madame Kanyi and the Jewish refugees.

Apart from Basil Seal and Rex Mottram, two civilised barbarians, Waugh's major male characters are civilised human beings, and although their attachment to the values of civilisation makes it difficult for them to live in Waugh's chaotic, uncivilised world, they are to be more admired than their uncivilised female counterparts. What should be noted is that while we can laugh that rather shocked, embarrassed laugh at either the macabre death of Simon Balcairn putting his head in the gas oven, or on hearing that Prudence has been eaten, Waugh, himself, gets more perverse delight out of killing off his female characters than he does his male ones. Basil Seal's pleasure in Mrs Youkoumian being kicked by the mules, or women having their scalps eaten by ants is akin to the schoolboy's pleasure in pulling the legs off a spider. And Basil's responses 'You seem to me a good chap' to Youkoumian, or 'I like to see them scared' to the Minister are like the 'clear English drawl' that, on hearing someone say of Dame Mildred Porch and Miss Sarah Tin that 'I dare say they've been raped', answers 'I hope so' (*Black Mischief*, p.196).

---

[36] Waugh wrote: 'Satire is a matter of period. It flourishes in a stable society and presupposes homogeneous moral standards – the early Roman Empire and eighteenth-century Europe. It is aimed at inconsistency and hypocrisy. It exposes polite cruelty and folly by exaggerating them. It seeks to produce shame. All this has no place in the Century of the Common Man where vice no longer pays lip service to virtue.' 'Fan-Fare', *Essays*, p.304.

[37] Julian Jebb, 'The Art of Fiction: Evelyn Waugh', *Paris Review* 30 (Summer – Fall, 1963), p.82.

Waugh likes seeing women at a disadvantage. There is no doubt that he liked to shock, and to tease, as witnessed by the macabre letter he sent to his daughter Margaret when he had taken her sister to a debutantes' cocktail party:

> There were 250 pimply youths and 250 hideous girls packed so tight together they could not move hand or foot. So I sat with the butler in the hall and that is the last anyone has seen of Teresa. I suppose she was crushed to death & the corpse too flat to be recognised. About 100 dead girls were carried out & buried in a common pit. R.I.P. I shall never let you, my ewe lamb, become a debutante. (*Letters*, p.469)

His favourite daughter was not to be sacrificed, but women, in general, were; and, to conclude, Waugh's schoolboy delight in degrading them can be seen in that famous entry in the diaries where he and Randolph Churchill enjoyed bullying Wanda Baillie-Hamilton at a cocktail party:

> A delightful day. There was one row. Randolph Churchill threw a cocktail in Wanda's face. I came up after it happened and made things no better by saying, 'Dear Wanda, how hot you look.' She left the party in a rage. (*Diaries*, p.315)

CHAPTER EIGHT

Women as Vandals

There is the Devil of Crazy Pavement constantly tugging at most English Women. (*Essays*[1])

The destruction of the 'great house' in Waugh's novels as a recurring theme has been noted by James Carens[2] and other critics, but it has not been fully appreciated that Waugh saw not only the modern movement in architecture as his enemy but women as well ... for, whereas his heroes live in a nostalgic and romantic past, most of his heroines meet the practical and unromantic future head-on.

Waugh, very early, was drawn to his aunts' house in Midsomer Norton saying that all his life he had 'sought dark and musty seclusions, like an animal preparing to whelp'.[3] This taste was fulfilled at his aunts' house which had hardly been changed since the 1870s. It was dark, full of oil paintings and 'curiosities', and interesting smells pervaded the house whereas in his own home the windows were always open and smells never lingered. What Waugh admired about the house was that it obviously belonged to another age, and he later wrote: 'I am sure that I loved my aunts' house because I was instinctively drawn to the ethos I now recognise as mid-Victorian.'[4] The house was falling apart but the decay did not bother Waugh. What did concern him was that his aunts gradually modernised the place:

> Late but ineluctable the twentieth century came seeping in. Plush gave place to chintz, gas to electric-light; the primitive geyser was susperseded; water came from the main and the pumps rusted; the accumulation of brackets and occasional tables and china was dispersed; the walls were stripped of their old papers and painted. The clocks stopped and their bronze and marble and ormolu cases were replaced with bright new time-pieces. Aunt Elsie conceived that stuffed birds and mounted butterflies were no longer in good taste and had them removed to the 'dark pantry'. Instead she indulged a liking for deplorable china animals, which her friends gave her in profusion, comic pre-Disney puppies and kittens, trios of monkeys covering eyes, mouth and ears.[5]

[1] Evelyn Waugh, 'A Call to the Orders', *Essays*, p.217.
[2] James F. Carens, *The Satiric Art of Evelyn Waugh* (1966), pp.24-31.
[3] *A Little Learning*, p.44.
[4] Ibid., p.48.
[5] Ibid., p.53.

Midsomer Norton influenced Waugh to the extent that before buying Combe Florey he once suggested to Laura Waugh that he should buy her a farm and that he should take over his aunts' house. He reasoned that this would solve the problem of Laura wanting to bring up the children on a farm in the country which was irreconcilable with his desire for a 'harmonious place to write in' which was suitable for his 'ineradicable love of collecting bric-a-brac'. He actually toyed with the idea of turning the house into a museum of Victorian art, and restoring the rooms to the splendid state that they would have been in 1870.[6] In fact, on the death of his aunts the house was sold and converted into local government offices. Waugh never went back after that but Midsomer Norton had played its part. Waugh's own Victorianized homes were to show his admiration for the past and his rejection of contemporary taste.

In 1925 the Decorative Arts Exhibition had opened in Paris and the exhibition gave its name to the style which became known as 'Modernistic' and 'Functional'. The new materials were plastics, ferro-concrete and vita-glass. While Waugh was writing articles against the new trends, *Vogue* was promoting the new decor by showing pictures of 'tastefully-decorated' flats. The fashion was for pale stippled walls or an all-white decor. Wood was faced in mirror-glass; aluminium and chromium were popular. Furniture was tubular, or, very often, painted, as were wall panels. Mechanical gadgets such as electric cocktail-shakers were popular and it was an age for disguise: radios masqueraded as tea-caddies, cabinets turned out to be gramophones and small bronze sculptures would open to reveal a cigarette-lighter. *Vogue* also promoted Le Corbusier, who had said that 'a house is a machine for living'. Women sat up and took notice of *Vogue* while Waugh watched what was happening with despair. In 1938 when the Le Corbusier phase had passed and people were once again turning towards civilised buildings, Waugh wrote:

> From Tromso to Angora the horrible little architects crept about – curly-headed, horn-spectacled, volubly explaining their 'machines for living'. Villas like sewage farms, mansions like half-submerged Channel steamers, offices like vast bee-hives and cucumber frames sprang up round their feet, furnished with electric fires ... We suffered less from the concrete-and-glass functional architecture than any other country in Europe. In a few months our climate began to expose the imposture. The white flat walls that had looked as cheerful as a surgical sterilising plant became mottled with damp; our east winds howled through the steel frames of the windows. The triumphs of the New Architecture began to assume the melancholy air of a deserted exhibition, almost before the tubular furniture within had become bent and tarnished.[7]

[6] *Letters*, p.109. It would appear that Laura never answered his question, for later he wrote saying: 'Did you ever get a letter from me expressing the wish to retain the little house at Midsomer Norton? You have never commented on that idea' (*Letters*, p.199).

[7] Evelyn Waugh, 'A Call to the Orders', *Essays*, p.216. The article was rejected by *Harper's Bazaar*, and Waugh wrote in his diary (p.428): 'Miss Reynolds returned an article I had written her about architecture on the grounds that her paper stood for "contemporary" design. I could have told her all about Corbusier fifteen years ago when she would not have known the name. Now that we are at last recovering from that swine-fever, the fashionable magazines take it up.'

Had Waugh ever liked anything modern? In 1917, when he was fourteen, he had written an essay, *In Defence of Cubism*, mainly because he had come under the influence of his brother's fiancée, Barbara Jacobs, of whom he was later to say: 'Barbara, in fact, made an aesthetic hypocrite of me. It was many years before I would freely confess that the Paris school and all that derived from it were abhorrent to me.'[8] It was Harold Acton who led Waugh away from the influence both of Barbara Jacobs and Francis Crease, who had given him 'illumination lessons' at Lancing. Waugh's preferences at Oxford were for Lovat Fraser and Eric Gill, but Acton introduced him to 'the baroque and the rococo and to the *Waste Land*'.[9]

Waugh's anti-modernistic feelings are easily apparent in his novels. Modern architects are ridiculed hilariously and, also, those men who support them such as Lord Copper, whose country seat is a 'frightful mansion' in East Finchley and whose offices rudely shock William Boot when he sees the 'Byzantine vestibule and Sassanian lounge of Copper House' which contains a 'chryselephantine effigy of Lord Copper in coronation robes'.

Waugh's brash 'hard-faced' businessmen support modern trends just as his heroines do; and he has the same lack of respect for both. His heroines, however, suffer more at his hands for the simple reason that Waugh appreciates that it is women who normally take charge of decorating the home and therefore pose more of a threat to the impractical and romantic past that he and his heroes prefer to live in.

The indifferent moderns

In *Decline and Fall* the great house King's Thursday, which is 'the finest piece of domestic Tudor in England', suffers a cruel fate at the hands of the destructive Margot Beste-Chetwynde. Her brother-in-law, Lord Pastmaster, is aware that his house which has been the seat of the Earls of Pastmaster since the reign of Bloody Mary, and was once considered 'rather a blot on the progressive landscape', is admired because it has stayed unchanged throughout the various 'succeeding fashions that fell upon domestic architecture'; and he takes a certain pride in showing people over the house and pointing out the closet in which the third Earl had imprisoned his wife for 'wishing to rebuild a smoking chimney' – a chimney that still smokes when the wind is in the east. Lord Pastmaster, however, has to reach the decision to sell King's Thursday as he can no longer accept the discomforts nor afford to make the changes that 'modern democracy' demands – the servants require such conveniences as 'lifts and labour-saving devices'. Believing that his rich sister-in-law will be able to afford to make the necessary changes while still keeping up King's Thursday as a historic stately home, he sells the

---

[8] *A Little Learning*, p.122.

[9] Ibid., p.197. And in 1959 Waugh wrote: 'I spent three days in Bavaria last summer and enjoyed the rococo churches.' Anthony W. Riley, 'Waugh on Germany: an Unpublished Postcard', *Evelyn Waugh Newsletter*, vol. 16, no.3 (Winter, 1982), p.4.

house to her. The neighbours are delighted, as is Mr Jack Spire[10] who, before the news, was promoting a 'Save King's Thursday Fund' to buy the house for the nation which unfortunately only raised a small amount of the 'very large sum that Lord Pastmaster was sensible enough to demand'. The sale is reported in all the fashionable illustrated papers, but the reporter to whom Mrs Beste-Chetwynde said, 'I can't think of anything more bourgeois and awful than timbered Tudor architecture' (p.118), doesn't report her revealing statement because he thought that he must have misunderstood what she said.

When Margot arrives to view her new purchase she says: 'It's worse than I thought, far worse ... Liberty's new building cannot be compared with it' (p.118). Liberty's new building (which was the new addition to the store) should, of course, never be compared to it as it is mock tudor – but the point is that Margot prefers the imitation to the real thing. Waugh when he was worrying about the trend to imitation Georgian in his article 'A Call to the Orders' said: '... we are in danger of doing to the styles of the eighteenth century what our fathers and grandfathers did to Tudor and Jacobean. It is a serious danger, because imitation, if extensive enough, really does debauch one's taste for the genuine.'[11]

Margot's act of razing King's Thursday to the ground is seen as 'no single act in Mrs Beste-Chetwynde's eventful and in many ways disgraceful career had excited quite so much hostile comment as the building, or rather the rebuilding, of this remarkable house' (p.15). Margot hires Professor Silenus, one of her 'finds', who had attracted her attention with his 'rejected design for a chewing-gum factory' which had been illustrated in a 'progressive Hungarian quarterly' (p.119). As the bulldozers move in, the neighbours raid the grounds, carrying away carved stonework for their rockeries so that they can say that they have preserved a little of the great house for the country; and meanwhile the panelling goes to the museum in South Kensington to be admired, says Waugh cynically, by 'Indian students'.

Margot asks Silenus for 'something clean and square' and as his philosophy is that the 'only perfect building must be the factory, because that is built to house machines not men' (p.120) he produces a factory-like horror. Waugh mocks at Le Corbusier here, for the journalist who interviews Silenus records that Silenus's amazing forecast is 'Will machines live in houses?' (p.120) – a nice inversion of Le Corbusier's philosophy of 'A house is a machine to live in'.[12] As Silenus believes in 'the elimination of the human element from the

---

[10] Jack Spire of the *London Hercules* is based on J.C. Squire (1884-1958), who was editor of the *London Mercury*. Squire was interested in the preservation of churches, which was the reason for the name 'Spire'. In his diaries Waugh recorded: 'I took a strong dislike to the man Squire' (p.165).

[11] Evelyn Waugh, 'A Call to the Orders', *Essays*, pp.216-17. The idea of destroying King's Thursday could have been indirectly prompted by the Mitfords' house, Swinbrook. Lord Redesdale had bulldozed an eighteenth-century house to make way for a Victorian/Tudor monstrosity. Margot destroys real Tudor in favour of a modern monstrosity.

[12] Silenus is likely to be based on a combination of Le Corbusier and Walter Gropius of the Bauhaus, for Waugh says in *Decline and Fall* that Silenus was 'at the Bauhaus in Dessau' (p.122). Le Corbusier was a contemporary of Gropius who was founder of the Bauhaus, an architectural school that flourished in Germany between 1919 and 1933.

consideration of form' (p.120), his creation is a cold, lifeless building made of ferro-concrete and glass with aluminium lifts, blinds and balustrades, pneumatic rubber furniture, porcelain ceilings, and leather-hung walls. There are india-rubber fungi in the conservatory, and one of the floors in the house is a large kaleidscope which is operated electrically.

Reactions to the house are mixed. The hero, Paul Pennyfeather, is entranced by the paradisiacal grounds of King's Thursday:

> The temperate April sunlight fell through the buddening chestnuts and revealed between their trunks green glimpses of parkland and the distant radiance of a lake. 'English spring,' thought Paul. 'In the dreaming ancestral beauty of the English country.' Surely, he thought, these great chestnuts in the morning sun stood for something more enduring and serene in a world that had lost its reason and would so stand when the chaos and confusion were forgotten? And surely it was the spirit of William Morris that whispered to him in Margot Beste-Chetwynde's motor car about seed-time and harvest, the superb succession of the seasons, the harmonious interdependence of rich and poor, of dignity, innocence and tradition? But at a turn in the drive the cadence of his thoughts was abruptly transected. They had come into sight of the house. (pp.123-4)

The new King's Thursday is not the romantic image that Paul has been building in his dream but a nightmare – the idealised vision of the past has become a monstrosity of the present. The anti-climax is extremely ironic. The opinion of the county is harsh, with such members of the aristocracy as Lady Vanbrugh[13] saying that the drains are satisfactory but that that is all she can find to say. While the neighbours rage, the Society for the Preservation of Ancient Buildings tries to get a guarantee from Margot that she will not demolish her castle in Ireland.

How does Margot herself regard the house? She is aware that the county does not approve, but that doesn't worry her. More important is that she quickly becomes bored with it; and by the time Paul Pennyfeather is in prison she is writing to tell him that she doesn't really like it and that she is 'having it redone'. Professor Silenus's batik tie worn by the head gardener is, as Waugh says with irony, the 'last relic of a great genius'. The point is that Margot will never like anything that she has done for her in the way of design for she never chooses anything personally. She left Silenus to deal with the house while she went on a world tour, telling him to have it finished by the spring when she returned. Margot has her houses redone each year as the fashions change and she simply goes along with the current trend, never putting the mark of her own personality on anything.

She thinks in practical and financial terms rather than romantically. Asked by her brother-in-law for more money for King's Thursday, as he says he would have demanded more if he had known she was going to demolish it,

---

[13] Waugh wrote: 'Vanbrugh gave up writing plays to build the most lovely houses in England.' 'General Conversation: Myself', *Essays*, p.192. Sir John Vanbrugh (1664-1726) was an architect of the English Baroque period, and Waugh is implying that Vanbrugh, who designed Castle Howard, the model for Brideshead, would consider King's Thursday an eyesore.

she says simply that it is not logical of him, for 'the less I valued this house, the less I ought to have paid, surely?' (p.135). She does however pay him the money, as she is afraid that otherwise he might go and get married and she wants her son, Peter, to inherit the title.

Nouveau riche, Margot epitomises modern taste. Like Margot, Angela Lyne is also *nouveau riche*, and although she doesn't demolish houses she follows in Margot's fashionable footsteps. Her flat, in a block in Grosvenor Square,[14] in *Put Out More Flags*, has been 'done up by David Lennox just before the war' and is 'empty' and 'uncommunicative' – a reflection of herself:

> This place was a service flat and as smart and non-committal as herself, a set of five large rooms high up in the mansard floor of a brand new block in Grosvenor Square. The decorators had been at work there while she was in France; the style was what passes for Empire in the fashionable world. Next year, had there been no war, she would have had it done over again during August. (p.118)

Angela, like Margot, belongs to a breed of women who are a decorator's delight. On a 'Pompeian side table' there is an electric cocktail-shaker which she likes to use. Like Margot she admires 'gadgets' and the decorators who come to do up the houses of fashionable ladies recognise this and 'litter' the place with expensive trifles. 'Parsimonious clients' send them back, but most of the others, like Angela, think that they are probably gifts from people whom they have forgotten to thank and pay for them a year later when the decorator sends in his bill.

Angela's first husband is Cedric Lyne, of whom she says to Basil: 'He was most romantic – genuinely. I'd never met anyone like him. Father's friends were all hard-boiled and rich – men like Metroland and Copper ... and then I met Cedric who was poor and very, very soft-boiled and tall and willowy and very unhappy in a boring smart regiment because he only cared about Russian Ballet and baroque architecture' (p.163). (In 1927, Waugh wrote: 'Looking back upon the last few months in London, I think of three typical artistic events: M. Michel Sevier's Exhibition of Paintings, the Magnasco Society's Exhibition of Baroque Drawings, and the production of *Mercury* by the Russian ballet. These, with the Charvet ties and shell buttonholes, Lord Latham's interior decorations, the paper boys crying the news of Mrs Bonati's murder, and the gossip in the constricted foyer of the Prince's Theatre make up the "period". They go together the vital with the trivial ...').[15] Apart from liking baroque architecture, Cedric likes Angela's money because it means he can afford to buy 'rare and beautiful things'. He and Angela chose Cedric's Folly (the name later given to the house) for the cascades of water that poured down from the hillside. Angela, again like Margot, thinks in financial terms. Looking down at the 'symmetrical, rectangular building below' she says,

---

[14] On 5 May 1927 'details were released of the gigantic block of service flats which were to be erected on the site of Grosvenor House'. Andrew Barrow, *Gossip: A History of High Society from 1920 to 1970* (1978), p.33.

[15] Evelyn Waugh, 'Preface to the Decorative Designs of Francis Crease', *Essays*, p.22.

'It'll do ... I'll offer them fifteen thousand.'

When Angela and Cedric are first together, it is her money that buys the first temple for Cedric's grottoes; and in the humiliating years after that, when she leaves him alone in the summer to be with Basil Seal, it is her money that buys each yearly monument, from which Cedric obtains immense pleasure, because his grottoes are 'always the same; joys for ever; not like men and women with their loves and hate'. And the year that Cedric agrees not to divorce Angela, as she can see no point in the scandal, he adds another monument; he spans the stream with 'a bridge in the Chinese Taste, taken direct from Batty Langley'.[16]

Cedric views Angela's flat with distaste, as does their son Nigel. He abhors the David Lennox grisailles,[17] telling his son 'No ... they are not old', and when Nigel says 'They're awfully feeble', he agrees:

> 'They are.' Regency: this was the age of Waterloo and highwaymen and duelling and slavery and revivalist preaching and Nelson having his arm off with no anaesthetic but rum, and Botany Bay– and *this* is what they make of it. (p.171)

There is no doubt of Waugh's dislike of modern art in *Put Out More Flags*, as one can see from his mockery of Poppet Green, the surrealist painter, who paints away like a 'mowing machine'. Her art is so tasteless to Waugh that he has Basil draw a ginger moustache across her 'Aphrodite of Melos', which is a 'buttercup-coloured head ... poised against a background of bull's-eyes and barley-sugar'. Of Poppet, Ambrose Silk remarks: 'My dear ... you can positively hear her imagination *creaking* as she does them, like a pair of old, old *corsets*, my dear, on a harridan'[18] (pp.30-1).

Jeffrey Heath has said that Ambrose has 'allowed his artistic tastes to become contaminated by politics; indeed, as a member of Poppet Green's Communist cell he even expresses approval of her ghastly jaundice-coloured head of Aphrodite'.[19] If we look at the passage we will see that this is not so, for Ambrose only approves of the painting because of the moustache that Basil has so mischievously added:

> '... *that* I consider *good*. I consider it *good*, Poppet. The moustache ... it shows you have crossed one of the artistic rubicons and feel strong enough to be facetious. Like those wonderfully dramatic old *chestnuts* in Parsnip's *Guernica Revisited*. You're growing up, Poppet, my dear.' (p.34)

[16] Batty Langley (1696-1751), English architect, master builder and landscape gardener.

[17] David Lennox was based on Cecil Beaton. See Sykes, p.129. *Grisaille* is a technique of monochrome painting in shades of grey, as in an oil painting or a wall decoration, imitating the effect of relief.

[18] Poppet Green could well have been inspired by Poppet John, Augustus John's daughter, whom Carrington described as 'slightly enfeebled in the head with falling "in love" every day with a new young man'. *Carrington: Letters and Extracts from her Diaries*, edited by David Garnett (1979), p.408. Although Waugh had admired Augustus John's portraits in 1920, as he had admired Picasso and Cubism, he became anti-modern in later life.

[19] Jeffrey Heath, *The Picturesque Prison: Evelyn Waugh and his Writing*, (1982), p.154. Waugh notes on his travels that the 'Aphrodite of Melos was competent'. *Diaries*, p.240.

The calculating touch

Celia Ryder, an unfaithful wife, who has little time for her husband apart from the fact that he is successful, is only interested in how she can further promote his career and in the commissions she can obtain for him – even if those commissions offend his integrity.

When they married, Charles Ryder's father gave him as a wedding present 'the price of a house', and he consequently bought an 'old rectory' in Celia's part of the country. On his return from his travels in Latin America, Ryder is told by his wife that while he was away she has had the old barn converted into a studio for him; her unspoken reason being that she wishes him to be seen as a fashionable artist. Apparently it has been such a success that an article has been published about it in *Country Life* which says that it is a '... *happy example of architectural good manners ... Sir Joseph Emden's tactful adaptation of traditional material to modern needs ...*'.

Ryder is dismayed by the photographs in the magazine, for all the features that he admired about the barn have been destroyed. The earth floor has been covered by wide oak boards and the 'great timbered roof', which 'before had been lost in shadow, now stood out stark, well lit, with clean white plaster between the beams'; and a window has been put in the north wall (p.221). Ryder (like Waugh) likes musty smells and he realises that the smell of the barn as he knew it would now be lost. The place looks like a 'village hall' to him, and sadly he says: 'I rather liked that barn.'

Celia is constantly after work for Charles, and on board ship she invites two Hollywood magnates to her party to meet her husband because, as he says, 'it had occurred to her that, with my interest in architecture, my true *métier* was designing scenery for the films' (p.229). Celia does not manage to ingratiate Charles with the movie moguls:

> 'Did you say anything to Mr Kramm about working in Hollywood?'
> 'Of course not.'
> 'Oh, Charles, you are a worry to me. It's not enough just to stand about looking distinguished and a martyr for Art.' (p.233)

Nor does Celia manage to persuade him to unpack some of his paintings and 'stick them round the cabin for her cocktail party', but one way or another she is determined to push Charles. She informs him that there is a 'lot of work' waiting for him as she has promised Lady Anchorage that he will 'do Anchorage House' as soon as he gets back. Anchorage House is coming down to make way for shops with two-roomed flats above them.

(Anchorage House is first mentioned in *Vile Bodies* and in Waugh's terms is a symbol of the threat of the modern world. The passage is worth quoting in full:

> This last survivor of the noble town houses of London was, in its time, of dominating and august dimensions, and even now, when it had become a mere

'picturesque bit' lurking in a ravine between concrete skyscrapers, its pillared façade, standing back from the street and obscured by railings and some wisps of foliage, had grace and dignity and other worldliness enough to cause a flutter or two in Mrs Hoop's heart as she drove into the forecourt.

Can't you just see the *ghosts?*' she said to Lady Circumference on the stairs. 'Pitt and Fox and Burke and Lady Hamilton and Beau Brummel and Dr Johnson' (a concurrence of celebrities, it may be remarked, at which something memorable might surely have occurred). 'Can't you just *see* them – in their buckled shoes?' (p.126)

Whereas Mrs Hoop has a 'confused but very glorious dream of eighteenth-century elegance', the down-to-earth Lady Circumference has no such illusions. She answers tartly, 'That's all my eye', for what she sees is something quite different. Apart from the usual crowd such as Mr Outrage, Lord Metroland, Lady Metroland, Lady Throbbing, Mrs Blackwater and others, of whom she doesn't much approve, she sees a 'great concourse of pious and honourable people ... their women-folk well gowned in rich and durable stuffs, their men-folk ablaze with orders; people who had represented their country in foreign places and sent their sons to die for her in battle ... brave and rather unreasonable people, that fine phalanx of the passing order ...' (pp.126-7). What Lady Circumference sees with a clear eye is that both Anchorage House and the noble people who pass through it are threatened by the encroachment of the modern world with its skycrapers, its business, its land and property taxes. She sees both the house and the old aristocracy as doomed.)

Celia Ryder wonders whether all the 'exotic' work that Charles has been doing will 'spoil' him for such a job as Anchorage House:

'Why should it?'
'Well, it's so different. Don't be cross.'
'It's just another jungle closing in.'
'I know just how you feel, darling. The Georgian Society made such a fuss, but we couldn't do anything.' (p.221)

One really cannot believe that Celia cares about preserving old buildings after what she has had done to Charles's barn. Like Mrs Beaver in *A Handful of Dust* she is only too ready to move in for the kill. Celia is the kind of lioness who will survive in any jungle and who is willing to let her mate pay the price.

The most disturbing fact about Celia Ryder is that she does understand Ryder's attitude to art – as is shown when she says that she knows that he has taken against the ice swan that the purser has had created for her party, but tells him that if it had been part of a 'description of a sixteenth-century banquet in Venice' he would have said that 'those were the days to live'. Charles's barbed response in 'in sixteenth-century Venice it would have been a somewhat different shape' doesn't affect her in the slightest. She also recognises that Charles's drawings of Latin America are 'perfectly brilliant and really rather beautiful in a sinister way, but somehow I don't feel they are quite *you*' (p.218).

Celia understands Charles's architectural preferences but it doesn't stop her getting him involved in projects that she knows he will despise. Ryder has produced numerous books on architecture. As Celia says to her friends, 'After all, he has said the last word about country houses, hasn't he?' Although she tells everyone that her husband is looking for new avenues to explore, she hastens to add that he'll still 'do' one or two more houses for 'friends'.

Celia, an unflagging hostess, is capable of saying such nauseating things to people as 'You see Charles lives for one thing – Beauty'; and, even worse, 'Whenever I see anything lovely nowadays – a building or a piece of scenery – I think to myself, "That's by Charles". I see everything through his eyes. He *is* England to me.' Such comments in the past have caused Ryder plenty of anguish but once he is in love with Julia Flyte he finds that Celia's remarks can no longer hurt him.

Celia, who married Charles at the time of his first, successful exhibition, and has done much since then, as Charles puts it, to 'push our interests', cares nothing for art or architecture except what they mean in terms of social and financial success. It is Celia's idea to have the private viewing on a Friday to be sure to 'catch the critics' and she tries to get Charles to dedicate the new book to the Duchess of Clarence, replying when Ryder says that he hasn't thought of 'dedicating it to anyone' that it is 'typical' of him – 'Why miss an opportunity to give pleasure.' In Celia's terms, no opportunity should ever be missed.

The feminine touch

While on the subject of Charles Ryder it is worth mentioning Lady Marchmain's attitude to modern decor. Her sitting room at Brideshead has already been unfavourably compared with Nanny Hawkins's room in Chapter Six, but it is worth pointing out a few facts again.

Lady Marchmain doesn't raze Brideshead to the ground as her husband's ancestors did (Brideshead Castle was originally near the village, but its owners suddenly preferred the setting of the valley, so they pulled the castle down and used the stones to build a new house), but she does vandalise her own sitting-room so that it appears as though it belongs to a completely different house. She lowers the ceiling so that the elaborate cornice, which graces all the rooms in Brideshead, is 'lost to view' and she has the old wallpaper stripped off and has one wall panelled in brocade and the others 'washed blue'.

Charles Ryder dislikes the room intensely:

> I closed the door behind me, shutting out the *bondieuserie*, the low ceiling, the chintz, the lambskin bindings, the views of Florence, the bowls of hyacinth and potpourri, the *petit-point*, the intimate feminine, modern world, and was back under the coved and coffered roof, the columns and entablature of the central hall, in the august, masculine atmosphere of a better age. (p.133)

Jeffrey Heath has said that Lady Marchmain's room is a 'mother's room, from which the unperceptive Charles Ryder escapes after his "talks" into the

"masculine atmosphere" of what he mistakenly thinks is a "better age" ' –
and Heath also believes that Lady Marchmain's room is the 'last bulwark of
faith' in Brideshead.[20] This argument doesn't hold water, for Lady
Marchmain's room is like her – suffocating, and full of *bondieuserie* (cloying
piety); and during the summer that Charles and Sebastian are at Brideshead
they 'keep out of his mother's room' because of its stifling feminine
atmosphere. Charles Ryder is not unperceptive, for he realises that his little
'talks' with her are designed to make him 'one of the bonds' with which to tie
Sebastian to her and Brideshead; and as his intimacy with her grows he
knows that he is gradually becoming part of the world from which Sebastian
wishes to escape.

If there is a room that is the 'last bulwark of faith' in *Brideshead Revisited* it is
Nanny Hawkins's room which Heath sees, with its jumble of souvenirs and
pictures, as the kind of 'motley taste' which he says is 'an established Waugh
cue for lack of reason and discipline'; and he suggests that Nanny Hawkins's
rosary which lies 'loosely' between her hands is confirmation of this.[21]
Where such an idea comes from is hard to know. Waugh's own idea of taste
was 'motley' and Nanny Hawkins's room is a reflection of his own nursery,
which was full of 'curiosities', and of his later homes, Piers Court and Combe
Florey, which were 'Victorianized' and full of bric-à-brac. Heath also says
that Sebastian's room, like Nanny Hawkins's room, is 'indiscriminating' in
its taste and therefore reflects his 'lack of discipline' which is a criticism on
Waugh's part of Sebastian.[22] Sebastian's room is described as follows:

> His room was filled with a strange jumble of objects – a harmonium in a
> gothic case, an elephant's foot waste-paper basket, a dome of wax fruit, two
> disproportionately large Sèvres vases, framed drawings by Daumier – made all
> the more incongruous by the austere college furniture and the large luncheon
> table. (p.33)

Auberon Waugh's study at Combe Florey is the room that his father used
and one of the valued relics from his father's past, which didn't go to Austin,
Texas, is Evelyn Waugh's rhinoceros waste-paper basket. Also, in Victorian
times Sèvres vases (Waugh once said of Stephen Spender that to read his
'fumbling with our rich and delicate language is to experience all the horror
of seeing a Sèvres vase in the hands of a chimpanzee')[23] were popular, as were
Covent Gardens of wax fruit.

Waugh, although he believed in the Augustan ideals of order and discipline
in architecture (and in writing), was a true Palladian at heart; and the point
about Palladianism is that, although it uses a plain type of exterior of strict
symmetry and harmonious grouping of all the parts, it was often combined
with a richly baroque treatment of the interior; and the true Palladian villa
often had an informal rococo garden. In England, Lord Burlington neglected

[20] Jeffrey Heath, *The Picturesque Prison*, p.174.
[21] Ibid., p.168.
[22] Ibid., p.176.
[23] Evelyn Waugh, 'Two Unquiet Lives', *Essays*, p.395.

the baroque interior when he designed Chiswick House; and it was, in fact, James Gibbs who, although he modified the eloquent late baroque style he had learnt in Rome, used it effectively in his design for St Martin-in-the-Fields which is one of the handsomest churches in the classical style in London and has the unusual distinction of being decorated inside with late baroque stucco ornament.

Waugh uses the Palladian ideal to impose order on the fantasy of his novels just as the severe exterior of a Palladian villa imposes order on the fantasy inside. Waugh was fond of incongruity; witness the copy he ordered from Wiltons of the carpet that was used at the 1851 exhibition at the Crystal Palace – a carpet of the most florid colours with coarsely adapted Persian motifs. It certainly went with his collection of Victorian furniture and pictures, his squatting Ethiopian wooden camel and other amazing objects, but hardly reflected the exterior of Combe Florey House which was built in 1680, or the carved pedestal shelves in the library which was to be its home.

Also, the idea that because Nanny holds her rosary 'loosely' it means a 'lack of reason and discipline' seems extremely far-fetched for, if anything, it is Nanny Hawkins who instils religion in the children. She, as we have seen, is the one who disciplines and guides them; and it is to her that they turn for advice and 'unsuffocating' warmth. Heath's understanding of the 'loosely' held rosary is small. Nanny Hawkins is fast asleep in her chair – not a time when she would be holding the rosary tightly; if anything the symbolism of the rosary conveys that Nanny's religion is always with her, awake or asleep.

Heath also believes that the 'miscellaneous taste of the pagan fountain connotes fraud, and Ryder compounds the fraud by painting a picture of it. Such a picture is not a suitable gift for Lady Marchmain, so Charles gives it to Nancy Hawkins who, in characteristic Waugh fashion, unthinkingly adds it to her collection.'[24] Waugh does not view the fountain with 'hostility' as Heath suggests. Charles Ryder sits for hours before the fountain 'probing its shadows, tracing its lingering echoes, rejoicing in all its clustered feats of daring and invention' (p.79). Ryder feels as he sits there a 'whole new system of nerves alive' within him and sees the water spurting and bubbling among the stones as a 'life-giving spring'. The fountain is not a 'bogus' design. It is, as Heath says, a baroque fountain that was found in a piazza in southern Italy a century before and brought to Brideshead by Sebastian's ancestors. More important, it has been 're-erected in an alien but welcoming climate'. The fountain was in fact based on the fountain at Castle Howard (the seat of an old-established Catholic family), which in turn was based on Bernini's Four Rivers Fountain in the Piazza Navona in Rome;[25] and Waugh once wrote that 'the man who can enjoy the flimsy and fantastic decorations of Naples is much more likely to appreciate the grandeur of Roman baroque, than the prig who demands Michelangelo or nothing'.[26] Bernini's Four Rivers Fountain (1648-51), designed for Pope Innocent X, is a great island rock from which the Four Rivers of the World spring; each of them is

[24] Jeffrey Heath, *The Picturesque Prison*, p.168.
[25] See Sykes, p.342.
[26] Evelyn Waugh, 'Literary Style in England and America', *Essays*, p.479.

personified by a statue and the whole is surmounted by a pagan Egyptian obelisk which, in its setting in Rome, rises in obeisance to the church of Sant' Agnese, which was built to commemorate the martyrdom of St Agnes and which stands on the original site that was used for pagan festivities. The fountain symbolises a re-awakened Rome, which dominates the earth not by its military power but by its faith, and the triumph of the papacy.

The simple reason why Charles doesn't give Lady Marchmain his 'passable echo of Piranesi'[27] is that, as Sebastian says, 'You don't know her' – not for religious reasons. If Charles did know her, in the way he did later, he would realise that Lady Marchmain would not admire such a drawing. The fountain is baroque, as the house is – and Lady Marchmain's room does not require echoes of Piranesi but 'little water colours'. The fact that Nanny Hawkins, on being given the drawing, adds it ' unthinkingly' to her collection is also disputable; for when Charles gives it to her she remarks that it has 'quite the look of the thing, which she had often heard admired but could never see the beauty of, herself' (p.79). Adding it to the collection is a compliment to Charles. It means that as Sebastian's friend, he has found a place in her heart; and the treasures he brings her will be added to those of the Flyte children and will be 'carefully dusted' and cherished.

Heath puts the fountain, with what he sees as its falsity, in the same context as Lady Marchmain's chapel. The two are entirely different. The fountain has the grandeur of Roman baroque; the chapel is 'art-nouveau', a period which Everlyn Waugh was ambivalent about – 'the "nineties", odious as they now seem to us with their "greenery-yallery" artiness';[28] and his dislike shows in his description of the chapel:

> The whole interior has been gutted, elaborately refurnished and redecorated in the arts-and-crafts style of the last decade of the nineteenth century. Angels in printed cotton smocks, rambler roses, flower-spangled meadows, frisking lambs, texts in Celtic script, saints in armour, covered the walls in an intricate pattern of clear, bright colours. There was a triptych of pale oak, carved so as to give it the peculiar property of seeming to have been moulded in Plasticine. The sanctuary lamp and all the metal furniture were of bronze, hand-beaten to the patina of a pock-marked skin; the altar steps had a carpet of grass-green, strewn with white and gold daisies. (pp.39-40)

The *art nouveau* chapel was the only architectural reference, according to Lady Dorothy Lygon,[29] that Waugh drew on from Madresfield. Built for

[27] Giambattista Piranesi (1720-1778) was an Italian architect and etcher. His etchings of Roman ruins were highly subjective and dramatic. He had an extravagant imagination but never tampered with the archaelogical correctness of his views. His presentation of classical architecture brought Rome into the foreground again, and he inspired Robert Adam and Sir John Soane.

[28] Evelyn Waugh, 'Why Glorify Youth?' *Essays*, p.126.

[29] See Lady Dorothy Lygon, 'Madresfield and Brideshead', *Evelyn Waugh and his World*, pp.53, 54. Daphne Fielding writes that the chapel was 'decorated with murals painted in a pre-Raphaelite style. On either side of the altar there were life-size portraits of himself [Lord Beauchamp] and Lady Beauchamp, kneeling in prayer and wearing peer's and peeress's robes, their coronets lying beside them on the daisy-strewn grass. The children appeared as winged cherubs flying round the walls.' *Mercury Presides* (1954), p.99.

Lady Marchmain as a wedding present, we are never actually told whether it was to her taste, but we must presume it was. Brideshead, who knows nothing about art, asks Charles Ryder what he thinks of the chapel aesthetically – 'Is it Good Art?' – to which Charles replies diplomatically:

'I think it's a remarkable example of its period. Probably in eighty years it will be greatly admired.'
'But surely it can't be good twenty years ago and good in eighty years, and not good now?'
'Well, it may be *good* now. All I mean is that I don't happen to like it much.' (p.89)

Cordelia, interestingly, thinks the chapel is 'beautiful' although, later, when Brideshead and the Bishop agree to close the chapel she watches as the priest goes through the necessary rituals, and comments that 'suddenly, there wasn't any chapel there any more, just an oddly decorated room' (p.121). The beauty of the chapel for Cordelia was brought about by her faith – and while the sanctuary lamp of 'deplorable design' burns, the chapel means everything to her; without the 'flame of religion' it is nothing. Cordelia tells Charles that if he had been to Tenebrae[30] he would know 'what the Jews felt about their temple. *Quomodo sedet sola civitas* ... it's a beautiful chant'.[31] Waugh, was, of course, very distressed that in England Catholics must 'meet in modern buildings, often of deplorable design, and are usually served by simple Irish missionaries';[32] and the Brideshead chapel is of deplorable design in Waugh's eyes and is served by Father Mackay, a 'genial Glasgow Irishman' of low intellect.

Interestingly, in his memorandum for the filming of *Brideshead Revisited*, Waugh reversed his views, for he said that 'the chapel in the book is a new one, and Lord Marchmain is represented as a recent and half-hearted convert to Catholicism. For the purpose of the film the Chapel should be old and part of the original castle on the site of which the baroque palace has been built. The Flytes should be represented as one of the English noble families which retained their religion throughout the Reformation period.' He also saw the fountain as representing the 'wordly eighteenth century splendour of the family'.[33] These instructions on Waugh's part seem to show a certain amount of dissatisfaction with the architectural details he had described in the book; and certainly if the chapel had been an old one the Catholic viewpoint in the book might well have been strengthened.

Of Julia Flyte's taste we learn very little. All we know from Anthony Blanche is that there is no 'greenery-yallery about her' – a compliment in

[30] Latin: *tenebrae* = darkness; in med.L. in the ecclesiastical sense. The name is given to the office of matins, and lauds of the following day, usually sung in the afternoon or evening of Wednesday, Thursday and Friday in Holy Week, at which the candles lighted at the beginning of the service are extinguished one by one after each psalm, in memory of the darkness at the time of the crucifixion (*OED*).

[31] 'How solitary lies the city ...' from 'Sorrows of Captive Zion', Lamentations 1:1.

[32] Evelyn Waugh, 'Come Inside', *Essays*, p.366.

[33] Evelyn Waugh, 'Memorandum for the Filming of *Brideshead Revisited*', 18 February 1947 (HRHRC).

Waugh's terms about Julia, but she is still an enigma. On the liner, which Charles sees as a modern montrosity and which has its wall panels painted the colour of blotting paper – 'kindergarten work in flat, drab colours' (a sure reminder of Lady Marchmain's childish attempts at mixing colours which always come out a 'kind of khaki'), he thinks: 'Here I am ... back from the jungle, back from the ruins. Here where wealth is no longer gorgeous, and power has no dignity. *Quomodo sedet sola civitas*' (p.225). While Charles is thinking this he actually passes Julia without noticing her, for Julia's beauty has faded into the 'cube of blotting paper' that she is sitting in.[34] Julia cannot understand why her maid should complain about her cabin, which to her 'seems a lap' (meaning the lap of luxury), and yet we know that the cabins are miniature versions of the 'monstrous hall above'.

Julia's attitude to the historic houses of England is a confused one, and a selfish one. When Lord Marchmain sells the 'historic' Marchmain House[35] to pay off his debts, and it is to be turned into a block of flats, Rex Mottram makes the great mistake of suggesting to Julia that they should live in the penthouse flat. It is the kind of insensitive gesture that Rex would make;[36] but although Cordelia says, 'He couldn't understand at all; he thought she would like to keep up with her old home' (p.211), Julia is worse than Rex in many ways, for she says she prefers to see Marchmain House turned into flats than have someone else live there. It shows a lack of generosity, and disregard for conservation, on Julia's part. Also, Rex might have expected her to like the idea; she did, after all, move into his house in Hertford Street which had 'lately been furnished and decorated by the most expensive firm'; and she didn't want a house in the country, saying, to Rex, that 'they could always take places furnished when they wanted to go away' (p.183).

On the other hand we know that Julia cares for Brideshead and when Lord Marchmain talks of leaving it to her rather than Bridey she feels she can accept it for, as she says, 'I don't think he cares much for the place. I do, you know. He and Beryl would be much more content in some little house somewhere' (p.306). This, however, is not completely true, for when Bridey tells Julia of his proposed marriage to Beryl Muspratt he says:

> 'I hope it's not going to be inconvenient for Rex moving out of here. You see, Barton Street is much too small for us and the three children. Besides, Beryl likes the country. In his letter papa proposed making over the whole estate right away.' (p.275)

Julia might care for Brideshead but, more than that, she is ambitious and selfish. If Lord Marchmain leaves the estate to her, she will not renounce it in favour of her elder brother.

[34] Robert Murray Davis sees Julia being 'introduced as a relief from the sterile modernity represented by the decor and Celia Ryder', *Evelyn Waugh, Writer* (1981), p.141.

[35] Most likely based on Halkyn House, the Beauchamp town house which Waugh often visited. Waugh records: 'Had arranged to meet Hubert at Halkyn House but Lady Beauchamp had just dropped dead so my arrival, tipsy with the Brownlows, was not opportune.' *Diaries*, p.395. Lady Marchmain dies at Marchmain House.

[36] Rex Mottram's insensitivity and bad taste is also shown in the tortoise that he gives Julia which has her initials in diamonds set into its shell.

Bridey, as has been mentioned, is not very artistic. He doesn't know whether the chapel is 'Good Art' and even has to ask Charles whether Marchmain House, a fine example of classical architecture, is 'good architecturally'. But although Waugh makes us aware of this he confuses the issue badly by having Brideshead understand that Beryl Muspratt's furniture is not suitable for Brideshead:

> 'Beryl's got some furniture of her own she's very attached to. I don't know if it would go very well here. You know, oak dressers and coffin stools and things. I thought she could put it in mummy's old room.' (p.276)

Lady Marchmain's 'modern' room was obviously not admired by Bridey nor, it would seem, either by Julia, who agrees with him that it 'would be the place'.

Lord Marchmain, who dislikes the English countryside, realises that it is 'a disgraceful thing to inherit great responsibilities and to be indifferent to them'. (p.96). He knows that he is behaving exactly as the 'Socialists' would have him behave but expects that his eldest son will 'change all that ... if they leave him anything to inherit ...'. However, he does not leave his estate to Bridey. He prefers to leave Brideshead to Julia – 'so beautiful always' – rather than to his son and Beryl Muspratt whom he thinks would not be 'quite in her proper element here'. Julia's beauty he sees as reflecting the beauty of Brideshead, but Julia, as decorous as she looks in her Chinese robe, is 'living in sin', whereas Bridey and Beryl are true to the faith. Lord Marchmain realises that there is no chance of the line continuing with Brideshead, as Beryl is too old to bear any more children; and with Julia there will be the chance of an heir. By making a 'sign' he manipulates Julia back into the faith so that she will not marry Charles; and, therefore, may in the future marry a Catholic (she could, most likely have her marriage to Rex legally dissolved) and return both faith and beauty to Brideshead. Lord Marchmain effectively destroys Charles Ryder's hopes of possessing Julia; remembering that when Charles first made love to her he saw himself as the 'freeholder of a property I would enjoy and develop at leisure'.

At the end of *Brideshead Revisited* the house has been vandalised by the army. The Quartering Commandant comments that Brideshead is a 'wonderful old place in its way ... pity to knock it about too much' (p.326). Although he covers up the painted walls of the Pompeian room the soldiers 'make hay' of Charles's paintings in the garden-room ... 'modern work but, if you ask me, the prettiest in the place'. The fountain described by Hooper as a 'frightful great fountain' and by the Quartering Commandant as a 'florid great thing' has been 'wired in', and the only thing it is good for is for the drivers to 'throw their cigarette-ends and the remains of their sandwiches there' (p.327).

The only thing that is not destroyed is the chapel, which shows no sign of its 'long neglect'. The *art nouveau* paint is as 'fresh and bright as ever'; and the chapel comes into its own again, for it has been opened up and the 'small red flame – a beaten copper lamp of deplorable design relit before the beaten-copper doors of a tabernacle ...' (p.331). The faith has been rekindled.

At first Charles Ryder thinks, seeing Brideshead as it is, that 'the place was desolate and the work all brought to nothing; *Quomodo sedet sola civitas*'; but then he realises that the lamp in the chapel would not have been lit without the 'builders and the tragedians' – the builders of Brideshead over the centuries and the people who had lived there and acted out their tragic scenarios. And he leaves looking 'more cheerful'.

Immoral surroundings

Julia Flyte's embroidered Chinese robe, which covers her so completely that her neck rises 'exquisitely from the plain gold circle at her throat', should reflect a modesty, a demureness that Waugh associated with the East[37] and approved of – but Julia is immoral. She wears her Chinese robe to have dinner with Charles in the 'Painted Parlour' with its 'prim Pompeian figures' on its dome, but the scene is misleading, for she is an adulteress and belongs more in the Chinese drawing room in which her 'mandarin coat' gives the death-bed scene an 'air of pantomime, of Aladdin's cave' – a room that reminds the Quartering Commandant of one of the 'costlier knocking-shops, you know – "*Maison Japonnaise*" ...' (p.327).

The decor of the 'Sports Room' in Margot Beste-Chetwynde's London house in *Decline and Fall* also reflects promiscuity. Decorated, once again, in her absence by David Lennox it has a carpet the colour of grass marked out with white lines, the walls are hung with netting, the lights are in glass footballs and 'athletic groups of the early nineties and a painting of a prize ram hung on the walls' (p.144). The room, which Margot, the procuress, sees as 'terribly common ... but it rather impresses the young ladies', is a parody of the other kind of athletics that the girls will be expected to perform; and the sexual symbol of the prize ram is crudely appropriate. Waugh also uses the symbol of the 'Balmoral tartan' which covers Margot's table in a highly ironic way, as it was the tartan that was created specially for Queen Victoria, who would hardly have been amused at Margot's line of work. In *Put Out More Flags*, Margot's London house is demolished by bombs.

Promiscuous decor runs rife in *A Handful of Dust*. Jenny Abdul Akbar,[38] who has escaped from a Moulay's harem, has a room that is 'furnished promiscuously', and Waugh uses the word in both its senses of sexual promiscuity and an indiscriminate collection of things; in this case,

[37] Waugh wrote of the Venetians that there was 'something of the East in the modesty of the women and the gravity of the men'. 'Sinking, Shadowed and Sad – the Last Glory of Europe', *Essays*, p.546.
[38] Jenny Abdul Akbar's name is similar in sound to that of the Maharanee of Cooch Behar who was the Hindoo lady whose house Waugh used to visit. In *A Little Learning* he said: 'Women sometimes resorted to fisticuffs in her house' (p.212). And Daphne Fielding in *Mercury Presides* writes of how the Bright Young People were fascinated by her and of the times they spent in her Hill Street house where they were met by the 'heavy scent of incense; lights were shaded and spirals of joss-stick smoke hung in the air. Indira Cooch Behar looked like a romantic princess out of *The Arabian Nights*' (1954), p.108. Olivia Plunket Greene used to attend these gatherings and this, more than the Mitfords' house, could have been the house that was full of 'bright cruel girls'.

furnishings. Jenny is seen to have a 'truly Eastern disregard of the right properties of things'; 'mats made for prayer' are strewn on the divan, and her treasures include a 'phallic fetish from Senegal'. Jenny herself wears crimson – a good colour for a harlot.

Jenny is sent to Hetton by the gang of thieves, their leader being Polly Cockpurse who, as her name suggests, has derived her fortune 'from men', to try to seduce Tony so that life will be easier for Brenda. Jenny does not succeed, but her attitude to Hetton is interesting, for she tries to denigrate Brenda in Tony's eyes. Tony, a loyal fellow, supports his wife, for he has no idea that Jenny is at Hetton for a highly immoral purpose. Jenny gushes about the house – 'a sweet old place'; 'its atmosphere'; 'such dignity and repose'; 'I love everything that's solid and homely and *good* after ...'; and she goes on to imply that, after her dreadful life with the Moulay, Tony and Hetton represent everything she desires. Realising that she is not succeeding with Tony she indirectly attacks Brenda when he shows her the morning room that Brenda is having redecorated – 'Oh, Teddy, what a shame. I do hate seeing things modernized'; to which Tony replies, 'It isn't a room we used very much.' Undaunted, Jenny is finally disloyal to Brenda saying that although she has been a 'wonderful friend' and she 'wouldn't say anything against her' she wonders whether Brenda 'really understands this beautiful place and all it means' to Tony. Again, Tony cuts her off sharply: 'Tell me more about your terrible life ...' (p.92). The point is that Brenda does understand what the place means to Tony but she cannot see any beauty in Hetton. She '*detests*' it because it is so 'appallingly ugly', not like her own family home, which was a 'really lovely house' built by Vanbrugh. She would, however, never tell Tony what she really thinks of Hetton because he is so 'crazy about the place'.

Although the country guide book describes Hetton as '*This, formerly one of the notable houses of the country, was entirely rebuilt in 1864 in the Gothic style and is now devoid of interest ...*', for Tony it is the house of his ancestors and there is not a 'glazed brick or encaustic tile' that isn't 'dear' to his 'heart'. Tony also realises that Hetton is unfashionable in the respect that people now preferred 'urns and colonnades'[39] to the 'half-timber and old pewter' of twenty years previously. The house has already been referred to as 'amusing' and Tony suspects that one day it will come into its own again. As he says to John Beaver, 'I know it isn't fashionable to like this sort of architecture now ... but I think it's good of its kind' (p.35).

The trouble is that Hetton isn't fashionable and, in Waugh's terms, it is the fashion of the day that reflects the morality of the day, which is why Tony's Gothic world 'comes to grief'. The fashion is for tearing down historic houses to make way for maisonette flats, which represent not a Gothic world of romance but a modern world of sordid intrigue and adultery.

Brenda is easily enticed by the modern world. At Hetton she already has a 'modern bed' and sleeps in a room called Guinevere – a name for a wanton or

---

[39] In 'A Call to the Orders', Waugh wrote of a 'formidable outcrop of urns' and pointed out that the builders of the eighteenth century had used urns 'liberally, but with clear purpose', whereas the present builders were scattering them 'indiscriminately' and seemed to have lost the 'art of designing them'. *Essays*, p.217.

adulteress; while her future lover, John Beaver, sleeps in Lancelot on his first visit to Hetton. From the beginning Waugh prepares us for Brenda's adultery, and that adultery is encouraged by the grasping Mrs Beaver, whose constant aim in life is to find 'another suitable house to split up' – the *double entendre* being obvious. She, sensing that Brenda is about to have an affair with her son, actively promotes it by persuading her to take a flat that has a 'slap-up' bathroom with every 'transatlantic refinement' and another room which has 'space for a bed'.

Ironically, Brenda taking on the flat from Mrs Beaver means that Tony will not be able to install the four new bathrooms that he had planned for Hetton 'without disturbing the character of the house'. As he says to Jock Grant-Menzies, 'We had to economise because of Brenda's economics.' In fact, he has to economise because of Brenda's adultery, and when he mentions to her that he will have to put off the improvements, her telling reply is 'I don't really deserve it ... I've been carrying on *anyhow* this week' (p.56).

Mrs Beaver, who has taught her son how to go over houses, 'as it was her hobby even before she started doing them up as a business', opens *A Handful of Dust*, revelling in the fact that a great house has burnt down, because it means another commission for her. Always on the lookout for work, she travels, with the 'gang of thieves', to Hetton to see what can be done with the morning room.

Mrs Beaver finds the room 'appalling'; Daisy thinks '*Everything's* horrible; Polly Cockpurse says 'It's a bit mouldy'; and Veronica wants to 'blow the whole thing sky-high'. Tony, interestingly, uses the same remark about the room as he did to Jenny earlier: 'It's not one we use a great deal.'

Brenda is determined to have the place redecorated, as she says she must have '*one* habitable room' downstairs as a small sitting-room for herself. The drawing room is not feasible because of its size, and the smoking-room and the library are obviously Tony's territory. Waugh wrote in 'The Philistine Age of English Decoration' that in the Victorian home the 'library-smoking-room' was an 'inviolable masculine sanctuary'[40] – obviously something he believed in all his life, judging by his own inviolable library at both Piers Court and Combe Florey.[41] Mrs Beaver wishes to cover the walls with white chromium[42] plating – a material that was used liberally in the twenties and thirties for bathrooms and living rooms in modern flats. Tony cannot believe that Brenda really wants chromium plating in the morning room, and although she says that it was only 'an idea' that is what she wants; and before

[40] *Essays*, p.220.
[41] Alec Waugh writes: 'Both at Stinchcombe and Combe Florey he furnished the best ground floor room with bookshelves that had some handsome bays. He had a fine writing desk. The room was sancrosanct. The children were not allowed to enter it.' *The Best Wine Last: an Autobiography through the Years 1932-1969* (1978), p.58.
[42] Waugh disliked chromium plating. He wrote of the Victorian householder who had his 'hip-bath before the bedroom fire' which 'provided a luxurious predecessor of the chromium and decalite cubicles of his degenerate grandchildren'. 'The Philistine Age of English Decoration', *Essays*, p.219. And in *Brideshead Revisited* Charles Ryder contrasts the old-fashioned, luxurious bathroom with 'the uniform, clinical little chambers, glittering with chromium-plate and looking-glass, which pass for luxury in the modern world' (p.149).

he knows it Tony is writing to tell her that the workmen are starting on the chromium plating next week and '... you know what I think about that'. Chromium plating is to play a large part in Tony's later hallucinations.

Brenda, by telling Tony that she understands that he will have to sell his beloved Hetton to pay her alimony, causes him to realise that his dream of a Gothic world has been shattered; and so he leaves the country as the associations of Hetton are too painful for him to contemplate for a while. He joins Dr Messinger's expedition, which is in search of a fabulous city in South America which Tony imagines as the idealised Gothic city of his dreams,[43] hoping that this Gothic world will not come to grief. But, sadly, it does for in his delirium Tony realises that Mrs Beaver has got there first. He learns:

'There is no City. Mrs Beaver has covered it with chromium plating and converted it into flats. Three guineas a week, each with a separate bathroom. Very suitable for base love. And Polly will be there. She and Mrs Beaver under the fallen battlements ...' (p.207)

There is no escape for Tony. He falls victim to Mr Todd and spends the rest of his life reading Dickens to him; and the symbol of keeping Dickens's novels alive amongst the savages is the equivalent of Tony trying to maintain Hetton in a savage, immoral, modern world. Brenda, 'practically starving' in her maisonette flat, learns that Tony, while he is away, is not only having bathrooms put in at Hetton but is having the morning room, which had been 'demolished', restored. She hasn't learnt very much by her experience, for she thinks it is 'mean' that he didn't go to Mrs Beaver for the bathrooms.

In the alternative ending to *A Handful of Dust*,[44] Brenda and Tony are re-united. Brenda tells Tony that she has 'turned against the flat' mainly because of the '*radiator smell*'.[45] Without Brenda knowing, and in collusion with Mrs Beaver, Tony takes the flat on himself, for unstated but obvious reasons, and Mrs Beaver, for the price of a table for the flat, observes 'absolute discretion', making sure that Tony's name is not on the board downstairs.

If this had been the true ending of *A Handful of Dust* it would have weakened Waugh's whole argument. Tony becoming the same as everybody else is not the answer; and the solution in the book, although it might not seem so, is a much more realistic and optimistic one. While Tony languishes in the jungle, his cousins take over Hetton. Death duties have caused them to shut most of the house and they live in the morning room, smoking room and what had been Tony's study. Teddy Last, who breeds silver foxes, hopes that they will

[43] There is a parallel with Waugh here who, when he was travelling in Brazil, had a vision of Boa Vista, but wrote on his arrival that 'the Boa Vista of my imagination had come to grief ... ploughed like Carthage, bought, demolished and transported brick by brick to another continent as though it had taken the fancy of Mr Hearst ...'. 'A Journey to Brazil in 1932' from 'Ninety Two Days' in *When The Going Was Good* (1978), p.229.

[44] The alternative ending to the serialised version of *A Handful of Dust* was called *By Special Request* and can be found in Evelyn Waugh, *Mr Loveday's Little Outing and Other Sad Stories* (1936), pp.23-47.

[45] There was no central heating at Combe Florey during Evelyn Waugh's lifetime.

be the means to restore Hetton to 'the glory that it has enjoyed in the days of his Cousin Tony'. James F. Carens sees this as the 'final irony of this novel'.[46] Ironic it is, but optimistic too, for the Lasts are a united family. They work together and have a much better understanding of the modern world. If the modern woman wants angora and silver fox to wear, they are prepared to breed the animals to supply such a demand, and by doing so will probably manage to preserve Hetton for future generations. They also reject Mrs Beaver's plans for a monument to Tony at Hetton (an ambitious suggestion of redecorating the chapel as a chantry) in favour of a plain stone that has come from their own quarries and been cut by their own workmen. They can survive in the modern world, whereas a romantic like Tony cannot.

The large historic house in Waugh's terms is nearly always seen as masculine. Brideshead is almost aggressively masculine; Hetton is full of the kinds of discomforts that Waugh expects men will put up with while women won't; Anchorage House with its 'august dimensions' is masculine; Boot Magna, although ruled by nannies, exhudes a masculine atmosphere, as does Doubting Hall with its lofty Palladian façade, its equestrian statue pointing a baton imperiously down the drive, and its overtly masculine library. John Plant's father's house in St John's Wood retains its 'own smell – an agreeable, rather stuffy atmosphere of cigar smoke and cantaloup; a masculine smell – women had always seemed a little out of place there, as in a London club on Coronation Day' (p.128).

There is one house which is an exception and that is Malfrey, which is inhabited by Barbara Sothill and her husband. Malfrey has something 'female and voluptuous' about its beauty; and whereas other houses maintain an 'original modesty' or a 'manly defence', Malfrey lies 'spread out, sumptuously at ease, splendid, defenceless and provocative; a Cleopatra among houses' (*Put Out More Flags*, p.9). Barbara Sothill abandoned her brother, Basil Seal, and their vaguely incestuous relationship, not for an affair with her husband, but for Malfrey – 'It was for Malfrey that she loved her prosaic and slightly absurd husband.' Barbara's feelings for Basil are, however, only lying dormant, and when Freddie no longer wants to talk about Basil when she does, she leads him down his 'favourite paths' to a 'gothic pavilion' where she knows that he likes to make love; and while she surrenders herself, not to him but to Malfrey, she thinks of Basil. Barbara, although one of Waugh's most sympathetic female characters, prostitutes herself for a house. Her saving grace in Waugh's eyes is that Malfrey is a beautiful house and Barbara never has any ideas of modernising it. Everything about Malfrey is 'splendid and harmonious' except for the incongruity of the visiting evacuee, Doris, who lurks in Barbara's and Basil's path in the marble pedestalled corridor 'rubbing herself on a pilaster *like* a cow on a stump'.

Deceptive first appearances

In *Work Suspended*, John Plant comes home to arrange, as he says, for the

---

46 James F. Carens, *The Satiric Art of Evelyn Waugh*, p.29.

'destruction of his father's house'. He knows that the property developers are after it and that it is likely that another 'great uninhabitable barrack' of flats will appear in its place; but he sells it because he has no desire to live there as the district is already ruined and he wants to get out of London. His decision to settle in the country is well received by his friends, for country houses are seen as 'bolt holes' … places where one could take a girl during a love affair, or convalesce, or retire to write a book; and the owners of country houses are 'by their nature, a patient race, but repeated abuse was apt to sour them; new blood in their ranks was highly welcome' (p.145). Another more 'amicable' reason for Plant's friends being interested in his move is that they, like him, have a 'specialised' enthusiasm for domestic architecture which is one of the 'peculiarities' of Plant's generation. Their admiration is mainly for the classical tradition, and even Lucy Simmonds's husband, Roger, 'compromised with his Marxist austerities so far as to keep up with his collection of the works of Batty Langley and William Halfpenny' (p.146).

Roger shows Plant a 1767 engraving[47] of *A Composed Hermitage in the Chinese Taste* which is still standing near Bath and which he would like Plant to buy.

> Roger's engraving showed a pavilion, still rigidly orthodox in plan, but, in elevation decked with ornament conceived in wild ignorance of oriental forms; there were balconies and balustrades of geometric patterns; the cornices swerved upwards at the corners in the lines of a pagoda; the roof was crowned with an onion cupola which might have been Russian, bells hung from the capitals of barley-sugar columns; the windows were freely derived from the Alhambra; there was a minaret. To complete the atmosphere the engraver had added a little group of Turkish military performing the bastinado upon a curiously complacent malefactor, an Arabian camel and a mandarin carrying a bird in a cage. (p.168)

Lucy Simmonds's reaction to this is to say 'I can't think why John would like to have a house like that', which strikes Plant with a 'keen sense of pleasure. She and I were on the same side' (p.159).

First impressions in *Work Suspended* are deceiving, for Lucy and Plant are not on the same side. Lucy doesn't like the house because, as a Marxist, she cannot share the group's 'nostalgia for the style of living' which was enjoyed by the noble classes in the eighteenth century, whereas Plant realises that the reason his friends want him to have the house is that 'it *was* just the house one would want someone else to have. I was graduating from the exploiting to the exploited class.' However, as Plant's preoccupation is in finding a house that is suitable for him, rather than a house that is an open invitation for all his friends to come and stay, that 'quest' becomes the 'structure' of their friendship. (Interestingly, Plant sees the openness of Lucy's friendship as enabling him to enter her mind, to be able to 'wander at will over the rich estate'; rather as Charles Ryder sees Julia as a 'property'. And of course, neither Plant nor Ryder fulfil their relationships with Lucy and Julia.) Their

---

[47] Jeffrey Heath has said that the engraving shows the kind of architectural joke that Waugh had 'deplored only a year before in *A Call to the Orders*', *The Picturesque Prison*, p.146. But this view is questionable. See below, Appendix Four.

tastes are poles apart. Plant, like his father, and like Waugh, is looking for a house that is 'at least a hundred years old' with 'high ceilings', a 'marble chimney piece in the drawing room', a 'walled kitchen garden', a 'paddock' – and the standard of gentility he is aiming at is 'something between the squire's and the retired admiral's'. Whereas Plant's taste is for the dark and Victorian, Lucy has a 'womanly love of sunlight and a Marxist faith in the superior beauties of concrete and steel'. Lucy thinks Plant's search for such a house and his wish to enrol himself with the 'rural bourgeois' milieu is 'grotesque', and she goes with him in a 'cheerful and purely sporting spirit as one may hunt a fox which one has no taste to eat' (p.175).

Ironically, Lucy's own house is full of 'bourgeois furniture' and 'chintz cushions' which do not suit her ideals at all; but she has taken the house furnished and does nothing with it. Mr Benwell even congratulates her on it, saying that he likes a 'London house to look like a London house'; but Plant realises that Lucy 'looks out of place there', as does Roger with his new artistic pose. Plant finally buys the house without Lucy being there, as she is heavily pregnant. Lucy's interest in her baby overrides any interest that she had in Plant and his house and, although he tells her that she will be his 'first guest', she never visits it; and he never lives there, for in wartime it is 'requisitioned' and symbolically 'filled with pregnant women, and through five years bit by bit befouled and dismembered'.

In *Helena*, too, first appearances are deceptive. Helena and Calpurnia are shown over the building site of Diocletian's new palace which is being built on the shores of the Adriatic. They are shown the 'concrete mixers, the system of central heating, all of the latest pattern ...' and the following conversation ensues:

> 'It's not a style that would ever go down in Britain,' said Helena at length.
> 'I suppose it's very modern, dear.'
> 'Not a window in the whole place.'
> 'On our lovely coast.'
> 'I never met Diocletian. My husband had a great respect for him, but I don't think he can be very nice.'
> 'The coast will never be the same again if he comes to live here.' (p.71)

Diocletian has already 'modernized' Nicomedia, which is being called the 'New Rome' and which Helena sees as a 'name of ill omen'. Helena is also aware of the modernization of Rome, for as she travels across the city to get to the dower house, the Sessorian Palace, she sees that behind the 'façades of temples and the historic buildings of the Republic' there are 'shabby apartment houses ... ten storeys high ... tottering with the weight of humanity'. But Helena isn't all she appears to be. When Constantine wants his arch decorated with sculptured figures like those on the arch of Trajan he is told by Professor Emolphus (another Silenus) and the sculptor Carpicius that it can't be done – modern sculptors are not capable of creating 'traditional symbolic figures'. Infuriated, he screams: 'Then, God damn it, go and pull the carvings of Trajan's arch and stick them on mine. Do it at once. Start this afternoon' – to which Helena says, 'Spoken like a man, my son' (p.108). Helena does not approve of Constantine's plan for a 'New Rome'. She doesn't like 'new things ... No one does in the land I come from.' In search of the True Cross, she learns in Aelia Capitolina that the marble steps to Government House are the 'identical' ones which 'our Lord had descended on his way to death'. When she hears that news she orders the staircase to be dismantled to be sent to the Pope for the Lateran, and successfully makes Government House 'uninhabitable'. All in a good cause, and in Helena's mind an absolute necessity. Whereas others had done their duty in the arena, Helena's is a 'gentler task'. She gathers wood and with her 'precious cargo' sails 'joyfully away' – leaving behind a demolished city for the hopeful rebirth of Rome.

First appearances are also deceptive in *Love Among The Ruins*. When Miles first meets Clara he is enchanted not only by her golden beard but by her surroundings, which remind him of Mountjoy, a stately home, full of splendid antiques, which has become a prison. Clara's 'cubicle' in her 'Nissen hut' is 'unlike anyone else's quarters in Satellite city'. She has pictures 'unlike anything approved by the Ministry of Art' which have been left to her by her mother, along with some 'cracked Crown Derby', antique fans and embroideries, and along with these she embodies all the vitality of the past. Her 'cubicle' reminds Miles 'of prison', which is the 'highest praise' he can give. But appearances are deceptive; such an idyllic setting and such a love affair cannot last in a modern world. Clara discovers that despite her Klugman operation she is pregnant, and has an abortion. By the time Miles finds her in hospital her golden beard has been replaced by a hideous mask.

Clara's beauty, along with her idyllic surroundings have become associated in Miles's mind with the pleasurable time he spent at Mountjoy, that civilised prison with its silks and tapestries, its panelling, its chandeliers and its marble temple in the grounds. Miles destroys Mountjoy just as the State destroyed Clara:

> Once before, he had burned his childhood. Now his brief adult life lay in ashes; the enchantments that surrounded Clara were one with the splendours of Mountjoy; her great golden beard, one with the tongues of flame that had leaped and expired among the stars; her fans and pictures and scraps of old embroidery, one with the gilded cornices and silk hangings, black, cold, and sodden. He ate his sausage with keen appetite and went to work. (p.216)

Having destroyed the past, Miles visits Clara in hospital. He finds her bored because everything is 'so dull today. Nothing except this prison that has been burnt down'; and when he reminds her how often he talked to her of Mountjoy she is surprised and says, 'Did you, Miles ? ... I've such a bad memory for things that don't concern me' (p.219). Mountjoy, and consequently, Miles, mean little to Clara. She is only interested in herself, and although she has some of her property, like an old shawl, with her in hospital, she is prepared to sell out to the State if there is some benefit to herself. Clara has none of the civilised values of the things she surrounds herself with.

As the only graduate of Mountjoy, everyone else having been killed because of the fire, Miles is required by the State to lecture to the nation as the 'whole future of Penology' is in his hands. He will travel with Miss Flower (rather in the manner of Trimmer and Virginia), who will show the model for the new Mountjoy that will 'arise from the ashes', the model being a 'standard packing-case'. Miles is expected to marry the ugly Miss Flower, and it looks as though the State's plan for the future will succeed. However, appearances are again deceptive, for at the marriage ceremony Miles fingers the lighter in his pocket and 'instantly, surprisingly, there burst out a tiny flame – gemlike, hymeneal, auspicious' (p.223). The conclusion one must reach is that Miles commits suicide rather than marry Miss Flower and become a puppet for the State. It is a 'hymeneal' and 'auspicious' flame, so Waugh sees Miles's swansong as a poetic and propitious action. Without Miles, the only graduate left of Mountjoy, the State will flounder.

*

All in all, Waugh blamed the modern age for the destruction of the great houses, even more than the war and the destruction that was caused by the German bombs which he saw as a 'negligible addition to the sum of our own destructiveness ... our surviving fine buildings and corner of landscape only serve to accentuate the prevailing desolation'.[48]

The great houses for him represented civilisation, and Waugh sees the destruction of them as the break-down of civilisation. Modern morals and values threaten the beauty and dignity of life, which is why the Bright Young People come in for plenty of attack. In *Vile Bodies* he wrote of them living in Edward Throbbing's house in Hertford Street: 'I think we shall have to move soon. Everything's getting rather broken up, too, and dirty, if you know what I mean. Because you see, there aren't any servants, only the butler and his wife, and they are always tight now' (p.29). They are always drunk because of the influence of Agatha Runcible and her friends. Waugh abhorred such carelessness; and in the main, as we have seen, it is women who come in for the lash of his pen.

Waugh's letters and diaries are full of references to art and architecture, but those references are rarely flattering to women. Such comments are made as 'Lord C's last act was to give Pam the house he had taken for Randolph. Randolph has been peremptorily evicted & Pam is tearing out fine Queen Anne woodwork'.[49] In 1959 he wrote to Ann Fleming on hearing that she had found a house:

> There are few pleasures to touch those of embellishing a building ... You are
> one of the very few women I have met who have positive good taste in visual
> things. When a woman has taste it is quite different from a man's and still more
> from a bugger's. I am sure you will make something fine.[50]

[48] Evelyn Waugh, 'What to do with the Upper Classes', *Town and Country* (September, 1946), p.260.

[49] *Letters*, p.425.

[50] Ibid., p.526.

To Sir Maurice Bowra he wrote first:

> We went to see Ann's house. It is no beauty; nor yet an eye sore. A typical English country house that has been buggered about for 350 years. Rather large. She talks of demolition. I urge that it is almost as expensive to destroy as to build and that (except for carpets) large rooms are much cheaper to furnish well than small.[51]

And then later:

> I wish I had the opportunity to conduct you round Ann's edifice pointing out its deplorable qualities. She has spent as much on it as the rebuilders of Downing Street. It has almost every deficiency.[52]

Mrs Fleming's taste was questionable after all. Almost the only one of Evelyn Waugh's female friends who comes through unscathed as far as taste is concerned is Lady Diana Cooper – the model for Mrs Stitch – a very exceptional lady.

---

[51] Ibid., p.530.

[52] Ibid., p.615. Also Ann Fleming writes: 'He and Laura spent a weekend in the house which Ian and I had built; he was persistently critical of all we had done and Laura bade him write an apology. It starts: "I am apt to pick holes." "Your Affec: Evelyn".' *Evelyn Waugh and His World*, p.237.

CHAPTER NINE

Julia Stitch: An Exceptional Case

I have a friend whom I have more than once attempted to portray in fiction under the name of 'Mrs Stitch'.[1]

Julia Stitch is based on Lady Diana Cooper; and Mark Amory has said that it is the 'most direct portrait to appear in Waugh's work'[2] – a statement that is borne out by Lady Diana herself; her acceptance of her character was so great that once when Waugh sent her a telegram asking if he could stay with her in Paris her response was a postcard which simply read 'oh yes please Stitch'.[3] Christopher Sykes says that Mrs Stitch is a 'caricaturist's impression of Diana Cooper ... not only did she recognise her image in the distorting mirror but she rejoiced at it; she was indeed positively irritated by well-meaning people who affected to see no semblance between herself and this extraordinary figure of fiction.'[4] Lady Diana has confirmed that this is correct.[5]

The point is, however, that Mrs Stitch is not a caricature, the image has not been distorted, and 'this extraordinary figure of fiction' is the very real and very extraordinary figure of Lady Diana. Most critics have noted that Mrs Stitch's idiosyncratic driving habits are similar to Lady Diana's own; but Mrs Stitch and Lady Diana have far more in common than their driving. A comparison of the real and the fictional character will show that they are one.

Mrs Stitch first appears in *Scoop*, and when we first meet her she is in bed – her face hidden under a mud pack. Lady Diana has always received her morning visitors in bed[6] and in fact Waugh recorded the following in his diary:

Message to call on Diana; found her with face expressionless in mud mask.[7]

---

[1] Evelyn Waugh, *A Tourist to Africa* (1960), p.18. 'Stitch' can either mean, in slang, a nickname for a tailor or 'lying with a woman', *c*.18-20c.ob. See Francis Grose, *A Classical Dictionary of the Vulgar Tongue*, edited by Eric Partridge (1963).

[2] *Letters*, p.650.

[3] *Diaries*, p.645.

[4] Sykes, p.237. Lady Diana was delighted with *Scoop*. She read 'Mr Wu's book' aloud to her friends and called it 'Pride of Boot'. See Diana Cooper, *The Light of Common Day* (1959), p.154.

[5] Lady Diana has been kind enough to read this chapter and to make a number of helpful comments. Letter, and chapter returned, to J. McDonnell 17 February 1983.

[6] Including myself when Lady Diana granted an interview on 16 November 1981.

[7] *Diaries*, p.391.

and when he started *Scoop* three months later:

> On Thursday 15th made a very good start with the first page of a novel describing Diana's early morning.[8]

Mrs Stitch's early morning in *Scoop* consists of dictating details on the telephone to a designer about the costumes for a charity show; signing cheques; talking to her secretary; helping her daughter[9] with her Latin homework; giving instructions to the elegant young man who is painting castles on the ceiling, and doing the crossword all at the same time. Mrs Stitch's morning has much in common with that of Lady Diana:

> As always with Diana's houses, her bedroom was the heart of the establishment. The bed itself rose sixteen feet from a shoal of gold dolphins and tridents to a wreath of dolphins at the crown, while ropes made fast the sea-blue satin curtains. Here she would hold court every morning; seeing friends; dictating letters; planning a raid on some ministry of works storehouse; reading or listening to music.[10]

The room described was in Admiralty House, and Waugh frequently visited Lady Diana there. In 1963 he wrote to tell her that 'Admiralty House has gone downhill since baby's time. The fine dining room is transformed into offices, the dolphin furniture banished with the Capt. Cook paintings. White paint everywhere. Baby's bedroom is the drawing room.'[11]

Waugh thought that Lady Diana had superb taste and said of the Embassy in Paris when she was there that it was a 'house of dazzling beauty, Borghese decorations in a Louis XV structure, brilliantly rearranged by Diana'.[12]

Having ruined castles painted on the ceiling of the bedroom in a house that was 'a superb creation by Nicolas Hawksmoor' might at first glance seem tasteless, but it is not entirely so. According to Lady Diana, the young painter was based on Rex Whistler,[13] and his style[14] was one that Lady Diana enjoyed in her own house in Gower Street. Her main regret on leaving that house was the loss of the drawing room decorated by Rex Whistler with Roman plaques and vases in *trompe l'oeil*.[15]

Lady Diana has said that Waugh and Whistler did not get on particularly well – 'There were never two characters more opposite. Evelyn liked his work

---

[8] Ibid., p.409.

[9] The character of Josephine has been substituted for Lady Diana's son, Viscount John Julius Norwich who, when young, used to spend his early mornings with his mother.

[10] Philip Ziegler, *Diana Cooper* (1981), p.182.

[11] *Letters*, p.605.

[12] Ibid., p.646.

[13] Lady Diana's comments on this chapter.

[14] Rex Whistler's style was an amalgam of Wren, classical Rome and Gothic. It was a style that had nothing to do with the experimentalism of the twenties but had a touch of the rococo and found its inspiration in the seventeenth and eighteenth centuries, and later on in the nineteenth century.

[15] Waugh, although he collected 'narrative pictures', had some *trompe l'oeil* ones because of Lady Diana's influence. See Sykes, p.516.

but never would have bought any as his taste was for narrative pictures.'[16] Waugh's attitude to Whistler was a complex one. He approved of Whistler's classically influenced work but wasn't so much in favour of that which was influenced by the nineteenth century;[17] and in his diaries he said of Eddie Marsh that he hadn't 'any taste ... He likes Rex Whistler'.[18] However, it is likely that Waugh is here denigrating the man as much as the artist. Lady Diana was extremely fond of Rex Whistler. He was well-liked, witty, charming, and great fun to be with; qualities that Waugh would have resented, particularly if Rex Whistler took Lady Diana's attention away from him; and as they attended some of the same social events that was likely.

To return to the ceiling in question, the only difference between Mrs Stitch and Lady Diana is that Lady Diana has said that she 'would never have the ceiling painted only the walls'.[19] The subject of the painting is in itself most interesting. The young man is being reprimanded by Mrs Stitch for 'putting too much ivy on the turret ... the owl won't show up unless you have him on the bare stone'. As Lady Diana has pointed out, the reference here is to Thomas Gray's *Elegy Written in a Country Churchyard*:[20]

> Save that from yonder ivy-mantled tower
> The moping owl does to the moon complain.

The ceiling has an eighteenth-century subject – most suitable for an eighteenth-century house.

When we first meet Mrs Stitch, Waugh creates a speech for her which, as it ripples along, sums up her character and personality immediately and forcefully:

> '... *Munera*, darling, like tumtiddy; always a short a in neuter plurals. It sounds like an anagram: see if "Terracotta" fits. I'm *delighted* to see you, John. Where have you been? You can come and buy carpets with me; I've found a new shop in Bethnal Green; kept by a very interesting Jew who speaks no English; the most extraordinary things keep happening to his sister. Why should I go to Viola Chasm's Distressed Area; did she come to my Model Madhouse?' (*Scoop*, p.7)

Waugh, here, has satirised the speech and activities of society ladies. The speech, however, is not unlike Lady Diana's own. Once, when she thought

---

[16] Lady Diana's comments on this chapter.

[17] In 'Let Us Return to the Nineties but Not to Oscar Wilde', Waugh wrote of the 'early Victorian tide' which had retreated and how, among other things, the 'Rex Whistler decorations' had 'dried out very drab and disappointing'. *Essays*, pp.122-3. It should be noted that Waugh's book *Wine in Peace and War* had illustrations by Rex Whistler.

[18] *Diaries*, pp.312-13.

[19] Lady Diana's comments on this chapter.

[20] Ibid. Jeffrey Heath has said that Mrs Stitch urges the elegant young man who is painting the ceiling to 'copy a lion's head from a photograph taken at Twisbury Manor', *The Picturesque Prison: Evelyn Waugh and his Writing* (1982), pp.127 & 133. The reference to the lion's head is to do with the design for a centurion's breastplate for a charity show which Mrs Stitch is discussing with the designer on the telephone.

that bankruptcy lay ahead of her and Duff Cooper[21] after he lost his position as Ambassador in Paris, she wrote to her son, John Julius Norwich (and she writes as she talks):

> We'll not be able to live in France, and I and Papa will drive to your home to ask for shelter, and your beastly tart-wife will be like Goneril and Reagan merged and bang the flimsy door in our nose, and we'll get a hulk on Bosham marshes as Peggoty did before us, and Papa will make love to the paid help and I will be Mrs Gummidge.[22]

Mrs Stitch's language is typical of Lady Diana's language, and she uses similar slang terms. Mrs Stitch has such expressions as 'Wasters' – short for the title of a book in *Scoop* called *Waste of Time*; and 'Foregonners' – also in *Scoop* meaning a foregone conclusion.[23] Lady Diana uses such expressions as 'jolly old chlorers' – short for chloroform; and 'get off scotters' – meaning scot-free.[24] The only other Waugh heroine who uses such slang is Brenda Last in *A Handful of Dust* who is responsible for 'badders' – meaning bad news; and 'lawner' – meaning refreshment served on the lawn at a meet.[25]

Mrs Stitch also uses other slang expressions such as 'she's driven three men into the bin';[26] 'hot sit-upon'; 'bang right'; and 'just the ticket'. Lady Diana's language is full of slang – and she says that 'such expressions as "looney-bin"; "bang right" and "bang wrong" were used by all our world'.[27]

Mrs Stitch's language is also peremptory. When Guy Crouchback in *Officers and Gentlemen* politely tries to refuse the offer of a gift of Forster's *Alexandria* she says, 'Take it, fool'; and when he tries to open the door of her car for her, she barks: 'Other side, fool. Jump in.' Also, when the Commander in Chief, at luncheon, says he knows the best poem, she snaps 'recitation', and when someone interrupts him she demands 'Hush'. Lady Diana has a similar manner. Waugh records in his diary that when Peter Quennell mentioned that he had 'more or less asked a girl' to dine with him, Diana snapped: 'Do I know her? Name? Who is she?'[28]

Mrs Stitch's demand for 'recitation' is directly patterned on Lady Diana, for she was encouraged as a child to learn great tracts of poetry. She carried on the tradition with her son – 'Learning by heart was all-important;

---

[21] 'I do not remember his ever talking to me of Mr Stitch. I do remember thinking what a good picture it was of Duff.' Letter from Lady Diana to J. McDonnell, 4 February 1983. For the identification of Duff Cooper as Algernon Stitch, also see Sykes, p.237.

[22] Philip Ziegler, *Diana Cooper*, p.264.

[23] *Scoop*, pp.8, 11.

[24] Philip Ziegler, *Diana Cooper*, pp.54, 234.

[25] ' "Ers" for the end of a word was Oxfordian and inherited by me – it was in use before my day.' Lady Diana's comments on this chapter. Also see Morris Marples, *University Slang* (1950), pp.77-8.

[26] 'Bin' is short for 'looney-bin', slang for a mental asylum. The *OED* (Supplement) credits Waugh – '1938, E. Waugh. *Scoop*. "To my certain knowledge she's driven three men into the bin".'

[27] Lady Diana's comments on this chapter.

[28] *Diaries*, p.647.

pocket-money had to be earned by recitation.'[29] Even her daughter-in-law came under fire when Lady Diana discovered that her grand-daughter did not know any nursery rhymes – 'so do make her learn poems – too old for her but with simple metres. *"Come Live with Me and be My Love"* for instance.'[30] Recitation was common practice when she entertained her friends to lunch or dinner. In 1963 Cecil Beaton recorded of a luncheon at her house: 'Diana winking and joking about her old age; talk about the new President, poems of Thomas Moore recited – a treat.'[31] Performance was necessary, and Evelyn Waugh was expected to read his latest novel aloud. Waugh also records that at the Embassy in Paris, when Peter Quennell said at dinner 'I wonder if anyone ever reads Browning nowadays?', Duff Cooper recited Browning's *Sordello* for twenty minutes.[32]

Apart from demanding 'recitation' in *Officers and Gentlemen*, Mrs Stitch also tries to get her daughter, Josephine, to perform in *Scoop*. Waugh is obviously gently mocking Lady Diana here, for Josephine will do nothing that she is told to do:

> 'Show him your imitation of the Prime Minister.'
> 'No.'
> 'Sing him your Neapolitan song.'
> 'No.'
> 'Stand on your head. Just once for Mr Boot.'
> 'No.'
> 'Oh dear ...' (*Scoop*, p.9)

Mrs Stitch also uses allusive language. She remembers Guy in *Officers and Gentlemen* because he was previously known to her when, during lunch, a cow had escaped – '*C'è scappata la mucca*' – and she had chased and caught it. Consequently she introduces Guy to her husband with 'Algie, you remember the underground cow?' Her remark leads the two local millionairesses to believe that Guy is her lover and that '*La vache souterraine? Ou la vache au Métro?*' is the 'new chic euphemism' which they will now remember to use with effect themselves on some other smart occasion.

Waugh's allusive idea of the cow escaping is again directly based on Lady Diana's personal experience. In 1941 she had a farm at Bognor and bought her first cow:

> Ever since my possession of Princess I have felt I cannot be complete without a cow. I had one called Fatima in Algiers and I have one today in France. Princess was a constant trouble before she got too attached to me, her

[29] Philip Ziegler, *Diana Cooper*, p.159.
[30] Ibid., p.290.
[31] Ibid., p.305.
[32] *Diaries*, p.647. Lady Diana in her comments on this chapter said that her husband would have 'read any other intelligible poem by Browning but definitely not *Sordello*. It is typical of Evelyn Waugh to have written such a thing – he was not fond of Duff.' In *PRB*, his essay on the Pre-Raphaelite brotherhood, Waugh said that Rosetti 'knew the greater part of *Sordello* by heart at a time when everyone else was exclaiming that it was totally unintelligible' (repr. 1982), p.27. *PRB* was first printed privately by Alastair Graham in 1926.

mistress-calf, to want to escape. How often in that first spring would I come to her with pail and stool under arm, beneath some radiant morning's stainless sky, larks exulting above, a warm sun already up and white-hoar frost underfoot, and find her vanished, the gardener already out in pursuit, the refugees barricaded in for fear of her being at large. Cows find it hard to hide, and I would generally find her at the old dairy-yard, knee-deep in valuable rationed cowfeed, grazing herself to the horns. I would fling a rope over her dear silly head and she would trot home by my side, more agile than I who stumbled along in huge rubber boots as unsuitable for a walk as were my nightcap and greasy face, so that I dreaded being seen by some early-rising acquaintance. The Princess, having no boots, once off the rope would evade me again.[33]

Waugh visited the farm at Bognor and, if not a witness to one of many Princess's escape attempts, had certainly heard stories about it. The lunch where Mrs Stitch mentions the 'escaped cow' is also reminiscent of a dinner in Algiers where Lady Diana sat next to General De Gaulle whose opening remark to her was '*Qu'avez vous fait de votre vache?*', having heard of her passion for cows, and their escapades, from his wife.[34] When asked if the idea of the escaping cow was based on her experiences, Lady Diana said, 'Most likely; my cows were always escaping!'[35]

Mrs Stitch, like Lady Diana, is indifferent to convention. At a luncheon party in Alexandria where the Pasha and the Commander-in-Chief are present she, 'never the slave of etiquette', puts Guy Crouchback on her right but 'thereafter talked beyond him at large'. Philip Ziegler reveals that Lady Diana, when ambassadress in Paris, 'could not bring herself to take seriously the French preoccupation with *place à table*. At a grand dinner Princess Radziwill conceived herself ill-placed and lit a cigarette before the fish to signal her displeasure: her neighbour, Gaston Palewski, thought this entirely proper; to Diana it seemed insane.'[36]

Mrs Stitch's indifference to convention also shows in the eccentricity of her apparel. At that particular lunch in *Officers and Gentlemen* she wears white linen, a Mexican sombrero and crimson slippers which are both 'fine and funny, with high curling toes'. Her outfit evokes cries of adulation from the local millionairesses who think it must be the height of fashion: 'Lady Steetch, Lady Steetch your hat ... Lady Steetch your shoes', to which Mrs Stitch replies affably, 'Five piastres in the bazaar' (p.129). Zeigler points out that Lady Diana 'always enjoyed dressing up, but even on the grandest occasion her appearance was apt to be unconventional.'[37] In Algiers a friend was asked to help entertain some important guests and found her in full Arab dress; and at another lunch party she wanted to bathe in the pool but had no costume. She rejected the loan of one – plunging into the pool in her 'lettuce-green lunch dress and Chinese coolie hat and swam to and fro at a stately

[33] Lady Diana Cooper, *Trumpets From the Steep* (1960), p.84. Also see Philip Ziegler, *Diana Cooper*, pp.204, 265.
[34] Ibid., p.86.
[35] Interview with Lady Diana.
[36] Philip Ziegler, *Diana Cooper*, p.227.
[37] Ibid., p.245.

breast-stroke'. This occasion was at Sir John Slessor's and she lunched after her dip in underclothes and his mackintosh.[38] She never believed in spending a great deal of money on clothes; and her trademark was always a very large hat.

One of Julia's Stitch's idiosyncrasies is the fact that she 'grew up with the conviction that comfort was rather common' and consequently she does not like any of her 'male guests to live soft' (*Officers and Gentlemen*, p.237). Ivor Claire, although he thought of moving in with her rather than staying in the nursing home in Alexandria, tells Guy that he decided not to, one of his reasons being that 'one can't be sure that Julia will give an invalid quite all he needs' (p.125). Tommy Blackhouse, on hearing that Guy is leaving the hospital to stay with Julia, remarks: 'I love Julia, but you have to be jolly well to stay with her' (p.237). Guy learns the truth of these remarks when Mrs Stitch puts him in a barely furnished basement room full of cockroaches. She dumps some tuberoses into the basin, surveys the room with 'unaffected pleasure' and throws in some cats to 'keep down the beetles' (p.237).

Bachelors suffer more at Mrs Stitch's hands than married men, for she believes that all men should be married; and if they are not, they get treated harshly. Guy, who had dined on Mrs Stitch's yacht when it had put into Santa Dulcina had thought it was 'a lap of luxury', but as Ivor Claire points out to him:

> 'Not the bachelors' cabins, Guy. Julia was brought up in the old tradition of giving hell to bachelors. There was mutiny brewing all the time. She used to drag one out of the casino like a naval picket rounding up a red-light quarter.'
> (*Officers and Gentlemen*, p.98)

Lady Diana grew up with the same conviction that 'male guests should not live soft', even extending her belief to her own son. Once when he was to stay with her sister Marjorie, she told her: 'I like him to have as much discomfort as possible ... No feather-beds or painted rooms. Give him a soldier's bed in a loft or basement or under the wide and starry.'[39] She also had no patience with illness – 'With a doctor pain was a suitable matter for discussion since it might be an aid to diagnosis; to complain of it otherwise was common. Diana inherited the attitude from her mother and applied it ruthlessly throughout her life to herself and her friends. Ann Fleming, in agony, once tried to escape from a dinner-party at the last moment. Diana was outraged: "Only menials have pains!" Obediently Mrs Fleming attended the dinner and was operated on next day for a twisted gut!'[40]

Waugh liked his comfort, and particularly liked eating in grand places. He wrote of Lady Diana:

[38] Ibid., p.222.
[39] Ibid., p.215. In *Put Out More Flags*, Waugh wrote of Malfrey in the war years: 'What had once been known as the "bachelors' wing", in the Victorian days when bachelors were hardy fellows who could put up with collegiate and barrack simplicity, was given over to the evacuees' (p.75).
[40] Philip Ziegler, *Diana Cooper*, p.15. Ziegler's text reads: 'Only servants have pains.' Lady Diana changed 'servants' to 'menials' in her comments on this chapter.

The one perennial discussion between Mrs Stitch and me is that I like to eat in marble halls under lofty chandeliers while Mrs Stitch insists on candlelit garrets and cellars. She thinks my preference hopelessly middle-class and tells me I am like Arnold Bennett.[41]

Julia Stitch is obviously a force to be reckoned with, and her reputation is such that when the men in *Officers and Gentlemen* are arguing about their sleeping quarters on the troopship Ivor Claire says, 'What they need is Julia Stitch to keep them in order' (p.103). This is again reminiscent of Lady Diana, for she was one of Waugh's few friends who could call him to order. On one famous occasion when he mischievously gave a man the wrong directions to the station she refused to speak to him until he ran after the man, apologised for his prank and helped him some of the way with his case. 'At times he was just too much,' says Lady Diana.[42]

Numerous other facets of Mrs Stitch's character belong to Lady Diana. Mrs Stitch has 'many interests but only one interest at a time' which, when she is with Guy Crouchback in Alexandria, is Alexandrian history. Lady Diana too is inclined to get sudden spurts of enthusiasm for a subject, though history, for her, has always been a staple of life. When Mrs Stitch stops her car in the centre of a crossing to point out Alexander's tomb – 'Forster says the marble was so bright that you could thread a needle at midnight' – Waugh is actually describing his own irritation with Lady Diana, who loved to stop and look at things. Ziegler writes:

> Diana did not find him altogether easy to travel with. He objected to her habit of dropping in at every hotel where she had ever stayed to gossip with the proprietor, and hated having things pointed out: '...."Don't miss the swans," sort of thing; so it's sealed lips when I see the spring's pageant.'[43]

In *Officers and Gentlemen* the King gives Mrs Stitch an amazing watch which her husband and his staff feel she should not accept; but Julia Stitch is not one to turn down a gift; and as she says, 'I can't help it, I *like* the King' (p.232). Again this is based on Lady Diana, who rarely turned down gifts. When she was eighteen Claud Russell, a grandson of the Duke of Bedford, presented her with a diamond-and-ruby pendant and a proposal of marriage. She kept the pendant and turned him down.[44]

Mrs Stitch's main idiosyncratic habit is, of course, her driving. Traffic jams are a bore and not to be put up with, so Mrs Stitch simply bowls along the pavement in her mass-produced, black baby car – 'tiny and glossy as a midget's funeral hearse' (*Scoop*, p.9). As she says, 'One of the things that I like about these absurd cars is that you can do things with them that you couldn't do in a real one' (p.10). Julia Stitch is above the law – a policeman might take her number and order her back into the road, but it doesn't mean anything to

[41] Waugh, *A Tourist to Africa*, p.19.
[42] Interview with Lady Diana.
[43] Philip Ziegler, *Diana Cooper*, p.266.
[44] Ibid., p.31. Lady Diana said: 'I was 18 – he was pushing 40. It was a petty pendant which I never wore.' Lady Diana's comments on this chapter.

her except that 'It's such a nuisance for Algy'. Algernon Stitch, her husband and a cabinet minister, deals with the police for her every time it happens.

Julia Stitch never understands the fuss that people make about such things. When she has driven down the steps to the gentlemen's lavatory in Sloane Street, after someone whom she thought she knew and wanted to talk to, she is surrounded by police and reporters. She has a '*great* deal to do', so simply says: 'I do think some of you might help, instead of standing there and asking questions' (p.40). The result of this composed statement is that she and her car are lifted up and placed back on the road – the police clearing a passage for her. Mrs Stitch isn't charged, for the police have been bribed and have 'pocketed their tips'.

Whether she's bowling across Hyde Park in *Scoop* – 'dextrously swerving between the lovers' – to try to catch a baboon that has escaped from the zoo and is up a tree in Kensington Gardens (p.48), or stopping in *Officers and Gentlemen* in the centre of a crossing – 'Why are they making such a fuss? There is all the time in the world. No one here ever lunches before two' (p.128), or climbing over the windscreen and sliding down the bonnet of the car because its mudguards are grating against the walls of a narrow alley and she can't get any further – Mrs Stitch does everything with panache. She remarks blithely when she has to get a taxi back because she and Guy cannot get her car out – 'Algie doesn't like my driving myself anyhow' (p.129).

Lady Diana's driving is legendary, and when asked about her driving compared with that of Julia Stitch she replied: 'Well that was not actually, but reasonably true.'[45] Ziegler reports that after driving a mini for the first time she said, 'It's like driving a swallow', which, as he says, 'shows as much about her technique as about the car itself'.[46] When in New York, Duff Cooper wrote of her, 'She understands neither the workings of the car, nor the traffic laws of New York';[47] and her son, John Julius has never been able to 'accept her conviction that in city traffic it was a case of *sauve qui peut* and damned be he who first cried, "Hold, enough!"'[48]

Mrs Stitch, like Lady Diana, is beautiful, witty and intelligent. Waugh, in fact, sometimes makes her more intelligent than the males she comes into contact with; and gives her a certain kind of superiority, which is unusual in the light of how he normally presents his female characters. Lord Copper, a colonial, is presented as being ignorant, for he has never heard of John Boot,[49] and Mrs Stitch makes him so 'Boot conscious' that he is resolved to question his literary secretary on the subject. (His bewilderment on first hearing that the Prime Minister always sleeps with 'a Boot by his bed' is understandable.)

[45] Interview with Lady Diana.

[46] Philip Ziegler, *Diana Cooper*, p.315.

[47] Ibid., p.131.

[48] Ibid., p.160, and for other stories of Lady Diana's driving see pp.115, 247, 250, 314-15.

[49] Jeffrey Heath in *The Picturesque Prison* (p.127) writes: 'John Courteney Boot's style is "a very nice little style", according to Lord Copper.' It should be pointed out that when Lord Copper says this he is talking to William Boot, not John Boot, and he actually has no idea of what either of them writes; apart from what he has learnt about John Boot from Mrs Stitch and his 'literary secretary'.

In *Officers and Gentlemen* Mrs Stitch says to Colonel Tickeridge and Guy Crouchback when she joins them, 'Have you your pistols? Have you your sharp-edged axes? Halberdiers! O Halberdiers!'[50] The men do not know what she is talking about so Mrs Stitch moves on to another subject. Also, when she offers her copy of E.M. Forster's *Alexandria* to Guy Crouchback, he says, 'Well, thanks awfully. I know his *Pharos and Pharillon*,[51] of course' – to which she replies, rather ironically, 'Of course', and goes on to add: 'The guide is topping too.'

Although Guy Crouchback is put in his place, even Waugh's favourite lady does not go unscathed as far as her intelligence is concerned ... 'topping' is extremely tongue-in-cheek. Also, rather as with Virginia Troy and her pronunciation of 'homosexual', Waugh denigrates Mrs Stitch's pronunciation. When, in *Officers and Gentlemen*, she asks the pasha to 'explain Cavafy to us', he obviously doesn't know what she is talking about and says that he leaves such things to His Excellency. The murmur goes round, 'Who is Cavafy? What is he?', and the Minister who has read all of the author's works in Greek explains. However, the lady on Guy Crouchback's right says: ' "Do they perhaps speak of Constantine Cavafis?" ' pronouncing the name quite differently from Mrs Stitch' (p.130).[52]

As with Helena, Waugh gives Mrs Stitch an ingenuous schoolroom manner at times. When she tells Guy Crouchback the story that she and Ivor Claire had concocted about Claire's desertion, she tells him 'as though at repetition in the schoolroom' (p.234). Robert Murray Davis believes that Waugh inserted the simile 'as though at repetition in the schoolroom' to 'emphasise the falsity of the line';[53] which is a possibility, but to my mind it is more likely that he is denigrating Mrs Stitch and not being able to accept her on equal terms, particularly as later, when Algernon Stitch brings the news of the invasion of Russia, Waugh has Mrs Stitch ask 'the simple question of the schoolroom' ... 'Is it a Good Thing?' (p.239).

Waugh would have been aware of Lady Diana's feelings about Russia, which were entirely different from his own. He despised the Communist regime. She, however, saw some point in it and thought it was preferable to Nazism, as she explained to her son:

> People hate Russians because they are Communists ... and have done atrocious things to their own people and would like to convert us all to their highly unsuccessful ways, but I prefer Russians infinitely to Huns and fear their

[50] Waugh has actually adapted some lines from Walt Whitman's *Pioneers! O Pioneers!* (1865): Come my tan-faced children, / Follow well in order, get your weapons ready, / Have you your pistols? Have you your sharp-edged axes? / Pioneers! O Pioneers!

[51] Waugh wrote in 'Literary Style in England and America' (*Essays*, p.479): 'Mr E.M. Forster, particularly in the first half of *Pharos and Pharillon*, set a model of lucidity and individuality in which the elegance is so unobtrusive as to pass some readers unnoticed.' Lady Diana has read *Pharos and Pharillon*.

[52] The lady pronounces the name correctly, but Waugh does not give it the correct Greek spelling. 'Cavafy, Constantine, Greek name *Kavafis*. 1863-1933, Greek poet of Alexandria in Egypt' *OED*.

[53] Robert Murray Davis, *Evelyn Waugh, Writer* (1981), p.277.

creed so much less than Nazism that I have no swallowing trouble over fighting on their side. Communism has at least an idealist aim – men are equals, no nations, all races are brothers, share your cow with your neighbour. Never be caught by people who say that Russia is worse than Germany – just consider if they are rich or poor.[54]

Mrs Stitch, like Helena, and Lucy in *Work Suspended*, has her intelligence repressed. Helena, as we have seen, repressed her intelligence to the stereotyped roles of wife, mother, deserted wife and Empress. She regained her curiosity and intellect late in life. Lucy Simmonds's intelligence was repressed because of her maternal instincts. Mrs Stitch is not allowed to be a hundred per cent intelligent either; she resorts to cajolery rather than brains when she wants something ... as one can see so clearly in *Scoop* and *Officers and Gentlemen*.

Kätchen is supposed to be the heroine of *Scoop*, but Julia Stitch, although the actual space she occupies in the book is small,[55] is the prime mover. The provider of the 'Stitch Service', she makes things happen even if they are not exactly what she intended. She is obviously known for the strings she can pull, for 'like all in her circle John Boot habitually brought his difficulties to her for solution' (p.5); and her influence can be clearly seen in her conversation with Lord Cooper who, as a colonial, out of place in the social world of London, is easy prey. Exploiting his social unease, she directs upon him 'some of her piercing shafts of charm' until he is 'first numb, then dazzled, then extravagantly receptive' (p.11). Lord Cooper is unaware that he is being got at, but the rest of the party are aware of the 'familiar process' and Mrs Stitch's power is such that once the luncheon party get the message that she is after a job for Boot they loyally back her up, although Lady Metroland and Lady Cockpurse are not in her league.

Mrs Stitch uses some fairly obvious feminine wiles to try to get John Boot the job. She implies to Lord Copper that Boot, the ideal man, would be hard to get; and such lines as 'I don't suppose you could persuade *him* to go, but someone like him' and 'Well, of course, if you *could* get him, Boot is your man' also give Waugh the chance to satirise Lord Copper by having him defend his empire with such pompous remarks as 'It has been my experience, dear Mrs Stitch, that the *Daily Beast* can command the talent of the world. Only last week the Poet Laureate wrote us an ode to the seasonal fluctuation of our net sales. We splashed it on the middle page. He admitted it was the most poetic and highly-paid work he had ever done' (p.13). Mrs Stitch is successful in getting Boot the job, but unfortunately the wrong Boot is sent to

---

[54] Philip Ziegler, *Diana Cooper*, p.207.
[55] According to Robert Murray Davis (*Evelyn Waugh, Writer*, p.94), Mrs Stitch only appeared in the basic manuscipt twice after the first chapter and the second appearance was many pages removed from the first. Waugh realised that this was too long and he inserted two major scenes in which she figures centrally – the action at the gentlemen's lavatory, and the scene at the ball where she discusses what could have gone wrong about the job for John Boot. And finally, though never represented in manuscript stage, she is included in the series of futures for the various characters at the end of the novel.

Ishmaelia; the 'Stitch Service' comes undone a little.[56]

Lady Diana was renowned for pulling strings. When a vacancy occurred in the Foreign Office, when Churchill was in power, she sent a telegram from Boston to Churchill 'Please look after Duffy'. Churchill never mentioned the wire, but her husband heard about it and wrote to her saying: 'I am sorry you telegraphed to Winston – If one can get on without intrigue – and I'm sure I can – it is much better not to indulge in it.'[57] Quite often her string-pulling went wrong. On one occasion when her son wanted, for his first diplomatic posting, to be sent to Moscow, he was delighted to hear that he had got the position but then found that Belgrade had been substituted instead. It turned out that his mother, newly widowed, had wanted him posted within reach or somewhere near. Although Eden wouldn't interfere, he did say that he would come to the rescue if the posting was too far afield.[58] Belgrade didn't suit John Julius Norwich or his mother – the 'Stitch Service' had come undone again.

Lord Copper was partly based on Lord Beaverbrook,[59] a great admirer of Lady Diana, and she asked him more than once to pull strings for her. At one time, if he had published some critical remarks that her husband had made about his political opponent of the time, life could have been a little difficult. Ziegler writes:

> Diana went to plead with him. 'I know what you've come for,' he grunted, and promised not merely to suppress the news himself but to try to get the press as a whole to do the same. He succeeded.[60]

Mrs Stitch's powers of cajolery run high, but it is her looks that get her what she wants, not her brains. Waugh said the following of Lady Diana when they were in Genoa together:

> Her first business was at the railway station which, for a reason that was never clear to me, was harbouring a coat of unlovely squalor abandoned somewhere by one of her more irresponsible cronies. Without authority or means of identification Mrs Stitch cajoled a series of beaming officials and possessed herself of the sordid garment. 'How different from the French,' Mrs Stitch said, '*they* would never have let me have it.' I sometimes suspect that one of the reasons she gets on so badly with the French is that she speaks their language well. In Italy she has to rely purely on her looks and always gets her way without argument.[61]

Cajolery, string-pulling and amoral behaviour abound in *Officers and*

---

[56] A short story based on Mrs Stitch's failure called 'Mrs Stitch Fails For the First Time' was published in the *Bystander* (Christmas issue, 1937); and *Town and Country* (New York) offered 250 dollars for the story in September 1937.

[57] Philip Ziegler, *Diana Cooper*, p.154.

[58] Ibid., p.287.

[59] Sykes (p.247) says that Lord Copper is based on 'an imaginary portrait (by Evelyn's own admission) of Lord Beaverbrook'.

[60] Philip Ziegler, *Diana Cooper*, p.164. Lady Diana in her comments on this chapter said: 'It was a very little indiscretion in an election speech.'

[61] *A Tourist to Africa*, p.19.

Gentlemen, where Mrs Stitch is protectress of X Commando in Alexandria. They feel her presence as that of 'a beneficent, alert deity, their own protectress' (p.159). Through Mrs Stitch the doors of wealthy Greek houses are opened to them; and while they relax, Mrs Stitch finds out about the plans for their future. Long before Major Hound learns that X Commando are off to Crete, Mrs Stitch has already informed Ivor Claire of the orders, who in turn has told Guy Crouchback. As Ivor Claire points out – 'When there's anything really up I shall hear from Julia Stitch before Tommy does. She is a mine of indiscretion' (p.125).

When Ivor Claire escapes from Crete, he, like John Boot, goes to Julia Stitch to solve his problem for him: that of being an officer who has deserted his men and disobeyed orders to be taken prisoner. Ivor is one of Julia's charmed circle, and when Guy, visited by Julia in hospital and not realising exactly what has happened, says that it is really delightful that Ivor is all right, Mrs Stitch remarks, 'Well, of course I think so ... I'm on Ivor's side always.' Guy does not realise exactly what lies behind Julia's comment but is shaken to the core when he realises that the aristocratic Ivor Claire – 'the fine flower of them all – quintessential England, the man Hitler had not taken into account' – has reasoned that 'honour' is 'a thing that changes' and has managed with Julia's help to make his way to India out of reach of any court martial. Mrs Stitch is about to leave the hospital when Guy remarks that he was with Ivor the last evening in Crete – and at that point Mrs Stitch settles down to quiz him:

> 'Were you, Guy?'
> 'We had a long gloomy talk about the surrender. I can't understand what happened after that.'
> 'I imagine everything was pretty complete chaos.'
> 'Yes.'
> 'And everyone too tired and hungry to remember anything.'
> 'More or less everyone.'
> 'No one making much sense.'
> 'Not many.'
> 'No one with much reason to be proud of themselves.'
> 'Not a great many.'
> 'Exactly what I've said all along,' said Mrs Stitch triumphantly. 'Obviously, by the end there *weren't* any orders.'
> It was Guy's first conversation since his return to consciousness. He was a little dizzy, but it came to him, nevertheless, that an attempt was being made at – to put it in its sweetest form – cajolery.
> 'There were orders, all right,' he said, 'perfectly clear ones.'
> 'Were there, Guy? Are you sure?'
> 'Quite sure.'
> Mrs Stitch seemed to have lost her impatience to leave. (pp.233-4)

From this point on Mrs Stitch takes a serious interest in Guy, for although she tells him the story that she and Ivor have put out – 'our story' – she realises that Guy could be the spanner in the works. She tells him that Tommy Blackhouse won't be interested in his notes – which Guy doesn't believe until he talks to Tommy and finds that, not only is Tommy not going to do anything about the situation, but also warns Guy off: 'Ivor's put up a pretty poor show. *We* know that – you won't find me applying for him a second time. Julia's got him out of the way. She had to work hard to do it, I can tell you. Now the best thing is for everyone to keep quiet and forget the whole business'(p.236).

Mrs Stitch moves quickly. By the afternoon she has Guy installed in her house, where she can keep an eye on him. Guy is disturbed by the day's events. He sees that for Julia Stitch there is no problem, because Ivor is an old friend who happens to be in trouble; but Tommy, from whom Guy would have expected support, also has no doubt that Ivor should be got out of the way, for in his mind a court martial is out of the question – 'in the narrowest view it would cause endless professional annoyance and delay; in the widest it would lend comfort to the enemy' (p.238). Guy, who lacks their 'simple rules of conduct' is in a turmoil. Mrs Stitch, although she has guests, never neglects him, visiting him three or four times a day with the 'hypodermic needle of her charm'. After learning of the development of the Russian alliance, Guy, unknown to Mrs Stitch, throws his pocket-book with its telling notes into the incinerator – his illusions shattered, for the Nazi-Soviet pact had prompted the beginning of his own chivalrous crusade. That evening, Colonel Tickeridge comes to dinner and Mrs Stitch learns that Guy is to go back with him as long as the Brigadier doesn't snap him up instead. Once again she is alert: she thought the Brigadier was dead and that was how Tommy Blackhouse had come to take over his command. On learning that he was only lost, she questions Tickeridge as to whether the Brigadier is a trouble-maker; she has heard something to that effect from Tommy. On being told that the Brigadier, if he is let down, is like a big-game hunter and will hound a man down, she again moves quickly. Two days later Guy finds himself with a move order that will take him back to England by the longest route possible. He tries to get it changed to no avail, and when he tries to speak to Julia that evening finds it hard to have a word alone with her. When he does, and asks her to do something about his plight, she says smoothly: 'Oh, no, Guy, I never interfere with the military. Algie wouldn't like it at all.'

The protectress can interfere with the military for a chum in distress but not for someone who might cause that same chum further distress. An early conversation between Ivor Claire and Guy Crouchback puts a perspective on their roles in relationship to Julia exactly:

> 'Trust Julia to keep in touch with chums.'
> 'No chum of mine, alas.'
> 'Everyone is a chum of Julia's.' (p.98)

But everyone isn't, as Guy finds out. Still not realising that Julia is behind the move to get him sent home, Guy does his packing and comes across the red identity disc that he had found on the body of a young soldier killed in Crete. He knows that 'the officer in command of a burial party is responsible for collecting the red identity discs and forwarding them to Records' and knows also that some officer has not done his duty and that the boy's relatives will never know what has happened to him unless he, Guy, passes the disc on to the right quarters. Consequently he puts the disc in an envelope and the next morning asks Julia if she could get Algie to deal with it for him. Asking what it is and hearing that it is 'a bit of unfinished business from Crete', she takes the envelope and, after Guy leaves, drops it into the waste-paper basket – thinking that it contains Guy's notes about the orders.

Mrs Stitch's actions in *Officers and Gentlemen* – the removal of Guy and the destroying of the envelope – are again based on Lady Diana. Once, in Paris, when one of her favourites was threatened with transfer, she 'wrote direct to the First Lord of the Admiralty to get the posting cancelled, without consulting Duff or the Naval Attache. "Very naughty of her," Duff remarked mildly.'[62] More important is the fact that Waugh consulted her about her final amoral action in the book. He told her that 'Mrs Stitch has behaved absolutely shockingly and I don't know whether you'll like it or bear it – I'm quite ready to change it or cut it'. On reading the passage she says that she was able to say: 'But Evelyn, it is exactly what I would have done – so that was all right!' She also considered the book 'very true to life and war and just as boring' and was worried that it wouldn't sell 'because he needed the money with those seven children'.[63]

Mrs Stitch's overtly criminal act of dropping the envelope in the waste-paper basket was not in the original manuscript. Robert Murray Davis says that the addition of her action was made so late that it did not appear in the American edition.[64] The lateness is because Waugh wanted to sound Lady Diana out about the passage and ask her permission to use it.

Julia Stitch's action has led James Carens to say that 'amoral to the core, Julia no longer appears as a delightful example of aristocratic indifference to convention'.[65] He feels that 'this pagan, this Cleopatra' has let the side down, just as Ivor Claire did, and believes that *Officers and Gentlemen* shows up not only the collapse of the class system but also the collapse of those upper-class people whom Waugh, for many years, had believed should embody the highest morals and ideals. But one cannot truly damn Julia Stitch or Ivor Claire for their behaviour, simply because neither of them has ever subscribed to any accepted code of morality. Julia, like Margot Beste-Chetwynde, is above the law – but more so.

What Carens has perhaps wrongly interpreted here is that Waugh never expected Julia Stitch/Lady Diana to behave in any way differently from the way he had written about her. He would have been most surprised if she had asked him to cut the passage, for he was well aware that her world was one where morality was no more than a charade, and the law was something to be flouted or evaded. His disillusionment with the aristocracy was no more than his disillusionment with life in general. As he said himself: 'Those who have read my works will perhaps understand the character of the world into which I exuberantly launched myself. Ten years of that world sufficed to

[62] Philip Ziegler, *Diana Cooper*, p.227.
[63] Interview with Lady Diana.
[64] Robert Murray Davis, *Evelyn Waugh, Writer*, p.278.
[65] James F. Carens, *The Satiric Art of Evelyn Waugh* (1966), p.164.

show me that life there, or anywhere, was unintelligible and unendurable without God.'[66] From *Decline and Fall* on he had seen the aristocracy, to which he would dearly have loved to belong, with the clear detached eye of a disappointed romantic ... depicting the society they dominated as a moral chaos, and clearly demonstrating how he thought they had betrayed the aristocratic ethos. As Cecil Beaton said of Waugh: 'Evelyn was attracted by the foibles of those who lived in large, aristocratic houses. He cultivated the Lygons at Madresfield, got elected to the 'best' clubs ... and fostered a fascination, though in many ways despising it, for the highest echelons of the Army and military etiquette. He drank port and put on weight, and attempted to behave in the manner of an Edwardian aristocrat.'[67]

In Waugh's preface to the *Sword of Honour* trilogy he said that in *Brideshead Revisited* he had written the obituary of the English upper class and in *Sword of Honour* the obituary of the Roman Catholic Church as it had existed for many centuries. More appropriate, I think, would be that in *Brideshead* he wrote of the death of his illusions about the aristocracy and in *Sword of Honour* wrote their obituary as well as that of the church.

Julia Stitch is no less lawless than Margot Beste-Chetwynde; the only difference being a nicety that she deals in dishonoured officers while Margot deals in prostitution. Beautiful and deadly, like Margot, Julia Stitch is associated with Cleopatra:

> Guy examined the yacht through his field-glasses.
> '*Cleopatra*,' he read.
> 'Julia Stitch,' said Claire. 'Too good to be true.' (p.97)

And when Julia drops the envelope into the waste-paper basket Waugh describes her eyes as 'one immense sea', which is an allusion to Hérédia's sonnet on Cleopatra.[68]

Interestingly, Waugh changed the name of Julia Stitch's yacht from *Nimbus* to *Cleopatra*, and Robert Murray Davis suggests that perhaps it was because 'direct reference to an aura prepared less effectively than its substitute for her emergence in Egypt as fascinating and capricious'.[69] The yacht that was at the disposal of Lady Diana and Duff Cooper when he was first Lord at the Admiralty was called the *Enchantress*: much nearer to *Cleopatra* than *Nimbus*.

Julia Stitch is an enchantress. Lord Copper is 'mesmerised, inebriated' by her; William Boot thinks that she is the most 'beautiful woman' he has ever seen; and Guy Crouchback sits silent 'quite soaked up by her'. Tommy Blackhouse and Ivor Claire are obvious admirers, but Julia Stitch has far more in her armoury than just her beauty: she has character. Ivor Claire

---

[66] Evelyn Waugh, 'Come Inside', *Essays*, p.367.

[67] Cecil Beaton, *Self Portrait with Friends: the Selected Diaries of Cecil Beaton, 1926-74* (1974), p.227.

[68] See above Chapter Three, n.16.

[69] Robert Murray Davis, *Evelyn Waugh, Writer*, p.277. Lady Diana was often associated with Cleopatra. Cecil Beaton's last photograph of her was taken when she was portrayed as Tiepolo's idea of Cleopatra at the Beistegui ball in Venice in 1951, and she used that photograph as her passport picture.

recognises her, when he is in the hospital, by her 'guttersnipe whistle'. Ian Littlewood has suggested that this is one of the 'manly traits' which is 'a passport to the author's favour'. He continues to say that characters such as Helena, Julia Stitch and Virginia Troy are characters who are 'prepared to meet men on equal terms. They play according to the same rules, in contrast to those, like Ryder's wife, who exploit the alien territory of their womanhood as a source of power.'[70]

It is true that Julia Stitch is 'prepared to meet men on equal terms'. She will fight as dirty as the next man, but it is completely untrue to say that she doesn't exploit the 'alien territory' of her womanhood. That is the essence of Julia Stitch and it is why she charms the Lord Coppers of the world. Jeffrey Heath has associated Julia Stitch (whom he sees as Lady Diana) with Diana – the goddess of the moon – because of her 'piercing shafts of charm'.[71] But the Roman goddess Diana had at least two roles: she was the goddess of the moon and the goddess of the hunt. There is no question which role Evelyn Waugh gave Julia Stitch to play: she is Diana the huntress. Her 'piercing shafts of charm' in *Scoop* and the 'hypodermic needle of her charm' in *Officers and Gentlemen* are the arrows with which she hunts her quarry.

Does Evelyn Waugh admire the lady? It is true that he dearly loved Lady Diana, although he sometimes suffered at her hands and perhaps the barbs at Mrs Stitch's intelligence might even have been brought about by the following exchange he had with her and thought important enough to enter in his diary after lunch with her at Admiralty House:

> Diana spoke, as I thought, of a 'morning with the electric'; she said it was a play everybody was excited about and she made me feel a bumpkin and wanted to. Got back a bit towards the end.[72]

In *Scoop* and *Officers and Gentlemen* there is a tone of gentle and rather loving mockery; and even the 'shocking' incident of the envelope is not so terrible, for Mrs Stitch appears only to take pity on Ivor Claire in his shame; and it is Claire who bothers Waugh more than Mrs Stitch. In *Scoop* the loving mockery is particularly apparent at the end of the novel when Mrs Stitch is included in the 'futures' for the characters – 'a future ... heaped with the spoils of every continent and every century, gadgets from New York and bronzes from the Aegean, new entrées and old friends' (p.221). Lady Diana loved the 'gadgets' she came across in New York, and Waugh, the 'old friend', teased her about them.

No critics appear to have noticed that Mrs Stitch appears briefly in the narrative of *Work Suspended*. Jeffrey Heath even makes the mistake of partly identifying Lady Diana with Lucy Simmonds which is highly unlikely as she

[70] Ian Littlewood, *The Writings of Evelyn Waugh* (1983), p.127.

[71] Jeffrey Heath, *The Picturesque Prison*, p.134.

[72] *Diaries*, p.429. The play referred to was Eugene O'Neill's *Mourning Becomes Electra* (1931). However, Harriet Waugh has said that they were all brought up to think Lady Diana 'immensely beautiful' and the rather cruel 'sentence game' that they played on other visitors would never have been 'played on Lady Diana'. Harriet Waugh in an interview with Maureen Cleave, *Evening Standard*, 17 April 1969, p.11.

appears, once again, as Mrs Algernon Stitch.[73] Her role is worth mentioning because she is out of character, and by that I mean out of the character of Mrs Stitch as Lady Diana. The passage occurs when John Plant is talking about the party his father[74] gives before sending-in day at the Academy:

> ... Mrs Algernon Stitch paid 500 guineas for his picture of the year – a tableau of contemporary life conceived and painted with elaborate mastery. My father attached great importance to suitable titles for his work, and after toying with 'The People's Idol', 'Feet of Clay', 'Not on the First Night', 'Their Night of Triumph', 'Success and Failure', 'Not Invited', 'Also Present', he finally called this picture rather enigmatically 'The Neglected Case'. It respresented the dressing room of a leading actress at the close of a triumphant first night. She sat at the dressing-table, her back turned on the company, and her face visible in the mirror, momentarily relaxed in fatigue. Her protector with proprietory swagger was filling the glasses for a circle of admirers. In the background the dresser was in colloquy at the half-open door with an elderly couple of provincial appearance; it is evident from their costume that they have seen the piece from the cheaper seats, and a commissionaire stands behind them uncertain whether he did right in admitting them. He did not do right; they are her old parents arriving most inopportunely. There was no questioning Mrs Stitch's rapturous enjoyment of her acquisition. (pp.118-19)

The Mrs Stitch of *Scoop* and *Officers and Gentlemen* and *A Tourist to Africa* would never have paid 500 guineas for the picture and neither would Lady Diana, who says: 'I would never have bought a picture for £500. Had I been given it, I might or might not have appreciated it.' The snobbery of not wanting the old parents involved is obviously Waugh's own snobbery, which Lady Diana concurs with but adds that he would not have been embarrassed by his father of whom he spoke often. Asked whether she approved of Mrs Stitch being characterised in this manner, she said 'Pardonable'.[75]

Waugh wrote of the way he portrayed his characters as follows: 'None except one or two negligible minor figures is a portrait ... Men and women as I see them would not be credible if literally transcribed',[76] which is a contradiction to the quotation that opens this chapter. The reason why Julia Stitch was not a direct portrait in *Work Suspended* is, and Lady Diana agrees

---

[73] Jeffrey Heath, *The Picturesque Prison*, p.148.

[74] In *Work Suspended* (p.115), John Plant's father is described as 'an intransigently old-fashioned young man, for he was brought up in the hey-day of Whistlerian decorative painting, and his first exhibited work was of a balloon ascent in Manchester – a large canvas crowded with human drama ...' Waugh was referring here to the American, James Abbot McNeil Whistler (1834-1903) of whom he did not approve as can be seen in 'The Death of Painting', *Essays*, p.506.

[75] Letter from Lady Diana to J. McDonnell, 4 February 1983. The picture depicts an actress and Lady Diana starred in Max Reinhardt's production of *The Miracle*, and Waugh accompanied her on her tour of the provinces. In 1933 the *Bystander* rejected a short story of Waugh's entitled 'An Ill Wind'. Waugh, not knowing that they had already received it, wrote to Roughead at A.D. Peters asking him to change a few facts. He said: 'I think the name Lady Priscilla looks too much like Diana Cooper so please have it altered throughout to Elsa Branch, no title. Mme. Branch when spoken to and omit the reference to peers daughter & stage' (HRHRC).

[76] Evelyn Waugh, 'Fan-Fare', *Essays*, p.302-3.

with this, that Lady Diana never took to Victorian narrative paintings and Waugh is having a little joke here at her expense. (The titles of the paintings mentioned recall the kind of titles that some of Waugh's own pictures had, such as 'Into the Cold World', a painting of a widow taking her small son into a raging blizzard from an empty house.)

Mrs Stitch's other roles,[77] however, are literally transcribed and entirely credible. Lady Diana is a tailor-made Waugh character, and in her case the truth is often stranger than fiction. If anything, Waugh, I suspect, had to tone down the original – and maybe this is why she is the strongest and the most interesting of all his female characters.

[77] Lady Diana has also been portrayed as Lady Artemis Hooper in D.H. Lawrence's *Aaron's Rod*; Lady Leone in Nancy Mitford's *Don't Tell Alfred*; Lady Queenie Paul in Arnold Bennett's *The Pretty Lady*; and Lady Maclean in Enid Bagnold's *The Loved and the Envied*.

CHAPTER TEN

Conclusion

He was also an irrepressible advocate of Female Suffrage. Visiting Boscastle
with his mother and aunts, he placarded the harbour with home-made labels
championing 'Votes for Women'; and on one occasion, when we were giving a
garden party, and half the guests had disappeared alike from the lawn and
tea-room, they were found crowded into the boys' play-room upstairs, where
Evelyn was delivering an impassioned address on the injustice of the male sex,
and the imperative necessity of a franchise extended to women before the next
General Election. His impromptu oratory was the success of the party. Indeed, it
is the only memory of the afternoon to survive after nearly twenty years.

(Arthur Waugh, *One Man's Road*, p.334)

This statement gives us some insight into Evelyn Waugh's feelings at
preparatory-school age, feelings that were inspired not just by his mother and
aunts but also by Barbara Jacobs (his brother's fiancée) and her mother who
were ardent feminists. Such feelings were not to last. Lady Betjeman, on
being told that Waugh campaigned for the Suffragettes, said 'Never', in
amazement, and then added that she would not have believed it possible –
'That's most interesting ... He always thought that a wife's place was in the
home.'[1]

Lady Betjeman's opinion is justified in the light of Waugh's own comments
in his works. Seth, in *Black Mischief*, in his war of 'Progress against
Barbarism' says that at his 'stirrups run woman's suffrage, vaccination and
vivisection. I am the New Age. I am the Future' (p.17). He is, however, told
by Basil Seal, that if his country had been modernised fifty years ago 'it
would have meant ... women's suffrage'; an idea that has now 'ceased to be
modern' (p.128). In *Remote People* he records seeing an 'abysmal British
drama ... *The Woman Who Did*[2] ... about a feminist and an illegitimate child
and a rich grandfather' (p.137); he also notes, on having dinner with the
Grants, that he met 'a prominent English feminist,[3] devoted to the
fomentation of birth-control and regional cookery in rural England, but the
atmosphere of Kenya had softened these severe foibles a little' (p.197).
Mockery is also made of Margot Beste-Chetwynde in *Decline and Fall* when
she interviews potential candidates for her prostitution business. She is

[1] Interview with Lady Betjeman, 16 September 1982.
[2] Waugh would have been referring to the film made of Grant Allen's novel, *The Woman Who
Did*, which was published in 1895.
[3] The prominent feminist was Lady Denman. See *Diaries*, p.346.

described as the 'very embodiment of the Feminist movement', a highly
ironic description in the context in which it is placed.

Women are rarely seen as equals in Waugh's work. To recapitulate: Angela
Lyne can talk like 'a highly intelligent man' but she doesn't act like one and
still needs Basil Seal; Lucy Simmonds can write 'like a man' but her
intelligence is repressed in favour of motherhood; Helena who rides and looks
'like a boy' and has a 'masculine mind' is rarely allowed to use it; and
Fausta, who has been told by Eusebius that she has 'a man's mind in her
grasp of a problem', is being mocked at, for her grandfather was a 'nameless
illiterate' and Fausta understands nothing of the theology she expounds.

Other women who either look or act like men are seen in an unflattering
light. In *A Handful of Dust*, Joyce, 'the shorter one' of Mrs Beaver's helpers, is
described as 'handling the crates like a man' (p.10), and Waugh makes her
lack of femininity obvious. In *Vile Bodies*, Chastity's comment that Mrs
Panrast 'looks like a man and – and she goes on like a man' (p.94) is hardly
flattering, for Mrs Panrast is a lesbian; and in his diaries Waugh made a note
of a lesbian party that he went to, saying that it was attended 'by a whole lot
of perverse young women with eyeglasses and whisky' (p.265). The picture of
the girl partisans in *Unconditional Surrender* shows what Waugh thought of
women who wanted equality:

> Even when we have anaesthetics the girls often refuse to take them. I have
> seen them endure excruciating operations without flinching, sometimes
> breaking into song as the surgeon probed, in order to prove their manhood ... It
> is a transforming experience. (p.165)

And in career terms Waugh simply sees men as more important:

> 'Now you can't sit here coffee-housing.⁴ You're keeping the men from the
> tables and *they* have work to do.' (Mrs Whale to Virginia and Kerstie in
> *Unconditional Surrender*, p.76)

Men also have more freedom and are to be envied by women: when Tony
Last tells Thérèse de Vitré about the journey he is to take, she pathetically
says, 'How I wish I was a man' (*A Handful of Dust*, p.164).

There is one female character, Kerstie Kilbannock, who is described as
having 'nuances in her way with men which suggested she had once worked
with them and competed on equal terms' (*Officers and Gentlemen*, p.133); but
this is no accolade, for Kerstie is morally outraged when she learns that Guy
is to remarry Virginia and calls him a 'poor bloody fool'; and then, in a
remark that is a clue to so much, says, 'You're being *chivalrous* – about
Virginia. Can't you understand men aren't chivalrous any more ...'
(*Unconditional Surrender*, p.151).

⁴ 'Coffee-housing' is slang for 'gossiping' and most likely originates from the fact that when
coffee-houses were opened in the eighteenth century they were treated as fashionable meeting
places for all kinds of discussion: Or to some coffee-house I stray, / For news, the manna of a
day, / And from the hipp'd discourses gather / That politics go by the weather. Matthew Green,
The Spleen, 1737.

Waugh would like to have been the ideal knight; he would like to have felt some kinship with Guy Crouchback's canonised knight, Sir Roger of Waybrooke, but his problem was that a chivalric attitude was hard to maintain in the world he knew, the world of Metroland, where women were emancipated, morals were loose and fair ladies did not require knights in shining armour. In his novels Waugh actually makes Brenda Last the 'imprisoned princess of fairy story' and Julia Flyte the 'heroine of a fairy story', but both characters, both of them adulteresses, cannot, and do not deserve to, win gallant knights. Brenda leaves her chivalrous knight, Tony, and wins 'Beaver, the joke figure they had all known and despised'; while of Julia, Charles, the narrator, says that she had only to stroke her 'magic ring' for the 'earth to open at her feet and belch forth her titanic servant, the fawning monster who could bring her whatever she asked, but bring it, perhaps, in unwelcome shape' (*Brideshead Revisited*, p.173). Julia's knight appears in the form of Rex Mottram who is, finally, 'unwelcome'.

It is true that Guy Crouchback is chivalrous and comes to Virginia's aid, but Guy needs to be chivalrous for his own salvation. He is not being chivalrous in the respect of helping the weak, for he admits that 'Virginia is tough. She would have survived somehow. I shan't be changing her by what I am doing' (p.151). Guy plays the knight errant to save the soul of Trimmer's child, not to save Virginia. In *Put Out More Flags* Basil Seal is also chivalrous; he comes to Angela Lyne's aid when she is drinking too much and prescribes that she should drink with him and not alone. Basil describes himself, to Susie, as 'drunk with chivalry' as a result of his drinking bout with Angela; but this knight errant hardly treats Angela chivalrously. Comments such as 'if you want a drink you might drink fair with a chap' (p.160), show that Basil is treating Angela like one of the boys (and being one of the boys is not an asset in Waugh's eyes), and instead of being, as a chivalrous knight might be, appalled at the way she takes her drink, he views her with respect because she takes it 'good and strong' (p.161). In Waugh's terms, Angela deserves her barbarian knight.

Waugh expected too much from women, as can be seen from the entries in his diaries. In the early stages of his relationship with Olivia Plunket Greene, he wrote of her: 'I have been allowing her to become a focus for all the decencies of life, which is foolish of me and not very fair to her' (p.204). It was foolish, for Olivia could not live up to being put on a pedestal, as the later entries reveal:

> I was also very vexed with Olivia who kissed Tony in the box and drank too much cherry brandy. (p.198)

> Olivia as usual behaved like a whore and was embraced on a bed by various people ... (p.234)

> ... Olivia did that disgusting dance of hers. (p.238)

When Olivia visited him, with friends, at the school where he was teaching, at Aston Clinton, he wrote: 'Suddenly some ladies were announced' (p.228). Waugh had differentiated between 'ladies' and 'females' at the age of thirteen, saying of a show he had seen that '... the ladies – I mean females – were so aged and cockney and so dreadfully painted that they simply spoilt the show' (p.10). And of a train journey at the same period of his life he wrote: 'We had a tremendous rush to get the train and only just bundled into a carriage where there were *three* babies and two females who drank evil-smelling stout to revive themselves the whole time' (p.11). Interestingly, Virginia Troy who, although she has 'class', is no lady, drinks stout when she has dinner with Uncle Peregrine in *Unconditional Surrender*. Waugh obviously used the term 'female' for what he considered a common class of woman, but it is interesting that Olivia and her friends are defined as 'some ladies' – the inference being that although of a superior class (superior in Waugh's terms) they left much to be desired. (In *Vile Bodies*, a man looks at Agatha Runcible who is dressed in trousers and says 'with feeling': '*Lady* ...'*Trousers*' (p.155).)

After the experiences of Olivia, Waugh was equally, if not more, disillusioned in his relationship with Evelyn Gardner – 'Evelyn has been pleased to make a cuckold of me with Heygate' (*Letters*, p.38) – and Teresa Jungman in 1933 refused to marry him: 'Stiff upper lip and dropped cock' (*Letters*, p.81).

Disappointed in love, he was also disappointed in the female sex. Waugh was quite often shocked and offended by the wayward, emancipated, violent and often mindless behaviour of the young women he came into contact with, as can once again be illustrated from the diaries:

> I came back to find an amazing orgy in progress. Everyone drunk or pretending drunkenness, except — who was sitting in the middle of it all unusually sedate. — almost naked was being slapped on the buttocks and enjoying herself ecstatically. Every two minutes she ran to the lavatory and as soon as she was out of the room everyone said, 'My dear, the things we are finding out about—.' It was all rather cruel. She looked so awful, with enormous shining legs cut and bleeding in places and slapped rosy in others and her eyes shining with desire. She kept making the most terrible remarks, too, whether consciously or unconsciously I do not know, about blood and grease and to my surprise Olivia saw them all. These girls must talk a terrible lot of bawdy amongst themselves ... I went to bed, as always, with rather a heavy heart. (p.208)

> Irene was put next to the Emperor and was translated with excitement. Coming back she said, 'That has shown all those Bartons, I have come out on top. I am Baroness Ravensdale in my own right.' Also: 'There was an idiotic woman on the other side who talked in platitudes. I knew the Emperor wanted to talk to me. I was terrified, Evelyn, quite cold inside, but I knew I had to find new subjects for him – new angles that would be of interest. I saw everyone's eyes on me looking to see whether I was making a success of it. Something outside me, greater than myself, came to my aid. Each time I was able to find something original and appropriate to say.' I think I must be a prig, people do shock me so. (p.334)

> ... a woman with the smile of the Gioconda and the voice of a parrot. (p.278)

It is hardly surprising that Waugh should have such characters in his novels as the 'Miss Strapper' of *Vile Bodies*. Her father, General Strapper, whip in hand, wants the 'damnable lie' that his daughter was at a nightclub retracted by the social editress of the *Daily Excess* – 'To anyone better acquainted with Miss Strapper's habits of life the paragraph was particularly reticent' (p.89).[5] The social editress points the General in the direction of Simon Balcairn, and Nina, later, finds Adam's story of Simon's whipping 'amusing' (p.90).

(One must note, however, that much of the violence that Waugh depicts comes from within himself. Mr Youkoumian, for example, who treats his wife so abominably, was based on Mr Bergebedgian whom Waugh met in Harar on his travels. Of Mr Bergebedgian he said, 'I do not think I have ever met a more tolerant man.'[6] While watching a girl dancing he records that 'Mr Bergebedgian pulled her shawl off. "Look," he said, "hasn't she got nice hair?" She recovered it crossly and Mr Bergebedgian began teasing her, twitching it back every time she passed. But he was a soft-hearted fellow and he desisted as soon as he realised that he was causing genuine distress.'[7] Mr Bergebedgian was perhaps more civilised than Waugh and his friends. A revealing letter of 1962 to Lady Diana Cooper recalls events of twenty years or so before when Lady Diana's birthday party was spoilt because Sir Richard Sykes 'stubbed out a cigarette on the hand of a tobacco heiress', and he also mentioned an incident where the Earl of Rosse boxed his future wife's ears 'with some violence' when she stepped 'innocently on to a balcony with another man'.[8] A savage society.)

Waugh most often portrays his women as civilised savages, and the diary entry of page 208 also brings up another insight into his personality, where he says, in a very schoolboyish tone, that 'these girls must talk a terrible lot of bawdy amongst themselves'. Waugh, as has been pointed out, had an immaculate ear for the language of women but he also, apparently, felt left out of their conversation at times. The 'bright cruel girls' in *The Ordeal of Gilbert Pinfold* (p.105) speak their own 'thieves' slang' – a situation which caused Mr Pinfold discomfort and which is reflected in *A Handful of Dust*:

> ... occasionally there were bursts of general conversation between the women; they had the habit of lapsing into a jargon of their own which Tony did not understand; it was a thieves' slang, by which the syllables of each word were transposed. Tony sat just outside the circle reading under another lamp. (p.80)

Waugh was an onlooker, an outsider, and rarely joined in such things as orgies unless he was drunk. The detached, rather despairing tone of the

[5] Waugh was not alone in his view of girls and violence. Elinor Glyn in *The Flirt and the Flapper* (1930) has the flapper telling the flirt that love is '... just wanting to hug and snatch – and even get beaten up'. She likes 'brute force' being used and talks of having 'to grab thrills from wherever we can' (pp.119-20).

[6] Evelyn Waugh, *Remote People* (Duckworth 1931), p.99.

[7] Ibid., p.107.

[8] *Letters*, p.591.

diaries shows his disillusionment with life, and with women. He found it hard to accept that a woman like the Baroness Ravensdale could be so egocentric and stupid, or that a woman who had the smile of the Mona Lisa squawked like a parrot.

Waugh wanted his women to be perfect, and they never were. Of his daughter, Margaret, who was 'robust and popular at school', he reflected sadly that she was full of 'new common tastes' and added that his 'Pre-Raphaelite preference' was for the 'wistful and difficult'.[9] Even when he fell in love with Laura Herbert, described by Lady Betjeman as 'the ethereal pre-Raphaelite girl of his dreams',[10] she could not live up to those dreams. There was a despicable side to Waugh that made him, along with the entries in the diaries where he admits to loving Laura, record such things as:

> Laura came ... looking fifteen years years old and very grubby. (p.533)

> Laura arrived looking very plain and dirty ... (p.534)

> Laura is busy and happy with agriculture and has lost all her Californian chic. (p.676)

Hardly a way to talk about the wife you are supposed to love. The distaste is not dissimilar to that recorded when Elizabeth Ponsonby wanted to make love to him – 'She has furry arms' (p.244).

Waugh's female characters, as we have seen with Virginia Troy, are often passed from one male to another. Of Alastair Trumpington we learn that:

> For a year, at the age of twenty-one, he had been Margot Metroland's lover; it was an apprenticeship many of his friends had served ... (*Put Out More Flags*, pp.44-5)

John Plant in *Work Suspended* says:

> We had all ... from time to time passed on girls from one to the other, borrowed and lent freely. (pp.133-4)

And

> Trixie had been Roger's last girl. Basil had passed her on to him, resumed the use of her for a week or two, then passed her back. None of us liked Trixie. She always gave the impression that she was not being treated with the respect she was used to. (pp.148-9)

Women were an interchangeable commodity. In *The Loved One* the first mortician is described as the 'standard product. A man could leave such a girl in a delicatessen shop in New York, fly three thousand miles and find her again in San Francisco' (p.45). A Major in *Unconditonal Surrender* tells Guy

---

[9] *Diaries*, p.745.
[10] Penelope Chetwode (Lady Betjeman), 'Recollections', in *Evelyn Waugh and His World*, p.100.

about his WAAF girlfriends – 'of his last WAAF and of the WAAF before her. The differences were negligible' (p.158). This is the same Major who says: 'A woman's only a woman but a good cigar is a smoke', using Rudyard Kipling's famous line from *The Betrothed*. Nina becomes an interchangeable commodity between Adam and Ginger in *Vile Bodies*, and Chastity has been 'called lots of things' because she's constantly handed from one male to another. Susie, in *Put Out More Flags*, who is one of Basil's 'remarkably silly' girls, is called a 'slut' by her lover Colonel Plum who has taken her from a Colonel in the pensions office. She ends up with Basil.

Waugh used a particular expression to describe some of his women: 'a grand girl.' He uses it in relation to Prudence Courteney, Angela Lyne, Virginia Troy, Brenda Last and Lucy Simmonds. For Basil Seal, Prudence is sexually 'a grand girl ... I'd like to eat you'; while Angela Lyne is 'a grand girl' while he's in bed with her because she's giving him some money. Virginia Troy is 'a grand girl' because she's so available; and Brenda Last is the ultimate in 'grand girls' because the expression is used of her nine times. It is first used by Jock Grant-Menzies to describe her to John Beaver, and after that it is Jock who always tells Tony that he is fond of Brenda and follows that with 'She's a grand girl', to which Tony echoes 'She's a grand girl'. Brenda was expected to marry Jock, and at the end of the book, deserted by both Beaver and Tony, she does. Lucy is 'a grand girl' because she is different – and John Plant cannot regard her 'as being, like Trixie, "one of Roger's girls" ' (p.163).

What then does 'grand girl' mean in Waugh's terms? Lucy is, perhaps, the only girl who is accorded the respect that the phrase might imply – but a better interpretation of it is that these 'grand girls' are 'good chums'. It is an immature way of describing a woman.

Waugh was stunted in growth; he remained a schoolboy in his attitude to women, and his immaturity is shown in the lack of successful relationships in his work. Romance is only connected with a woman in the respect of the hero having fond memories. Tony, after Brenda has left him, can reflect on their honeymoon in a villa on the Italian Riviera with the 'Cypress and olive trees', the enchanting 'café where they sat out in the evening, watching the fishing boats and the lights reflected in the quiet water' (*A Handful of Dust*, p.156), but he doesn't reflect on his relationship with Brenda; and Tony cannot cope with the Brenda who suddenly becomes, not the princess of the fairy story, but a real woman who is fallible. Tony's sexual relationship with Brenda is hardly satisfactory. She rarely sleeps with him, because she is always 'so tired'. Tony's sexual prowess is called into question by Brenda's affair with Beaver, whom she can teach 'a whole lot of things'. Tony is sexually unsuccessful. Jenny Abdul Akbar is thrown at his head, but Tony doesn't take up the invitation and Polly Cockpurse says of him that he's 'a slow starter'. When he takes Millie to Brighton for the weekend so that he can get a divorce he doesn't sleep with her; and before he goes he asks Jock's advice about taking a girl, saying, 'If you suggest going the whole hog it's rather fresh' (p.129). The word 'hog' is a telling one, for in *A Handful of Dust* women are spoken of in the same breath as pigs by Jock Grant-Menzies – 'After all, there are other things in life besides women and pigs' (p.66). Being a chivalrous knight, Tony actually takes a girl to Brighton of whom he says 'You can trust her to behave anywhere', which is very ironic in light of the fact that she is a prostitute and can be trusted to behave while Tony's trust in Brenda, a lady, is destroyed. Tony never manages to sleep with Thérèse de Vitré either – the romantic shipboard acquaintance is finished by her as soon as she learns that he is married.[11]

Guy Crouchback is similar to Tony but a little more mature: he remembers his honeymoon at the Castello, with Virginia, as the Castello being 'a place of joy and love' and the time as being one when 'frustrated love had found its first satisfaction' (*Men at Arms*, p.11). But Guy's memory of his sexual prowess on honeymoon does not reflect Virginia's memory of the same event of which she says: 'If I remember our honeymoon correctly, you weren't so experienced then. Not a particularly expert performance as I remember' (*Men at Arms*, p.131).

In *Unconditional Surrender*, Uncle Peregrine has been to bed with a woman 'twice' – and tells Virginia that some men of his age go to doctors for 'expensive treatments' to make them '*want*' women'. Uncle Peregrine thinks that that is something which is unexplainable, but Virginia in her direct way says: 'Why is it different from going for a walk to get up an appetite for luncheon?' In Uncle Peregrine's book it is 'wrong' because of his religion, and he goes on to say about sex: 'There's another thing. You only have to look at the ghastly fellows who are a success with women to realise that there isn't much point in it' (p.137).

Charles Ryder has been cuckolded by his wife, Celia, and his sexuality is in question, for when people see his paintings they are heard to say: 'Ryder's is the last name would have occurred to me. They're so virile, so passionate' (*Brideshead Revisited*, p.255). The two women 'Death's Head' and 'Sickly Child' think that Charles and Sebastian are 'fairies', and Charles notes that 'it had clearly raised us in Julia's estimation that we had been out with women' (p.118).

Waugh wrote of the sexual scenes in Brideshead:

> I am not sure of my success. I feel very much the futility of describing sexual emotions without describing the sexual act; I should like to give as much detail as I have of the meals, to the two coitions – with his wife and Julia. It would be no more or less obscene than to leave them to the reader's imagination which in this case cannot be as acute as mine. There is a gap in which the reader will insert his own sexual habits instead of those of my characters. (*Diaries*, pp.564-65)

The reader needs to insert his own sexual habits, for both coitions are immature in the extreme. Let us take the two relevant passages:

[11] *A Handful of Dust* is reminiscent of Waugh's short story 'Love in the Slump' which can be found in *Mr Loveday's Little Outing and Other Sad Stories* (1936). Angela Trench-Troubridge's marriage to Tom Watch is 'completely typical of all that was most unremarkable in modern social conditions'. Angela does not find sex very satisfactory with Tom, so cuckolds him with his Eton and Oxford friend. This story which was edited out of Waugh's later collections of short stories is very similar to Waugh's own situation with Evelyn Gardner.

She talked in this way while she undressed, with an effort to appear at ease; then she sat at the dressing table, ran a comb through her hair, and with her bare back towards me, looking at herself in the glass, said: 'Shall I put my face to bed?'

It was a familiar phrase, one that I did not like; she meant, should she remove her make-up, cover herself with grease and put her hair in a net.

'No,' I said, 'not at once.'

Then she knew what was wanted. She had neat, hygienic ways for that too, but there were relief and triumph in her smile of welcome; later we parted and lay in our twin beds a yard or two distant, smoking. (p.219)

In that minute, with her lips to my ear and her breath warm in the salt wind, Julia said, though I had not spoken, 'Yes, now,' and as the ship righted herself and for the moment ran into calmer waters, Julia led me below.

It was no time for the sweets of luxury; they would come, in their season, with the swallow and the lime flowers. Now on the rough water there was a formality to be observed, no more. It was as though a deed of conveyance of her narrow loins had been drawn and sealed. I was making my first entry as the freeholder of a property I would enjoy and develop at leisure. (p.248)

Both women take the initiative and both acts of sex are mechanical. It is obvious in Celia's case that Ryder resents the 'relief and triumph' in her smile, for the next morning when Celia presumes that by making love to her they are back on their old footing, and he has forgiven her adultery, she is quickly disillusioned. When Celia says that she is 'not worrying any more' and she knows that they can 'start again exactly where we left off', Charles reminds her of her adultery, and although Celia says 'It's all over and forgotten' he retorts in a cruel and adolescent manner:

'I just wanted to know,' I said. 'We're back as we were the day I went abroad, is that it?'

So we started that day exactly where we left off two years before, with my wife in tears. (p.223)

Charles is not capable of an act of generosity. He is prepared to have sex with Celia because he needs the physical release, but he cannot forgive her her frailty. In the first draft of *Brideshead* the ending to this particular scene was different. After Celia had said that she wasn't worrying any more, and she knew that they could start again where they left off, the scene ended there with the concluding passage: 'So we started that day exactly as we had left off two years before.'[12] Waugh obviously changed the passage because it wouldn't fit in with Ryder's future affair with Julia, but one also suspects that he rewrote it in the light of his own feelings. Charles Ryder cannot accept his wife again; neither can Tony Last, who says to Reggie St. Cloud of Brenda: 'I don't want her back ... I just couldn't feel the same about her again' (*A Handful of Dust*, p.147). How reminiscent this is of how Waugh felt about Evelyn Gardner.

[12] See Robert Murray Davis, *Evelyn Waugh, Writer* (1981), p.149.

If we now look at the sexual act between Ryder and Julia we shall see that Waugh also changed that passage for the 1960 edition. The original passage read:

> So at sunset I took formal possession of her as her lover. It was no time for the sweets of luxury: they would come, in their season, with the swallow and the lime flowers. Now on the rough water, as I was made free of her narrow loins and, it seemed now, in assuaging that fierce appetite, cast a burden which I had borne all my life, toiled under, not knowing its nature – now, while the waves still broke and thundered on the prow, the act of possession was a symbol, a rite of ancient origin and solemn meaning.

Bernard Bergonzi has said that the passage shows 'that for Charles becoming Julia's lover was not just a personal transaction, but had a ritualistic, even a religious significance' and he believes that Waugh realised 'the exceedingly vulnerable implications' of the passage which implies that Charles 'is not merely taking possession of Julia as a woman, but is becoming carnally incorporated into the magic circle of Brideshead, a kind of earthly beatitude'.[13] One has to agree that in the 1945 edition this passage was out of keeping with Ryder's later attitude to Catholicism; when Lord Marchmain was dying, and until he gave his sign, Ryder was still talking of Catholicism as 'witchcraft' and 'mumbo jumbo'. Bergonzi sees the more restrained passage of the 1960 edition as not offering much of a 'fundamental improvement', for 'instead of a "rite of ancient origin" we have the taking legal possession of a property', and he goes on to say that the revision suggests 'that for Charles, Julia could never be just a woman he was in love with. She inevitably stood for much more – for Brideshead Castle and all its treasure, both material and spiritual.'[14]

There is no doubt in my mind that Waugh intended the double meaning – that Ryder loved Julia not for herself, but for Brideshead. During the storm on the ship, Julia recognises that Sebastian was 'the forerunner', and later at Brideshead she says, 'It's frightening ... to think how completely you have forgotten Sebastian', to which Charles replies: 'He was the forerunner.' Julia's concern is perhaps that she is 'only a forerunner, too', and when Charles tries to tell her that he has not forgotten Sebastian, that he is with him 'daily in Julia; or rather it was Julia I had known in him, in those distant Arcadian days', she says: 'That's cold comfort for a girl ... How do I know I shan't suddenly turn out to be somebody else? It's an easy way to chuck' (p.288).

Ryder, the narrator, tells us that he has not forgotten Sebastian – 'every stone of the house had a memory of him' – and when it looks as though Lord Marchmain is to leave Brideshead to Julia, Charles realises that:

> It opened a prospect; the prospect one gained at the turn of the avenue, as I had first seen it with Sebastian, of the secluded valley, the lakes falling away

[13] Bernard Bergonzi, 'Everlyn Waugh's Gentlemen', *Critical Quarterly* 5 (1963), p.28.
[14] Ibid., p.29.

one below the other, the old house in the foreground, the rest of the world abandoned and forgotten; a world of its own of peace and love and beauty; a soldier's dream in a foreign bivouac; such a prospect perhaps as a high pinnacle of the temple afforded after the hungry days in the desert and the jackal-haunted nights. Need I reproach myself if sometimes I was taken by the vision? (p.306)

Julia has said that she thinks that they could be 'very happy' at Brideshead, and whereas Julia is thinking in terms of their relationship Charles is only thinking in terms of Brideshead itself. Julia is a bonus to be thrown in, very little more.

In both passages relating to the sexual act with Julia, Charles shows no thought for her. He either takes 'formal possession' of her or makes his 'first entry as the freeholder of a property'. There is 'no time for the sweets of luxury'. No words of love, no response from Julia. She is used, as Celia is, to fulfil Ryder's needs. Also, after the act, when he and Julia dine together, the 'stars come out and sweep across the sky and the scene for Ryder is not seen as a romantic setting with Julia but reminds him of how he had seen the stars 'sweep above the towers and gables of Oxford'; in other words they remind him of Sebastian.

Ryder's reason for marrying Celia was: 'Physical attraction. Ambition. Everyone agrees she's the ideal wife for a painter. Loneliness, missing Sebastian' (p.245). His reasons for wanting to marry Julia are much the same.

Waugh's men are not sexually adequate. Prudence in *Black Mischief* tells William that he is 'effeminate and under-sexed' (p.45). Nina in *Vile Bodies* hardly finds Adam's first performance satisfactory – it gives her 'a pain' and she doesn't think that it is 'at all divine' (p.81). Ginger's performance with Nina is questioned too, for he appears to play golf all the time on their honeymoon. Virginia Troy wants to know why the Crouchback family do so little '——ing'; and even Basil Seal who obviously satisfies Prudence and his silly girls, in what Waugh sees as a coarse-grained way, has a 'morbid' relationship with Angela Lyne in which 'sensuality played a small part'. In the age of the predatory female, where Margot Beste-Chetwynde says of Chokey that 'I could eat you up every bit', it is, strangely, only Paul Pennyfeather who proves that he is good in bed. Tried out by Margot to make sure that they should marry, he achieves what he has to achieve. The thought must creep in that while writing *Decline and Fall* Waugh was living happily with Evelyn Gardner, and not until she deserted him does the sexually inadequate male figure appear in his works. There is one scene in *Vile Bodies* which sums up Waugh's anger and frustration at the female sex, and it is a passage in which he is quite conscious of what he is doing:

In his room ... There was also a rotund female bust covered in shiny red material, and chopped off short, as in primitive martyrdoms, at neck, waist and elbows; a thing known as a dressmaker's 'dummy' (there had been one of these in Adam's home which they used to call 'Jemima' – one day he stabbed 'Jemima' with a chisel and scattered stuffing over the nursery floor and was punished. A more enlightened age would have seen a complex in this action and worried accordingly. Anyway he was made to sweep up all the stuffing himself.) (p.157)

In the diaries Waugh wrote: 'Yesterday I became a man and put away childish things' (p.182). He may have believed so, but he retained his schoolboy attitude to women and it is reflected in his work; his heroines either treat males as children as has been seen in Chapter Six, or the male characters often seem themselves in that light.

Alastair Trumpington in *Put Out More Flags* has a 'firm, personal sense of schoolboy honour ... Since marriage he had been unfaithful to Sonia for a week every year during Bratts Club golf tournament at Le Touquet, usually with the wife of a fellow member. He did this without any scruple because he believed Bratts week to be in some way excluded from the normal life of loyalties and obligations ...' (p.45).

Paul Pennyfeather takes the rap for Margot's crimes because although his 'Boy Scout honour' tells him that Margot 'had got him into a row and ought to jolly well own up and face the music' he recognises the truth of Peter Pastmaster's statement – 'You can't see Mama in prison, can you?' (*Decline and Fall*, p.187).

Ginger in *Vile Bodies* says that he put on his 'bib and tucker and toddled off, hoping for a bit of innocent amusement' (p.118); while Whitemaid in *Scott-King's Modern Europe* wishes himself back in the dormitory so that he can imagine Miss Sveningen striding between the beds with a 'threatening hairbrush' (p.218).[15] Perhaps Waugh's nanny spanked him with a hairbrush. Certainly little John Andrew in *A Handful of Dust* wants to be spanked by the beautiful Jenny Abdul Akbar:

> They sat on John's small bed in the night-nursery. He threw the clothes back and crawled out, nestling against Jenny. 'Back to bed,' she said, 'or I shall spank you.'
> 'Would you do it hard? I shouldn't mind.' (p.88)

We have seen that Waugh cannot cope with the frailties of womankind, but there is also something else that he cannot cope with and that is motherhood. In life he was not present when his wife had 'her' babies (they are never referred to as his or theirs: see Appendix Three) and in fiction the heroes are also absent from such events. Even worse is the extreme lack of understanding:

> 'Isn't it true women sometimes go off their heads for a bit just after having a baby?'
> 'So I've heard.' (*Men at Arms*, p.215)

> 'D'you know there are cases of women going completely bald after childbirth? And permanently insane?' (*Work Suspended*, p.177)

[15] P.G. Wodehouse in *Portrait of a Disciplinarian* said: 'It is a moot point whether a man of sensibility can ever be entirely at his ease in the presence of a woman who has frequently spanked him with the flat side of a hairbrush.' See p.202 in *Meet Mr Mulliner* (1927).

'What's it like? I mean, it isn't a freak or anything?'

'No, I've been into that; two arms, two legs, one head, white – just a baby. Of course, you can't tell for some time if it's sane or not. I believe the first sign is that it can't take hold of things with its hands. Did you know that Lucy's grandmother was shut up?' (*Work Suspended*, pp.191-2)

'... Of course you must know all about child-birth. It has all been rather a surprise to me. I had never given it much thought but I had supposed that women just went to bed and that they had a sort of stomach ache and groaned a bit and then there was a baby. It isn't at all like that.'

'I always moved out when Angela had babies.'

'I was awfully interested. I moved out at the end but the beginning was quite a surprise – almost unnerving.' (*Unconditional Surrender*, p.185)

What is interesting to note in these examples is the amount of insanity that is mentioned. Frances Donaldson has said that she believes that Waugh was 'immensely attracted by madness';[16] and Lady Diana Cooper has said that 'he had some insanity'.[17] Madness has previously been noted in connection with the eyes of various characters as shown in Chapter Three, but this is something entirely different. This madness is a cover-up for Waugh's immaturity. As he cannot cope with real women, he cannot cope with the maternal instincts of those same women. Having a baby often changes a woman's entire being to the point of transforming her outlook and character. An expectant mother sees the world differently and the reason for her existence is at once apparently clear. Women sometimes assume, as Waugh so rightly detected in Lucy Simmonds, that 'incurious self-regarding expression which sometimes goes with a first pregnancy' (*Work Suspended*, p.153). It is a time that Waugh would most likely have felt left out of Laura's life: and for a man who clung to childhood memories he could well have seen himself as being displaced in her affections. He also, because of his religion, would have seen motherhood as something very sacred, and Laura, once she had fulfilled the role of mother, could hardly be regarded as the rather young and inexperienced girl he had married. As we laugh that shocked and embarrassed laugh at some of Waugh's vicious deaths, to cover up our horror, so Waugh uses the theme of madness in pregnancy to cover up his inability to cope with the subject. John Plant, who admits to feeling 'stifled' in the 'pastry-cook's atmosphere' of Lucy's bedroom, says to Roger that he knew a man who had five children – 'He felt just as you did until the fifth. Then he was suddenly overcome with love; he bought a thermometer and kept taking its temperature when the nurse was out of the room. I daresay it's a habit, like hashish' (p.191).

Waugh told Frances Donaldson that the father figure was 'a role in which I rather like to see myself'.[18] Perhaps he did, in later life, but certainly at one time it would not seem so:

There is a great deal of talk at the moment about the rocket guns which the

---

[16] Frances Donaldson, *Portrait of a Country Neighbour* (1967), p.62.

[17] Interview with Lady Diana Cooper, 16 November 1981.

[18] Frances Donaldson, *Portrait of a Country Neighbour*, p.41.

Germans are said to have set up in France, with a range to carry vast explosive charges to London ... I have accordingly given orders for the books I have been keeping at the Hyde Park Hotel to be sent to Piers Court. At the same time I have advocated my son coming to London. It would seem from this I prefer my books to my son. I can argue that fireman rescue children and destroy books, but the truth is that a child is easily replaced while a book destroyed is utterly lost; also a child is eternal; but most that I have a sense of absolute possession over my library and not over my nursery. (*Diaries*, p.555)

Waugh, although he appears not to know how to cope with the role of motherhood in his works, obviously saw the role of women as being in the home. He took great joy in denigrating women novelists, for example. In *Work Suspended* John Plant will not sell his stories as serials – 'the delicate fibres of a story suffer when it is chopped up into weekly or monthly parts and never completely heal' (p.107). Of his competitors who, interestingly, are not male but female, he observes:

> She was writing with an eye on the magazines. She had to close this episode prematurely; she had to introduce that extraneous bit of melodrama, so as to make each instalment a readable unit. 'Well,' I would reflect, 'she has a husband to support and two sons at school. She must not expect to do two jobs well, to be a good mother and a good novelist.'[19]

Waugh could have been talking about himself here, for he did adapt his work for serialisation and in the case of *A Handful of Dust* changed the end to suit the American market. The point is, however, that a woman cannot expect to be good at two jobs. As we have already seen, Waugh's view of women's intelligence was that it was extremely limited, and his view is borne out in a remark he made to Frances Donaldson. He told her that a woman friend of his had admired her prose style. She, sensing that he had been unflattering about her, said 'I hope you weren't beastly about it' to which he replied, shocked that she should think so – 'Oh no ... I was only amused at the poor beast thinking she knows one prose style from another.'[20]

The 'poor beast' is Waugh himself. One has to feel some pity as well as despair for a man who was so obviously crippled. He sees women as adulteresses, as incompetent mothers, as unintelligent, as disfigured by make-up, as ruining stately homes, and in many other unflattering lights. He cannot accept any kind of frailty. Even women being ill nauseates him. In *Brideshead Revisited*, during the storm, Celia Ryder makes a 'sacred, female rite even of seasickness' (p.239); while in *Remote People* he records the women on the ship, where there is also a storm, as 'Women passengers came up

---

[19] *Work Suspended*, pp.107-8. In *Vile Bodies*, Mr Benfleet is seen to be 'correcting proofs for one of his women novelists' (p.30); and in *Scott-King's Modern Europe* Scott-King thinks of Miss Bombaum: 'She did not look like a lady; she did not even look quite respectable, but he could not reconcile her typewriter with the callings of actress or courtesan; nor for that matter the sharp little sexless face under the too feminine hat and the lavish style of hair-dressing. He came near the truth in suspecting her of being, what he had often heard of but never seen in life, a female novelist' (pp. 205-6).

[20] Frances Donaldson, *Portrait of a Country Neighbour*, p.19.

squealing from their cabins below, with colourless, queasy faces' (p.222). They are not unlike the Bright Young People – that 'litter of pigs' who run 'squealing up the steps' of Lady Metroland's house in *Vile Bodies* (p.92).

The question, then, that one must ask is how Waugh achieves making his bad, beautiful heroines, as he sees them, attractive and sympathetic in the eyes of the reader. It is a remarkable feat. The answer, I believe, is relatively simple. When Waugh first started writing he was fascinated by the women he met and by their attitude of treating the world only on their own terms. His infatuation with upper-class women, and the upper class in general, is clearly apparent in the early works, and he watches with a detached, and quite tolerant, eye the antics of his early heroines, of whom we really learn very little. They are abstractions – and that is the clue. Waugh wrote in 1946:

> I believe that you can only leave God out by making your characters pure abstractions. Countless admirable writers, perhaps some of the best in the world, succeed in this. Henry James was the last of them. The failure of modern novelists since and including James Joyce is one of presumption and exorbitance. They are not content with the artificial figures which hitherto passed so gracefully as men and women. They try to represent the whole human mind and soul and yet omit its determining character – that of being God's creature with a defined purpose. So in my future books there will be two things to make them unpopular: a preoccupation with style and the attempt to represent man more fully, which, to me, means only one thing, man in his relation to God.[21]

It is a pity that Waugh was not content with artificial figures, for once he attempts to represent females more fully in their relation to God, he fails. The figure of Julia Flyte will never be as successful as the figure of Margot Beste-Chetwynde, and of the two of them one has to question who is the more believable, Margot with all her wicked ways and feminine wiles, or Julia with her questionable faith and her selfishness. In *Brideshead Revisited* Waugh did not describe Celia Ryder in relation to God, and Celia is a far better drawn character than Julia, for Waugh, perhaps quite unconsciously, made her an abstraction.

Julia Stitch, to my mind, is the finest female character in Waugh, and interestingly he portrayed her quite fully. In *Officers and Gentlemen* she reigns supreme. Waugh never managed to convert Lady Diana Cooper to Catholicism; this could be why, like Margot Beste-Chetwynde, she comes off the page like 'the first breath of spring'.

For her part, Lady Diana Cooper has always contended that 'Mr Wu' had 'an unhappy nature'.[22] One may conclude by quoting once more from the diaries:

> Father made a remark worth recording. The new puppy was howling dismally, during dinner, in the bathroom. Father said 'He's unhappy and wants to tell us all about it, which, after all, is all that most literature is!' (*Diaries*, p.95)

[21] Evelyn Waugh, 'Fan-Fare', *Essays*, p.302.
[22] Interview with Lady Diana.

APPENDIX ONE

Mr Wu

The name 'Mr Wu' was used by Lady Diana Cooper for Evelyn Waugh and the alias can be found in her memoir, *The Light of Common Day* (Rupert Hart-Davis, London, 1959), pp.153-4.

It was Rudolph Kommer who first coined the name, and Waugh and Kommer were rivals for Lady Diana's affection. It is interesting in *Scoop* that the heroine's name is Kätchen, for Kommer was called Kaetchen by Lady Diana after he had picked up a dog in a restaurant and said, 'Ah Kaetchen, Kaetchen, you mustn't crowl and park at the lady' (*Letters*, p.67, n.7). And Kätchen in *Scoop* has two men interested in her, William Boot and her German lover. Like Lady Diana, Kätchen is also blonde. The situation is not unlike the rivalry that existed between Waugh and Kommer, though Rudolph Kommer (von Czernowitz) was a Romanian Jew.

The name 'Mr Wu' was not new, however. Lady Diana met Waugh in 1932, but in 1927 the following was written in the *Weekly Dispatch* (13 March 927), p.5., by Lady Eleanor Smith:

> 'Pekingese,' I was told today, 'are apt to become violent when crossed in any way. Their tempers, from puppyhood onwards, can in no way be relied upon.'
>
> Whether this is or is not true, I cannot say, but I know one Pekingese who has for some years bitten anyone and everyone with whom he comes into contact, including the mistress who cherishes him to her bosom.
>
> He is appropriately named 'Wu'.

It has been thought that this was a reference to Waugh, but it is most unlikely. Barbara Cartland in *We Danced All Night* (Hutchinson, London, 1970, p.175) writes: 'I had seen very few plays before I came to London in 1919. One – called *Mr. Wu* – I had seen by mistake, when my governess took me to what she believed was a musical comedy. I can remember her embarrassment and also my bewilderment! I couldn't understand what *Mr. Wu* – Matheson Lang as the big Chinaman – wanted to do to a white woman.'

The reference in the *Weekly Dispatch* was probably to Matheson Lang, who became known as 'Mr Wu' after he had played the famous part. In 1927 Waugh was not a name in the gossip columns. After the play had appeared, a George Formby song 'Oh, Mr Wu what shall I do? I'm hanging out those Chinese Laundry Blues' became popular. It is likely that 'Mr Wu's' romantic advances in the play influenced the name given to Waugh by Kommer because of Waugh's attention to Lady Diana. 'Blues' from the Formby song would also have been appropriate to Waugh.

And finally 'Wu' could also have derived from 'Wuff', for in 1930 a conversation was recorded between Lady Lavery and Lord Berners, who was accompanied by Evelyn Waugh: ' "How nice to see you," she said, "and Mr Wuff, too" ' (*Daily Express*, 8 October, 1930, p.19). Waugh had also been known as 'Wuffles' at Lancing.

The Poetry in *The Loved One*

The Richard Middleton poem that Waugh uses in *The Loved One* was called
Any Lover, Any Lass. It reads as follows:

Why are her eyes so bright, so bright
    Why do her lips control
The kisses of a summer's night,
    When I would love her soul?

God set her brave eyes wide apart
    And painted them with fire,
They stir the ashes of my heart
    To embers of desire.

Her lips so tenderly are wrought
    In so divine a shape,
That I am servant to my thought
    And can no wise escape.

Her body is a flower, her hair
    About her neck doth play;
I find her colours everywhere,
    They are the pride of day.

Her little hands are soft and when
    I see her fingers move
I know in very truth that men
    Have died for less than love.

Ah, dear, live, lovely thing! my eyes
    Have sought her like a prayer;
It is my better self that cries
    'Would she were not so fair!'

Would I might forfeit ecstasy
    And find a calmer place,
Where I might undesirous see
    Her too desired face.

Nor find her eyes so bright, so bright,
    Nor hear her lips unroll
Dream after dream the lifelong night,
    When I would love her soul.

Waugh used verses 2, 4 and 5, and the first two lines of verse six. He liked Richard Middleton's work, and when he was seventeen he made an approving mark against his poems in Dudley Carew's copy of the *Oxford Book of Victorian Verse*.

In *The Loved One* we know that Dennis Barlow reads *The Oxford Book of English Verse*, and he also says that Aimée must 'draw from the bran-tub of anthologies' (p.84). Paul Doyle and Professor Donald Green (*Evelyn Waugh Newsletter*, vol.15, no.4, Winter, 1981, p.7) had some difficulty tracking the poem down, and Professor Green finally found it in the 'Poems of Love' section in *Stevenson's Home Book of Verse*. But the point is that there are a number of Oxford Books of Verse and the Middleton poem is in *The Oxford Book of Victorian Verse*, edited by Sir Arthur Quiller-Couch (Clarendon Press, Oxford, 1912).

Although Richard Middleton was a minor English poet, he was respected in his day. He wrote two volumes of poems and songs, and a number of stories (his most famous being *The Ghost Ship*). He used to write book reviews for the *Academy*, of which Lord Alfred Douglas was editor at the time; and Lord Alfred Douglas wrote an introduction to one of Middleton's books.

More interesting is that in 1921 a production of his play *The District Visitor* was produced by Edmonia Nolley (almost as good a name as Sophie Dalmeyer Krump) at the Vagabond Theater in Baltimore. Also in 1922, Small Maynard (America) published Henry Savage's *Richard Middleton: The Man and His Work*.

Mr Doyle presumes that all the poems mentioned in *The Loved One*, apart from the Middleton one, come from the *Oxford Book of English Verse*. This is not so. Dennis said that Aimée would need the 'bran-tub of anthologies' and she does. Poe's 'To Helen', Keats' 'Ode to a Nightingale', and Shakespeare's sonnet are in the *Oxford Book of English Verse*. Tennyson's 'Now sleeps the crimson petal, now the white' is in the *Oxford Book of English Verse* as 'Summer Night', whereas it is in the *Oxford Book of Victorian Verse* under its correct heading of 'Songs from "The Princess" ' No.V, Tennyson's 'I wither slowly in thine arms / Here at the quiet limit of the world' – lines 6 & 7 of 'Tithonus' are not in the *Oxford Book of English Verse* but can be found in any Tennyson anthology; and 'On the midnight pallet lying' – line one, section XI of A.E. Housman's *A Shropshire Lad* is again not in the *Oxford Book of English Verse* but can be found in any Housman anthology.

If Aimée is ignorant of Middleton she is also ignorant of Robert Burns, as are Dr Kenworthy and the American public. There is an inscription on the lovers' seat, and the words of the oath that the lovers take are cut into the step. The seat incorporates the ancient symbol of the Heart of the Bruce. Aimée asks Dennis if it was Bruce who wrote the vow, not realising that Robert Bruce (1274-1329) fought the English until the Treaty of Northampton (1328) recognised the independence of Scotland and his right to the throne. His heart was buried in Melrose Abbey. She is also not aware that the inscription and the oath come from two different poems by Burns.

The inscription says that the couples who '*join their lips through the Heart of the Bruce shall have many a canty day with ane anither and maun totter down hand in hand like the immortal Anderson couple'*. The words of the prescribed oath that the couples take is:

> Till a' the seas gang dry my dear
> And the rocks melt wi' the sun;
> I will luve thee still my dear,
> While the sands o' life shall run.

The inscription is based on Burns', 'John Anderson My Jo', and the oath is from Burns' 'A red, red rose'. Dennis also tells Aimée that the ending of the poem, of the oath, is:

> Now we maun totter down, John,
> And hand in hand we'll go,
> And sleep the gither at the foot,
> John Anderson, my jo.

which is the end of 'John Anderson, My Jo', not the end of 'A red, red rose'. Dennis however does this for a reason. By using the end of the Anderson poem with the Rose one he tries to tell Aimée that it is all right to sleep together. Aimée's reaction, though, is to ask why all the poetry he knows is 'so coarse', particularly as he is talking of becoming a minister. Dennis says that 'everything is ethical to engaged couples'; but that doesn't make any difference to Aimée who is determined to wait until marriage. Dennis realises of course that Aimée will not know the poem, and consequently will not recognise that it is about two old people who have had their day, rather than about two young people courting.

Evelyn Waugh and his Children

Evelyn Waugh never seemed to be present for the birth of his children. Waugh did not get on with his brother-in-law, Auberon Herbert, which was obviously one of the reasons, because Laura, apart from her first child, always had her babies at Pixton, the Herbert home. This was understandable in the war years but seems strange for the birth of the last two children. Why, one wonders, didn't Laura stay at Piers Court? Perhaps it was because she knew that Waugh would not be at home.

Waugh's letters and diaries record the following references to the birth of his children. Maria Teresa Waugh was born in March 1938, and as there was no diary that year the birth is not recorded; but in the *Letters* Waugh writes to A.D. Peters on 10 March 1938 to say: 'Laura's baby was born yesterday morning.' It would appear that he was at Piers Court at the time (*Letters*, p.116). In October 1939 Waugh writes that the doctor had visited and thought that Laura would probably give birth in November. 'Accordingly I decided to leave for Chagford in the hope of getting my novel finished, or nearly finished by the time I could take Laura from Pixton' (*Diaries*, p.447). Waugh was at Pixton for the birth of Auberon but stayed at a boarding house in the village, probably because he didn't get on with his in-laws. In November 1940, a child, Mary, was born but died twenty-four hours afterwards, shortly after his arrival. Waugh records: 'Poor little girl she was not wanted' (*Diaries*, p.489). Waugh had written in April 1940 to Laura sympathising with her about her pregnancy: 'It is sad news for you that you are having another baby.' He went on to try to explain that he found some consolation in the fact that new life was being given, while he, most likely, would have to take life during the war. He also expressed the thought that Laura's children would be a comfort to her if he died (*Letters*, p.139). Of Margaret, his favourite daughter's birth, he records in 1942: 'My daughter Margaret was born about 11th or 12th June. I arrived on Saturday morning at Pixton and found Laura very well and the asparagus in season' (*Diaries*, p.522). In May 1944, Friday 12, he was given six weeks leave, but although Laura was about to give birth he returned to Chagford to write (*Diaries*, p.565). He was informed on Saturday 13, by a telephone message, that 'Laura has had a daughter and is well' (*Diaries*, p.566). On 23 May he went to Pixton and found 'Laura in excellent health and her baby also' (*Diaries*, p.566). By 3 June he records that he has started work in Chagford again, 'retarded two weeks by my visits to Pixton and London' (*Diaries*, p.567). On

15 June 1946 he goes to Madrid, returning on 2 July, to find a telegram awaiting him in London – 'Laura delivered of a son' (*Diaries*, p.655). That was the Tuesday; he visits Pixton on the Saturday. (The son was James.) Septimus Waugh's birth is not recorded in the diaries, as Waugh did not keep one between 28 October 1948 and 28 September 1952.

It does however appear that he wrote to Laura from White's on 4 July 1950 to say that he was very sorry to learn that she was still bearing her 'great burden'. He continued: 'Your condition was surprisingly announced to the peoples of Amsterdam by my chairman who said: "Mr Waugh's great enthusiasm for the Holland Festival is exemplified by the fact that he has left his wife's side while she is bearing him a seventh child".' On 8 July, he wrote: 'I look eagerly in the columns of *The Times* but every day am disappointed. I am so very sorry for you in this tedious wait, but rejoice you are with your family & with a puppy to keep you amused, and all the coming and going of Pixton to distract you.' He then goes on to talk about the Court Ball being 'wholly delightful' ... and ends with 'I will come to Pixton soon. I am longing to see you.' Laura's reply (*Letters*, p.331, note 9) is revealing:

> I have been thinking deeply about whether it would be a good thing for you to come and visit me again and though I long for it I don't think it would be if Auberon is going to be here – I don't know yet that he is but it seems to be probable.
> I think the mixture of all the children and him would be intolerable to you and even though I know you would be polite to him I know I should be in a fever and miserable, feeling things were not right.

Obviously the tension that Waugh would have created by being there was not worth it, even to the loving Laura; and one suspects that she needed the comfort of her family at Pixton during her confinements.

APPENDIX FOUR

Waugh and Architecture

Jeffrey Heath in *The Picturesque Prison, Evelyn Waugh and His Writing* (1982, p.146) has said that the 1767 engraving of *A Composed Hermitage in the Chinese Taste* shows the kind of architectural joke that Waugh had 'deplored only a year before in "A Call to the Orders" '. But Waugh wrote: 'Gothic was made to be played with, and its misuse, like that of Oriental styles, has often had the most enchanting effect ... in the great age the classicicists were full of jokes – Gothic, Indian, Chinese but never classical jokes. They remained true to the Vitruvian canons ... It was by being drilled in those until the mind was conditioned to move automatically in the golden proportions, that the designers were able to indulge the most exuberant fancies. By studying 'the Orders' you can produce Chippendale Chinese; by studying Chippendale Chinese you will produce nothing but magazine covers' (*Essays*, pp.217-18).

And in 'Literary Style in England and America' he wrote:

> From the middle of the eighteenth century until the middle of the nineteenth there was published in England a series of architectural designs for the use of provincial builders and private patrons. The plates display buildings of varying sizes, from gate-lodges to mansions, decorated in various 'styles', Palladian, Greek, Gothic, even Chinese. The ground plans are identical, the 'style' consists of surface enrichment. At the end of this period it was even possible for very important works such as the Houses of Parliament in London to be the work of two hands, Barry designing the structure, Pugin overlaying it with medieval ornament. And the result is not to be despised. In the present half century we have seen architects abandon all attempt at 'style' and our eyes are everywhere sickened with boredom at the blank, unlovely, unlovable facades which have arisen from Constantinople to Los Angeles. *Essays*, pp.477-8

Roger Simmonds's Hermitage is 'rigidly orthodox in plan', and the 'elevation' which is the surface face of the building, not the structure, is what is decorated. Roger likes Batty Langley and William Halfpenny, and Waugh had books by both of them in his library. They were both architects of the eighteenth century. Langley (who is responsible for Cedric Lyne's bridge in *Put Out More Flags*) produced a number of books, including one called *A Sure Guide to Builders* (1726) which contained engravings of the 'orders', and Ancient Masonry (1734 or 1735) which gave designs for all kinds of architectural features drawn from English and foreign sources. Halfpenny's first book, *Magnum in Parvo* or *The Marrow of Architecture* (1722), gave engravings of the 'orders' as defined by Palladio. The books of Langley and

Halfpenny were to influence the movement of Palladianism in the USA and their works were republished at later dates. Halfpenny was also responsible for a number of books on Chinese architecture. *Rural Architecture in the Chinese Taste* (1750) was chiefly aimed at provincial builders and country gentlemen. The designs were in fact as much French rococo as Chinese, and the Chinese in the middle of the eighteenth century enjoyed a freedom somewhat akin to the rococo in France which sent occasional eddies of influence across Palladian England. As we know, Waugh was fond of the rococo ... and the rococo spirit in the eighteenth century finally proved as fertile in invention in England as in France and Germany with *Chinoiserie*. China and paper came in large quantities from the East. Furniture, plasterwork and panelling which embodied Chinese motifs were popular, and Chinese Chippendale was in great demand. Charles Ryder in *Brideshead Revisited* finds it an 'aesthetic education to live within those walls, to wander from the Soanesque library to the Chinese drawing room, adazzle with gilt pagodas and nodding mandarins, painted paper and Chippendale fretwork ...' And Waugh himself was fond of Chinese Chippendale – once writing to Ann Fleming about a furniture sale he told her of 'a very pretty Chinese-Chippendale overmantle £1400 ...' (*Letters*, p.484).

Harold Acton, a lifelong friend who lived in Peking from 1933 to 1939, has said of Waugh in *Memoirs of an Aesthete* (1948, p.318): 'He was primarily an artist in revolt against philistinism, and this was our lasting bond.' Interestingly, when Acton's book came out, Waugh wrote to him to say (*Letters*, p.277):

> I expected to find most interest in the Oxford section but, enormously though that did delight me, I found Peking even more enthralling. You have accomplished a great feat in communicating your own tenderness for the place to a bigoted Westerner.

Jeffrey Heath has said that, in *Work Suspended*, Lucy having 'one of her best friends live in the East' is 'always a sure sign of Waugh's disapproval' (*The Picturesque Prison*, p.149). As Harold Acton was a lifelong friend who lived in the East for many years, Heath's statement is disputable.

Waugh did not like communism, but he did admire certain things about the East. He approved of the modesty of the women, as mentioned previously in connection with Julia Flyte, and the eastern influence in art – witness his attitude to Chinese Chippendale, and his purchase of the carpet for Combe Florey with its coarsely adapted Persian motifs. He also in *A Little Learning* (p.24) said that he admired his half uncle in his 'costume of the gorgeous East'; and in a letter to his daughter Margaret he tells her: 'I am glad you are learning Chinese. The ideograms should be written with a brush. In old China calligraphy was regarded as one of the highest of the Arts ... Here is a picture of a Chinese lady for you. It is painted on rice-paper & will fall to pieces at the gentlest touch. So I shall not think ill of you if it does not survive long. But it is a pretty picture 100 years old. I should like you to be able to paint as well as this' (*Letters*, pp.392-3).

Bibliography

Primary Sources

Books and essays

Ackerly, J.R.	*Hindoo Holiday*. London: Chatto and Windus, 1932
Arlen, Michael	*The Green Hat*. London: Collins, 1924
	Lily Christine. London: Hutchinson, 1930
	May Fair. London: Collins, 1925
	Men Dislike Women. London: Heinemann, 1931
	Piracy. London: Collins, 1922
	Young Men in Love. London: Hutchinson, 1927
Bowen, Elizabeth	*The Death of the Heart*. London: Jonathan Cape, 1938
Bradley, H. Dennis	*Vile Bodies: A Play in Twelve Episodes*. London: Chapman & Hall, 1931
Firbank, Ronald	*Caprice*. London: Grant Richards, 1918
	The Flower Beneath The Foot. London: Grant Richards, 1923
	Inclinations. London: Grant Richards, 1917
	Valmouth. London: Grant Richards Ltd., 1919
	The Princess Zoubaroff in *The Works of Ronald Firbank*, vol. 3, London: Duckworth, 1929
Forster, E.M.	*Pharos and Pharillon*. London: Hogarth Press, 1923
Gardner, Evelyn	'The Modern Mother: A Young Wife's Challenging Plea'. *Evening Standard*, 9 January 1930, p.7
Gerhardi, William	*The Polyglots*. London: Cobden-Sanderson, 1925
Glyn, Elinor	*Three Weeks*. London: Duckworth, 1906
	'IT' and Other Stories. London: Duckworth, 1927
Greene, Graham	*The End of the Affair*. London: Heinemann, 1951
	England Made Me. London: Heinemann, 1935
Green, Henry	*Living*. London: Hogarth Press, 1929
	Party Going. London: Hogarth Press, 1939
Harwood, Ronald	*The Ordeal of Gilbert Pinfold*: (A play from the novel by Evelyn Waugh). Oxford: Amber Lane Press, 1983
Aldous Huxley	*Antic Hay*. London: Chatto & Windus, 1923
	Crome Yellow. London: Chatto & Windus, 1921
	Point Counter Point. London: Chatto & Windus, 1928
Kipling, Rudyard	'Mrs Bathurst' in *Traffics and Discoveries*. London: Macmillan, 1904
Lehmann, Rosamond	*Dusty Answer*. London: Chatto & Windus, 1927
Lewis, P. Wyndham	*Tarr*. London: The Egoist, 1918
Loos, Anita	*Gentlemen Prefer Blondes: the illuminating diary of a professional lady*. New York: Brentanos, 1926

Mansfield, Katherine — *The Garden Party and other stories.* London: Constable, 1922

Maugham, W. Somerset — *Cakes and Ale, or The Skeleton in the Cupboard.* London: Heinemann, 1930

May, Betty — *Tiger Woman.* London: Duckworth, 1929

Middleton, Richard — *Poems and Songs in Two Volumes.* London: Fisher Unwin, 1912 & 1913

Mitford, Nancy — Editor, *Noblesse Oblige: an enquiry into the identifiable characteristics of the English aristocracy.* London: Hamish Hamilton, 1956

Morton, J.B. — *Beachcomber: the Works of J.B. Morton.* Editor, Richard Ingrams, London: Frederick Muller, 1974

Nichols, Beverley — *Crazy Pavements.* London: Jonathan Cape, 1925

Powell, Anthony — *Afternoon Men.* London: Duckworth, 1931

Sykes, Christopher — *Evelyn Waugh: a biography.* London: Collins, 1975. Penguin Books, 1977

Usborne, Richard — *Wodehouse at Work. A study of the books and characters of P.G. Wodehouse across nearly sixty years.* London: Herbert Jenkins, 1961

Waugh, Alec — *The Fatal Gift.* London: W.H. Allen, 1973

Waugh, Evelyn — 'The Balance' in *Georgian Stories.* London: Chapman & Hall, 1926

Black Mischief. London: Chapman & Hall, 1932. Revised edition with preface. London: Chapman & Hall, 1962. Penguin Books, 1980

Charles Ryder's Schooldays (first published in *The Times Literary Supplement* in 1982) in *Work Suspended and other stories now including Charles Ryder's Schooldays.* Harmondsworth: Penguin, 1982

'The Curse of the Horse Race' in *Little Innocents: Childhood Reminiscences.* Preface, Alan Pryce-Jones. London: Cobden Sanderson, 1932

Brideshead Revisited. London: Chapman & Hall, 1945. Revised edition with preface. London: Chapman & Hall, 1960. Penguin Books, 1980

Decline and Fall. London: Chapman & Hall, 1928. Revised edition with preface. London: Chapman & Hall, 1962. Penguin Books, 1979

The Diaries of Evelyn Waugh. Editor, Michael Davie. London: Weidenfeld and Nicolson, 1976. Penguin, 1979

'Preface' to *The Duchess of Jermyn Street: The Life and Good Times of Rosa Lewis of the Cavendish Hotel.* Daphne Fielding. London: Eyre and Spottiswoode, 1964

Edmund Campion. London: Chapman & Hall, 1935

'Edward of Unique Achievement'. *Cherwell.* Oxford: 13 June 1925

The Essays, Articles and Reviews of Evelyn Waugh. Editor, Donat Gallagher. London: Methuen, 1983

A Handful of Dust. London: Chapman & Hall, 1934. Revised edition. London: Chapman & Hall, 1964.

Penguin Books, 1978.

Helena. London: Chapman & Hall, 1950. Penguin Books, 1979.

'Honeymoon Travel' in *The Book for Brides*. London: Forbes Publications, 1948, pp.51-5

Labels. London: Duckworth, 1930.

'Letters (and Post-cards) to Randolph Churchill'. *Encounter*. 31 July 1968, pp.3-19

The Letters of Evelyn Waugh. Editor, Mark Amory. London: Weidenfeld & Nicolson, 1980

A Little Learning. London: Chapman & Hall, 1964

Mr Loveday's Little Outing. (Includes 'By Special Request' the alternative ending to *A Handful of Dust*, originally written as a serial and called '*A Flat in London*'.) London: Chapman & Hall, 1936

Love Among The Ruins. London: Chapman & Hall, 1953

The Loved One. London: Chapman & Hall, 1948. Revised edition. London: Chapman & Hall, 1965. Penguin Books, 1979

'The Major Intervenes'. *Atlantic Monthly*, July 1949. pp.34-41

'Matter-of-Fact-Mothers of the New Age'. *Evening Standard*, 8 April 1929, p.7

Men at Arms. London: Chapman & Hall, 1952. Penguin Books, 1979

Officers and Gentlemen. London: Chapman & Hall, 1955. Penguin Books, 1979

The Ordeal of Gilbert Pinfold. London: Chapman & Hall, 1957. Published with *Tactical Exercise* and *Love Among The Ruins*. Penguin Books, 1980

PRB An Essay on the Pre-Raphaelite Brotherhood 1847-54. Westerham, Kent: Dalrymple Press, 1982. (Privately printed by Alastair Graham, 1926)

Put Out More Flags. London: Chapman & Hall, 1942. Revised edition, London: Chapman & Hall, 1966. Penguin Books, 1979

Remote People. London: Duckworth, 1931

Robbery Under Law: The Mexican Object-Lesson. London: Chapman & Hall, 1939

Ronald Knox. London: Chapman & Hall, 1959

Rossetti: His Life and Works. London: Duckworth, 1927

Scoop. London: Chapman & Hall, 1938. Revised edition. London: Chapman & Hall, 1964. Penguin Books, 1978

'Sloth' in *The Seven Deadly Sins*. London: Sunday Times Publications, 1962

Sword of Honour (the one volume edition of the war trilogy). London: Chapman & Hall, 1965

Tactical Exercise. Harmondsworth, Middlesex: Penguin Books, 1962

A Tourist in Africa. London: Chapman & Hall, 1960

	Unconditional Surrender. London: Chapman & Hall, 1961. Penguin Books, 1980
	Vile Bodies. London: Chapman & Hall, 1930. Revised edition. London: Chapman & Hall, 1965. Penguin Books, 1979
	When the Going was Good. London: Duckworth, 1946. Penguin Books, 1979.
	Wine in Peace and War. London: Saccone & Speed, 1949
	Work Suspended and Other Stories. London: Chapman & Hall, 1943. Penguin Books, 1978. Includes *Mr Loveday's Little Outing, Cruise, Period Piece, On Guard, An Englishman's Home, Excursion in Reality, Bella Fleace Gave A Party, Winner Takes All, Scott King's Modern Europe* (First published London: Chapman & Hall, 1946) and *Basil Seal Rides Again.* (First published London: Chapman & Hall, 1963)
Wodehouse, P.G.	'Portrait of a Disciplinarian' in *Meet Mr Mulliner.* London: Herbert Jenkins, 1927
Woolf, Virginia	*A Room of One's Own.* London: Hogarth Press, 1929

Transcriptions of interviews and talks

Betjeman, John	'*Living Writers II: Evelyn Waugh*'. BBC Third Programme, 14 December 1946
Freeman, John	'*Evelyn Waugh: Face to Face*'. BBC Television, 20 July 1960
Waugh, Evelyn	'*Up to London – III*'. BBC Third Programme, 21 June 1938

Secondary Sources

Memoirs and social history

Acton, Harold	*Memoirs of an Aesthete.* London: Methuen, 1948
	More Memoirs of an Aesthete. London: Methuen, 1970
	Nancy Mitford: A Memoir. London: Hamish Hamilton, 1975
Balfour, Patrick (Lord Kinross)	*Society Racket: A Critical Survey of Modern Social Life.* London: John Long, 1933
	'The Years with Kinross'. *Punch*, 9 August 1961, pp.210-11
Barrow, Andrew	*Gossip: A History of High Society from 1920-1970.* London: Hamish Hamilton, 1978
Beaton, Cecil	*The Glass of Fashion.* London: Weidenfeld & Nicolson, 1954
	Self Portrait with Friends: The Selected Diaries of Cecil Beaton, 1926-74. London: Weidenfeld & Nicolson, 1974
Bowra, C.M.	*Memories 1898-1939.* London: Weidenfeld & Nicolson, 1966

Carew, Dudley	*A Fragment of Friendship: A Memory of Evelyn Waugh When Young*. London: Everest Books, 1974
Cooper, Diana	*The Light of Common Day*. London: Rupert Hart-Davis, 1959
	Trumpets From the Steep. London: Rupert Hart-Davis, 1960
Donaldson, Frances	*Evelyn Waugh: Portrait of a Country Neighbour*. London: Weidenfeld & Nicolson, 1967
Fielding, Daphne	*The Duchess of Jermyn Street: The Life and Good Times of Rosa Lewis of the Cavendish Hotel*. London: Eyre & Spottiswoode, 1964
	Emerald & Nancy: Lady Cunard and her Daughter. London: Eyre & Spottiswoode, 1968
	Mercury Presides. London: Eyre & Spottiswoode, 1954
	The Nearest Way Home. London: Eyre & Spottiswoode, 1970
Garnett, David	*Carrington: Letters and Extracts from her Diaries*. Oxford: OUP, 1979
Goldring, Douglas	*The Nineteen Twenties*. London: Nicolas and Watson, 1945
Graves, Robert and Hodge, Alan	*The Long Weekend: A Social History of Great Britain, 1918-1939*. London: Faber & Faber, 1940
Green, Martin	*Children of the Sun: A Narrative of Decadence in England after 1918*. London: Constable, 1977
Guinness, Bryan	*Potpourri from the Thirties*. Oxford: Cygnet Press, 1982
Guinness, Jonathan and Catherine	*The House of Mitford*. London: Hutchinson, 1984
Harrison, Michael	*Rosa*. London: Peter Davies, 1962
Hollis, Christopher	*Oxford in the Twenties: Recollections of Five Friends*. London: Heinemann, 1976
Howell, Georgina	Editor, *In Vogue: Sixty Years of Celebrities and Fashions from British Vogue*. London: Allen Lane, 1975
Lancaster, Marie Jacqueline	Editor, *Brian Howard: Portrait of a Failure*. London: Anthony Blond, 1968
Mosley, Diana	*A Life of Contrasts*. London: Hamish Hamilton, 1977
Nichols, Beverley	*Twenty Five*. London: Jonathan Cape, 1926.
Ponsonby, Loelia	*Grace and Favour: The Memories of Loelia, Duchess of Westminster*. London: Weidenfeld & Nicolson, 1961
Powell, Anthony	*To Keep The Ball Rolling: The Memoirs of Anthony Powell, vol. 11: Messengers of Day*. London: Heinemann, 1978
Powell, Anthony; Acton, Harold; and Sutro, John	'Three Evocations of Evelyn Waugh', *Adam International Review*. No. 3. London: Curwen Press, 1966
Priestley, J.B.	*English Journey*. London: Heinemann, 1968
Pryce-Jones, David	Editor, *Evelyn Waugh & His World*. London: Weidenfeld & Nicolson, 1973
	Editor, *Cyril Connolly, Journal and Memoir*. London: Collins, 1983.
Robertson, W. Graham	*Time Was*. London: Hamish Hamilton, 1931.
Waugh, Alec	*The Best Wine Last: An Autobiography Through the Years 1932-1969*. London: W.H. Allen, 1978

Waugh, Alec   *My Brother Evelyn & Other Profiles*. London: Cassell, 1967
   A Year to Remember: A Reminiscence of 1931. London. W.H. Allen, 1975

Waugh, Arthur   *One Man's Road*. London: Chapman & Hall, 1931

Waugh, Harriet   A Maureen Cleave Interview, 'Harriet Waugh is in control of the moon but admits she finds it rather surburban. Perhaps she should have listened to father ...', *Evening Standard*, 17 April, 1969, p.11

Winn, Godfrey   *A Month of Sundays*. London: Cassell, 1938

Ziegler, Philip   *Diana Cooper*. London: Hamish Hamilton, 1981

Critical books and monographs

Bergonzi, Bernard   *The Situation of the Novel*. London: Macmillan, 1970

Bradbury, Malcolm   *Evelyn Waugh*. Writers and Critics series. Edinburgh: Oliver and Boyd, 1964

Breit, Harvey   *The Writer Observed*. London: Alvin Redman, 1957

Burgess, Anthony   *The Novel Now*. London: Faber & Faber, 1967

Carens, James F.   *The Satiric Art of Evelyn Waugh*. Seattle: University of Washington Press, 1966

Cook, William J.   *Makes, Modes and Morals: the Art of Evelyn Waugh*. Cranbury, NJ, USA, Fairleigh Dickinson UP, 1966

Davis, Robert Murray   *Evelyn Waugh, Writer*. Norman, Oklahoma, USA, Pilgrim Books, 1981

Devitis, A.A.   *Roman Holiday: The Catholic Novels of Evelyn Waugh*. New York: Bookman Associates, 1956

Fussell, Paul   *Abroad: British Literary Travelling Between the Wars*. Oxford: OUP, 1980

Greenblatt, Stephen Jay   *Three Modern Satirists: Waugh, Orwell and Huxley*. New Haven, Conn., USA: Yale UP, 1965

Heath, Jeffrey   *The Picturesque Prison: Evelyn Waugh and his Writing*. London: Weidenfeld and Nicolson, 1982

Hollis, Christopher   *Evelyn Waugh*. Writers and their Work, no.46. London: Longmans, Green, 1954

Johnstone, Richard   *The Will To Believe: Novelists of the 1930s*. Oxford: OUP, 1982

Karl, Frederick R.   *A Reader's Guide to the Contemporary English Novel*. London: Thames & Hudson, 1972

Lane, Calvin, W.   *Evelyn Waugh*. Boston, USA: Twayne, 1981

Littlewood, Ian   *The Writings of Evelyn Waugh*. Oxford: Blackwell, 1983

Lodge, David   *Evelyn Waugh: Columbia Essays on Modern Writers*. New York: Columbia UP, 1971

McCormick, John   *Catastrophe & Imagination*. London: Longmans, Green, 1957

Mikes, George   *Eight Humorists*. London: Allan Wingate, 1954

O'Donnell, Donat (Connor Cruise O'Brien)   *Maria Cross: Imaginative Patterns in a Group of Catholic Writers*. London: Chatto and Windus, 1953

O'Faolain, Sean — *The Vanishing Hero: Studies in Novelists of the Twenties.* London: Eyre and Spottiswoode, 1956

Philips, Gene D. — *Evelyn Waugh's Officers, Gentlemen and Rogues: the Fact Behind His Fiction.* Chicago, USA: Nelson-Hall, 1975

Reed, John R. — *Old School Ties: the Public Schools in British Literature.* Syracuse, NY: Syracuse UP, 1964

Robson, W.W. — *Modern English Literature.* London: OUP, 1970

Savage, D.S. — 'The Innocence of Evelyn Waugh' in *Focus Four*, Editor, B. Rajan. London: Dennis Dobson, 1948

Spender, Stephen. — *The Creative Element: a Study of Vision, Despair and Orthodoxy Among Some Modern Writers.* London: Hamish Hamilton, 1953

St John, John — *To The War With Waugh.* London: Leo Cooper, 1974

Stopp, Frederick J. — *Evelyn Waugh: Portrait of an Artist.* London: Chapman & Hall, 1958

Wilson, Edmund — ' "Never Apologise, Never Explain": the Art of Evelyn Waugh', *Classicals and Commercials*. London: W.H. Allen, 1951

Articles and essays

Bergonzi, Bernard — 'Evelyn Waugh's Gentlemen'. *Critical Quarterly*, vol.5, Spring 1963, pp.23-6

Davie, Michael — 'The Diary of a Somebody' in 'An introduction by Michael Davie to the Private Diaries of Evelyn Waugh'. *Observer Review*, 25 March 1973, p.29

Davis, Robert Murray — 'Evelyn Waugh on the Art of Fiction'. *Papers on Language and Literature*, 2, 1966, pp.243-52
'The Mind and Art of Evelyn Waugh'. *Papers on Language and Literature*, 3, 1967, pp.270-87

Dennis, Nigel — 'Fabricated Man'. *NY Review of Books*, vol.XXIV, no.20, 8 December 1977, pp.3-6

Dyson, A.E. — 'Evelyn Waugh and the Mysteriously Disappearing Hero'. *Critical Quarterly*, Spring, 1960, pp.72-9

Fitzherbert, Margaret — 'Waugh Juvenilia'. *Spectator*, 5 February 1983, pp.24-5

Gerhardi, William — 'The Ordeal of Evelyn Waugh'. *Times Literary Supplement*, 12 September 1967, p.961

Greene, George — 'Scapegoat with Style: The Status of Evelyn Waugh'. *Queens Quarterly*, LXXI, Winter, 1965, pp.72-85

James, Clive — 'Waugh's Last Stand'. *NY Review of Books*, vol.XXVII, no.19. 10 November 1980, pp.3-4

Jebb, Julian — 'The Art of Fiction XXX: Evelyn Waugh'. *Paris Review*, 30, Summer-Fall 1963, pp.72-85

Jervis, Stephen A. — 'Evelyn Waugh, *Vile Bodies*, and the Younger Generation'. *South Atlantic Quarterly* LXVI, Summer 1967, pp.440-8

Jones, Richard — 'Evelyn Waugh: A Man at Bay'. *Virginia Quarterly Review*, 54, no.3, 1978, pp.503-17

Kleine, Don, W. — 'The Cosmic Comedies of Evelyn Waugh'. *South Atlantic Quarterly*, LXI, April 1962, pp.533-9

Linck, Charles, E. and Davis, Robert Murray — 'The Bright Young People in *Vile Bodies*'. *Papers in Language and Literature* V, Winter 1969, pp.80-90

Macaulay, Rose — 'Evelyn Waugh'. *Horizon*, 14 December 1946, pp.360-76

Marcus, Steven — 'Evelyn Waugh and the Art of Entertainment'. *Partisan Review*, XXIII, Summer 1956, pp.548-57

Menen, Aubrey — 'The Baroque and Mr Waugh'. *Month*, V, April 1951, pp.225-37

Pritchett, V.S. — 'Books in General'. *New Statesman*, 7 May 1949, pp.473-4

Slater, Ann Pasternak — 'Waugh's *A Handful of Dust*: Right Things in Wrong Places'. *Essays on Criticism*, vol.XXXII, January, 1982, pp.48-68

Sheppard, R.Z. — 'Books: Fifty Years of Total Waugh'. *Time Magazine*, 12 February 1979, pp.56 & 59

Sykes, Christopher, Connolly, Cyril, et al. — 'A Critique of Waugh', *Listener*, 31 August 1967, pp.267-9

Waugh, Auberon — '*Brideshead:* Who Really Was Who'. *Daily Mail*, 13 October 1981, pp.20-1

'Entries and Exits' (Review of the diaries of Evelyn Waugh). *Spectator*, 4 September 1976, pp.13 & 14

'Father and Son'. *Books and Bookmen*, 19 October 1973, pp.110-11

'Waugh's World'. *New York Times Magazine*, 7 October 1973, pp.10, 11, 21-3

Bibliographies

Davis, Robert Murray, et al. — *Evelyn Waugh: a Checklist of Primary and Secondary Material.* Troy, NY: Whitston Publishing Company, 1972

Davis, Robert Murray — *A Catalogue of the Evelyn Waugh Collection at the Humanities Research Center, University of Texas at Austin.* Troy, NY: Whitston Publishing Company, 1981

Doyle, Paul — Editor. *The Evelyn Waugh Newsletter.* New York: Nassau Community College, State University of New York, Garden City, N.Y. 11530

Index